BARRON'S

HOW TO PREPARE FOR THE

LAST/ATS-W

LIBERAL ARTS AND SCIENCES TEST/ASSESSMENT OF TEACHING SKILLS-WRITTEN

NEW YORK STATE TEACHER CERTIFICATION EXAMINATIONS (NYSTCE)

WITH AN INTRODUCTION TO THE CST

2ND EDITION

Dr. Robert D. Postman
Professor, Mercy College,
Westchester County, New York

BARRON'S

To my wife
Liz
and my children
Chad, Blaire, and Ryan
This book is dedicated to you.

All inquiries should be addressed to:
Barron's Educational Series, Inc.
250 Wireless Boulevard
Hauppauge, New York 11788
http://www.barronseduc.com

Library of Congress Catalog Card No. 2003058301

International Standard Book No. 0-7641-2306-8

Library of Congress Cataloging-in-Publication Data

Postman, Robert D.
   LAST/ATS-W : how to prepare for the Liberal Arts and Sciences Test
Assessment of Teaching Skills-Written, with an introduction to the CST,
New York State teacher certification examinations (NYSTCE) / Robert
D. Postman.— 2nd ed.
         p.   cm.
   At head of title: Barron's.
   ISBN 0-7641-2306-8 (alk. paper)
   1. Teaching—New York (State)—Examinations—Study guides.   2. Teachers—
Certification—New York (State)   I. Title: Barron's LAST/ATS-W.   II. Title.

LB1763.N7P67   2004
371.12'09747—dc22   2003058301

PRINTED IN THE UNITED STATES OF AMERICA

9 8 7 6 5 4 3 2 1

CONTENTS

PREFACE

More than 200,000 prospective teachers used the first edition of this book to successfully prepare for the LAST and the ATS-W. This edition is updated to reflect the new test guidelines and the revised New York State teacher certification requirements.

This book shows you how to get a passing score on the LAST and ATS-W, introduces you to the other New York Teacher Certification Examination, and helps you get started in a teaching career. The book has been field-tested by college students and prospective teachers and reviewed by experienced teachers and subject matter specialists.

The practice tests in this book have the same question types and the same question-and-answer formats as the real tests. Review sections provide a clear overview of subject matter, strategies for passing the LAST and ATS-W, and extra LAST and ATS-W practice questions.

My wife, Liz, a teacher and a constant source of support, made significant contributions to this book. I hope she accepts my regrets for the lost months. My children Chad, Blaire, and Ryan have also been supportive as I worked on this and other books over the years.

I can attest that Barron's is simply the best publisher of test preparation books. The editorial department, under the leadership of Mark Miele, spared no effort to assure that this book is most helpful to you, the test-taker.

Darrell Buono did a masterful job with this manuscript. Many special touches in the book are due to his caring attention.

I am grateful to Martin Shields for reviewing the science reading section and to Ryan Postman for reviewing the mathematics section. Thanks also to my colleagues Bill Prattella, Andy Peiser, Reggie Marra, Demetra Keane, Mary Ellen Hoffman, and Connie Bond for their suggestions and insight.

Special thanks to the undergraduate and graduate students and those changing careers, particularly Joe Connell, who field-tested sections of this book, and to those at the Metropolitan Museum of Art for their assistance. I am also grateful to those at the New York Education Department for taking the time to talk with me about the LAST and ATS-W, and to those at other New York colleges who talked to me about their experiences with the testing.

You are entering teaching during a time of tremendous opportunity, and I wish you well in your pursuit of a rewarding and fulfilling career. The next generation awaits. You will help them prepare for a vastly different, technological world.

Robert D. Postman

TEST DATES AND REGISTRATION DEADLINES

TEST DATE	Regular	Late*	Emergency*		Report Mailing Date
	Internet RECEIPT Mail POSTMARK	*Internet RECEIPT*	*Internet*	*Phone (413) 256-2882 M–F 9:00 A.M.–5:00 P.M. Not on holidays*	*(Scores may be available earlier online)*
Oct. 18, 2003	Sept. 12, 2003	Sept. 26, 2003	Sept. 26–Oct. 10, 2003	Oct. 1–10, 2003	Jan. 23, 2004
Feb. 14, 2004	Jan. 9, 2004	Jan. 23, 2004	Jan. 23–Feb. 6, 2004	Jan. 28–Feb. 6, 2004	March 19, 2004
April 24, 2004	March 19, 2004	April 2, 2004	April 2–16, 2004	April 7–16, 2004	May 28, 2004
May 22, 2004	April 16, 2004	April 30, 2004	April 30–May 14, 2004	May 5–14, 2004	June 25, 2004
July 17, 2004	June 11, 2004	June 25, 2004	June 25–July 9, 2004	June 30–July 9, 2004	August 20, 2004

*Late Registration and Emergency Registration require additional fees.

YOUR REVIEW PLAN

This section helps you set up a review plan for the Liberal Arts and Sciences Test (LAST) and the Assessment of Teaching Skills-Written (ATS-W.) We begin with a brief discussion of the tests.

The LAST is primarily a multiple-choice reading comprehension test, with some long passages, and an essay that is evaluated for written English. The ATS-W is primarily a multiple-choice field-based test about teaching situations and an essay evaluated for the quality of the response to an education situation or problem. Most college students say the LAST is more difficult than the ATS-W. That is certainly true from the results I see.

I recently talked a group of college students who used this book to prepare for both tests. Yes, they all passed. Here is a brief summary of their reactions. Most students left the LAST feeling a little overwhelmed and pleased they reviewed and took the practice tests. Most said there was a lot of reading and it could be difficult to choose the correct answer. Most students left the ATS-W feeling more confident and pleased they had field experience and that they had taken a practice test. Some felt uncertain about the ATS-W because it seemed there might be more than one correct answer.

LAST REVIEW PLAN

Choose one of these review plans for the LAST. You can always change your mind later. You don't want to review more than you need, but it is better to be a little overprepared than a little underprepared. Read the plans over, put a check next to your review plan, and get started. Check off each step as you go.

☐ Quick Review

Use this plan if you are excellent at reading comprehension tests and writing essays under time pressure, or if you'll be taking the test in the very near future.

☐ Review Chapter 1 for an overview of the tests.	pages 1–10
☐ Review Chapter 2 for test preparation and test-taking strategies.	pages 11–26
☐ Take LAST 1 in Chapter 11.	pages 263–307
☐ Take LAST 2 in Chapter 12.	pages 308–344

☐ Core Review

Use this plan if you are fairly confident about the LAST. The Core Review gives more help with reading comprehension and writing essays. These areas make up more than 80 percent of the LAST.

☐ Review Chapter 1 for an overview of the tests.	pages 1–10
☐ Review Chapter 2 for test preparation and test-taking strategies.	pages 11–26
☐ Review Chapter 3, Reading.	pages 29–47
☐ Review Chapter 4, English and Writing.	pages 48–86
☐ Take LAST 1 in Chapter 11.	pages 263–307
☐ Take LAST 2 in Chapter 12.	pages 308–344

☐ **Extended Review**

There are some questions about mathematics, art interpretation, and English on the LAST. The extended review includes preparation for these additional LAST topics. Students report this extended review can help correctly answer another four to eight questions. Use this plan if you think you might need or want these additional points.

ATS-W REVIEW PLAN

Follow these additional steps to prepare for the ATS-W.

Take one of the practice ATS-Ws.

OTHER RESOURCES

Chapter 8 (page 141) and Chapter 9 (page 169) provide 85 reading comprehension items in science and social studies with explained answers for those who want more practice. These chapters may also help you strengthen your understanding of these subjects.

Chapter 15 (page 421) gives an overview of the teacher certification requirements in New York State.

Chapter 16 (page 433) suggests some steps for finding a teaching position and includes extensive job search resources, including a list of all the school districts in New York State.

Rip this page out and use it as a bookmark.

PART I

Quick Review

THE LAST, ATS-W, AND OTHER NEW YORK TEACHER CERTIFICATION TESTS

TEST INFO BOX

Every chapter begins with a Test Info Box. Read it for information about the LAST and the ATS-W.

The New York State Teacher Certification Tests are offered by National Evaluation Systems (NES). Contact NES for information about registration, admission tickets, testing accommodations, and test scores.

National Evaluation Systems
P.O. Box 160
Amherst, MA 01004-9008
413-256-2882
TTY for the deaf: 413-256-8032

Go to *www.nystce.nesinc.com* for a registration form, test dates, Internet registration, score reports, and other information.

THE TESTS
Passing scores on the Liberal Arts and Sciences Test (LAST) and the Assessment of Teaching Skills-Written (ATS-W) are required for most New York teaching certificates.

The LAST consists of 80 multiple-choice items and a written assignment. The written assignment is about a topic given on the test.

The ATS-W consists of 80 multiple-choice items and a written assignment. There is an elementary and a secondary version of the ATS-W. The written assignment is about teaching or a school-related situation.

PASSING SCORES
An overall scale score of 220 is passing for each test. The multiple-choice items contribute 80 percent to the final score, while the written assignment contributes 20 percent. About 50—54 correct answers on the multiple-choice section and 3 or 4 out of 6 points on the written assignment should earn a passing score.

OTHER NEW YORK STATE TESTS
The Content Specialty Test (CST) is also discussed in this chapter.

READ ME FIRST

NEW YORK STATE TEACHER CERTIFICATION TESTS

This section gives a brief overview of the tests required for New York teacher certification.

The LAST and the ATS-W

This book is about the LAST and the ATS-W. Passing scores on the LAST and the ATS-W are required for most initial New York State teaching certificates. These tests are summarized on the previous pages, and this book provides a comprehensive review for the LAST and the ATS-W. You will find two LAST practice tests and two ATS-W practice tests in Chapters 11–14.

Content Specialty Test (CST)

There is a CST for each certification area. Each CST consists of multiple-choice items and a constructed response item. Tests in languages other than English also include listening and speaking sections.

Multiple-Subject CST

The multi-subject CST is taken most frequently; given below is a brief list of the topics covered on this test. There is appropriate review in this book to prepare you for the multi-subject CST.

English Language Arts
Mathematics
Science
Technology
Social Studies
The Fine Arts
Health and Fitness
Family and Consumer Science/Career Development

CST Information

For extensive information about the Content Specialty test in your certification area, visit one of the web sites listed below and choose the link for your CST. Your computer will need an installed acrobat reader to access the files.

http://www.nystce.nesinc.com/NY_viewobjs_opener.htm

This section explains the steps you should take in the beginning of your preparation.

What Is the LAST All About?

The LAST is a test about the introductory level liberal arts courses you took in college. The tests consist of 80 multiple-choice items and a written assignment. You have four hours to complete the LAST. You decide how much time to spend on the multiple-choice items, and how much time to spend on the written assignment.

The LAST items are based on four broad liberal arts subareas. The test yields a score for each liberal arts area, a score for the written assignment, and a score for the entire test. The multiple-choice items contribute 80 percent to the final score, while the written assignment score contributes 20 percent to the final score. Even so, you may encounter the most difficulty with the written assignment.

Multiple-Choice Items

The multiple-choice items are drawn from the liberal arts subareas shown below. You get one raw score point for each correct answer. There is no penalty for incorrect answers.

LAST AREAS

- **Mathematics**
- **Science**
- **History/Social Science**
- **Art**
- **Literature**
- **Humanities**
- **English/Communication**

Written Assignment

Each LAST contains a written assignment. Usually, you are asked to summarize the topic or situation and then give your opinion or point of view. Written assignments are rated 0–3 by two readers based on how well you write edited English. The final written assignment score of 0–6 is the sum of these two scores.

What Is the ATS-W All About?

The ATS-W is a test about the education courses you took in college and about your experience in schools. The test consists of 80 multiple-choice items and a written assignment. You have four hours to complete the ATS-W. You decide how much time to spend on the multiple-choice items and how much time to spend on the written assignment.

The ATS-W items are based on four broad education-related subareas. The multiple-choice items contribute 80 percent to the final score, while the written assignment score contributes 20 percent to the final score. Even so, you may encounter the most difficulty with the written assignment.

Multiple-Choice Items

The multiple-choice items are drawn from the subareas shown below. You get one raw score point for each correct answer. There is no penalty for incorrect answers.

ATS-W AREAS

- **Knowledge of the Learner**
- **Instructional Planning/Assessment**
- **Instructional Delivery**
- **The Professional Environment**

Written Assignment

The ATS-W includes a written assignment. This written assignment may not be an essay. For example, past written assignments have asked for the outline of a curriculum and a lesson plan.

You may be asked to respond to a classroom situation, or some other education related situation. The written assignment must be written clearly enough to be understood, but the readers do not evaluate your writing ability. However, a well-written assignment always makes the best impression.

The written assignment is rated 0–3 by two readers based on the appropriateness of your response. Your final written assignment score is the sum of these two scores. The final written assignment score of 0–6 is the sum of these two scores.

GETTING A PASSING SCORE

Raw Scores and Scale Scores

Your raw score is the number of items you answer correctly, or the number of points you actually earn. Your scale score shows your raw score on a single scale compared to everyone else who has taken the LAST or the ATS-W.

It works this way. LAST and ATS-W test items and different forms of the test have different difficulty levels. For example, a mathematics item on one form of the LAST might be harder than a mathematics item on another form. To make up for this difference in difficulty, the harder mathematics item might earn 0.9 scale points, while the easier item might earn 0.8 scale points.

This is the fair way to do it. To maintain this fairness, LAST and ATS-W passing scores are given as scale scores. The scale scores for the LAST and the ATS-W, as well as for each area on the test and for the written assignment, range from 100 to 300.

Passing Scores

Passing these tests is about your ability to use, apply, and integrate information. Just memorizing the information isn't good enough.

Scale Scores

You pass if your overall scale score is 220 or better.

PASSING SCALE SCORES

LAST	**220**
ATS-W	**220**

Raw Scores

The table below shows the raw scores likely to earn minimum scale scores. These are estimates and somewhat higher or somewhat lower raw scores may be passing for the test you take.

ESTIMATED RAW SCORES NEEDED FOR PASSING SCALE SCORES

	Minimum
LAST	55–58 multiple-choice items correct and
	3 or 4 out of 6 written assignment points
ATS-W	55–58 multiple-choice items correct and
	3 or 4 out of 6 written assignment points

You can make up for a lower score on the multiple-choice items or the written assignment with a higher score on the other part of the test.

REGISTERING FOR THE LAST AND THE ATS-W

The New York State Teacher Certification Registration Bulletin contains registration forms for the LAST, ATS-W, and other New York Certification Tests. The bulletin is usually available in the summer for the following school year. If you are attending a college in New York State, you can usually find copies of the bulletin in the school or department of education.

When you get the bulletin, complete the registration form and send it in with the correct fee. Pay close attention to the registration deadlines.

ON THE WEB

You can also register through *www.nystce.nesinc.com*. Score reports, a registration bulletin, test dates, and other information are also available through this site.

TEST SITE

Recent tests have been given at the sites listed below. Some sites offer tests on only a few test dates.

Albany	New York City – Bronx
Binghamton	New York City – Brooklyn
Buffalo	New York City – Manhattan
Cortland	New York City – Queens
Geneseo	Plattsburgh
Long Island – Nassau	Potsdam
Long Island – Suffolk	Rochester
New Paltz	Syracuse
Niagara	Westchester County

Puerto Rico

Check the bulletin for sites near you and list as your first choice the site at which you will feel the most comfortable. List acceptable second and third choice alternatives, but never list an alternative you really don't want to go to. If you do, you may end up there.

Send in the registration form as soon as possible. Early registrants are more likely to get their first choice site.

REGISTRATION DEADLINES

There are regular, late, and emergency registration periods. Your registration form must be *postmarked* by the registration deadline shown in the bulletin. Emergency registration is by phone. The regular registration deadline is about six weeks before the test date. You will pay about 40 percent more to register during the late registration period, which ends about three weeks before the test date. You will double your registration costs during the emergency registration period, which ends about a week before the test date.

Regular registrants should receive an admissions ticket about three weeks before the test. Late registrants should receive the ticket about a week before the test. Emergency registrants complete their registration at the test site. If you don't get your registration ticket in a timely manner, or the ticket has errors, contact National Evaluation Systems at the phone number in the registration booklet.

TEST SCHEDULE

The LAST and the ATS-W each take four and a half hours with four hours of testing time and 30 minutes for instructions. The LAST is given from 8:00 A.M. to 12:30 P.M. and the ATS-W from 1:00 P.M. to 5:30 P.M. It takes nine hours if you take two tests. Most students take just one test at a time, unless it is an emergency.

ALTERNATIVE TEST ARRANGEMENTS

You may qualify for special test arrangements if your religious beliefs do not permit you to take tests on Saturday, or if you have a physical, cognitive, or emotional disability. All requests for alternative testing arrangements must be made during the regular registration period.

Alternative tests for religious reasons are given on the Sunday following the regular test dates at selected test sites. You should submit a regular registration form, an Alternative Testing Arrangements Request Form, and a letter from a clergy member on official letterhead.

If you have a disability, you can request more time on a regular test date or request alternative test arrangements. Some disabilities can be accommodated at all test sites, while others require a separate test site. You should submit a regular registration form, an Alternative Testing Arrangements Request Form, and complete documentation of your disability.

As a practical matter, you or your counselor should contact National Evaluation Systems well in advance of the registration deadline to explain your needs and to find out the sort of documentation they require.

2 LAST/ATS-W PREPARATION TECHNIQUES AND TEST-TAKING STRATEGIES

TEST INFO BOX

This chapter shows you essential test-taking strategies that will help you improve your score. It includes steps for written assignments and scored written assignment examples. The most important strategies are discussed below.

MULTIPLE-CHOICE

Eliminate and then guess. There is no penalty for wrong answers. Never leave any answer blank.

Suppose you eliminate just one incorrect answer choice on all the items and you guess every answer. On average you would get about 26 correct. Suppose you eliminate two incorrect answer choices on all the items and you guess every answer. On average, you would get 40 correct.

WRITTEN ASSIGNMENT

Write an outline first, then complete the written assignment.
Write 4, 5, or 6 paragraphs with 75 to 85 words in each paragraph.

The LAST written assignment is used to evaluate your writing ability. The ATS-W written assignment is used to evaluate your ability to respond to education related situations.

Topic Paragraph: Begin the written assignment with an introduction to orient the reader to the topic. The first paragraph should clearly state the main idea of your entire written assignment.
Topic Sentence: Begin each paragraph with a topic sentence that supports the main idea.
Details: Provide details, examples, and arguments to support the topic sentence.
Grammar, Punctuation, Spelling: Edit sentences to conform to standard usage. Avoid passive construction; write actively and avoid the passive voice. That is, write "I passed the test," rather than "The test was passed."
Conclusion: End the written assignment with a paragraph that summarizes your main points.

PREPARING FOR THE LAST AND THE ATS-W

By now you've sent in the registration form and the test is at least four to nine weeks away. This section describes how to prepare for the LAST and the ATS-W. The next chapter describes test taking strategies. Before we go on, let's think about what you are preparing for.

Wait! Why Test Me? I'm a Good Person!

Why indeed? Life would be so much easier without tests. If anyone tells you that they like to take tests, don't believe them. Nobody does. Tests are imperfect. Some people pass when they should have failed, while others fail when they should have passed. It may not be fair, but it is very real. So sit back and relax. You're just going to have to do it, and this book will show you how.

Who Makes Up These Tests and How Do They Get Written?

Consider the following scenario. It is late in the afternoon. Around a table sit teachers, deans of education, parents, and representatives of the state education department. In front of each person is a preliminary list of skills and knowledge that teachers should possess. The list comes from comments by an even larger group of teachers and other educational professionals.

Those around the table are regular people just like the ones you might run into in a store or on the street. They all care about education. They also bring to the table their own strengths and weaknesses—their own perspectives and biases. What's that? An argument just broke out. People are choosing up sides and, depending on the outcome, one item on the list will stay or go.

The final list goes to professional test writers to prepare test items. These items are tried out, refined, and put through a review process. Eventually the test question bank is established, and a test is born. These test writers are not geniuses. They just know how to write questions. You might get a better score on this test than some of them would.

Keep those people around the table and the test writers in mind as you use this book. You are preparing for their test. Soon, you will be like one of those people around the table. You may even contribute to a test like this one.

Get Yourself Ready for the Test

Most people feel at least a little bit uncomfortable about tests. You are probably one of them. No book is going to make you feel comfortable. But here are some suggestions.

Most people are less tense when they exercise. Set up a reasonable exercise program for yourself. The program should involve exercising in a way that is appropriate for you 30 to 45 minutes each day. This exercise may be just as important as other preparation.

Prepare with another person. You will feel less isolated if you have a friend or colleague to study with.

Accept these important truths. You are not going to get all the answers correct. You don't have to. You can take this test over again if you have to. There is no penalty for taking the test again. This is not a do or die, life or death situation.

WHAT COLLEGE STUDENTS SAY ABOUT THE TESTS

More than 500 students were surveyed just after they took the LAST and the ATS-W. Their reactions to the tests and their advice to future test-takers are summarized on the next page.

What College Students Say About the LAST

Students say you should take the LAST after the sophomore year. Most students say answer the multiple-choice items first and then write the essay. But other students report success when they write the essay first. Even the best test takers say that time pressure can be a real issue on the LAST. They advise using a watch or clock to monitor your time and to leave an hour for the essay. Check with your education advisor for advice about when to take the LAST.

Multiple Choice

Students say the LAST is primarily a reading comprehension test. The test consists mainly of passages followed by items about the passage. Some passages are difficult and some items are tricky. Passages and items may integrate liberal arts concepts.

Students say you will see some mathematics, reading graphs, charts and maps, and English usage items. The visual arts items often show a picture and ask for some common sense interpretation. Items related to these topics are not reading comprehension items.

Students say that almost all of the items can be answered just from the information in the passage.

Written Assignment

Students say the most important thing is to write an outline before you start to write. They say to be sure to write about the topic. The written assignment can be about anything. It is how you write, not your point of view that matters.

Students' Advice to You About Preparing for the LAST

1. Learn how to answer reading comprehension items and how to write an essay under time pressure.
2. Take practice tests in realistic situations.
3. Practice reading in the content areas of science, history, and social studies.
4. Get a broad overview of mathematics, reading graphs, charts, maps, and English.

What College Students Say About the ATS-W

Students say you should take the ATS-W after you finish most of your education courses and after you have field experience. Most students say answer the multiple-choice items first and then complete the written assignment. Check with your education advisor about when to take the ATS-W.

Multiple Choice

Students say the ATS-W is just as much about your teaching experience as about your college education courses. Most of the test consists of passages describing teaching or other education-related situations followed by items about the passage.

Students say most of the information needed to answer the items is found in the passage.

Students say you need to use common sense based on your education experience as you answer the questions. They say that between 35 percent and 55 percent of the items can be answered using informed common sense.

Students say you should have a broad general background in education related areas.

Written Assignment

Students say the most important thing is to write at least a brief outline before you start to write the assignment. They say to be sure to write about the topic. The written assignment will be about a teaching or school-related situation. It is how well you respond to the education-related situation, not your writing ability, that matters on this written assignment.

Students' Advice to You About Preparing for the ATS-W

1. Get lots of teaching experience.
2. Take practice tests in a realistic situation.
3. Get a broad overview of education-related areas.
4. Learn how to answer reading comprehension items and how to write essays and curricula. Practice reading and writing.

FOLLOW THIS FINAL WEEK PLAN

MONDAY

Make sure you have your admission ticket.
Make sure you know where the test is given.
Make sure you know how you're getting there.

TUESDAY

Visit the test site, if you haven't done it already. You don't want any surprises this Saturday.

WEDNESDAY

Get some sharpened No. 2 pencils, a digital watch or clock, and a good big eraser and put them aside.

THURSDAY

Take a break from preparing for the test, and relax.

FRIDAY

Complete any forms you have to bring to the test.
Prepare any snacks or food you want to bring with you.
Talk to someone who makes you feel good or do something enjoyable and relaxing.
Have a good night's sleep.

SATURDAY—TEST DAY

Dress comfortably. There are no points for appearance.
Eat the same kind of breakfast you've been eating each morning.
Don't stuff yourself. You want your blood racing through your brain, not your stomach.
Get together things to bring to the test including: registration ticket, identification forms, pencils, calculator, eraser, and snacks or food.

Get to the test room, not the parking lot, about 10 to 15 minutes before the start time.
Remember to leave time for parking and walking to the test site.
Hand in your forms—you're in the door. You're ready. This is the easy part.
Follow the test-taking strategies in the next section.

PROVEN TEST-TAKING STRATEGIES

Testing companies like to pretend that test taking strategies don't help that much. They act like that because they want everyone to think that their tests only measure your knowledge of the subject. Of course, they are just pretending; knowing test taking strategies can make a big difference.

However, there is nothing better than being prepared for the material on this test. If you are prepared, then these strategies can make a difference. Use them. Other people will be. Not using them may very well lower your score.

Be Comfortable

Get a good seat. Don't sit near anyone or anything that will distract you. Stay away from your friends. If you don't like where you are sitting, move or ask for another seat. You paid money for this test, and you have a right to favorable test conditions.

You Will Make Mistakes

You are going to make mistakes on this test. The people who wrote the test expect you to make them.

You Are Not Competing with Anyone

Don't worry about how anyone else is doing. Your score does not depend on theirs. When the score report comes out it doesn't say, "Nancy got a 661, but Blaire got a 670." You just want to get the score required for your certificate. If you can do better, that's great. Stay focused. Remember your goal.

MULTIPLE-CHOICE STRATEGIES

It's Not What You Know That Matters, It's Just Which Circle You Fill In

No one you know or care about will see your test. An impersonal machine scores all multiple-choice questions. The machine just senses whether the correct circle on the answer sheet is filled in. That is the way the test makers want it. If that's good enough for them, it should be good enough for you. Concentrate on filling in the correct circle.

Do Your Work in the Test Booklet

You can write anything you want in your test booklet. The test booklet is not used for scoring and no one will look at it. You can't bring scratch paper to the test so use your booklet instead.

Some of the strategies we recommend involve writing in and marking up the booklet. These strategies work and we strongly recommend that you use them.

Do your work for a question near that question in the test booklet. You can also do work on the cover or wherever else suits you. You may want to do calculations, underline important words, mark up a picture, or draw a diagram.

You Can Be Right but Be Marked Wrong

If you get the right answer but fill in the wrong circle, the machine will mark it wrong. We told you that filling in the right circle was what mattered. We strongly recommend that you follow this strategy.

Write the letter for your answer big in the test booklet next to the number for the problem. If you change your mind about an answer, cross off the "old" letter and write the "new" one. At the end of each section, transfer all the answers together from the test booklet to the answer sheet.

What number times 0.00708 is equal to 70.8?

(A) ~~100,000 × 0.00708 = 708~~

(B) $10,000 \times 0.00708 = 70.8$

(C) 1,000

(D) 0.01

B

The correct answer is (B) 10,000.

Watch That Answer Sheet

Remember that a machine is doing the marking. Fill in the correct answer circle completely. Don't put extra pencil marks on the answer section of the answer sheet. Stray marks could be mistaken for answers.

Some Questions Are Traps

Some questions include the words *not, least,* or *except.* You are being asked for the answer that doesn't fit with the rest. Be alert for these types of questions.

Save the Hard Questions for Last

You're not supposed to get all the questions correct, and some of them will be too difficult for you. Work through the questions and answer the easy ones. Pass the other ones by. Do these more difficult questions the second time through. If a question seems really hard, draw a circle around the question number in the test booklet. Save these questions until the very end.

They Show You the Answer

Every multiple-choice test shows you the correct answer for each question. The answer is staring right at you. You just have to figure out which one it is. There is a 20 or 25 percent chance you'll get it right by just closing your eyes and pointing.

Some Answers Are Traps

When someone writes a test question, they include distracters. Distracters are traps—incorrect answers that look like correct answers. It might be an answer to an addition problem when you should be multiplying. It might be a correct answer to a different question. It might just be an answer that catches your eye. Watch out for this type of incorrect answer.

Eliminate the Incorrect Answers

If you can't figure out which answer is correct, then decide which answers can't be correct. Choose the answers you're sure are incorrect. Cross them off in the test booklet. Only one left? That's the correct answer.

Guess, Guess, Guess

If there are still two or more answers left, then guess. Guess the answer from those remaining. Never leave any item blank. There is no penalty for guessing.

WRITTEN ASSIGNMENT STRATEGIES

Here's How They Score You

Written assignments are rated 0–3. The raters use these general guidelines.

3 A well developed, complete written assignment. Shows a thorough response to all parts of the topic. Clear explanations that are well supported. An assignment that is free of significant grammatical, punctuation, or spelling errors.

2 A fairly well developed, complete written assignment. It may not thoroughly respond to all parts of the topic. Fairly clear explanations that may not be well supported. It may contain some significant grammatical, punctuation, or spelling errors.

1 A poorly developed, incomplete written assignment. It does not thoroughly respond to most parts of the topic. Contains many poor explanations that are not well supported. It may contain some significant grammatical, punctuation, or spelling errors.

0 A very poorly developed, incomplete written assignment. It does not thoroughly respond to the topic. Contains only poor, unsupported explanations. Contains numerous significant grammatical, punctuation, or spelling errors

Unscorable Written Assignments

A written assignment is rated unscorable (U) if it is blank; unrelated to the topic, no matter how well written; not long enough to score; written in a language other than English; or illegible. A rating of U means the test is a failure regardless of the score on the multiple-choice section.

Your Responses Are Graded Holistically

Holistic rating means the raters assign a score based on their informed sense about your writing. Raters have a lot of essays to look at and they do not do a detailed analysis.

After each test date, National Evaluation Systems gets together a group of readers in Albany, New York. These readers typically consist of teachers and college professors. They put these readers up in an Albany area motel. At first, representatives of NES show the readers the topics for the recent test and review the types of responses that should be rated 0, 1, 2, or 3. The readers are trained to evaluate the responses according to the NES guidelines.

Each written assignment is evaluated twice, without the second reader knowing the evaluation given by the first reader. If the two evaluations differ significantly, other readers review the assignment. Your score is the sum of the evaluations.

Using This Section

This section shows you how to write passing essays. It goes without saying that readers have a tedious, tiring assignment. Think about those readers as you write. Write a response that makes it easy for them to give you a high score.

Steps for Writing Passing Written Assignments

Follow these steps to write a passing essay. You should allow about an hour to complete all the steps. The time estimates below are approximate.

1. **Understand the assignment. (2 minutes)**
   Each topic provides a subject and then describes the subject in more detail. Read the topic carefully to ensure that you understand each of these parts.

2. **Choose thesis statement. Write it down. (3 minutes)**
   Readers expect you to have one clear main point of view about the topic. Choose yours; make sure it addresses the entire topic, and stick to it.

3. **Write an outline. (10 minutes)**
   Write a brief outline summarizing the following essay elements.
   - Thesis statement
   - Introduction
   - Topic sentence and details for each paragraph
   - Conclusion
   Use this time to plan your essay.

4. **Write the assignment. (40 minutes)**
   Essays scoring 2 or 3 higher typically have five, six, or seven paragraphs totaling 300–600 words. Writing an essay this long does not guarantee a passing score, but most passing essays are about this long.
   Use this time to write well.

5. **Proofread and edit your writing. (5 minutes)**
   Read your essay over and correct any errors in usage, spelling, or punctuation. The readers understand that your essay is a first draft and they expect to see corrections.

Apply the Steps

Here's how to apply these steps for a particular written assignment. Follow along and write in your own ideas when called for. Remember, for any written assignment, there are many different thesis statements and essays that would receive a passing score.

WRITTEN ASSIGNMENT

Sample Written Assignment

Overall, do machines help people or do machines cause difficulty for people, and what type of machine fits the category you choose? The information below presents both sides of this question.

Overall, machines help people. Machines have lessened the workload for mankind and have enabled workers to be more productive. Other machines help keep people healthier and sustain life. Still other machines make life easier at home and help people travel easily from one place to the other to visit loved ones. Does anyone really want to do away with machines and return to earlier times when humans were consumed with manual labor? There can be no doubt that, overall, machines help people and there are many examples of helpful machines.

Overall, machines cause difficulty for people. Just look at one of our favorite machines, the automobile. More than 40,000 people are killed in automobile accidents each year and hundreds of thousands more are seriously injured or completely disabled. Other machines fill the atmosphere with poisonous fumes and may well lead to the ultimate destruction of mankind when there is no oxygen left to breathe. Sure there are *some* helpful machines. But, there can be no doubt overall that machines cause difficulty for people, and there are very many examples of machines that cause difficulty for people.

Overall, do machines help people or do machines cause difficulty for people?

Review and evaluate the opposing positions presented above.

Choose one of these positions. Support your position with a specific example of a machine that helps people or a machine that causes difficulty.

Write an essay that supports your position following the guidelines presented above.

1. **Understand the written assignment. (2 minutes)**

    The assignment is about machines. I have to decide whether to write about machines that causes difficulty for people OR about machines that help people. I have to give a specific example of a machine that is a difficulty or a machine that helps. It does not make any difference which one I pick.

    I've got to stick to this topic.

    I'm going to choose machines that help people.

    A complete response to the topic is an essay about a machine that helps people. There are many machines to choose from. An incomplete response will significantly lower the score.

2. **Choose thesis statement. Write it down. (3 minutes)**

    This important step sets the stage for your entire essay. Work through this section actively. Write down the names of several machines that help people. There is no one correct answer, so it does not have to be an exhaustive list.

    > Computers
    > Escalator
    > Car
    > Heart-lung machine
    > Fax machine

    Suppose you choose the heart-lung machine.

    Now write how, what, and why heart-lung machines help people.
    How: Circulate blood in place of the heart?
    What: Replaces the heart during heart surgery.
    Why: The heart is unable to pump blood when it is being operated on.

    Now write the choice from your list of machines. _____

    Thesis statement.

    My thesis statement is "Overall, machines help people." A heart-lung machine is an example of a helpful machine. Heart-lung machines are machines that help people by taking the place of the heart during heart surgery.

    The thesis statement establishes I have chosen the position that machines are helpful and the heart-lung machine is my example of a machine that helps people and explains the basis for my choice of the heart-lung machine. Both parts are needed for an effective thesis statement.

    Write your thesis statement.

    _____

3. Write an outline. (10 minutes)
   - Introduction, including the thesis statement

_____

   - A heart-lung machine saves lives.
    People would die if the machines were not available.

   - The machine circulates and filters blood during operations.
    Special membranes filter the blood, removing impurities.

_____

   - The heart can literally stop while the heart-lung machine is in use.
    Doctors have to restart the heart.

_____

   - Conclusion

Write an outline to plan your essay. Your outline consists of an introduction, topic sentences and supporting details for three paragraphs, and a conclusion. That's five paragraphs in all.

Write an outline for your written assignment.

_____

_____

_____

_____

_____

_____

_____

_____

_____

4. Write the assignment. (40 minutes)

I spent the time writing an outline to plan my essay. I am going to rely on that plan as I write my essay.
Use a separate piece of paper.
Write your own essay about the heart-lung machine—a machine that helps people.

5. Proofread and edit your essay. (5 minutes)
Edit your essay. Remember that readers expect to see changes.

Check

You will find five rated sample essays on this topic on this and the following pages. Compare your essays to these sample essays. Rate your essay 0–3 using these samples and the scoring guide on page 57.

Practice

Write, proofread, and edit an essay on your topic. Rate your essay 0–3. Try to show your essays to an English professor or an experienced essay evaluator. Ask that person to evaluate your essays and make recommendations for improving your writing.

SAMPLE WRITTEN ASSIGNMENTS

ESSAY 1

This essay would likely receive a total score of 0–2 out of 6.

I think that machines are mostly helpful to people,

Look at the heart-lung machine which are a medical miracle. Heart lung machines are use in hospitals all over the country. Doctors use this machine while doing surgery. Heart lung machines keep people alive during surgery and they use them to do open heart surgery. Lots of people can than the heart lung machine for keeping them alive.

Some people say that their are too many bypass surgerys done every year and this may cause more problems than it fixes. However, lots of people would die without the machine. Its a good thing that the heart lung machine was invented.

ESSAY 2

This essay would likely receive a total score of 2 or 3 out of 6.

Overall, machines are mostly helpful to people. A heart lung machine is an example of a machine that helps.

Heart lung machines are use in hospitals all over the world. They get use every day. People are hook up to them when they are having surgery like if they are having open heart surgery.

I will now present one way heart lung machines are in use. Once we didn't have heart lung machines to help a doctor. When the machine was invent we see lots of changes in surgry that a doctor can do. The doctor can operate during the person heart not work. My grandmother went to the hospital for have surgry and they use the machine. Where she would been without the machine.

And the machine keep blood move through the body. The doctor can take their time to fix a person heart while they are laying their on the operating room. I know someone who work in a hospital and they say didn't know how it was possible befour machine.

Last, that machine clean a bodies blood as it foes through. The blood won't poison the person wh blood it is. But it wood be better if body clean its own blood. A body better machine. I did tell you how the machine work and what it did. The machine can save a lifes.

ESSAY 3

This essay would likely receive a total score of 3–5 out of 6.

This is what this essay looked like after editing. Note the editorial changes the student made during the editing process. This is the essay raters would actually see. The raters expect to see these changes and marks.

Machines and People

Overall, machines are helpful to people. I have chosen the heart lung machine as an example of a machine that helps people. Heart lung machines are a ~~medicine~~ medical miracle. They are used in hospitals all over the world. Heart lung machines are used during open heart surgery to circulate a patient's blood and clean the blood.

These machines can save lots of ~~lifes~~ lives.

Heart-lung machines have made open heart surgery possible. Before they were invented, many people died of disease or during surgery. Surgery would not have been ~~impossible~~ before then. And many people are alive today because of them. Besides surgery can now go on for hours. Sometimes the surgery can last as long as 12 hours. The heart lung machine makes things ~~very~~ possible and saves lives. Heart lung machines circulate blood ~~thru~~ through the body. It pumps like a heart. The heart can stop and the heart lung machine will pump instead. Then the blood moves through the body just like the heart pumping. So the blood gets to all the veins. It is ~~too~~ unbelievable ~~why~~ how the heart lung machine can work and keep people from dying.

The heart lung machine can clean a person's blood. All the bad stuff gets taken out of the blood before it goes back into the body. That way the body won't get poison. I know of ~~someone~~ who had their blood cleaned by the machine while they were operated on. The person was ~~unconscience~~ unconscious. The doctor fixed his heart. ~~Since~~ Because the machine was going the person's heart was stopped. The doctor had to start it up again. It was pretty scary to think about that happening to a person. But the machine took the bad stuff out of the blood and the person lived.

To conclude, I believe that the heart lung machine is great for people who need open heart surgery. It pumps and cleans their blood too. They are a medical miracle.

ESSAY 4

This essay would likely receive a total score of 5 or 6 out of 6.

The Heart Lung Machine--Proof That Overall, Machines Help People

In my opinion, machines are likely to help people than to cause difficulty. I have chosen the heart-lung machine as an example of a helpful machine. In this essay I will explain what the heart-lung machine does and how it is helpful.

Every day the heart-lung machine saves someone's life. The heart-lung machine is a wonderful machine that makes open-heart surgery possible by pumping and cleaning a person's blood. Surgeons use the machine during open-heart surgery. Each day we walk by someone who is alive because of the heart-lung machine. Each day throughout the world skilled surgeons perform difficult surgery with the aid of a heart-lung machine.

The heart-lung machine makes open-heart surgery possible. Open-heart surgery means the doctor is operating inside of the heart. In order to operate on the inside of the heart, the flow of blood must be stopped. But without blood flow the patient would die. Researchers worked for decades to find a way to keep a patient alive while the hearty was stopped. They were eventually successful and they named the machine a heart-lung machine. The first heart-lung machines were probably very primitive, but today's machines are very sophisticated.

The heart-lung machine circulates blood while the heart is not pumping. The blood is taken from the body into one side of the machine and pumped back into the body though the other side. The blood pumped back into the body travels through the circulatory system.

However, just pumping blood is not enough. As blood passes through a person's body, the body uses oxygen stored in the blood. Blood starts from the heart full of oxygen and returns to the heart without much oxygen. The lungs take in oxygen and pass that oxygen on to the blood. But during surgery the heart-lung machine does the lung's work and puts oxygen in the blood as the blood passes through the machine.

The heart-lung machine makes open-heart surgery possible. The machine circulates and oxygenates a person's blood while the heart is stopped. Without the machine, many people would die from heart disease or would die during surgery. The heart-lung machine is a machine that helps people by keeping them alive and holds the promise of even more amazing machines to come.

PART II

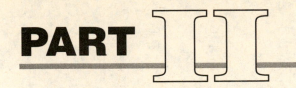

Core Review

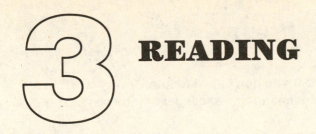

3 READING

VOCABULARY REVIEW

You can't read if you don't know the vocabulary. But you don't have to know every word in the dictionary. Follow this reasonable approach to understand the vocabulary on these tests.

CONTEXT CLUES

Many times you can figure out a word from its context. Look at these examples. Synonyms, antonyms, examples, or descriptions may help you figure out the word.

1. The woman's mind wandered as her two friends *prated* on. It really did not bother her though. In all the years she had known them, they had always *babbled* about their lives. It was almost comforting.
2. The wind *abated* in the late afternoon. Things were different yesterday when the wind had *picked up* toward the end of the day.
3. The argument with her boss had been her *Waterloo*. She wondered if the *defeat* suffered by Napoleon *at this famous place* had felt the same.
4. The events swept the politician into a *vortex* of controversy. The politician knew what it meant to be spun around like a toy boat in the *swirl of water* that swept down the bathtub drain.

Passage 1 gives a synonym for the unknown word. We can tell that *prated* means babbled. *Babbled* is used as a synonym of *prated* in the passage.

Passage 2 gives an antonym for the unknown word. We can tell that *abated* means slowed down or diminished because *picked up* is used as an antonym of *abated*.

Passage 3 gives a description of the unknown word. The description of *Waterloo* tells us that the word means *defeat*.

Passage 4 gives an example of the unknown word. This example of a *swirl of water* going down the bathtub drain gives us a good idea of what a *vortex* is.

ROOTS

A root is the basic element of a word. The root is usually related to the word's origin. Roots can often help you figure out the word's meaning. Here are some roots that may help you.

Root	Meaning	Examples
bio	life	biography, biology
circu	around	circumference, circulate
frac	break	fraction, refract
geo	earth	geology, geography
mal	bad	malicious, malcontent
matr, mater	mother	maternal, matron
neo	new	neonate, neoclassic
patr, pater	father	paternal, patron
spec	look	spectacles, specimen
tele	distant	telephone, television

PREFIXES

Prefixes are syllables that come at the beginning of a word. Prefixes usually have a standard meaning. They can often help you figure out the word's meaning. Here is a list of prefixes that may help you figure out a word.

Prefix	Meaning	Examples
a-	not	amoral, apolitical
il-, im-, ir-	not	illegitimate, immoral, incorrect
un-	not	unbearable, unknown
non-	not	nonbeliever, nonsense
ant-, anti-	against	antiwar, antidote
de-	opposite	defoliate, declaw
mis-	wrong	misstep, misdeed
ante-	before	antedate, antecedent
fore-	before	foretell, forecast
post-	after	postfight, postoperative
re-	again	refurbish, redo
super-	above	superior, superstar
sub-	below	subsonic, subpar

THE VOCABULARY LIST

Here is a list of a few hundred vocabulary words. This list includes everyday words and a few specialized education terms. Read through the list and visualize the words and their definitions. After a while you will become very familiar with them.

Of course, this is not anywhere near all the words you need to know for the exams. But they will give you a start. These words also will give you some idea of the kinds of words you may encounter on the examinations.

Another great way to develop a vocabulary is to read a paper every day and a news magazine every week, in addition to the other reading you are doing. There are also several inexpensive books, including *1100 Words You Need to Know*, *Pocket Guide to Vocabulary*, and *Vocabulary Success* from Barron's, which may help you develop your vocabulary further.

abhor To regard with horror
I abhor violence.

abstain To refrain by choice
Ray decided to abstain from fattening foods.

abstract Not related to any object, theoretical
Mathematics can be very abstract.

acquisition An addition to an established group or collection
The museum's most recent acquisition was an early Roman vase.

admonish To correct firmly but kindly
The teacher admonished the student not to chew gum in class.

adroit Skillful or nimble in difficult circumstances
The nine year old was already an adroit gymnast.

adversary A foe or enemy
The wildebeast was ever-alert for its ancient adversary, the lion.

advocate To speak for an idea; a person who speaks for an idea
Lou was an advocate of gun control.

aesthetic Pertaining to beauty
Ron found the painting a moving aesthetic experience.

affective To do with the emotional or feeling aspect of learning
Len read the Taxonomy of Educational Objectives: Affective Domain.

alias An assumed name
The check forger had used an alias.

alleviate To reduce or make more bearable
The hot shower helped alleviate the pain in her back.

allude To make an indirect reference to, hint at
Elaine only alluded to her previous trips through the state.

ambiguous Open to many interpretations
That is an ambiguous statement.

apathy Absence of passion or emotion
The teacher tried to overcome their apathy toward the subject.

apprehensive Fear or unease about possible outcomes
Bob was apprehensive about visiting the dentist.

aptitude The ability to gain from a particular type of instruction
The professor pointed out that aptitude alone was not enough for success in school.

articulate To speak clearly and distinctly, present a point of view
Chris was chosen to articulate the group's point of view.

assess To measure or determine an outcome or value
There are many informal ways to assess learning.

attest To affirm or certify
I can attest to Cathy's ability as a softball pitcher.

augment To increase or add to
The new coins augmented the already large collection.

belated Past time or tardy
George sent a belated birthday card.

benevolent Expresses good will or kindly feelings
The club was devoted to performing benevolent acts.

biased A prejudiced view or action
The judge ruled that the decision was biased.

bolster To shore up, support
The explorer sang to bolster her courage.

candid Direct and outspoken
Lee was well known for her candid comments.

caricature Exaggerated, ludicrous picture, in words or a cartoon
The satirist presented world leaders as caricatures.

carnivorous Flesh eating or predatory
The lion is a carnivorous animal.

censor A person who judges the morality of others; act on that judgment
Please don't censor my views!

censure Expression of disapproval, reprimand
The senate acted to censure the congressman.

cessation The act of ceasing or halting
The eleventh hour marked the cessation of hostilities.

chronic Continuing and constant
Asthma can be a chronic condition.

clandestine Concealed or secret
The spy engaged in clandestine activities.

cogent Intellectually convincing
He presented a cogent argument.

cognitive Relates to the intellectual area of learning
Lou read the Taxonomy of Educational Objectives: Cognitive Domain.

competency Demonstrated ability
Bert demonstrated the specified mathematics competency.

complacent Unaware self-satisfaction
The tennis player realized she had become complacent.

concept A generalization
The professor lectured on concept development.

congenital Existing at birth but non-hereditary
The baby had a small congenital defect.

contemporaries Belonging in the same time period, about the same age
Piaget and Bruner were contemporaries.

contempt Feeling or showing disdain or scorn
She felt nothing but contempt for their actions.

contentious Argumentative
Tim was in a contentious mood.

corroborate To make certain with other information, to confirm
The reporter would always corroborate a story before publication.

credence Claim to acceptance or trustworthiness
They did not want to lend credence to his views.

cursory Surface, not in depth
Ron gave his car a cursory inspection.

daunt To intimidate with fear
Harry did not let the difficulty of the task daunt him.

debacle Disastrous collapse or rout
The whole trip had been a debacle.

debilitate To make feeble
He was concerned that the flu would debilitate him.

decadent Condition of decline/decay
Joan said in frustration, "We live in a decadent society."

deductive Learning that proceeds from general to specific
He proved his premise using deductive logic.

demographic Population data
The census gathers demographic information.

denounce To condemn a person or idea
The diplomat rose in the United Nations to denounce the plan.

deter To prevent or stop an action, usually by some threat
The president felt that the peace conference would help deter aggression.

diligent A persistent effort; a person who makes such an effort
The investigator was diligent in her pursuit of the truth.

discern To perceive or recognize, often by insight
The principal attempted to discern which student was telling the truth.

discord Disagreement or disharmony
Gail's early promotion led to discord in the office.

discriminate To distinguish among people or groups based on their characteristics
It is not appropriate to discriminate based on race or ethnicity.

disdain To show or act with contempt
The professional showed disdain for her amateurish efforts.

disseminate To send around, scatter
The health organization will disseminate any new information on the flu.

divergent Thinking that extends in many directions, is not focused
Les was an intelligent but divergent thinker.

diverse Not uniform, varied
Alan came from a diverse neighborhood.

duress coercion
He claimed that he confessed under duress.

eccentric Behaves unusually, different from the norm
His long hair and midnight walks made Albert appear eccentric.

eclectic Drawing from several ideas or practices
Joe preferred an eclectic approach to the practice of psychology.

eloquent Vivid, articulate expression
The congregation was spellbound by the eloquent sermon.

emanate To flow out, come forth
How could such wisdom emanate from one so young?

embellish To make things seem more than they are
Art loved to embellish the truth.

empirical From observation or experiment
The scientist's conclusions were based on empirical evidence.

employment A job or professional position (paid)
You seek employment so you can make the big bucks.

enduring Lasting over the long term
Their friendship grew into an enduring relationship.

enhance To improve or build up
The mechanic used a fuel additive to enhance the car's performance.

enigma A mystery or puzzle
The communist bloc is an "enigma wrapped inside a mystery." (Churchill)

equity Equal attention or treatment
The workers were seeking pay equity with others in their industry.

equivocal Uncertain, capable of multiple interpretations
In an attempt to avoid conflict, the negotiator took an equivocal stand.

expedite To speed up, facilitate
Hal's job at the shipping company was to expedite deliveries.

exploit Take maximum advantage of, perhaps unethically
Her adversary tried to exploit her grief to gain an advantage.

extrinsic Coming from outside
The teacher turned to extrinsic motivation.

farce A mockery
The attorney objected, saying that the testimony made the trial a farce.

feign To pretend, make a false appearance of
Some people feign illness to get out of work.

fervent Marked by intense feeling
The spokesman presented a fervent defense of the company's actions.

fiasco Total failure
They had not prepared for the presentation, and it turned into a fiasco.

formidable Difficult to surmount
State certification requirements can present a formidable obstacle.

fracas A noisy quarrel or a scrap
The debate turned into a full-fledged fracas.

gamut Complete range or extent
Waiting to take the test, her mind ran the gamut of emotions.

glib Quickness suggesting insincerity
The glib response made Rita wonder about the speaker's sincerity.

grave Very serious or weighty
The supervisor had grave concerns about the worker's ability.

guile Cunning, crafty, duplicitous
When the truth failed, he tried to win his point with guile.

handicapped Having one or more disabilities
The child study team classified Loren as handicapped.

harass Bother persistently
Some fans came to harass the players on the opposing team.

heterogeneous A group with normal variation in ability or performance
Students from many backgrounds formed a heterogeneous population.

homogeneous A group with little variation in ability or performance
The school used test scores to place students in homogeneous groups.

hypocrite One who feigns a virtuous character or belief
Speaking against drinking and then driving drunk make him a hypocrite!

immune Protected or exempt from disease or harm
The vaccination made Ray immune to measles.

impartial Fair and objective
The contestants agreed on an objective, impartial referee.

impasse Situation with no workable solution
The talks had not stopped, but they had reached an impasse.

impede To retard or obstruct
Mason did not let adversity impede his progress.

implicit Understood but not directly stated
They never spoke about the matter, but they had an implicit understanding.

indifferent Uncaring or apathetic
The teacher was indifferent to the student's pleas for an extension.

indigenous Native to an area
The botanist recognized it as an indigenous plant.

inductive Learning that proceeds from specific to general
Science uses an inductive process, from examples to a generalization.

inevitable Certain and unavoidable
After the rains, the collapse of the dam was inevitable.

infer To reach a conclusion not explicitly stated
The advertisement sought to infer that the product was superior.

inhibit To hold back or restrain
The hormone was used to inhibit growth.

innovate To introduce something new or change established procedure
Mere change was not enough, they had to innovate the procedure.

inquiry Question-based Socratic learning
Much of science teaching uses inquiry-based learning.

intrinsic inherent, the essential nature
The teacher drew on the meaning of the topic for an intrinsic motivation.

inundate To overwhelm, flood
It was December, and mail began to inundate the post office.

jocular Characterized by joking or good nature
The smiling man seemed to be a jocular fellow.

judicial Relating to the administration of justice
His goal was to have no dealings with the judicial system.

knack A talent for doing something
Ron had a real knack for mechanical work.

languid Weak, lacking energy
The sunbather enjoyed a languid afternoon at the shore.

liaison An illicit relationship or a means of communication
The governor appointed his chief aid liaison to the senate.

lucid Clear and easily understood
The teacher answered the question in a direct and lucid way.

magnanimous Generous in forgiving
Loretta is a magnanimous to a fault.

malignant Very injurious, evil
Crime is a malignant sore on our society.

malleable Open to being shaped or influenced
He had a malleable position on gun control.

meticulous Very careful and precise
Gina took meticulous care of the fine china.

miser A money hoarder
The old miser had more money than he could ever use.

monotonous Repetitive and boring
Circling the airport, waiting to land, became monotonous.

mores Understood rules of society
Linda made following social mores her goal in life.

motivation Something that creates interest or action
Most good lessons begin with good motivation.

myriad Large indefinite number
Look skyward and be amazed by the myriad of stars.

naive Lacking sophistication
Laura is unaware, and a little naive, about the impact she has on others.

nemesis A formidable rival
Lex Luthor is Superman's nemesis.

novice A beginner
Her unsteady legs revealed that Sue was a novice skater.

nullified Removed the importance of
The penalty nullified the 20-yard gain made by the running back.

objective A goal
The teacher wrote an objective for each lesson.

oblivious Unaware and unmindful
Les was half asleep and oblivious to the racket around him.

obscure Vague, unclear, uncertain
The lawyer quoted an obscure reference.

ominous Threatening or menacing
There were ominous black storm clouds on the horizon.

palatable Agreeable, acceptable
Sandy's friends tried to make her punishment more palatable.

panorama A comprehensive view or picture
The visitors' center offered a panorama of the canyon below.

pedagogy The science of teaching
Part of certification tests focus on pedagogy.

perpetuate To continue or cause to be remembered
A plaque was put up to perpetuate the memory of the retiring teacher.

pompous Exaggerated self-importance
Rona acted pompous, but Lynne suspected she was very empty inside.

precarious Uncertain, beyond one's control
A diver sat on a precarious perch on a cliff above the water.

precedent An act or instance that sets the standard
The judge's ruling set a precedent for later cases.

preclude To act to make impossible or impracticable
Beau did not want to preclude any options.

precocious Very early development
Chad was very precocious and ran at six months.

prolific Abundant producer
Isaac Asimov was a prolific science fiction writer.

prognosis A forecast or prediction
The stock broker gave a guarded prognosis for continued growth.

provoke To stir up or anger
Children banging on the cage would provoke the circus lion to growl.

psychomotor Relates to the motor skill area of learning
I read the Taxonomy of Behavioral Objectives: Psychomotor Domain.

quagmire Predicament or difficult situation
The regulations were a quagmire of conflicting rules and vague terms.

qualm Feeling of doubt or misgiving
The teacher had not a single qualm about giving the student a low grade.

quandary A dilemma
The absence of the teacher aide left the teacher in a quandary.

quench To put out, satisfy
The glass of water was not enough to quench his thirst.

rancor Bitter continuing resentment
A deep rancor had existed between the two friends since the accident.

rationale The basis or reason for something
The speeder tried to present a rationale to the officer who stopped her.

reciprocal Mutual interchange
Each person got something out of their reciprocal arrangement.

refute To prove false
The lawyer used new evidence to refute claims made by the prosecution.

remedial Designed to compensate for learning deficits
Jim spent one period a day in remedial instruction.

reprove Criticize gently
The teacher would reprove students for chewing gum in class.

repudiate To reject or disown
The senator repudiated membership in an all male club.

resolve To reach a definite conclusion
A mediator was called in to resolve the situation.

retrospect Contemplation of the past
Ryan noted, in retrospect, that leaving home was his best decision.

revere To hold in the highest regard
Citizens of the town revere their long time mayor.

sanction To issue authoritative approval or a penalty
The boxing commissioner had to sanction the match.

scrutinize To inspect with great care
You should scrutinize any document before signing it.

siblings Brothers or sisters
The holidays give me the chance to spend time with my siblings.

skeptical Doubting, questioning the validity
The principal was skeptical about the students' reason for being late.

solace Comfort in misfortune
Her friends provided solace in her time of grief.

solitude Being alone
Pat enjoyed her Sunday afternoon moments of solitude.

stagnant Inert, contaminated
In dry weather the lake shrank to a stagnant pool.

stereotype An oversimplified generalized view or belief
We are all guilty of fitting people into a stereotype.

subsidy Financial assistance
Chris received a subsidy from her company so she could attend school.

subtle Faint, not easy to find or understand
Subtle changes in the teller's actions alerted the police to the robbery.

subterfuge A deceptive strategy
The spy used subterfuge to gain access to the secret materials.

superficial Surface, not profound
The inspector gave the car a superficial inspection.

tacit Not spoken, inferred
They had a tacit agreement.

taxonomy Classification of levels of thinking or organisms
I read each Taxonomy of Educational Objectives.

tenacious Persistent and determined
The police officer was tenacious in pursuit of a criminal.

tentative Unsure, uncertain
The athletic director set up a tentative basketball schedule.

terminate To end, conclude
He wanted to terminate the relationship.

transition Passage from one activity to another
The transition from college student to teacher was not easy.

trepidation Apprehension, state of dread
Erin felt some trepidation about beginning her new job

trivial Unimportant, ordinary
The seemingly trivial occurrence had taken on added importance.

ubiquitous Everywhere, omnipresent
A walk through the forest invited attacks from the ubiquitous mosquitoes.

ultimatum A final demand
After a trying day, the teacher issued an ultimatum to the class.

usurp To wrongfully and forcefully seize and hold, particularly power
The association vice president tried to usurp the president's power.

vacillate To swing indecisively
He had a tendency to vacillate in his stance on discipline.

valid Logically correct
The math teacher was explaining a valid mathematical proof.

vehement Forceful, passionate
The child had a vehement reaction to the teacher's criticism.

vestige A sign of something no longer there or existing
Old John was the last vestige of the first teachers to work at the school.

vicarious Experience through the activities or feelings of others
He had to experience sports in a vicarious way through his students.

virulent Very poisonous or noxious
The coral snake has a particularly virulent venom.

vital Important and essential
The school secretary was a vital part of the school.

waffle To write or speak in a misleading way
The spokesperson waffled as she tried to explain away the mistake.

wary Watchful, on guard
The soldiers were very wary of any movements in the field.

Xanadu An idyllic, perfect place
All wished for some time in Xanadu.

yearned Longed or hoped for
Liz yearned for a small class.

zeal Diligent devotion to a cause
Ron approached his job with considerable zeal.

STEPS FOR ANSWERING MULTIPLE-CHOICE READING ITEMS

Most of the LAST consists of passages followed by multiple-choice questions. You do not have to know what an entire reading passage is about. You just have to know enough to get the answer correct. Less than half, often less than 25 percent, of the information in any passage is needed to answer all the questions.

You do not have to read the passage in detail. In fact, careful slow reading will almost certainly get you into trouble. Strange as it seems, follow this advice—avoid careful, detailed reading at all costs.

Buried among all the false gold in the passage are a few valuable nuggets. Follow these steps to hit pay dirt and avoid the fool's gold.

READING ABOUT READING

Reading seems to be a natural process. Reading about reading and about steps to taking reading tests can seem contrived and confusing. However, we know that these steps and techniques work. Once you apply the steps to the practice exercises, your reading ability and scores will improve.

FIVE STEPS TO TAKING A READING TEST

During a reading test follow these steps.

1. Skim to find the topic of each paragraph.
2. Read the questions and answers.
3. Eliminate incorrect answers.
4. Scan the details to find the answer.
5. Choose the answer that is absolutely correct.

Skim to Find the Topic of Each Paragraph

Your first job is to find the topic of each paragraph. The topic is what a paragraph or passage is about.

The topic of a paragraph is usually found in the first and last sentences. Read the first and last sentences just enough to find the topic. You can write the topic in the margin next to the passage. Remember, the test booklet is yours. You can mark it up as much as you like.

Reading Sentences

Every sentence has a subject that tells what the sentence is about. The sentence also has a verb that tells what the subject is doing or links the subject to the complement. The sentence may also contain a complement that receives the action or describes what is being said about the subject. The words underlined in the following examples are the ones you would focus on as you preview.

1. The famous educator <u>John Dewey founded</u> an educational movement called <u>progressive education.</u>

2. Sad to say, we have learned <u>American school children</u> of all ages <u>are poorly nourished.</u>

You may occasionally encounter a paragraph or passage in which the topic can't be summarized from the first and last sentences. This type of paragraph usually contains factual information. If this happens, you will have to read the entire paragraph.

Fact, Opinion, or Fiction

If it is a factual passage, the author will present the fact and support it with details and examples. If the passage presents an opinion, the author will give the opinion and support it with arguments, examples, and other details. Many passages combine fact and opinion. If it is a fictional passage, the author will tell a story with details, descriptions, and examples about people, places, or things.

Once you find the topic, you will probably need more information to answer the questions. But don't worry about this other information and details now. You can go back and find it after you have read the questions.

Read the Questions and the Answers

Now read the questions—one at a time. Read the answers for the question you are working on. Be sure that you understand what each question and its answer mean.

Before you answer a question, be sure you know whether it is asking for a fact or an inference. If the question asks for a fact, the correct answer will identify a main idea or supporting detail. We'll discuss more about main ideas and details later. The correct answer may also identify a cause-and-effect relationship among ideas or be a paraphrase or summary of parts of the passage. Look for these.

If the question asks for an inference, the correct answer will identify the author's purpose, assumptions, or attitude and the difference between fact and the author's opinion. Look for these elements.

Eliminate Incorrect Answers

Read the answers and eliminate the ones that you absolutely know are incorrect. Read the answers literally. If you know it's wrong, cross it off.

Distracters

Test writers try to fool you. They deliberately write incorrect answer choices designed to distract your attention from the correct answer choice. These distracters can be tempting and you should be aware of them as you take the LAST, the ATS-W, and the CST. Use them to help you eliminate incorrect answers.

There are four main types of distracters described below. You can frequently arrive at the correct answer by just eliminating incorrect answers.

Misstatement

This distracter occurs most commonly, and more often on the LAST than on the ATS-W or the CST. A misstatement distracter often looks like it came right from the passage. But it changes ever so slightly the meaning of the passage, turns words around, or uses words out of context. The slightest change from the original passage may make the answer choice incorrect.

Look at these examples.

Passage: The area near the coast had deciduous and evergreens. The evergreens included a live oak and some magnolia trees. The evergreens had crowded out the deciduous trees as time went on.

Here are some examples of misstatements about this passage that might be incorrect answer choices.

(A) The area near the ocean had both deciduous and evergreen trees.

This misstates the passage. The passage mentions only the coast and not an ocean.

(B) The area is crowded with deciduous and evergreen trees.

The word "crowded" is taken out of context because nothing in the passage indicates that the area was crowded with trees.

(C) The area near the coast had some magnolia trees that were deciduous.

All of these words are from the passage but they are "turned around" to completely misstate the passage.

Right Answer—Wrong Question

This distracter gives a correct answer from the passage, but not a correct one for the question you are trying to answer. This distracter appears on the LAST, ATS-W, and the CST.

Passage: The area near the coast had deciduous and evergreens. The evergreens included a live oak and some magnolia trees. The evergreens had crowded out the deciduous trees as time went on.

Question: What best describes the trees near the coast?

(A) A live oak and some magnolias.

This answer is directly from the passage. And it is the correct answer to "What are some of the evergreen trees near the coast?" But it does not answer the question above. It also does not answer the question "What evergreen trees are near the coast?" because the passage just says what the evergreens included. There may have been more.

Appealing Language

This distracter draws your attention because it has very appealing language or appears to be fundamentally true. This distracter appears on the LAST and the ATS-W, but is a particular favorite on the ATS-W and the CST.

Passage: Stan Gozeki is a physical education teacher with a very unruly student in the class. The student has refused to follow instructions and challenged authority many times in the past and school officials have indicated that if he continues in this way he may have to be removed from school.

1. Suddenly the student acts out and verbally challenges Mr. Gozeki's authority causing Mr. Gozeki to correctly

(A) use corporal punishment because this is an emergency case, and if Mr. Gozeki does not quiet the student down administrators may hear of the incident and the student may be suspended from school and forced to go home where there is no one to watch over him.

   Everything in the answer choice after "use corporal punishment" is appealing language. The language seeks to make it seem that Mr. Gozeki is well motivated and is doing the right thing. But a teacher in New York may not employ corporal punishment and all of these words are just meant to distract.

Always—Never

This distracter uses extreme words such as "always" and "never." Appealing language can make an incorrect answer seem correct; always-never distracters can make a seemingly correct answer incorrect. If you can think of one exception, or if the answer is debatable, then the extreme answer choice is incorrect. Not every extreme answer choice is incorrect, but you should be aware when you see them. This distracter appears on the LAST, ATS-W, and the CST.

Passage: Stan Gozeki is a physical education teacher with a very unruly student in the class. The student has refused to follow instructions and challenged authority many times in the past and school officials have indicated that if he continues in this way he may have to be removed from school.

2. Mr. Gozeki discusses the student with the school guidance counselor and the counselor gives this appropriate advice:

(A) Never go in the locker room when this student is there.

That's unrealistic. There are just too many things that might cause Mr. Gozeki to go into the locker room when the student is in there. This extreme answer is incorrect. A correct choice might be "Do your best not to go into the locker room when this student is there."

Scan the Details to Find the Answer

Once you have eliminated answers, compare the other answers to the passage. When you find the answer that is confirmed by the passage—stop. That is your answer choice. Follow these other suggestions for finding the correct answer.

You will often need to read details to find the main idea of a paragraph. The main idea of a paragraph is what the writer has to say about the topic. Most questions are about the main idea of a paragraph. Scan the details about the main idea until you find the answer. Scanning means skipping over information that does not answer the question.

Look at this paragraph.

> There are many types of boats. Some are very fast while others could sleep a whole platoon of soldiers. I prefer the old putt-putt fishing boat with a ten-horsepower motor. That was a boat with a purpose. You didn't scare many people, but the fish were sure worried.

The topic of this paragraph is boats. The main idea is that the writer prefers small fishing boats to other boats.

Unstated Topic and Main Idea

Sometimes the topic and main idea are not stated. Consider this passage.

> The Chinese were the first to use sails thousands of years ago, hundreds of years before sails were used in Europe. The Chinese also used the wheel and the kite long before they were used on the European continent. Experts believe that many other Chinese inventions were used from three hundred to one thousand three hundred years before they were used in Europe.

The topic of this paragraph is inventions. The main idea of the paragraph is that the Chinese invented and used many things hundreds and thousands of years before they appeared in Europe.

Some Answers Are Not Related to the Main Idea

Some answers are not related to the main idea of a paragraph. These questions may be the most difficult to answer. You just have to keep scanning the details until you find the correct answer.

Who Wrote This Answer?

People who write tests go to great lengths to choose a correct answer that cannot be questioned. That is what they get paid for. They are not paid to write answers that have a higher meaning or include great truths.

Test writers want to be asked to write questions and answers again. They want to avoid valid complaints from test takers like you who raise legitimate concerns about their answers.

They usually accomplish this difficult task in one of two ways. They may write answers that are very specific and based directly on the reading. They may also write correct answers that seem very vague.

A Vague Answer Can Be Correct

How can a person write a vague answer that is correct? Think of it this way. If I wrote that a person is 6 feet 5 inches tall, you could get out a tape measure to check my facts. Since I was very specific, you are more likely to be able to prove me wrong.

On the other hand, if I write that the same person is over 6 feet tall you would be hard pressed to find fault with my statement. So my vague statement was hard to argue with. If the person in question is near 6 feet 5 inches tall, then my vague answer is most likely to be the correct one.

Don't choose an answer just because it seems more detailed or specific. A vague answer may be just as likely to be correct.

Choose the Answer That Is Absolutely Correct

Be sure that your choice answers the question. Be sure that your choice is based on the information contained in the paragraph. Don't choose an answer to another question. Don't choose an answer just because it sounds right. Don't choose an answer just because you agree with it.

There is no room on tests like these for answers that are partially wrong. The correct answer will be absolutely, incontrovertibly, unquestionably, indisputably, and unarguably the best answer among the choices given.

APPLYING THE STEPS

Let's apply the five steps to this passage and questions.

> Many vocational high schools in the United States give off-site work experience to their students. Students usually work in local businesses part of the school day and attend high school the other part. These programs have made American vocational schools world leaders in making job experience available to teenage students.

According to this paragraph, American vocational high schools are
world leaders in making job experience available to teenage students
because they
(A) have students attend school only part of the day.
(B) were quick to move their students to schools off-site.
(C) require students to work before they can attend the school.
(D) involve their students in cooperative education programs.

Step 1: Skim to find the topic of each paragraph. Both the first and last sentences tell
us that the topic is vocational schools and work experience.

Step 2: Read the questions and answers. Why are American vocational education high
schools the world leaders in offering job experience?

Step 3: Eliminate incorrect answers. Answer (C) is obviously wrong. It has to do with
work before high school. Answer (B) is also incorrect. This has to do with attending
school off-site. This leaves answers (A) and (D).

Step 4: Scan the details to find the answer. Scan the details and find that parts of
answer (A) are found in the passage. In answer (D) you have to know that cooperative
education is another name for off-site work during school.

Step 5: Choose the answer that is absolutely correct. It is down to answer (A) or
answer (D). But answer (A) contains only part of the reason that vocational education
high schools have gained such acclaim. Answer (D) is the absolutely correct
answer.

Here's how to apply the steps to the following passage.

*Problem
Solving*

Problem solving has become the main focus of mathematics learning.
Students learn problem-solving strategies and then apply them to
problems. Many tests now focus on problem solving and limit the number
of computational problems. The problem-solving movement is traced
to George Polya who wrote several problem-solving books for high
school teachers.

*Problem
Solving
Strategies*

Problem-solving strategies include guess and check, draw a diagram,
and make a list. Many of the strategies are taught as skills, which
inhibits flexible and creative thinking. Problems in textbooks can also
limit the power of the strategies. However, the problem-solving movement will be with us for some time, and a number of the strategies are
useful.

Step 1: Skim to find the topic of each paragraph. The topic of the first paragraph is
problem solving. You find the topic in both the first and last sentences. Write the
topic next to the paragraph. The topic for the second paragraph is problem-solving
strategies. You can write the topic next to each paragraph.

Now we are ready to look at the questions. If the question is about problem solving "in general" we start looking in the first paragraph for the answer. If the question is about strategies, we start looking in the second paragraph for the answer.

Step 2: Read the questions and answers.

According to this passage, a difficulty with teaching problem-solving strategies is:
(A) The strategies are too difficult for children.
(B) The strategies are taught as skills.
(C) The strategies are in textbooks.
(D) The strategies are part of a movement.

Step 3: Eliminate incorrect answers. Answer (A) can't be right because difficulty is not mentioned in the passage. That leaves (B), (C), and (D) for us to consider.

Step 4: Scan the details to find the answer. The question asks about strategies so we look immediately to the second paragraph for the answer. The correct answer is (B). Choice (C) is not correct because the passage does not mention strategies in textbooks. There is no indication that (D) is correct.

Step 5: Choose the answer that is absolutely correct. The correct choice is (B).

PRACTICE PASSAGE

Apply the five steps to this practice passage. Darken the letter of the correct answer. Follow the directions given below. The answers to these questions are found on pages 44–47. Do not look at the answers until you complete your work.

Read the following passage. After reading the passage, choose the best answer to each question from among the four choices. Answer all the questions following the passage on the basis of what is stated or implied in the passage.

Today's students have hand-held calculators that can graph one or even many equations. Students can even type in several equations and the calculator will "solve" them. This is the best way just to see a plotted graph quickly.

This is the worst way to learn about graphing and equations. The calculator can't tell the student anything about the process of graphing and does not teach them how to plot a graph.

Left to this electronic graphing process, students will not have the hands-on experience patterns needed to see the patterns and symmetry that characterize graphing and equations. They may become too dependent on the calculator and be unable to reason effectively about equations and the process of graphing.

It may be true that graphing and solving equations is taught mechanically in some classrooms. There is also something to be said for these electronic devices, which give students the opportunity to try out several graphs and solutions quickly before deciding on a final solution.

For all their electronic accuracy and patience, these graphing calculators cannot replace the process of graphing and solving equations on your own. For mastery of equations and graphing comes not just from seeing the graph automatically displayed on a screen; it also comes from a hands-on involvement with graphing.

1. The main idea of the passage is that

   (A) a child can be good at graphing equations only through hands-on experience.
   (B) teaching approaches for graphing equations should be improved.
   (C) accuracy and patience are the keys to effective graphing instruction.
   (D) the new graphing calculators have limited ability to teach students about graphing.

2. According to this passage, what negative impact will graphing calculators have on students who use them?
   (A) They will not have experience with four-function calculators.
   (B) They will become too dependent on the calculator.
   (C) They can quickly try out several graphs before coming up with a final answer.
   (D) They will get too much hands-on experience with calculators.

3. According to the passage, which of the following is a major drawback of the graphing calculator?
   (A) It graphs too many equations with their solutions.
   (B) It does not give students hands-on experience with graphing.
   (C) It does not give students hands-on experience with calculators.
   (D) This electronic method interferes with the mechanical method.

4. The passage includes information that would answer which of the following questions?
   (A) What are the shortcomings of graphing and solving equations as it sometimes takes place?
   (B) How many equations can you type into a graphing calculator?
   (C) What hands-on experience should students have as they learn about graphing equations?
   (D) What is the degree of accuracy and speed that can be attained by a graphing calculator?

5. The description of a graphing calculator found in this passage tells about which of the following?

      I.   The equations that can be graphed
      II. The approximate size of the calculator
     III. The advantages of the graphing calculator
   (A) I only
   (B) II only
   (C) I and II only
   (D) II and III only

Practice Passage Answers

Don't read this section until you have completed the practice passage.
    Here's how to apply the steps.

Step 1: Skim to find the topic of each paragraph. You may have written a topic next to each paragraph. Suggested topics are shown next to the following selection. Your topics don't have to be identical, but they should accurately reflect the paragraph's content.

Graphing Calculators

Today's students have hand-held calculators that can graph one or even many equations. Students can even type in several equations and the calculator will "solve" them. This is the best way to see a plotted graph quickly.

This is the worst way to learn about graphing and equations. The calculator can't tell the student anything about the process of graphing and does not teach them how to plot a graph.

Problem with Graphing Calculators

Left to this electronic graphing process, students will not have the hands-on experience needed to see the patterns and symmetry that characterize graphing and equations. They may become too dependent on the calculator and be unable to reason effectively about equations and the process of graphing.

Why its a Problem

It may be true that graphing and solving equations is taught mechanically in some classrooms. There is also something to be said for these electronic devices, which give students the opportunity to try out several graphs and solutions quickly before deciding on a final solution.

Good Points

For all their electronic accuracy and patience, these graphing calculators cannot replace the process of graphing and solving equations on your own. For mastery of equations and graphing comes not just from seeing the graph automatically displayed on a screen; it also comes from a hands-on involvement with graphing.

Apply Steps 2 through 5 to each of the questions.

1. The main idea of the passage is that
    (A) a child can be good at graphing equations only through hands-on experience.
    (B) teaching approaches for graphing equations should be improved.
    (C) accuracy and patience are the keys to effective graphing instruction.
    (D) the new graphing calculators have limited ability to teach students about graphing.

Step 2: Read the question and answers. You have to identify the main idea of the passage. This is a very common question on reading tests. Remember that the main idea is what the writer is trying to say or communicate in the passage.

Step 3: Eliminate incorrect answers. Answers (B) and (C) are not correct. Answer (C) is not at all correct based on the passage. Even though (B) may be true, it does not reflect what the writer is trying to say in this passage.

Step 4: Scan the details to find the answer. As we review the details we see that both answer (A) and answer (D) are both stated or implied in the passage. A scan of the details, alone, does not reveal which is the main idea. We must determine that on our own.

Step 5: Choose the answer that is absolutely correct. Which answer is absolutely correct? The whole passage is about graphing calculators, and they must be an important part of the main idea. The correct answer is (D). The author certainly believes that (A) is true, but uses this point to support the main idea.

2. According to this passage, what negative impact will graphing calculators have on students who use them?
   (A) They will not have experience with four-function calculators.
   (B) They will become too dependent on the calculator.
   (C) They can quickly try out several graphs before coming up with a final answer.
   (D) They will get too much hands-on experience with calculators.

Step 2: Read the questions and answers. This is a straightforward comprehension question. What negative impact will calculators have on students who use them? The second and third paragraphs have topics related to problems with calculators. We'll probably find the answer there.

Step 3: Eliminate incorrect answers. Answer (C) is not a negative impact of graphing calculators. Scan the details to find the correct answer from (A), (B), and (D).

Step 4: Scan the details to find the answer. The only detail that matches the question is in paragraph 3. The authors says that students may become too dependent on the calculators. That's our answer.

Step 5: Choose the answer that is absolutely correct. Answer (B) is the only correct choice.

3. According to the passage, which of the following is a major drawback of the graphing calculator?
   (A) It graphs too many equations with their solutions.
   (B) It does not give students hands-on experience with graphing.
   (C) It does not give students hands-on experience with calculators.
   (D) This electronic method interferes with the mechanical method.

Step 2: Read the question and answers. This is another straightforward comprehension question. This question is somewhat different from Question 2. Notice that the question asks for a drawback of the calculator. It does not ask for something that is wrong with the calculator itself. The topics indicate that we will probably find the answer in paragraph 1 or paragraph 2.

Step 3: Eliminate incorrect answers. Answer (C) is obviously wrong. Graphing calculators do give students hands-on experience with calculators. Be careful! It is easy to mix up (C) and (B). Answer (A) is a strength of the calculator and is also incorrect. Let's move on to the details.

Step 4: Scan the details to find the answer. Choices (B) and (D) remain. The details in paragraph 2 reveal that the correct answer is (B).

Step 5: Choose the answer that is absolutely correct. Answer (B) is the only absolutely correct answer. Notice that answers (B) and (C) are similar. The absolutely correct answer for this question was a possible correct answer for the previous question. Just because an answer seems correct doesn't mean that it is the absolutely correct answer.

4. The passage includes information that would answer which of the following questions?
   (A) What are the shortcomings of teaching about graphing equations as it sometimes takes place?
   (B) How many equations can you type into a graphing calculator?
   (C) What hands-on experience should students have as they learn about graphing equations?
   (D) What is the degree of accuracy and speed that can be attained by a graphing calculator?

Step 2: Read the question and answers. This is yet another type of reading comprehension question. You are asked to identify the questions that could be answered from the passage.

Step 3: Eliminate incorrect answers. Choices (B) and (D) are not correct. None of this information is included in the passage. This is not to say that these questions are not important. Rather it means that the answers to these questions are not found in this passage.

Step 4: Scan the details to find the answer. Both (A) and (C) are discussed in the passage. However, a scan of the details reveals that the answer to (C) is not found in the passage. The passage mentions hands-on experience, but it does not mention what types of hands-on experience students should have. There is an answer for (A). Graphing is taught mechanically in some classrooms.

Step 5: Choose the answer that is absolutely correct. Answer (A) is the absolutely correct answer. This is the only question that can be answered from the passage. The answer is not related to the writer's main idea and this may make it more difficult to answer.

5. The description of a graphing calculator found in this passage tells about which of the following?
   I.   The equations that can be graphed
   II. The approximate size of the calculator
   III. The advantages of the graphing calculator
   (A) I only
   (B) II only
   (C) I and II only
   (D) II and III only

Step 2: Read the question and answers. This is another classic type of reading comprehension question. You are given several choices. You must decide which combination of these choices is the absolutely correct answer.

Step 3: Eliminate incorrect answers. If you can determine that Statement I, for example, is not addressed in the passage, you can eliminate ALL answer choices that include Statement I.

Step 4: Scan the details to find which of the original three statements are true.
   I. No, there is no description of which equations can be graphed.
  II. Yes, paragraph 1 mentions that the calculators are hand-held.
 III. Yes, paragraph 4 mentions the advantages.
Both II and III are correct.

Step 5: Choose the answer that is absolutely correct. Choice (D) is absolutely correct. It lists both II and III.

READING PRACTICE ITEMS

You will find 85 multiple-choice practice reading items in the Reading in a Content Area section, beginning on page 139. All the items have explained answers.

   The Reading about Science chapter has 30 practice items, beginning on page 141. There are 55 practice items in the Reading about History, Humanities, and Social Science chapter, which begins on page 169.

   We recommend that you try the first 10 or so items in each chapter now. Then you can decide whether that is enough, whether you want to do more now, or whether you will go back to that section later for more practice.

 # ENGLISH AND WRITING

<table>
<tr><td align="center">TEST INFO BOX</td></tr>
</table>

The LAST and the ATS-W each include a written assignment. The written assignment contributes 20 percent to your overall score for each test. This chapter contains a thorough English review and sample LAST written assignments. Chapter 10 contains sample ATS-W written assignments. Refer to Chapter 2 to review the Steps for Writing Passing Written Assignments.

WRITTEN ASSIGNMENTS

LAST
LAST written assignments usually present both sides of an issue and ask you to pick one of the sides and to support your choice. Written assignments are rated 0–3 by two readers based on how well you write edited English. The final written assignment score of 0–6 is the sum of these two scores.

ATS-W
You may be asked to respond to a classroom situation, or some other education-related situation. The written assignment must be written clearly enough to be understood, but the readers do not evaluate your writing ability. However, a well-written assignment always makes the best impression.

The written assignment is rated 0–3 by two readers based on the appropriateness of your response. The final written assignment score of 0–6 is the sum of these two scores.

USING THIS CHAPTER

Choose one of these approaches.

I want a quick English/Writing review.

❏ Take and correct the English Review Quiz on page 50.
❏ Complete the English Practice Items on pages 58–80.
❏ Complete the Practice Written Assignment on page 81.

I want a thorough English/Writing review.

❏ Take the English Review Quiz on page 50.
❏ Correct the Review Quiz and read the indicated parts of the review.
❏ Complete the English Practice Items on pages 58–80.
❏ Complete the Practice Written Assignment on page 81.

I just want to practice English/Writing activities.

❏ Complete the English Practice Items on pages 58–80.
❏ Complete the Practice Written Assignment on page 81.

ENGLISH REVIEW QUIZ

The English Review Quiz assesses your knowledge of the English topics included in the tests. The quiz also provides an excellent way to refresh your memory about these topics. The first part of the quiz consists of sentences to mark or correct. Make your marks or corrections right on the sentences. In the second part of the quiz, you are asked to write a brief essay.

This quiz will be more difficult than the questions on the actual certification test. The idea here is to find out what you do know and what you don't know. It's not important to answer all these questions correctly and don't be concerned if you miss many of them.

The answers are found immediately after the quiz. It's to your advantage not to look at them until you have completed the quiz. Once you have completed and marked this review quiz, use the checklist to decide which sections to study.

PART I—SENTENCE CORRECTION

> Correct the sentence. Some sentences may not contain errors.

1. Ron and James fathers each sent them to players camp to learn the mysterys of sport.

2. They go the camp, ridden horses while they were there, and had write letters home.

3. Ron and James called his coach. The operator never answered, and they wondered what happened to her.

4. Bob and Liz went to the store and got some groceries.

5. Dad want me to do my homework. My sisters try their best to help me.

> Underline the subject in each sentence.

6. Chad's project that he showed the teacher improved his final grade.

7. The legs pumped hard, and the racer finished in first place.

8. Through the halls and down the stairs ran the harried student.

9. Where is the dog's leash?

> Correct the sentence. Some sentences may not contain errors.

10. Chad was sure correct; the food tastes bad and the singer sang bad but Ryan played really well. Ryan was more happy than Chad, who sat closer to the stage than Ryan.

11. The waiter brought food to the table on a large tray. The waiter wanted a job in the suburbs that paid well.

12. Waiting for the food to come, the complaining began.

       he was in the suburbs for 3 weeks

13. After three weeks in the suburbs, the *his* job was lost.

✓ 14. Juan and Rita spent two days at the beach before going to the mountains.

15. Neither Ryan or Bob wanted to shovel the drive. However, some things must be done not only when you want to but *also* when you have to do them.

Underline the prepositional phrases.

16. The two friends walked among the flowers before the sunset. They stepped without fear beside the waterfall as they thought about the future.

Correct the sentence. Some sentences may not contain errors.

17. Ryan knew that the coach wouldn't do anything that would not be helpful. The coach thought it was better to do nothing than to make a mistake. Ryan thought there was no truth to the belief that nothing could be done.

18. Ryan hoped his coach, professor Lois Minke, would help him get a tryout with the United States national team. Dr. Minke, a professor of physical education recommended that Ryan read *Sports: a Guide to Survival*.

19. The coach realized that new selection rules to go into effect in May. She also knew what it would take for Ryan to be selected. Ryan winning every game. But the coach and Ryan had a common goal. To see Ryan on the team.

20. Ryan's parents wanted a success rather than see him fail. They knew he stayed in shape by eating right and exercising daily. Ryan is a person who works hard and has talent.

21. Chad was dog tired after soccer practice. He became a coach for the purpose of helping the college to the soccer finals. During the rein of the former coach, the team had miserable seasons. Chad would stay at the job until such time as he could except the first place trophy.

22. Chad was satisfied but the players were grumbling. The players wanted to practice less have more free time. The players didn't like their light blue uniforms. The finals began in May 1996. The first game was scheduled for Tuesday May 9 at 1:00 P.M. The time for the game was here the players were on the field. Chad had the essential materials with him player list score book soccer balls and a cup of hope.

PART II—ESSAY

Time yourself for one hour. Use the following lined page to write a brief essay that answers this question.

Should high school students have to pass a standardized test before they graduate? The information below presents both sides of this question.

High school students should have to pass a standardized test before they graduate. The only way to ensure that students have covered required high school work is to have a standardized test. It would be best if every student in the country took the same test. That would give an objective way of comparing students and there would be no doubt which students and which schools were meeting their responsibilities. Really, who could object to the test if students and school are doing their jobs?

High school students should not have to pass a standardized test before they graduate. Even with all the standardized tests given in this country research shows that success in college is more related to how students do in the real world of high school, not how they do on tests. In fact, standardized tests can lower standards because teachers teach to the tests and ignore other important areas. Really, who believes you can find out about a student's high school achievement in a few hours on a Saturday?

Should high school students have to pass a standardized test before they graduate?

Review and evaluate the opposing positions presented above.

Choose one of these positions. Support your position with specific reasons.

Write an essay that supports your position following the guidelines presented above.

ANSWER CHECKLIST

PART I—Sentence Correction

The answers are organized by review sections. Check your answers. If you miss any item in a section, check the box and review that section.

❏ *Nouns, page 58*
  1. <u>Ron's</u> and <u>James's</u> fathers each sent them to <u>players'</u> camp to learn the <u>mysteries</u> of sport.

❏ *Verbs, page 59*
  2. They <u>went</u> to the camp, <u>rode</u> horses while they were there, and <u>wrote</u> letters home.

❏ *Pronouns, page 60*
  3. Ron and James called (<u>Ron's, James's, their</u>) coach. The operator never answered, and they wondered what happened to <u>him or</u> her.

❏ *Subject-Verb Agreement, page 62*
  4. No error
  5. Dad <u>wants</u> me to do my homework. My sisters try their best to help me.
  6. Chad's <u>project</u> that he showed the teacher improved his final grade.
  7. The <u>legs</u> pumped hard, and the <u>racer</u> finished in first place.
  8. Through the halls and down the stairs ran the harried <u>student</u>.
  9. Where is the dog's <u>leash</u>?

❏ *Adjectives and Adverbs, page 63*
  10. Chad was <u>surely</u> correct; the food tastes bad and the singer sang <u>badly</u> but Ryan played really well. Ryan was <u>happier</u> than Chad, who sat closer to the stage than Ryan <u>did</u>.

11. The waiter brought food <u>on a large tray to the table</u>. The waiter wanted <u>a well-paying job in the suburbs</u>.
12. Waiting for the food to come, the (<u>patrons, diners</u>) complained. The (<u>patrons, diners</u>) complained about waiting for the food to come.
13. After (<u>he, the waiter</u>) was in the suburbs for three weeks (<u>his</u>) job was lost. <u>He</u> lost <u>his</u> job after he was in the suburbs for three weeks.

❏ *Conjunctions, page 65*
  14. No error
  15. Neither Ryan <u>nor</u> Bob wanted to shovel the drive. However, some things must be done not only when you want to but <u>also</u> when you have to do them.

❏ *Prepositions, page 66*
  16. The two friends walked <u>among the flowers</u> <u>before the sunset</u>. They stepped <u>without fear beside the waterfall</u> as they thought <u>about the future</u>.

❏ *Negation, page 66*
  17. Ryan knew that the coach <u>would be helpful</u>. The coach thought it was better to do nothing than to make a mistake. Ryan thought <u>something could be done</u>.

❏ *Capitalization, page 67*
  18. Ryan hoped his coach, <u>Professor</u> Lois Minke, would help him get a tryout with the United States <u>National Team</u>. Dr. Minke, a professor of physical education, recommended that Ryan read *Sports: A Guide to Survival*.

❏ *Sentence Fragments, page 68*

19. The coach realized that new selection rules <u>would</u> go into effect in May. She also knew what it would take for Ryan to be selected. Ryan <u>would have to win</u> every game. But the coach and Ryan had a common goal. <u>They wanted</u> to see Ryan on the team.

❏ *Parallelism, page 69*

20. Ryan's parents wanted a success rather than <u>a failure</u>. (wanted success rather than failure) They knew he stayed in shape <u>by</u> eating right and by exercising daily. Ryan was a person who works hard and <u>who</u> has talent. (Ryan is hardworking and talented.)

❏ *Diction, page 69*

21. Chad was [delete "dog"] tired after soccer practice. He became a coach <u>to help</u> the college <u>ascend</u> to the soccer finals. During the <u>reign</u> of the former coach, the team had miserable seasons. Chad would stay at the job until [delete "such time as"] he could <u>accept</u> the first place trophy.

❏ *Punctuation, page 71*

22. Chad was satisfied, but the players were grumbling. The players wanted to practice less <u>and</u> have more free time. The players didn't like their light blue uniforms. The finals began in May 1996. The first game was scheduled for Tuesday, May 9, at 1:00 P.M. The time for the game was here; the players were on the field. Chad had the essential materials with him: player list, score book, soccer balls, (optional) and a cup of hope.

PART II—ESSAY

Evaluation Guidelines

Find an English professor or a high school English teacher. Ask that person to *rigorously* rate your essay using the criteria below.

A rating of 3 indicates that your writing is very good.

A rating of 2 indicates that your writing is acceptable, but you may need more practice.

A rating of 1, 0, or U indicates that you need a significant amount of help writing essays. You should practice writing essays until you can consistently achieve a rating of 2. You should get regular help at a writing center or from a writing tutor. Ask the person who rated your essay for other recommendations. Follow those recommendations.

Raters use these general guidelines

3 A well-developed, complete written assignment.
Shows a thorough response to all parts of the topic.
Clear explanations that are well supported.
The assignment is free of significant grammatical, punctuation, or spelling errors.

2 A fairly well-developed, complete written assignment.
It may not thoroughly respond to all parts of the topic.
Fairly clear explanations that may not be well supported.
It may contain some significant grammatical, punctuation, or spelling errors.

1 A poorly developed, incomplete written assignment.
It does not thoroughly respond to most parts of the topic.
Contains many poor explanations that are not well supported.
It may contain some significant grammatical, punctuation, or spelling errors.

0 A very poorly developed, incomplete written assignment.
It does not thoroughly respond to the topic.
Contains only poor, unsupported explanations.
Contains numerous significant grammatical, punctuation, or spelling errors.

U Any of these factors leads to a "U" rating:
A blank paper
An essay unrelated to the topic no matter how well written
An essay not long enough to score
An essay written in a language other than English
An illegible essay

ENGLISH REVIEW

NOUNS AND VERBS

Every sentence has a subject and a predicate. Most sentences are statements. The sentence usually names something (subject). Then the sentence describes the subject or tells what that subject is doing (predicate). Sentences that ask questions also have a subject and a predicate. Here are some examples.

Subject	Predicate
The car	moved.
The tree	grew.
The street	was dark.
The forest	teemed with plants of every type and size.

Many subjects are nouns. Every predicate has a verb. A list of the nouns and verbs from the preceding sentences follows.

Noun	Verb
car	moved
tree	grew
street	was
forest, plants	teemed

Nouns

Nouns name a person, place, thing, characteristic, or concept. Nouns give a name to everything that is, has been, or will be. Here are some simple examples.

Person	Place	Thing	Characteristic	Concept (Idea)
Abe Lincoln	Lincoln Memorial	beard	mystery	freedom
judge	courthouse	gavel	fairness	justice
professor	college	chalkboard	intelligence	number

Singular and Plural Nouns

Singular nouns refer to only one thing. Plural forms refer to more than one thing. Plurals are usually formed by adding an *s* or dropping a *y* and adding *ies*. Here are some examples.

Singular	Plural
college	colleges
professor	professors
Lincoln Memorial	Lincoln Memorials
mystery	mysteries

Possessive Nouns

Possessive nouns show that the noun possesses a thing or a characteristic. Make a singular noun possessive by adding *'s*. Here are some examples.

The *child's* sled was in the garage ready for use.
The *school's* mascot was loose again.
The rain interfered with *Jane's* vacation.
Ron's and *Doug's* fathers were born in the same year.
Ron and *Doug's* teacher kept them after school.

Make a singular noun ending in *s* possessive by adding *'s* unless the pronunciation is too difficult.

The teacher read *James's* paper several times.
The angler grabbed the *bass'* fin.

Make a plural noun possessive by adding an apostrophe (') only.

The *principals'* meeting was delayed.
The report indicated that *students'* scores had declined.

Verbs

Some verbs are action verbs. Other verbs are linking verbs that link the subject to words that describe it. Here are some examples.

Action Verbs	Linking Verbs
Blaire *runs* down the street.	Blaire *is* tired.
Blaire *told* her story.	The class *was* bored.
The crowd *roared*.	The players *were* inspired.
The old ship *rusted*.	It *had been* a proud ship.

Tense

A verb has three principal tenses: present tense, past tense, and future tense. The present tense shows that the action is happening now. The past tense shows that the action happened in the past. The future tense shows that something will happen. Here are some examples.

Present: I *enjoy* my time off.
Past: I *enjoyed* my time off.
Future: I *will enjoy* my time off.

Present: I *hate* working late.
Past: I *hated* working late.
Future: I *will hate* working late.

Regular and Irregular Verbs

Regular verbs follow the consistent pattern noted previously. However, a number of verbs are irregular. Irregular verbs have their own unique forms for each tense. A partial list of irregular verbs follows. The past participle is usually preceded by *had, has* or *have.*

SOME IRREGULAR VERBS

Present Tense	Past Tense	Past Participle
am, is, are	was, were	been
begin	began	begun
break	broke	broken
bring	brought	brought
catch	caught	caught
choose	chose	chosen
come	came	come
do	did	done
eat	ate	eaten
give	gave	given
go	went	gone
grow	grew	grown
know	knew	known
lie	lay	lain
lay	laid	laid
raise	raised	raised
ride	rode	ridden
see	saw	seen
set	set	set
sit	sat	sat
speak	spoke	spoken
take	took	taken
tear	tore	torn
throw	threw	thrown
write	wrote	written

PRONOUNS

Pronouns take the place of nouns or noun phrases and help avoid constant repetition of the noun or phrase. Here is an example.

Blaire is in law school. *She* studies in *her* room every day.
[The pronouns *she* and *her* refer to the noun *Blaire*.]

Clear Reference

The pronouns must clearly refer to a particular noun or noun phrase. Here are some examples.

Unclear

Ashley and Blaire took turns feeding *her* cat.
[We can't tell which person *her* refers to.]

Ashley gave it to Blaire. [The pronoun *it* refers to a noun that is not stated.]

Clear

Ashley and Blaire took turns feeding Blaire's cat. [A pronoun doesn't work here.]

Ashley got the book and gave it to Blaire. [The pronoun works once the noun is stated.]

Agreement

Each pronoun must agree in number (singular or plural) and gender (male or female) with the noun it refers to. Here are some examples.

Nonagreement in Number

The children played all day, and *she* came in exhausted.
[*Children* is plural, but *she* is singular.]

The child picked up the hat and brought *them* into the house.
[*Child* is singular, but *them* is plural.]

Agreement

The children played all day, and *they* came in exhausted.

The child picked up the hat and brought *it* into the house.

Nonagreement in Gender

The lioness picked up *his* cub. [*Lioness* is female, and *his* is male.]

A child must bring in a doctor's note before she comes to school.
[The child may be a male or female but *she* is female.]

Agreement

The lioness picked up *her* cub.

A child must bring in a doctor's note before *he* or *she* comes to school.

SUBJECT-VERB AGREEMENT

Singular and Plural

Singular nouns take singular verbs. Plural nouns take plural verbs. Singular verbs usually end in *s*, and plural verbs usually do not. Here are some examples.

Singular:	My father want*s* me home early.
Plural:	My parents want me home early.

Singular:	Ryan runs a mile each day.
Plural:	Ryan and Chad run a mile each day.

Singular:	She tries her best to do a good job.
Plural:	Liz and Ann try their best to do a good job.

Correctly Identify Subject and Verb

The subject may not be in front of the verb. In fact, the subject may not be anywhere near the verb. Say the subject and the verb to yourself. If it makes sense, you probably have it right.

• Words may come between the subject and the verb.

Chad's final exam score, which he showed to his mother, improved his final grade.

The verb is *improved*. The word *mother* appears just before improved.

Is this the subject? Say it to yourself. [Mother improved the grade.]

That can't be right. Score must be the subject. Say it to yourself. [Score improved the grade.] That's right. *Score* is the subject, and *improved* is the verb.

The racer running with a sore arm finished first.

Say it to yourself. [Racer finished first.] *Racer* is the noun, and *finished* is the verb.

It wouldn't make any sense to say the arm finished first.

• The verb may come before the subject.

Over the river and through the woods romps the merry leprechaun.

Leprechaun is the subject, and *romps* is the verb. [Think: Leprechaun romps.]

Where are the car keys?

Keys is the subject, and *are* is the verb. [Think: The car keys are where?]

Examples of Subject-Verb Agreement

Words such as *each, neither, everyone, nobody, someone,* and *anyone* are singular pronouns. They always take a singular verb.

> Everyone *needs* a good laugh now and then.
> Nobody *knows* more about computers than Bob.

Words that refer to number such as *one-half, any, most,* and *some* can be singular or plural.

> One-fifth of the students *were* absent. [*Students* is plural.]
> One-fifth of the cake *was* eaten. [There is only one cake.]

ADJECTIVES AND ADVERBS

Adjectives

Adjectives modify nouns and pronouns. Adjectives add detail and clarify nouns and pronouns. Frequently, adjectives come immediately before the nouns or pronouns they are modifying. At other times, the nouns or pronouns come first and are connected directly to the adjectives by linking verbs. Here are some examples.

Direct	With a Linking Verb
That is a *large* dog.	That dog is *large*.
He's an *angry* man.	The man seems *angry*.

Adverbs

Adverbs are often formed by adding *ly* to an adjective. However, many adverbs don't end in *ly* (for example, *always*). Adverbs modify verbs, adjectives, and adverbs. Adverbs can also modify phrases, clauses, and sentences. Here are some examples.

Modify verb:	Ryan *quickly* sought a solution.
Modify adjective:	That is an *exceedingly* large dog.
Modify adverb:	Lisa told her story *quite* truthfully.
Modify sentence:	*Unfortunately*, all good things must end.
Modify phrase:	The instructor arrived *just* in time to start the class.

Avoiding Adjective and Adverb Errors

- Don't use adjectives in place of adverbs.

Correct	Incorrect
Lynne read the book quickly.	Lynne read the book quick.
Stan finished his work easily.	Stan finished the book easy.

- Don't confuse the adjectives *good* and *bad* with the adverbs *well* and *badly*.

Correct	Incorrect
Adverbs	
She wanted to play the piano well.	She wanted to play the piano good.
Bob sang badly.	Bob sang bad.
Adjectives	
The food tastes good.	The food tastes well.
The food tastes bad.	The food tastes badly.

- Don't confuse the adjectives *real* and *sure* with the adverbs *really* and *surely*.

Correct	Incorrect
Chuck played really well.	Chuck played real well.
He was surely correct.	He was sure correct.

Comparison

Adjectives and adverbs can show comparisons. Avoid clumsy modifiers.

Correct	Incorrect
Jim is more clingy than Ray.	Jim is clingier than Ray.
Ray is much taller than Jim.	Ray is more taller than Jim.
Jim is more interesting than Ray.	Jim is interesting than Ray.
Ray is happier than Jim.	Ray is more happy than Jim.

Review word comparisons carefully to be sure that the comparison is clear.

Unclear:	Chad lives closer to Ryan than Blaire.
Clear:	Chad lives closer to Ryan than Blaire does.
Clear:	Chad lives closer to Ryan than he does to Blaire.

Unclear:	The bus engine is bigger than a cars.
Clear:	The bus engine is bigger than a car's engine.

Misplaced and Dangling Modifiers

Modifiers may be words or groups of words. Modifiers change or qualify the meaning of another word or group of words. Modifiers belong near the words they modify.

Misplaced modifiers appear to modify words in a way that doesn't make sense.

The modifier in the following sentence is *in a large box*. It doesn't make sense for *in a large box* to modify *house*. Move the modifier near *pizza* where it belongs.

Misplaced:	Les delivered pizza to the house in a large box.
Revised:	Les delivered pizza in a large box to the house.

The modifier in the next sentence is *paid well*. *Paid well* can't modify *city*. Move it next to *the job* where it belongs.

Misplaced:	Gail wanted the job in the city that paid well.
Revised:	Gail wanted the well-paying job in the city.

Dangling modifiers modify words not present in the sentence. The modifier in the following sentence is *waiting for the concert to begin*.

This modifier describes the audience, but *audience* is not mentioned in the sentence. The modifier is left dangling with nothing to attach itself to.

Dangling:	Waiting for the concert to begin, the chanting started.
Revised:	Waiting for the concert to begin, the audience began chanting.
Revised:	The audience began chanting while waiting for the concert to begin.

The modifier in the next sentence is *after three weeks in the country*. The modifier describes the person, not the license. But the person is not mentioned in the sentence. The modifier is dangling.

Dangling:	After three weeks in the country, the license was revoked.
Revised:	After he was in the country for three weeks, his license was revoked.
Revised:	His license was revoked after he was in the country three weeks.

CONJUNCTIONS

Conjunctions are words that connect and logically relate parts of a sentence.

- These conjunctions connect words: *and, but, for, or, nor*.

    Dan *and* Dorie live in Pittsburgh.

    Tim *or* Sarah will get up to feed the baby.

- These conjunctive pairs establish a relationship among words: *either–or, neither–nor, not only–but also*. Words in these pairs should not be mixed.

    Neither David *nor* Noel wants to get up to feed the baby.

    The baby cries *not only* when she is hungry, *but also* when she is thirsty.

• These conjunctions connect and modify clauses in a sentence: *nevertheless, however, because, furthermore.*

Matt's mother was coming to visit; *however,* a snow storm prevented the trip.

Because the baby was sleeping, Julie and Bill decided to get some sleep too.

PREPOSITIONS

Prepositions connect a word to a pronoun, noun, or noun phrase called the object of the preposition. A partial list of prepositions follows.

PREPOSITIONS

above	across	after	among
as	at	before	below
beside	by	except	for
from	in	into	near
of	on	over	to
toward	up	upon	without

A prepositional phrase consists of a preposition, its object and any modifiers. Here are some examples.

Preposition	Object
in	the book
with	apparent glee
without	a care

Some sentences with prepositional phrases follow.

Chad found his book *in the room.*
Liz rode *on her horse.*
Schroeder is the dog *with the brown paws.*
Over the river and *through the woods to grandmother's house* we go.

NEGATION

Words such as *no, never, nobody, nothing,* and *not* (with contractions such as *would not—wouldn't*) are used to express a negative. However, only one of these words is needed to express a negative thought. Two negative words create a double negative, which is not standard English.

Incorrect:	The politician *didn't say nothing* that made sense.
Revised:	The politician *didn't say anything* that made sense.
Revised:	The politician *said nothing* that made any sense.

Incorrect:	The politician *wouldn't do nothing* that did no good. [A triple negative.]
Revised:	The politician *would do nothing* good.
Revised:	The politician *wouldn't do* good things.

CAPITALIZATION

- Capitalize the first word in each sentence.
- Capitalize *I*.
- Capitalize proper nouns. In a title, capitalize proper and common nouns, but not articles or short prepositions. Proper nouns are specific names for people, places, or things.
- Capitalize proper adjectives. Proper adjectives can be formed from some proper nouns.

PROPER NOUNS

George Bush	Taj Majal
Bob Postman	Thanksgiving
Alabama	July
North America	Wednesday

COMMON NOUNS

president	building
author	fall
state	month
continent	day

PROPER NOUNS AND PROPER ADJECTIVES

Pennsylvania	Pennsylvanian
California	Californian
New York	New Yorker
Italy	Italian

PROPER NOUNS WITH COMMON NOUNS AND ARTICLES

United States of America
the Mississippi River
Lake Michigan

- Capitalize titles before, but not after, proper nouns.

Professor Jeremy Smails	Jeremy Smails, professor of history
President Otto Smart	Otto Smart, president of Limelight Ltd.

- Titles, alone, may be capitalized if they indicate a very high rank.

President of the United States

Secretary of State

- Capitalize titles of books except for short articles, prepositions, and conjunctions unless they are the first or last words or follow a colon (:).

How to Prepare for the Praxis Examinations

The How to Survive in College Book

Derek: A Study in Perseverance

SENTENCE FRAGMENTS

English sentences require a subject and a verb. Fragments are parts of sentences written as though they were sentences. Fragments are writing mistakes that lack a subject, a predicate, or both subject and predicate. Here are some examples.

Since when.
To enjoy the summer months.
Because he isn't working hard.
If you can fix old cars.
What the principal wanted to hear.

Include a subject and/or a verb to rewrite a fragment as a sentence.

Fragment	Sentence
Should be coming up the driveway now.	The *car* should be coming up the driveway now.
Both the lawyer and her client.	Both the lawyer and her client *waited* in court.
Which is my favorite subject.	I *took math*, which is my favorite subject.
If you can play.	If you can play, *you'll improve with practice.*

Verbs such as *to be, to go, winning, starring*, etc., need a main verb.

Fragment	Sentence
The new rules to go into effect in April.	The new rules *will* go into effect in April.
The team winning every game.	The team *was* winning every game.

Often, a fragment is related to a complete sentence. Combine the two to make a single sentence.

Fragment:	Reni loved vegetables. *Particularly corn, celery, lettuce, squash, and eggplant.*
Revised:	Reni loved vegetables, particularly corn, celery, lettuce, squash, and eggplant.

Fragment:	*To see people standing on Mars.* This could happen in the 21st century.
Revised:	To see people standing on Mars is one of the things that could happen in the 21st century.

Sometimes short fragments can be used for emphasis. However, you should not use fragments in your essay. Here are some examples.

Stop! Don't take one more step toward that apple pie.

I need some time to myself. *That's why.*

PARALLELISM

When two or more ideas are connected, use a parallel structure. Parallelism helps the reader follow the passage more clearly. Here are some examples.

Not Parallel:	Toni stayed in shape by eating right and exercising daily.
Parallel:	Toni stayed in shape by eating right and *by* exercising daily.

Not Parallel:	Lisa is a student who works hard and has genuine insight.
Parallel:	Lisa is a student who works hard and *who* has genuine insight.

Not Parallel:	Art had a choice either to clean his room or take out the garbage.
Parallel:	Art had a choice either to clean his room or *to* take out the garbage.

Not Parallel:	Derek wanted a success rather than failing.
Parallel:	Derek wanted a success rather than a failure.
Parallel:	Derek wanted success rather than failure.

DICTION

Diction is choosing and using appropriate words. Good diction conveys a thought clearly without unnecessary words. Good diction develops fully over a number of years; however, there are some rules and tips you can follow, especially when writing for the LAST.

• Do not use slang, colloquialisms, or other nonstandard English. One person's slang is another person's confusion. Slang is often regional, and slang meanings change rapidly. We do not give examples of slang here for that very reason. Do not use slang words in your formal writing.

   Colloquialisms are words used frequently in spoken language. This informal use of terms such as *dog tired, kids,* and *hanging around,* is not generally accepted in formal writing. Save these informal terms for daily speech and omit or remove them from your writing except as quotations.

Omit any other non-standard English. Always choose standard English terms that accurately reflect the thought to be conveyed.

• Avoid wordy, redundant, or pretentious writing. Good writing is clear and economical.

Wordy: I chose my career as a teacher because of its high ideals, the truly self-sacrificing idealism of a career in teaching, and for the purpose of receiving the myriad and cascading recognition that one can receive from the community as a whole and from its constituents.

Revised: I chose a career in teaching for its high ideals and for community recognition.

Given below is a partial list of wordy phrases and the replacement word.

WORDY PHRASES AND REPLACEMENTS

at the present time	now	because of the fact that	because
for the purpose of	for	in the final analysis	finally
in the event that	if	until such time as	until

Choosing the Correct Word

Homonyms

Homonyms are words that sound alike but do not have the same meaning. These words can be confusing and you may use the incorrect spelling of a word. If words are homonyms, be sure you choose the correct spelling for the meaning you intend.

HOMONYMS

accept (receive)	ascent (rise)
except (other than)	assent (agreement)
board (wood)	fair (average)
bored (uninterested)	fare (a charge)
led (guided)	lessen (make less)
lead (metal)	lesson (learning experience)
past (gone before)	peace (no war)
passed (moved by)	piece (portion)
rain (precipitation)	to (toward)
reign (rule)	too (also)
rein (animal strap)	two (a number)
their (possessive pronoun)	its (shows possession)
there (location)	it's (it is)
they're (they are)	

Idioms

Idioms are expressions with special meanings, and they often break the rules of grammar. Idioms are acceptable in formal writing, but they must be used carefully. Here are some examples.

IDIOMS

in accordance with	inferior to
angry with	occupied by (someone)
differ from (someone)	occupied with (something)
differ about (an issue)	prior to
independent of	rewarded with (something)

PUNCTUATION

The Period (.)

Use a period to end every sentence, unless the sentence is a direct question, a strong command, or an interjection.

> You will do well on the LAST.

The Question Mark (?)

Use a question mark to end every sentence that is a direct question.

> What is the passing score for the ATS-W?

The Exclamation Point (!)

Use an exclamation point to end a sentence that is a strong command or interjection. Do not overuse exclamation points.

Interjection:	Oh, please!
Command:	Avalanche, head for cover!

The Comma (,)

The comma may be the most used punctuation mark. This section details a few of these uses.

A clause is part of a sentence that could be a sentence itself. If a clause begins with a conjunction, use a comma before the conjunction.

Incorrect:	I was satisfied with the food but John was grumbling.
Correct:	I was satisfied with the food, but John was grumbling.

Incorrect:	Larry was going fishing or he was going to paint his house.
Correct:	Larry was going fishing, or he was going to paint his house.

A clause or a phrase often introduces a sentence. Introductory phrases or clauses should be set off by a comma. If the introductory element is very short, the comma is optional. Here are some examples.

However, there are other options you may want to consider.

When the de-icer hit the plane's wing, the ice began to melt.

To get a driver's license, go to the motor vehicle bureau.

It doesn't matter what you want, you have to take what you get.

Parenthetical expressions interrupt the flow of a sentence. Set off the parenthetical expression with commas. Do not set off expressions that are essential to understanding the sentence. Here are some examples.

Tom, an old friend, showed up at my house the other day.

I was traveling on a train, in car 8200, on my way to Florida.

John and Ron, who are seniors, went on break to Florida.
[Use a comma. The phrase "who are seniors" is extra information.]

All the students who are seniors take an additional course.
[Don't use a comma. The phrase "who are seniors" is essential information.]

Commas are used to set off items in a list or series. Here are some examples.

Jed is interested in computers, surfing, and fishing.
[Notice the comma before the conjunction *and*. You may omit this comma.]

Mario drives a fast, red car.
[The sentence would make sense with *and* in place of the commas.]

Andy hoped for a bright, sunny, balmy day.
[The sentence would make sense with *and* in place of the commas.]

Lucy had a pale green dress.
[The sentence would not make sense with *and*. The word *pale* modifies *green*. Don't use a comma.]

Randy will go to the movies, pick up some groceries, and then go home.
[Remember, the comma before *and* is optional.]

Commas are used in other writing. Here are some examples.

Dates

Tuesday, February 8, 1994

July 4, 1776, was the first Independence Day.

School begins on Wednesday, September 6, at 8:00 A.M.

His parents immigrated in October 1936.
[No comma is needed.]

Addresses

Closter, New Jersey 07624

321 Forest Street, Phoenix, Arizona

The distance to Hauppauge, Long Island is 37 miles.

16 Martins Avenue, Room 220

The Semicolon (;)

Use the semicolon to connect main clauses not connected by a conjunction. Include a semicolon with very long clauses connected by a conjunction. Here are some examples.

The puck was dropped; the hockey game began.

The puck was dropped, and the hockey game began.

The general manager of the hockey team was not sure what should be done about the player who was injured during the game; but he did know that the player's contract stipulated that his pay would continue whether he was able to play or not.

The Colon (:)

Use the colon after a main clause to introduce a list. These examples show when to use a colon and when not to use a colon.

Liz kept these items in her car: spare tire, jack, flares, and a blanket.

Liz kept a spare tire, jack, flares, and a blanket in her car.

ENGLISH PRACTICE ITEMS

These questions are designed to help you practice the concepts and skills presented in this chapter. For that reason, questions 1–20 are not at all like the items on the real LAST. The other questions may have a different emphasis than the real test.

Mark your choice, then check your answers on page 84.

PART A

1 Ⓐ Ⓑ Ⓒ Ⓓ Ⓔ   5 Ⓐ Ⓑ Ⓒ Ⓓ Ⓔ   9 Ⓐ Ⓑ Ⓒ Ⓓ Ⓔ   13 Ⓐ Ⓑ Ⓒ Ⓓ Ⓔ   17 Ⓐ Ⓑ Ⓒ Ⓓ Ⓔ
2 Ⓐ Ⓑ Ⓒ Ⓓ Ⓔ   6 Ⓐ Ⓑ Ⓒ Ⓓ Ⓔ   10 Ⓐ Ⓑ Ⓒ Ⓓ Ⓔ   14 Ⓐ Ⓑ Ⓒ Ⓓ Ⓔ   18 Ⓐ Ⓑ Ⓒ Ⓓ Ⓔ
3 Ⓐ Ⓑ Ⓒ Ⓓ Ⓔ   7 Ⓐ Ⓑ Ⓒ Ⓓ Ⓔ   11 Ⓐ Ⓑ Ⓒ Ⓓ Ⓔ   15 Ⓐ Ⓑ Ⓒ Ⓓ Ⓔ   19 Ⓐ Ⓑ Ⓒ Ⓓ Ⓔ
4 Ⓐ Ⓑ Ⓒ Ⓓ Ⓔ   8 Ⓐ Ⓑ Ⓒ Ⓓ Ⓔ   12 Ⓐ Ⓑ Ⓒ Ⓓ Ⓔ   16 Ⓐ Ⓑ Ⓒ Ⓓ Ⓔ   20 Ⓐ Ⓑ Ⓒ Ⓓ Ⓔ

PART B

21 Ⓐ Ⓑ Ⓒ Ⓓ
22 Ⓐ Ⓑ Ⓒ Ⓓ
23 Ⓐ Ⓑ Ⓒ Ⓓ
24 Ⓐ Ⓑ Ⓒ Ⓓ
25 Ⓐ Ⓑ Ⓒ Ⓓ

PART C

26 Ⓐ Ⓑ Ⓒ Ⓓ
27 Ⓐ Ⓑ Ⓒ Ⓓ
28 Ⓐ Ⓑ Ⓒ Ⓓ
29 Ⓐ Ⓑ Ⓒ Ⓓ
30 Ⓐ Ⓑ Ⓒ Ⓓ

PART A

> Choose the letter that indicates an error, or choose (E) for no error.

1. Kitty and Harry's anniversary will fall on
   (A)   (B)
   Father's Day this year. No error.
   (C)   (D)   (E)

2. The trees leaves provide a fall festival
   (A)   (B)
   called "Fall Foliage"
               (C)
   in most New England states. No error.
               (D)   (E)

3. Most colleges require
   (A)   (B)
   a specific number
   (C)
   of academic credits for admission.
               (D)
   No error.
   (E)

4. My brother Robert
   (A)
   loves to read novels but would enjoy
   (B)   (C)
   good mystery's more. No error.
   (D)   (E)

5. Louise had lay her mitt on the bench
   (A)   (B)   (C)
   when she got a glass of water.
               (D)
   No error.
   (E)

6. It seems to me that I had spoke to my
   (A)   (B)
   landlord about the crack in the ceiling
               (C)
   about two months ago. No error.
   (D)   (E)

7. The committee on fund-raising
   (A)   (B)
   gathers in the hall,
   (C)
   but Joe went to the room. No error.
   (D)   (E)

8. The administrator wanted
   (A)   (B)
   all lesson plan books
   (C)
   handed in by Friday. No error.
   (D)   (E)

9. Behind the tree, she was reading a book,
   (A)   (B)
   eating a banana, and she waited for the
      (C)   (D)
   sunset. No error.
               (E)

10. Is Washington, D.C. closer to Arlington
    (A)   (B)   (C)
    Cemetery than Charleston? No error.
               (D)   (E)

11. The student would not do nothing
        (A)   (B)
    to redeem himself
        (C)
    in the eyes of the principal. No error.
                (D)   (E)

12. Good teachers are distinguished by
        (A)   (B)
    their enthusiasm and organization.
               (C)   (D)
    No error.
       (E)

13. The principle of the middle school
        (A)   (B)
    wanted to reorganize
        (C)
    the lunch schedule. No error.
            (D)   (E)

14. Grandmother's shopping list consisted of
        (A)   (B)
    mustard, green beans, buttermilk, and
                              (C)
    included some eggs. No error.
            (D)   (E)

15. Unless you arm yourself with
           (A)
    insect repellent, you will get a bight.
            (B)   (C)   (D)
    No error.
       (E)

16. Graduation exercises will be held on _
                (A)   (B)
    Friday_ June 19th at 7:00 P.M. No error.
       (C)   (D)   (E)

17. With a quick glance the noisy room
    (A)   (B)   (C)
    was silenced. No error.
        (D)   (E)

18. Without even trying, the sprinter
        (A)   (B)
    passed the world record
            (C)
    by five tenths of a second. No error.
        (D)   (E)

19. Prior to the passage of PL 94–142,
        (A)   (B)
    special-education students
            (C)
    were not unrepresented legally.
            (D)
    No error.
       (E)

20. Combine the sugar, waters, cornstarch,
    (A)   (B)   (C)
    and eggs. No error.
        (D)   (E)

PART B

> Choose the letter of the best choice for the underlined section, without changing the meaning of the sentence. If the original is best, choose (A). Otherwise, select one of the suggested changes.

21. Postman's talents were missed <u>not any more</u> as a student but also in his extracurricular activities on campus.
    (A) not any more
    (B) not
    (C) not only
    (D) never any

22. <u>Piled on the table, the students started sorting through their projects</u>.
    (A) Piled on the table, the students started sorting through their projects.
    (B) The students started sorting through their projects, which were piled on the table.
    (C) Piled on the table, the students sorted through their projects.
    (D) The students sorted through their projects as they piled on the table.

23. All the soccer players, <u>who are injured,</u> must not play the game.
    (A) , who are injured,
    (B) , who are injured
    (C) who are injured,
    (D) who are injured

24. The plumber kept these tools in his <u>truck; plunger, snake, washers and faucets</u>.
    (A) truck; plunger, snake, washers and faucets
    (B) truck (plunger, snake, washes and faucets)
    (C) truck: plunger; snake; washers and faucets
    (D) truck: plunger, snake, washers, and faucets.

25. The two <u>attorneys meet</u> and agreed on an out-of-court settlement.
    (A) attorneys meet
    (B) attorney's meet
    (C) attorney's met
    (D) attorneys met

PART C

Read the passage and answer the questions.

(1) Shop-at-home networks are the latest television craze. (2) You can order just about anything you want from the comfort of your home. (3) I heard a story recently about someone who claims to have picked up the phone and ordered while this person was _____.
(4) It seems to me that television shopping is the final step in our descent to an isolated society. (5) Malls will be like ghost towns, libraries will be empty, town centers will be deserted, and we will, each of us, be alone in our own cubicles, glued to our television sets.

26. How does the writer of the passage intend the word glued in the last sentence to be interpreted?
    (A) literally
    (B) ironically
    (C) figuratively
    (D) emphatically

27. Which of the following best fits in the blank in Sentence 3?
    (A) flying
    (B) asleep
    (C) undecided
    (D) shopping

28. Which of the following sentences contain opinions?
    (A) 1 only
    (B) 4 and 5 only
    (C) 3 only
    (D) 1 and 3 only

29. Which of the following best describes the technique the author uses in this paragraph?
    (A) argumentation
    (B) exposition
    (C) description
    (D) characterization

30. Which sentence contains a simile?
    (A) 2
    (B) 3
    (C) 4
    (D) 5

PRACTICE WRITTEN ASSIGNMENT

Use the following lined pages to write a brief essay based on this topic. Use one hour.

Teachers may base their own classroom practices on the way they were taught as children. Teachers may embrace practices or approaches they liked as a child or avoid practices or approaches they found distasteful.

Assume that this is true and choose an elementary school teacher who had a style or approach that you would either use or avoid.

Write an essay appropriate for a group of teachers in New York State that

- identifies the teacher and grade level and describes the approach you would use or avoid

- explains why the approach was appropriate or inappropriate

- explains what made the approach appropriate or inappropriate

ANSWERS

Part A

1. A	5. A	9. D	13. A	17. E
2. A	6. B	10. D	14. D	18. C
3. E	7. C	11. B	15. D	19. D
4. D	8. E	12. E	16. C	20. C

Part B

21. C   22. B   23. D   24. E   25. D

Part C

26. C   27. B   28. B   29 A   30. E

Practice Essay

Show your essay to two people for evaluation. Ask an English teacher or English professor to look at it. Use the rating scale shown on page 15. Add their rating together to find your total score.

ESSAY 1

This essay would likely receive a total score of 1–2 out of 6.

Miss Willis was my second grade teacher who I respected very much. Good teachers are very important if we expect to have good students.

Miss Willis would have come to school every day with a sunny attitude even when there was some other problem at home or at school. She never got mad at us or yelled at us when we did stuff that was not good.

That was the style that Miss Willis had that I would use as a teacher. She never made me feel bad and she was always trying to be helpful and nice. I would try my very best to be as nice as she was and to follow her examples. If I could be as good a teacher as she was then I would be a teacher my supervisor would have to say that she thought that I was doing all the things that she had done to make her a good teacher.

So, Miss Willis is the teacher I would try to be most like.

ESSAY 2

This essay would likely receive a total score of 3–4 out of 6.

Miss Stendel – The Teacher I Want to be Like

It has been a long time since I have been in elementary school, and the school I went to is not even there anymore. I would choose Miss Dorothea T. Stendel as the teacher I want to be like. She was my fifth grade teacher In Emerson School and she liked to visit Native American reservations. She used to spend a lot of time in the western states.

The main appropriate technique she used was to be very nice to me. She seemed to understand boys, which a lot of teachers do not. I worked hard because she was nice to me and I would try to use that same approach in my classroom. It may not be scientific but it certainly was a very appropriate approach for me.

The approach was appropriate because it motivated me. I guess you would call it intrinsic motivation. I did not want to work hard for grades. I wanted to work hard just for the work itself.

Miss Stendel used an approach that I thought was not appropriate. I will avoid this approach when I am a teacher. She had piles of mathematics worksheets all around the window sill. You had to work your way around the window sill to do the math program. When you reached the last window you were done.

The approach was inappropriate because the sheets were boring and you really got nothing out of them. There was just a lot of exercises and skill problems on the sheets. You could do the entire windowsill and not learn anything.

The reason the approach was inappropriate is because it did not teach anything, and because it did not show real world applications of mathematics or how mathematical ideas were connected. In my classroom I would make sure students mastered mathematics concepts and be sure to show how to transfer the learning to real world situations. I would emphasize the meaning of mathematics and show students how mathematics ideas were connected.

I do not know where Miss Stendel is today, but I would like to be able to thank her for helping me so much. I guess motivating someone to learn can be more important than teaching them mathematics. The more I think about it, I realize now that she certainly understood more and was more strategic than I ever understood. I want to be like that.

PART 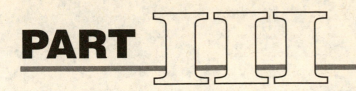 III

Extended Review

5 MATHEMATICS

USING THIS CHAPTER

This chapter prepares you to do the Mathematics items on the LAST. Choose one of the approaches.

I want a quick Mathematics review. (Best for most people.)

❑ Take and correct the Mathematics Review Quiz on page 91.
❑ Look over the sections on graphs, maps, and test strategies on pages 109–115.

I want a more thorough Mathematics review.

❑ Take and correct the Mathematics Review Quiz on page 91.
❑ Correct the Review Quiz and review the indicated parts of this chapter.
❑ Look over the sections on graphs, maps, and test strategies on pages 109–115.

MATHEMATICS REVIEW QUIZ

This quiz uses a short answer format to help you find out what you know about the Mathematics topics reviewed in this chapter. The quiz results direct you to the portions of the chapter you should reread.

This quiz will also help focus your thinking about Mathematics, and these questions and answers are a good review in themselves. It's not important to answer all these questions correctly, and don't be concerned if you miss many of them.

The answers are found immediately after the quiz. It's to your advantage not to look at them until you have completed the quiz. Once you have completed and corrected this review quiz, use the answer checklist to decide which sections to review.

> Write the answers in the space provided or on a separate sheet of paper.

<u>Questions 1–3:</u> *Use symbols for less than, greater than, and equal to, and compare these numbers:*

1. 23 $<$ 32

2. 18 $=$ 4 + 14

3. 9 $<$ 10 $<$ 11

4. Write the place value of the digit 7 in the numeral 476,891,202,593.
   seventy billion

5. $4^3 =$ 104

6. $6^9 \div 6^7 =$ 36

7. $3^2 \times 2^3 =$ 9/8

8. Write the place value of the digit 4 in the numeral 529.354.
   four hundredths

<u>Questions 9–10:</u> *Use symbols for less than, greater than, and equal to, and compare these numbers:*

9. 9,879 $<$ 12,021

10. 98.1589 $<$ 98.162

11. 203.61 + 9.402 + 0.78 213.792

12. 30.916 − 8.72 22.196

230.916
− 8.720
22.196

13. 3.4×0.0021 _____

14. $0.576 \div 0.32$ _____

15. Write these fractions from least to greatest.

$$7/8, \; 11/12, \; 17/20$$

17/20, 11/12, 7/8

16. $1^2/_3 \times 3^3/_4$ _____

17. $1^2/_3 \div 3/_8$ _____

18. $1^4/_9 + 5/_6$ _____

19. $4^5/_6 - 2^3/_5$ _____

<u>Questions 20–23:</u> *Change among decimals, percents, and fractions to complete the table.*

Decimal	Percent	Fraction
0.56	20. 56%	$^{14}/_{25}$
0.152	15.2%	21. _____
22. _____	23. _____	$^3/_8$

24. What percent of 120 is 40? _____

25. 15 percent of what number is 6? _____

26. What is the probability of rolling one die and getting a 7? 0

Questions 27–29: *Find the mean, median, and mode of this set of data*

$$10, 5, 2, 1, 8, 5, 3, 0$$

27. Mean _4.25_   8 7 2 3 5 5 8 10
    3+5 = $\frac{8}{2}$ = 4

28. Median _4_

29. Mode _5_

30. $^-8 + {}^+4 =$ _−4_

31. $^+85 + {}^-103 =$ _18_

32. $^-12 - {}^+7 =$ _−19_

33. $^-72 - {}^-28 =$ _−44_

34. $^-9 \times {}^+8 =$ _72_

35. $^-12 \times {}^-6 =$ _72_

36. $^-28 \div {}^+7 =$ _−4_

37. $^-72 \div {}^-9 =$ _8_

38. Find the area of a triangle with a base of 3 and a height of 2. _3_ $\frac{b \times h}{2}$

39. Find the volume of a cube with a side of 5.
    Lxwxh = 5×3 = 15

Write the value of the variable.

40. $x - 35 = 26$ _61_

41. $x + 81 = 7$ _−74_

42. $y \div 8 = 3$ _24_

43. $3z = 54$ _18_

44. $4y - 9 = 19$ _7_

45. $k \div 6 + 5 = 17$ _72_

ANSWER CHECKLIST

The answers are organized by review sections. Check your answers. If you miss any questions in a section, check the box and review that section.

❏ *Understand and Order Whole Numbers, page 94*
   1. <
   2. =
   3. <, <

❏ *Place Value, page 94*
   4. 10 billion

❏ *Positive Exponents, page 95*
   5. 64
   6. 36
   7. 72

❏ *Understand and Order Decimals, page 95*
   8. thousandths

❏ *Comparing Whole Numbers and Decimals, page 95*
   9. <
   10. <

❏ *Add, Subtract, Multiply, and Divide Decimals, page 96*
   11. 213.792
   12. 22.196
   13. 0.00714
   14. 1.8

❏ *Understand and Order Fractions, page 97*
   15. $^{17}/_{20}$, $^{7}/_{8}$, $^{11}/_{12}$

❏ *Multiply, Divide, Add, and Subtract Fractions and Mixed Numbers, page 99*
   16. $6\,^{1}/_{4}$
   17. $4\,^{4}/_{9}$
   18. $2\,^{5}/_{18}$
   19. $2\,^{7}/_{30}$

❏ *Percent, page 100*

Decimal	Percent	Fraction
0.56	**20.** 56%	14/25
0.152	15.2%	**21.** 19/125
22. 0.375	**23.** 37.5%	3/8

❏ *Three Types of Percent Problems, page 101*
   24. $33\,^{1}/_{3}$%
   25. 40

❏ *Probability, page 103*
   26. zero

❏ *Statistics, page 103*
   27. 4.25
   28. 4
   29. 5

❏ *Add and Subtract Integers, page 104*
   30. −4
   31. −18
   32. −19
   33. −44

❏ *Multiply and Divide Integers, page 105*
   34. −72
   35. +72
   36. −4
   37. +8

❏ *Formulas, page 105*
   38. 3
   39. 125

❏ *Equations, page 107*
   40. 61
   41. −74
   42. 24
   43. 18
   44. 7
   45. 72

☑ *Reading and Interpreting Graphs, page 109*

☑ *Reading and Interpreting Maps, page 112*

☑ *Mathematics Test Strategies, page 113*

MATHEMATICS REVIEW

UNDERSTAND AND ORDER WHOLE NUMBERS

Whole numbers are the numbers you use to tell how many. They include 0, 1, 2, 3, 4, 5, 6 . . . . The dots tell us that these numbers keep going on forever.

You can visualize whole numbers evenly spaced on a number line.

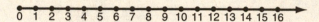

You can use the number line to compare numbers. Numbers get smaller as we go to the left and larger as we go to the right. We use the terms *equal to* (=), *less than* (<), *greater than* (>), and *between* to compare numbers.

12 equals 10 +2	2 is less than 5	9 is greater than 4	6 is between 5 and 7
12 = 10 + 2	2 < 5	9 > 4	5 < 6 < 7

Place Value

We use ten digits, 0–9 to write out numerals. We also use a place value system of numeration. The value of a digit depends on the place it occupies. Look at the following place value chart.

millions	hundred thousands	ten thousands	thousands	hundreds	tens	ones
3	5	7	9	4	1	0

The value of the 9 is 9,000. The 9 is in the thousands place. The value of the 5 is 500,000. The 5 is in the hundred thousands place. Read the number three million, five hundred seventy-nine thousand, four hundred ten.

Some whole numbers are very large. The distance from earth to the planet Pluto is about six trillion (6,000,000,000,000) yards. The distance from earth to the nearest star is about 40 quadrillion (40,000,000,000,000,000) yards.

Completed Examples

A. What is the value of 8 in the numeral 47,829?

The value of the 8 is 800; this is because the 8 is in the hundreds place.

B. Use >, <, or = to compare 2 and 7.
Use the number line to see that 2 < 7 (2 is less than 7).

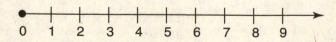

POSITIVE EXPONENTS

You can show repeated multiplication as an exponent. The exponent shows how many times the factor appears.

$$\text{Base—}3^5 = 3 \times 3 \times 3 \times 3 \times 3 = 243$$

[Exponent]

[Factors]

Rules for Exponents

Use these rules to multiply and divide exponents with the *same base*.

$$7^8 \times 7^5 = 7^{13} \qquad a^n \times a^m = a^{m+n}$$
$$7^8 \div 7^5 = 7^3 \qquad a^n \div a^m = a^{n-m}$$

Completed Examples

A. $4^3 + 6^2 \quad = 4 \times 4 \times 4 + 6 \times 6 \quad = 64 + 36 = 100$

B. $(2^3)(4^2) \quad = (2 \times 2 \times 2) \times (4 \times 4) \qquad = 8 \times 16 \quad = 128$

C. $(3^2)^2 \qquad = 3^4 \quad = 3 \times 3 \times 3 \times 3 = 81$

D. $(10 - 9)^2 = 1^2 \quad = 1$

UNDERSTAND AND ORDER DECIMALS

Decimals are used to represent numbers between 0 and 1. Decimals can also be written on a number line.

We also use ten digits 0–9 and a place value system of numeration to write decimals. The value of a digit depends on the place it occupies. Look at the following place value chart.

ones	tenths	hundredths	thousandths	ten-thousandths	hundred-thousandths	millionths	ten-millionths	hundred-millionths	billionths
0 .	3	6	8	7					

The value of 3 is three tenths. The 3 is in the tenths place. The value of 8 is eight thousandths. The 8 is in the thousandths place.

Comparing Whole Numbers and Decimals

To compare two numbers line up the place values. Start at the left and keep going until the digits in the same place are different.

Compare	9,879 and 16,459	23,801 and 23,798	58.1289 and 58.132
Line up the place values	9,879 16,459 9,879 < 16,459 Less than	23,**8**01 23,798 23,801 > 23,798 Greater than	58.1289 58.1**3**2 58.1289 < 58.132 Less than

Completed Examples

A. What is the value of the digit 2 in the decimal 35.6829?

The 2 is in the thousandths place. $2 \times 0.001 = 0.002$.
The value of the 2 is 0.002 or 2 thousandths.

B. Use $<$, $>$, or $=$ to compare 1248.9234 and 1248.9229

1248.9234 $>$ 1248.9229 The digits in the numerals are the same until you reach the thousandths place where $3 > 2$. Since $3 > 2$, then 1248.9234 $>$ 1248.9229.

ADD, SUBTRACT, MULTIPLY, AND DIVIDE DECIMALS

Add and Subtract Decimals

Line up the decimal points and add or subtract.

Add: $14.9 + 3.108 + 0.16$ Subtract $14.234 - 7.14$

$$
\begin{array}{r}
14.9 \\
3.108 \\
+\ 0.16 \\
\hline
18.168
\end{array}
\qquad
\begin{array}{r}
14.234 \\
-7.14 \\
\hline
7.094
\end{array}
$$

Multiply Decimals

Multiply as with whole numbers. Count the total number of decimal places in the factors. Put that many decimal places in the product. You may have to write leading zeros.

Multiply: 17.4×1.3 Multiply: 0.016×1.7

$$
\begin{array}{r}
17.4 \\
\times\ 1.3 \\
\hline
522 \\
174 \\
\hline
22.6\,2
\end{array}
\qquad
\begin{array}{r}
0.016 \\
\times\ 1.7 \\
\hline
112 \\
16 \\
\hline
0\,2\,7\,2
\end{array}
$$

Divide Decimals

Make the divisor a whole number. Match the movement in the dividend and then divide.

$$
0.16\overline{)1.328} \qquad 0.16\overline{)1.328} \qquad
\begin{array}{r}
8.3 \\
16\overline{)132.8} \\
\underline{128} \\
48 \\
\underline{48} \\
0
\end{array}
$$

UNDERSTAND AND ORDER FRACTIONS

A fraction names a part of a whole or of a group. A fraction has two parts, a numerator and a denominator. The denominator tells how many parts in all. The numerator tell how many parts you identified.

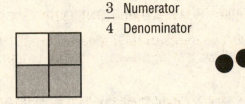

$\dfrac{3}{4}$ Numerator
Denominator

Equivalent Fractions

Two fractions that stand for the same number are called equivalent fractions. Multiply or divide the numerator and denominator by the same number to find an equivalent fraction.

$$\frac{2\times3}{5\times3}=\frac{6}{15} \qquad \frac{6\div3}{9\div3}=\frac{2}{3} \qquad \frac{6\times4}{8\times4}=\frac{24}{32} \qquad \frac{8\div2}{10\div2}=\frac{4}{5}$$

Fractions can also be written and ordered on a number line. You can use the number line to compare fractions. Fractions get smaller as we go to the left and larger as we go to the right. We use the terms equivalent to (=), less than (<), greater than (>), and between to compare fractions.

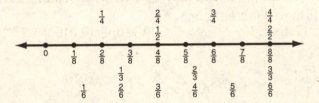

½ is equivalent to ²/₄   ²/₃ is less than ³/₄   ⅝ is greater than ½   ⅓ is between ¼ and ³/₈

$$\frac{1}{2}=\frac{2}{4} \qquad\qquad \frac{2}{3}<\frac{3}{4} \qquad\qquad \frac{5}{8}>\frac{1}{2} \qquad\qquad \frac{1}{4}<\frac{1}{3}<\frac{3}{8}$$

Compare Two Fractions

Use this method to compare two fractions. For example, compare $^{13}/_{18}$ and $^{5}/_{7}$. First write the two fractions and cross multiply as shown. The larger cross product appears next to the larger fraction. If cross products are equal then the fractions are equivalent.

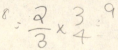

$$91 = \qquad\qquad = 90$$

$$91 > 90 \text{ so } \frac{13}{18} > \frac{5}{7}$$

Completed Examples

A. Compare $\dfrac{5}{7}$ and $\dfrac{18}{19}$,

Use cross multiplication.

$\dfrac{5}{7} \times \dfrac{18}{19}$, $5 \times 19 = 95$ and $7 \times 18 = 126$, therefore $\dfrac{5}{7} < \dfrac{18}{19}$.

B. Write $\dfrac{27}{7}$ as a mixed number.

$$7)\overline{27} \quad \begin{array}{c} 3 \text{ R6} \\ \hline 21 \\ 6 \end{array}$$

$\dfrac{27}{7} = 3\dfrac{6}{7}$

C. Write $6\dfrac{5}{8}$ as a fraction.

$6 \times 8 = 48$. Multiply the denominator and the whole number.
$48 + 5 = 53$. Add the numerator to the product.

$6\dfrac{5}{8} = \dfrac{53}{8}$

Mixed Numbers and Improper Fractions

Change an improper fraction to a mixed number:

$$\dfrac{23}{8} = 8)\overline{23}\,^{2\frac{7}{8}}$$

Change a mixed number to an improper fraction:

$$3\dfrac{2}{5} = \dfrac{17}{5}$$

Multiply denominator and whole number. Then add the numerator.

$$\dfrac{(3 \times 5) + 2}{5} = \dfrac{15 + 2}{5} = \dfrac{17}{5}$$

MULTIPLY, DIVIDE, ADD, AND SUBTRACT FRACTIONS AND MIXED NUMBERS

Multiply Fractions and Mixed Numbers

Write any mixed number as an improper fraction. Multiply numerator and denominator. Write the product in simplest form. For example, Multiply $^3/_4$ and $^1/_6$.

$$\frac{3}{4} \times \frac{1}{6} = \frac{3}{24} = \frac{1}{8}$$

Now, multiply $3^1/_3$ times $^3/_5$.

$$3\frac{1}{3} \times \frac{3}{5} = \frac{10}{3} \times \frac{3}{5} = \frac{30}{15} = 2$$

Divide Fractions and Mixed Numbers

To divide $1^4/_5$ by $^3/_8$:

$$1\frac{4}{5} \div \frac{3}{8} = \frac{9}{5} \div \frac{3}{8} = \frac{9}{5} \times \frac{8}{3} = \frac{72}{15} = 4\frac{12}{15} = 4\frac{4}{5}$$

Write any mixed numbers as improper fractions   Invert the divisor and multiply   Write the product   Write in simplest form

Add Fractions and Mixed Numbers

Write fractions with common denominators. Add and then write in simplest form.

Add: $\dfrac{3}{8} + \dfrac{1}{4}$

$$\frac{3}{8} = \frac{3}{8}$$
$$+\frac{1}{4} = \frac{2}{8}$$
$$\frac{5}{8}$$

Add: $\dfrac{7}{8} + \dfrac{5}{12}$

$$\frac{7}{8} = \frac{21}{24}$$
$$+\frac{5}{12} = \frac{10}{24}$$
$$\frac{31}{24} = 1\frac{7}{24}$$

Add: $2\dfrac{1}{3} + \dfrac{5}{7}$

$$2\frac{1}{3} = 2\frac{7}{21}$$
$$+\frac{5}{7} = \frac{15}{21}$$
$$2\frac{22}{21} = 3\frac{1}{21}$$

(handwritten) $\dfrac{7}{3} + \dfrac{5}{7}$ $\dfrac{49}{21} + \dfrac{15}{21} = \dfrac{64}{21}$ $3\dfrac{1}{21}$

Subtract Fractions and Mixed Numbers

Write fractions with common denominators. Subtract and then write in simplest form.

Subtract: $\dfrac{5}{6} - \dfrac{1}{3}$

$$\frac{5}{6} = \frac{5}{6}$$
$$-\frac{1}{3} = \frac{2}{6}$$
$$\frac{3}{6} = \frac{1}{2}$$

Subtract: $\dfrac{3}{8} - \dfrac{1}{5}$

$$\frac{3}{8} = \frac{15}{40}$$
$$-\frac{1}{5} = \frac{8}{40}$$
$$\frac{7}{40}$$

Subtract: $3\dfrac{1}{6} - 1\dfrac{1}{3}$

$$3\frac{1}{6} = 3\frac{1}{6} = 2\frac{7}{6}$$
$$-1\frac{1}{3} = 1\frac{2}{6} = 1\frac{2}{6}$$
$$1\frac{5}{6}$$

PERCENT

Percent comes from per centum, which means per hundred. Whenever you see a number followed by a percent sign it means that number out of 100.

Decimals and Percents

To write a decimal as a percent, move the decimal point two places to the right and write the percent sign.

$$0.34 = 34\% \qquad 0.297 = 29.7\% \qquad 0.6 = 60\% \qquad 0.001 = 0.1\%$$

To write a percent as a decimal, move the decimal point two places to the left and delete the percent sign.

$$51\% = 0.51 \qquad 34.18\% = 0.3418 \qquad 0.9\% = 0.009$$

Fractions and Percents

Writing Fractions as Percents

- Divide the numerator by the denominator. Write the answer as a percent.

Write $^3/_5$ as a percent.

$$5\overline{)3.0}^{\,0.6} \qquad 0.6 = 60\%$$

Write $^5/_8$ as a percent.

$$8\overline{)5.000}^{\,0.625} \qquad 0.625 = 62.5\%$$

- Write an equivalent fraction with 100 in the denominator. Write the numerator followed by a percent sign.

Write $^{13}/_{25}$ as a percent.

$$\frac{13}{25} = \frac{52}{100} = 52\%$$

- Use these equivalencies.

$$\frac{1}{4} = 25\% \qquad \frac{1}{2} = 50\% \qquad \frac{3}{4} = 75\% \qquad \frac{4}{4} = 100\%$$

$$\frac{1}{5} = 20\% \qquad \frac{2}{5} = 40\% \qquad \frac{3}{5} = 60\% \qquad \frac{4}{5} = 80\%$$

$$\frac{1}{6} = 16\frac{2}{3}\% \qquad \frac{1}{3} = 33\frac{1}{3}\% \qquad \frac{2}{3} = 66\frac{2}{3}\% \qquad \frac{5}{6} = 83\frac{1}{3}\%$$

$$\frac{1}{8} = 12\frac{1}{2}\% \qquad \frac{3}{8} = 37\frac{1}{2}\% \qquad \frac{5}{8} = 62\frac{1}{2}\% \qquad \frac{7}{8} = 87\frac{1}{2}\%$$

Writing Percents as Fractions

Write a fraction with 100 in the denominator and the percent in the numerator. Simplify.

$$18\% = \frac{18}{100} = \frac{9}{50} \qquad 7.5\% = \frac{7.5}{100} = \frac{75}{1000} = \frac{3}{40}$$

Completed Examples

A. Write 0.567 as a percent.

Move the decimal two places to the right and write a percent sign; therefore, $0.567 = 56.7\%$.

B. Write $\frac{1}{4}$ as a percent.

Write $\frac{1}{4}$ as a decimal $(1 \div 4) = 0.25$

Write 0.25 as a percent $0.25 = 25\%$

C. Write 26% as a fraction.

Place the percent number in the numerator and 100 in the denominator.

$$26\% = \frac{26}{100} = \frac{13}{50}$$

Simplify: $\frac{26}{100} = \frac{13}{50}$

THREE TYPES OF PERCENT PROBLEMS

Finding a Percent of a Number

To find a percent of a number, write a number sentence with a decimal for the percent and solve.

$$\text{Find } 40\% \text{ of } 90.$$

$$0.4 \times 90 = 36$$

It may be easier to write a fraction for the percent.

$$\text{Find } 62\tfrac{1}{2}\% \text{ of } 64.$$

$$\frac{5}{8} \times 64 = 5 \times 8 = 40$$

Finding What Percent One Number Is of Another

To find what percent one number is of another, write a number sentence and solve to find the percent.

What percent of 5 is 3?

$$n \times 5 = 3$$

$$n = {}^3\!/_5 = 0.6 = 60\%$$

Finding a Number When a Percent of It Is Known

To find a number when a percent of it is known, write a number sentence with a decimal or a fraction for the percent and solve to find the number.

5% of what number is 2?

$$0.05 \times n = 2$$

$$n = 2 \div 0.05$$

$$n = 40$$

Completed Examples

A. What percent of 70 is 28?

$\square \times 70 = 28$

$\square = \dfrac{28}{70} = \dfrac{4}{10}$

$\square = 40\%$

(handwritten: $nx\ 70 = 28$, $\dfrac{70}{70}$, $\dfrac{4}{10} = \dfrac{2}{5}$ *)*

B. 30% of 60 is what number?

$30\% \times 60 = \square$

$0.3 \times 60 = \square$

$\square = 18$

(handwritten: $\begin{array}{r} 60 \\ \times .3 \\ \hline 18.0 \end{array}$ *)*

C. 40% of what number is 16?

$0.40 \times \square = 16$

$\square = \dfrac{16}{0.4}$

$\square = 40$

(handwritten: $.4 \times n = \dfrac{16}{.4} = 40$, $\dfrac{}{.4}$ *)*

PROBABILITY AND SIMPLE STATISTICS

Probability

The probability of an occurrence is the likelihood that it will happen. Most often, we write probability as a fraction.

Flip a fair coin and the probability that it will come up heads is 1/2. The same is true for tails. Write the probability this way.

$$P\,(\text{H}) = 1/2 \qquad P\,(\text{T}) = 1/2$$

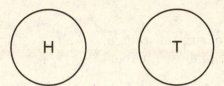

If something will never occur the probability is 0. If something will always occur, the probability is 1. Therefore, if you flip a fair coin,

$$P\,(7) = 0 \qquad P\,(\text{H or T}) = 1$$

Statistics

Descriptive statistics are used to explain or describe a set of numbers. Most often we use the mean, median, or mode to describe these numbers.

Mean (Average)

The mean is a position midway between two extremes. To find the mean:

1. Add the items or scores.

2. Divide by the number of items.

    For example, find the mean of 24, 17, 42, 51, 36.

$$24 + 17 + 42 + 51 + 36 = 170 \qquad 170 \div 5 = 34$$

The mean or average is 34.

Median

The median is the middle number. To find the median:

1. Arrange the numbers from least to greatest.

2. If there are an odd number of scores, then find the middle score.

3. If there is an even number of scores, average the two middle scores.

For example, find the median of these numbers.

$$6, 9, 11, \underline{17}, \underline{21}, 33, 45, 71$$

There are an even number of scores. The middle scores are 17 and 21.

$$17 + 21 = 38 \qquad 38 \div 2 = 19$$

The median is 19.

Don't forget to arrange the scores in order before finding the middle score!

Mode

The mode is the number that occurs most often.
For example, find the mode of these numbers.

$$6, 3, 7, 6, 9, 3, 6, 1, 2, 6, 7, 3$$

The number 6 occurs most often so 6 is the mode.

Not all sets of numbers have a mode. Some sets of numbers may have more than one mode.

INTEGERS

The number line can also show negative numbers. There is a negative whole number for every positive whole number. Zero is neither positive nor negative. The negative whole numbers and the positive whole numbers together are called integers.

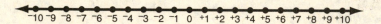

Add and Subtract Integers

Add

When the signs are the same keep the sign and add.

$$
\begin{array}{r}
^{+}7 \\
+\ ^{+}8 \\
\hline
^{+}15
\end{array}
\qquad
\begin{array}{r}
^{-}3 \\
+\ ^{-}11 \\
\hline
^{-}14
\end{array}
$$

When the signs are different, disregard the signs, subtract the numbers, and keep the sign of the larger number.

$$
\begin{array}{r}
^{+}28 \\
+\ ^{-}49 \\
\hline
^{-}21
\end{array}
\qquad
\begin{array}{r}
^{-}86 \\
+\ ^{+}135 \\
\hline
^{+}49
\end{array}
$$

Subtract

Change the sign of the number being subtracted. Then add using the preceding rules.

$$
\begin{array}{cccc}
^+13 & ^-43 & ^+29 & ^-92 \\
-\,^-18 & -\,^-17 & -\,^-49 & -\,^+135 \\
\downarrow & \downarrow & \downarrow & \downarrow \\
^+13 & ^-43 & ^+29 & ^-92 \\
+\,^+18 & +\,^+17 & +\,^+49 & +\,^-135 \\
\hline
^+31 & ^-26 & ^+78 & ^-227
\end{array}
$$

Multiply and Divide Integers

Multiply

Multiply as you would whole numbers. The product is *positive* if there are an even number of negative factors. The product is *negative* if there are an odd number of negative factors.

$$^-2 \times {}^+4 \times {}^-6 \times {}^+3 = {}^+144 \qquad {}^-2 \times {}^-4 \times {}^+6 \times {}^-3 = {}^-144$$

Divide

Forget the signs and divide. The quotient is *positive* if both integers have the same sign. The quotient is *negative* if the integers have different signs.

$$^+24 \div {}^+4 = {}^+6 \qquad {}^-24 \div {}^-4 = {}^+6 \qquad {}^+24 \div {}^-4 = {}^-6 \qquad {}^-24 \div {}^+4 = {}^-6$$

FORMULAS

Evaluating an Expression

Evaluate an expression by replacing the variables with values. Remember to use the correct order of operations. For example, evaluate

$$3x - \frac{y}{z} \text{ for } x = 3, \ y = 8, \text{ and } z = 4$$

$$3\left(3\right) - \frac{8}{4} = 9 - 2 = 7$$

Using Formulas

Using a formula is like evaluating an expression. Just replace the variables with values. Here are some important formulas to know. The area of a figure is the amount of space it occupies in two dimensions. The perimeter of a figure is the distance around the figure. Use 3.14 for π.

Figure	Formula	Description
Triangle	Area = $\frac{1}{2} bh$ Perimeter = $s_1 + s_2 + s_3$	
Square	Area = s^2 Perimeter = $4s$	
Rectangle	Area = lw Perimeter = $2l + 2w$	
Parallelogram	Area = bh Perimeter = $2s + 2b$	
Trapezoid	Area = $\frac{1}{2} h(b_1 + b_2)$ Perimeter = $b_1 + b_2 + s_1 + s_2$	
Circle	Area = πr^2 Circumference = $2\pi r$ or $\qquad\qquad\quad = \pi d$	
Cube	Volume = s^3	

Pythagorean Formula

The Pythagorean formula for right triangles states that the sum of the square of the legs equals the square of the hypotenuse:

$$a^2 + b^2 = c^2$$

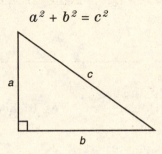

Completed Examples—Distance and Area

Let's solve the distance and area problems.

A. How many meters is it around a regular hexagon with a side of 87 centimeters?
A hexagon has 6 sides. It's a regular hexagon, so all the sides are the same length.
$6 \times 87 = 522$. The perimeter is 522 centimeters, which equals 5.22 meters.

B. What is the area of this figure?

The formula for the area of a circle is πr^2.
The diameter is 18, so the radius is 9. Use 3.14 for π.
$A = 3.14 \times (9)^2 = 3.14 \times 81 = 254.34$ or about 254.

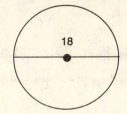

EQUATIONS

The whole idea of solving equations is to isolate the variable on one side of the equal sign. The value of the variable is what's on the other side of the equal sign. Substitute your answer into the original equation to check your solution.

Solve Equations by Adding or Subtracting

Solve: $y + 19 = 23$
Subtract 19 $y + 19 - 19 = 23 - 19$
$y = 4$

Check: Does $4 + 19 = 23$? Yes. It checks.

Add 23   Solve: $x - 23 = 51$
$x - 23 + 23 = 51 + 23$
$x = 74$

Check: Does $74 - 23 = 51$. Yes. It checks.

Solve Equations by Multiplying or Dividing

$$\text{Solve: } \frac{z}{7} = 6$$

Multiply by 7 $\qquad \frac{z}{7} \times 7 = 6 \times 7$

$$z = 42$$

Check: Does $\frac{42}{7} = 6$? Yes. It checks.

$$\text{Solve: } 21 = -3x$$

Divide by $^-3$ $\qquad \dfrac{21}{-3} = \dfrac{-3x}{-3}$

$$-7 = x$$

Check: Does $21 = (-3)(-7)$? Yes. It checks.

Solve Two-Step Equations

Add or subtract before you multiply or divide.

$$\text{Solve: } 3x - 6 = 24$$

Add 6 $\quad 3x - 6 + 6 = 24 + 6$
$$3x = 30$$

Divide by 3 $\quad \dfrac{3x}{3} = \dfrac{30}{3}$

$$x = 10$$

Check: Does $3 \times \mathbf{10} - 6 = 24$? Yes. It checks.

$$\text{Solve: } \frac{y}{7} + 4 = 32$$

Subtract 4 $\quad \dfrac{y}{7} + 4 - 4 = 32 - 4$

$$\frac{y}{7} = 28$$

Multiply by 7 $\quad \dfrac{y}{7} \times 7 = \big(28\big)\big(7\big)$
$$y = 196$$

Check: Does $\dfrac{\mathbf{196}}{7} + 4 = 32$? Yes. It checks.

READ AND INTERPRET GRAPHS

You will likely encounter graphs on the test. Examples of the four main types of graphs are shown below. Answer the questions that accompany the graphs and review the answers on page 111.

The Pictograph

The pictograph uses symbols to stand for numbers. In the following graph, each picture represents 1,000 phones. This pictographs shows that Closter has 8,000 phones.

Number of Phones in Five Towns
(in thousands)

Try these questions:

1. According to this graph, about how many more phones are there in Bergenfield than in Emerson?
   (A) 10,000
   (B) 15,000
   (C) 1,000
   (D) 1.5 thousand

2. This graph *best* demonstrates which of the following?
   (A) More people live in Bergenfield.
   (B) People in Alpine make the fewest calls.
   (C) There are about twice as many phones in Emerson as in Alpine.
   (D) There are about four times as many phones in Bergenfield as in Alpine.

The Bar Graph

The bar graph represents information by the length of a bar. The graph below shows the rainfall during two months in each of five towns. This graph shows that Dumont had 1.5 inches of rain in July and August.

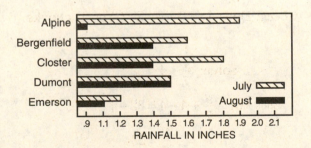

Rainfall in July and August for Five Towns

Try these questions:

3. You wanted to get the least rainfall. Based on this graph, which town would you go to in July and which town would you go to in August?
   (A) Closter, Bergenfield
   (B) Alpine, Dumont
   (C) Closter, Alpine
   (D) None of the above

4. This graph *best* demonstrates which of the following?
   (A) The rainiest town yearly is Closter.
   (B) Alpine has the largest rainfall difference between July and August.
   (C) The driest town yearly is Emerson.
   (D) In August, Alpine has more rain than Emerson.

The Line Graph

The line graph plots information against two axes. The graph below shows monthly sales for two corporations. This graph shows that the NOP Corp. had $600,000 in sales during November.

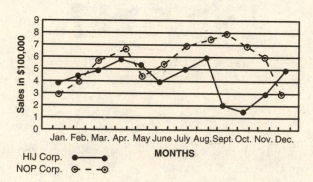

HIJ Corp. ●──●
NOP Corp. ○──○
MONTHS

Sales for Two Companies During the Year

You might be asked two types of questions.

5. What was the approximate difference in sales between the HIJ and the NOP Corporations in June?
   (A) $15,000
   (B) $150,000
   (C) $400,000
   (D) $4.5 million

6. This graph *best* demonstrates which of the following?
   (A) NOP has more employees.
   (B) From August to September, the differences in sales grew by 400%.
   (C) In October, NOP had over $600,000 more in sales than HIJ.
   (D) In total, HIJ had more sales this year than NOP.

The Circle Graph

The circle represents an entire amount. In the graph below, each wedge-shaped piece of the graph represents the percent of tax money spent on different town services. This graph shows that if the town collects $1,400,000 in taxes, the town will spend $84,000 (0.06 × $400,000) on planning.

Percent of Tax Money Spent for Town Services

Use the circle graph to answer these questions.

7. The town collects $1,400,000 in taxes. How much will the town spend on schools?
   - (A) $320,000
   - (B) $60,000
   - (C) $600,000
   - (D) $448,000

8. The town collects $1,400,000 in taxes. The town needs to spend $392,000 for police. Any needed money will come from sanitation. The percents in the pie chart are recalculated. What percent is left for sanitation?
   - (A) 21%
   - (B) 17%
   - (C) 13%
   - (D) 10%

Explained Answers

1. **D** Writing answers in a different format (1.5 thousand instead of 1,500) is common.

2. **D** You can't draw any valid conclusions about the populations or calls made. Some towns might have more businesses, own fewer phones, or make more calls per household.

3. **D** Emerson, Alpine are the towns you would choose. No need to compute. Find the smallest bar for each month.

4. **B** That fact is clear. We only have information about July and August, so we can't be sure about (A) or (C). Choice (D) is not true.

5. **B** Each space represents $100,000 and there are 1.5 spaces between the sales figures in June.

6. **B** You can't predict the number of employees from this information. Choices (C) and (D) are false.

7. **D** Multiply 0.32 × $1,400,000.

8. **C** It takes 28 percent of the taxes to get $392,000. That's 4 percent more than the police get now. Sanitation loses 4 percent, leaving 13 percent.

READ AND INTERPRET MAPS

Use the map to answer the items.

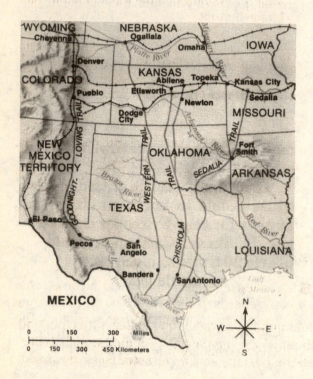

Western cattle trails and railroads about 1875

1. Which cattle trail goes from San Antonio to Abilene?
   (A) Chisholm
   (B) Sedalia
   (C) Goodnight-Loving
   (D) Western Trail

2. Which cattle trail crosses the Pecos River?
   (A) Chisholm
   (B) Sedalia
   (C) Goodnight-Loving
   (D) Western Trail

3. Which cattle trail passes through the fewest states?
   (A) Chisholm
   (B) Sedalia
   (C) Goodnight-Loving
   (D) Western Trail

4. About how far is it by train from Sedalia to Abilene?
   (A) 150 miles
   (B) 300 miles
   (C) 450 miles
   (D) 600 miles

5. The Goodnight-Loving Trail turns north after Pecos because
   (A) that's the way to Denver
   (B) cattle drovers did not want to go into Mexico
   (C) of the mountains
   (D) of the Rio Grande River

6. Which state contains the final railhead for the largest number of cattle trails?
   (A) Texas
   (B) Kansas
   (C) Oklahoma
   (D) Nebraska

7. If drovers move a herd of cattle about 25 kilometers per day, about how many days would it take to move a herd from Fort Smith to Sedalia on the Sedalia Trail?
   (A) 8
   (B) 16
   (C) 24
   (D) 32

Explained Answers

1. **A** Find San Antonio in southern Texas and trace the Chisholm Trail to Abilene, Kansas. Notice that the trail splits as it gets into Kansas.

2. **C** The Pecos River flows through Pecos in southwest Texas. You can trace the Goodnight-Loving Trail across the river.

3. **A** The Chisholm Trail passes through just three states, while the other four trails pass through at least four states. Notice that the trails go generally south-north while the railroads go generally east-west.

4. **B** Use the scale at the bottom of the page to see that the distance is about 300 miles. The scale shows miles on the top and kilometers on the bottom.

5. **C** The map shows that the Goodnight-Loving Trail turns north because of the mountains.

6. **B** Two trails have rail heads in Kansas, at Dodge City and at Abilene.

7. **B** Use the kilometer scale to find that it is about 400 kilometers from Fort Smith to Sedalia. Divide 400 by 25 to find that it would take about 16 days to make the trip.

MATHEMATICS TEST STRATEGIES

The mathematics tested is the kind you probably had in high school and in college. It is the kind of mathematics you will use as you teach and go about your everyday life. Computational ability alone is expected but is held to a minimum. Remember to use the general test strategies discussed on pages 13–15.

Circle Important Information and Key Words and Cross Out Information You Don't Need

This approach will draw your attention to the information needed to answer the question. A common mistake is to use from the question information that has nothing to do with the solution.

Example:

> In the morning, a train travels at a constant speed over an 800 kilometer distance. In the afternoon the train travels back over this same route. There is less traffic and the train travels four times as fast as it did that morning. However, there are more people on the train during the afternoon. Which of the following do you know about the train's afternoon trip?

(A) The time is divided by four

(B) The time is multiplied by four

(C) The rate and time are divided by four

(D) The distance is the same so the rate is the same

To solve the problem you just need to know that the speed is constant, four times as fast, and the same route was covered. Circle the information you need to solve the problem.

The distance traveled or that there were more people in the afternoon is extra information. Cross off this extra information, which may interfere with your ability to solve the problem.

In the morning, a train travels at a ⟨constant speed⟩ ~~over an 800-kilometer distance.~~ In the afternoon the train travels back over this ⟨same route.⟩ ~~There is less traffic~~ and the train travels ⟨four times as fast⟩ as it did that morning. ~~However, there are more people on the train during the afternoon.~~ Which of the following do you know about the train's afternoon trip?

The correct answer is (A), the time is divided by four. The route is the same, but the train travels four times as fast. Therefore, the time to make the trip is divided by four. Rate means the same thing as speed, and we know that the speed has been multiplied by four.

Estimate to Be Sure Your Answer Is Reasonable

You can use estimation and common sense to be sure that the answer is reasonable. You may make a multiplication error or misalign decimal points. You may be so engrossed in a problem that you miss the big picture because of the details. These difficulties can be headed off by making sure your answer is reasonable.

A few examples follow.

A question involves dividing or multiplying. Multiply: 28×72.

Estimate first: $30 \times 70 = 2,100$. Your answer should be close to 2,100. If not, then your answer is not reasonable. A mistake was probably made in multiplication.

A question involves subtracting or adding. Add: $12.9 + 0.63 + 10.29 + 4.3$.

Estimate first: $13 + 1 + 10 + 4 = 28$. Your answer should be close to 28. If not, then your answer is not reasonable. The decimal points may not have been aligned.

A question asks you to compare fractions to $^{11}/_{10}$.

Think: $^{11}/_{10}$ is more than 1. Any number 1 or less will be less than $^{11}/_{10}$. Any number $1^{1}/_{8}$ or larger will be more than $^{11}/_{10}$. You have to look closely only at numbers between 1 and $1^{1}/_{8}$.

A question asks you to multiply two fractions or decimals.

The fractions or decimals are less than 1. The product of two fractions or decimals less than 1 is less than either of the two fractions or decimals. If not, you know that your answer is not reasonable.

Stand back for a second after you answer each question and ask, "Is this reasonable? Is this at least approximately correct? Does this make sense?"

Check answers to computation, particularly division and subtraction. When you have completed a division or subtraction example, do a quick, approximate check. Your check should confirm your answer. If not, your answer is probably not reasonable.

Work from the Answers

If you don't know how to solve a formula or relation, try out each answer choice until you get the correct answer. Look at this example.

What percent times $^1/_4$ is $^1/_5$?

(A) 25%

(B) 40%

(C) 80%

(D) 120%

Just take each answer in turn and try it out.

$$0.25 \times \frac{1}{4} = \frac{1}{4} \times \frac{1}{4} = \frac{1}{16}$$ That's not it.

$$0.40 \times \frac{1}{4} = \frac{4}{10} \times \frac{1}{4} = \frac{4}{40} = \frac{1}{10}$$ That's not it either.

$$0.8 \times \frac{1}{4} = \frac{4}{5} \times \frac{1}{4} = \frac{4}{20} = \frac{1}{5}$$

You know that 0.8 is the correct answer, so choice (C) is correct.

Try Out Numbers

Look at the preceding question.

Work with fractions at first. Ask: What number times $^1/_4$ equals $^1/_5$?

Through trial and error you find out that $^4/_5 \times ^1/_4 = ^1/_5$.

The answer in fractions is $^4/_5$.

$$\frac{4}{5} = 0.8 = 80\%$$

The correct choice is (C).

In this example, we found the answer without ever solving an equation. We just tried out numbers until we found the one that works.

Eliminate and Guess

Use this approach when all else has failed. Begin by eliminating the answers you know are wrong. Sometimes you know with certainty that an answer is incorrect. Other times, an answer looks so unreasonable that you can be fairly sure that it is not correct.

Once you have eliminated incorrect answers, a few will probably be left. Just guess among these choices.

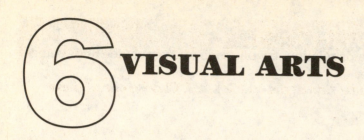

6 VISUAL ARTS

USING THIS CHAPTER

This chapter prepares you to take the Visual Arts items on the LAST. Choose one of these approaches.

I want a Visual Arts review.

❏ Read the Visual Arts Review.
❏ Complete the Visual Arts Practice Items on page 121.

I want to practice Visual Arts questions.

❏ Complete the Visual Arts Practice Items on page 121.

VISUAL ARTS REVIEW

VISUAL ARTS

Visual art includes paintings, photographs, prints, carvings, sculpture, and architecture. *Representational* art presents a recognizable representation of real people, places, or things. *Abstract* art presents nonrecognizable representations of real things or thoughts, perhaps using geometric shapes or designs. *Nonrepresentational* art is unrelated to real things or thoughts and represents only itself.

Visual arts are built around certain visual elements.

Points are represented by dots and are the simplest visual element. **Lines** are created when points move and may be horizontal, vertical, diagonal, straight, jagged, or wavy. Lines come in many thicknesses and lengths. Lines in a painting or drawing may suggest three-dimensional images or outline a shape.

Shapes are bounded forms in two-dimensional art. The boundary of a shape is usually a line, but it may also be created by color, shading, and texture. A shape may be geometric or fluid.

Space refers to the area occupied by the art. Paintings occupy two-dimensional space, while sculpture occupies three-dimensional space. Sculptors manipulate three-dimensional space and forms to create the desired effect, while painters often manipulate two-dimensional space to create the illusion of three-dimensional space.

Color: The colors of the spectrum are red, orange, yellow, green, blue, indigo, and violet. White is actually the combination of all the spectral colors, and black is an absence of color. Colors communicate mood (blue is cold, yellow is warm). Warm colors appear to expand a work's size while cold colors appear to contract its size. Color has three properties.

1. **Hue** is the color itself. It describes a color's placement in the color spectrum.
2. **Value** refers to the amount of lightness or darkness in a color. Low value shades are dark, while high value shades are light. You can raise the value of a color by adding white, and lower the value by adding black.
3. **Saturation** (also called chroma or intensity) describes the brightness or dullness of a color.

Perspective refers to methods of manipulating two-dimensional space to create the illusion of three-dimensional space. *Foreshortening* means exaggerating linear perspective by drawing the near parts of an object in close proximity to the far parts of the same object. *Linear perspective* means drawing objects smaller as they get further away. Still photographs naturally employ linear perspective.

Principles of Design

These elements of design are frequently used to analyze and describe an artwork.

Balance refers to the equilibrium of elements that create a work. Balance can be achieved through both symmetrical and asymmetrical arrangements.

Symmetry is achieved when one half of an artwork more or less reflects the other half. Symmetrical works tend to create a sense of formality.

Asymmetry is achieved when color and the lightness of different parts of a work create a sense of balance. For example, a lighter area may balance a darker area. Asymmetrical works tend to create a sense of informality.

Rhythm refers to the repetition of elements in an artwork. Effective repetition of design elements tends to create a more dynamic work.

Dominance means to use color or positioning to draw the attention of the viewer to the most important element or elements in a work.

Painting

Painting techniques include oil, watercolor, gouache, and fresco. The paint for all of these techniques consists of a pigment (color), binder (e.g., egg, oil, wax), which holds the pigment together, and solvents (water, turpentine), which permit the paint to spread on a surface.

Oil is the primary painting form. The oil can be applied as thinly or thickly as desired and dries slowly so that the artist can rework it until the desired result is obtained.

Watercolor presents a thin wispy appearance and is widely used for landscape painting. Gouache is an opaque watercolor that is often applied to a board. Acrylic paints combine most of the advantages of oil paint with easy clean up. Acrylics are often applied with an airbrush.

Analyzing Art Forms

Art appears in many incarnations, including paintings, photographs, prints, carvings, sculpture, and architecture. When asked to analyze any work of art, you can comment on the content, the form, the style, and the method used by the artist.

The *content* is what actually appears in a work of art. It is the subject matter of the art. Don't take the obvious subject matter for granted when considering your analysis. Choose descriptive words as you search for ways to capture the content of the image in front of you. For example, a landscape may contain peaceful blue skies, a raging river, cows and horses grazing, or seemingly endless grassy fields. A portrait may show a happy person or someone filled with concern or worry. A sculpture may show a smoothly muscled athlete. A building may have cascading stairs or a series of columns that thrust upward to the ceiling.

The *form* of a work of art is the order imposed by the artist. Form is the design of the work regardless of the content. A painting or photograph may show strong horizontal or vertical orientation. Perhaps the work is symmetrical, with one part a mirror image of the other. Some works may be tilted or asymmetrical.

The *style* refers to the artist's way of expressing ideas including formal styles such as gothic, high renaissance, baroque, or impressionist. In a painting or picture you can notice how the artist uses color. The colors may blend or clash. There may be an overall dark tone to the picture, or it may be light and airy. Perhaps the artist used dots of paint to produce the image.

The *method* is the medium used by the artist to create the work. It may be an oil painting or a watercolor. Perhaps the artist created prints or an etching. A three-dimensional work of art may have been sculpted, cast, carved, molded, or turned on a potter's wheel.

Keep these elements of content, form, style, and method in mind as you respond to the questions on the LAST.

VISUAL ARTS PRACTICE ITEMS

These items will help you practice for the real LAST. These items have the same form and test the same material as the LAST items. The items you encounter on the real LAST may have a different emphasis and may be more complete.

Instructions

Mark your answers on the sheet provided below. Complete the items in 20 minutes or less. Correct your answer sheet using the answers on page 125.

1 Ⓐ Ⓑ Ⓒ Ⓓ		5 Ⓐ Ⓑ Ⓒ Ⓓ		9 Ⓐ Ⓑ Ⓒ Ⓓ	
2 Ⓐ Ⓑ Ⓒ Ⓓ		6 Ⓐ Ⓑ Ⓒ Ⓓ		10 Ⓐ Ⓑ Ⓒ	
3 Ⓐ Ⓑ Ⓒ Ⓓ		7 Ⓐ Ⓑ Ⓒ Ⓓ		11 Ⓐ Ⓑ Ⓒ	
4 Ⓐ Ⓑ Ⓒ Ⓓ		8 Ⓐ Ⓑ Ⓒ Ⓓ		12 Ⓐ Ⓑ Ⓒ	

A.

The Metropolitan Museum of Art, Charles Stewart Smith Collection, Gift of Mrs. Charles Stewart Smith, Charles Stewart Smith Jr. and Howard Casell Smith, in memory of Charles Stewart Smith, 1914. (14.76.37)

B.

The Metropolitan Museum of Art, Purchase Rogers & Fletcher Funds, Erving & Joyce Wolf Fund, Raymond J. Horowitz Gift, Bequest of Richard De Wolfe Brixey, by Exchange, & John Osgood & Elizabeth Amis Cameron Blanchard Memorial Fund, 1978. (1978.203)

C.

The Metropolitan Museum of Art, Gift of Mr. and Mrs. Joseph G. Blum, 1970. (1970.527.1)

1. Picture A expresses
   (A) anger.
   (B) pensiveness.
   (C) distraction.
   (D) assertiveness.

2. Picture A could be best described as
   (A) an abstract work whose primary meaning is the work itself.
   (B) a central figure surrounded by rectangular border.
   (C) an impressionistic work in which the figure represents an animal.
   (D) an 18th century American work.

3. Picture A is distinctive because
   (A) the border is decorated.
   (B) the figure is horned.
   (C) The sword has a carved, ornamental handle.
   (D) The figure is thrust forward.

4. Picture B depicts a
   (A) rocky shore.
   (B) seaport.
   (C) sloping shore.
   (D) turgid sea.

5. Picture B could be best described as
   (A) a bucolic scene.
   (B) an active scene.
   (C) a morning scene.
   (D) a languid scene.

6. Which of the following best describes Picture B?
   (A) A scene with people talking
   (B) A scene with children playing
   (C) A commercial scene
   (D) A scene dominated by the sky

7. Picture C primarily depicts
   (A) geometric contrasts.
   (B) a swirling sky.
   (C) a skyward needle.
   (D) a supported walkway.

8. Which of the following best describes Picture C?
   (A) A brick plaza sweeping by open latticed rectangles
   (B) A surreal world visited by real people
   (C) A visitors center at a spaceport
   (D) A central spire framed by sphere, semi-circle, and sky

9. Picture C is most likely
   (A) an artist's rendering of buildings to be constructed.
   (B) a set for a futuristic movies.
   (C) a three-dimensional model of a NASA visitors center.
   (D) a picture of an actual structure.

10. Which picture best depicts determination?
    (A)
    (B)
    (C)

11. Which picture does not include a semicircular shape?
    (A)
    (B)
    (C)

12. Which picture shows multiple events?
    (A)
    (B)
    (C)

7 LITERATURE AND COMMUNICATION

TEST INFO BOX

This chapter helps you prepare for the Literature and Communication items on the LAST. It includes a review of the topics included on the LAST.

On the LAST, you may be asked to analyze or critique literature or to identify faulty logic in a passage. You may also be asked to identify an author's purpose and tone or to identify the meaning of figurative language or figures of speech.

USING THIS CHAPTER

This chapter prepares you for the Literature items on the LAST. Choose one of these approaches.

I want a Literature and Communication review.

❑ Read the Literature and Communication Review on page 128.
❑ Complete the Literature and Communication Practice Items on page 133.

I want to practice Literature items.

❑ Complete the Literature and Communication Practice Items on page 133.

LITERATURE

APPROACHES TO READING AND INTERPRETING LITERATURE

Recognize the Author's Purpose

The author's primary purpose explains why the author wrote the passage. The purpose is closely related to the main idea. You might think. "Fine, I know the main idea. But why did the author take the time to write about that main idea?" "What is the author trying to make me know or feel?"

The author's purpose will be in one of the following five categories.

Describe	Present an image of physical reality or a mental image.
Entertain	Amuse, Perform
Inform	Clarify, Explain, State
Narrate	Relate, Tell a Story
Persuade	Argue, Convince, Prove

There is no hard and fast rule for identifying the author's purpose. Rely on your informed impression of the passage. Once in a while a passage may overtly state the author's purpose. But you must usually figure it out on your own. Remember, one of the answer choices will be correct. Your job is to decide which one it is.

Distinguish Between Fact and Opinion

Facts can be proven true *or* false by some objective means or method. *A fact refers to persons, things, or events that exist now or existed at some time in the past.* Note that a fact does not have to be true. For example, the statement "The tallest human being alive today is 86 inches tall" is false. This statement is a fact because it can be proven false.

Opinions, however, cannot be proved or disproved by some objective means or method. Opinions are subjective and include attitudes and probabilities. Some statements, which seem true, may still be opinions. For example, the statement "A car is easier to park than a bus" seems true. However, this statement is an opinion. There is no way to objectively prove this statement true or false.

Examples:

Fact: <u>Abraham Lincoln was President of the United States during the Civil War</u>. We can check historical records and find out if the statement is true. This statement of fact is true.

Fact: <u>Robert E. Lee went into exile in Canada after the Civil War</u>. We can check historical records. This factual statement is true. Lee later became president of Washington College, now called Washington and Lee University.

Fact: <u>It is more than 90°F. outside</u>. We can use a thermometer to prove or disprove this statement.

Fact: <u>More people were born in November than in any other month</u>. We can check statistical records to prove or disprove this statement.

Opinion: <u>If Lincoln had lived, Reconstruction would have been better</u>. This sounds true, but there is no way to prove or disprove this statement.

Opinion: <u>Lee was the Civil War's most brilliant general</u>. Sounds true, but there is no way to prove it.

Opinion: <u>It will always be colder in November than in July</u>. Sounds true! But we can't prove or disprove future events.

Detect Bias

Bias

A statement or passage reveals bias if the author has prejudged or has a predisposition to a doctrine, idea, or practice. Bias means the author is trying to convince or influence the reader through some emotional appeal or slanted writing.

Bias can be positive or negative.

Positive Bias: She is so lovely, she deserves the very best.
Negative Bias: She is so horrible, I hope she gets what's coming to her.

Forms of Bias

Biased writing can often be identified by the presence of one or more of the following forms of bias.

Emotional Language	Language that appeals to the reader's emotions, and not to common sense or logic.
	Positive: If I am elected, I will help your family get jobs.
	Negative: If my opponent is elected, your family will lose their jobs.
Inaccurate Information	Language that presents false, inaccurate, or unproved information as though it were factual.
	Positive: My polls indicate that I am very popular.
	Negative: My polls indicate that a lot of people disagree with my opponent.
Name Calling	Language that uses negative, disapproving terms without any factual basis.
	Negative: I'll tell you, my opponent is a real jerk.
Slanted Language	Language that slants the facts or evidence toward the writer's point of view.
	Positive: I am a positive person, looking for the good side of people.
	Negative: My opponent finds fault with everyone and everything.
Stereotyping	Language that indicates that a person is like all the members of a particular group.
	Positive: I belong to the Krepenkle party, the party known for its honesty.
	Negative: My opponent belongs to the Perplenkle party, the party of increased taxes.

Recognize the Author's Tone

Tone
The author's tone is the author's attitude as reflected in the passage. Answering this question means choosing the correct tone word. How do you think the author would sound while speaking? What impression would you form about the speaker's attitude or feeling? The answer to the latter question will usually lead you to the author's tone. A partial list of tone words is given below.

absurd	excited	outraged
amused	formal	outspoken
angry	gentle	pathetic
apathetic	hard	pessimistic
arrogant	impassioned	playful
bitter	indignant	prayerful
cheerful	intense	reverent
comic	intimate	righteous
compassionate	joyous	satirical
complex	loving	sentimental
concerned	malicious	serious
cruel	mocking	solemn
depressed	nostalgic	tragic
distressed	objective	uneasy
evasive	optimistic	vindictive

LITERARY TERMS

Allegory In allegory, the characters, story, and setting actually represent other people, settings, or abstract ideas. This symbolic meaning is more important than the literal meaning. For example, Jonathan Swift's book *Gulliver's Travels* is allegorical when it uses horses and other creatures to represent people. Aesop's *Fables* use allegory to represent moral or ethical ideas. Parables such as the prodigal son use allegory to teach a lesson.

Alliteration Alliteration is the repetition of an initial consonant in nearby words. For example, the selections "Neither rain, nor sleet nor dark of night," and "Peas?—Please. Peanuts?—Possibly. Potatoes?—Potentially. Pigs knuckles?—Please!" use alliteration.

Anthropomorphism Anthropomorphism attributes the human body or human qualities to nonhuman things or entities. Initially, anthropomorphism meant depicting a god or gods as humans with human qualities.

Figures of speech Figures of speech refer to figurative language not meant to be taken literally; rather, figures of speech are used to create some special meaning or imagery.

Euphemism Euphemism is substituting an inoffensive term for one that may be offensive or cause distress. For example, "pass away" may be substituted for "die," and "indisposed" may be substituted for "ill."

Hyperbole Hyperbole is a drastic overstatement or understatement not meant literally. Hyperbole may be used to emphasize a point or for comic effect. For example, after an argument between friends one might exclaim, "You are the worst person who has ever lived." In another example, the winner of the Olympic decathlon may be referred to as "Not that bad an athlete."

Metaphor A metaphor speaks of one thing as though it were something else, without the words "like" or "as." For example, the sentences "My life's a tennis match, but I never get to serve" and "The night crept through 'til dawn" are metaphors.

Mixed metaphor A mixed metaphor combines two or more unrelated metaphors. For example, the sentence "Running on empty, the soccer player plowed through the rest of the match" is a mixed metaphor.

Onomatopoeia This figure of speech refers to words that imitate natural sounds. Onomatopoeia appears in the words of a once popular song, "*Buzz, buzz, buzz* goes the bumble bee, *twiddely, diddely, dee* goes the bird."

Simile A simile compares two different things, usually using the words "like" or "as." For example, the sentences "Her eyes are like deep, quiet pools" or "Her nails are like tiger claws" are similes.

COMMUNICATION

RHETORICAL CONVENTIONS OF ARGUMENTATION, EXPOSITION, NARRATION, AND REFLECTION

In **argumentation** the writer or speaker tries to convince the readers or listeners to accept a particular view or idea. There are several rules to follow to construct a well-ordered argument. Your presentation should appear moderate and reasoned, and you should acknowledge the reasonableness of those who differ with you.

The statements must be believable in form and in fact. That is, the statements must distinguish among fact, opinion, and the conclusions you have drawn. The presentation should clarify the meanings of key ideas and words. The presentation must also squarely address the question and not beg the question.

The presentation must support any views or conclusions with solid evidence and arguments. The arguments can be inductive or deductive. However, these arguments must avoid the invalid and fallacious arguments noted previously.

> **Expository** presentations simply explain. This book is essentially expository presentation. It explains about the LAST and how to pass it.

> **Narration** presents a factual or fictional story. A written fictional account or a spoken presentation about your life as a child is a narration.

> **Reflection** describes a scene, person, or emotion. A spoken description of your neighborhood or a written note describing how you felt when you graduated from high school are reflections.

LITERATURE AND COMMUNICATION PRACTICE ITEMS

These items will help you practice the concepts in this chapter. The items you encounter on the LAST may have a different emphasis and may be more complete.

Instructions
Mark your answers on the sheet provided below. Correct your answer sheet using the answers on page 137.

1 Ⓐ Ⓑ Ⓒ Ⓓ	5 Ⓐ Ⓑ Ⓒ Ⓓ	9 Ⓐ Ⓑ Ⓒ Ⓓ	13 Ⓐ Ⓑ Ⓒ Ⓓ	17 Ⓐ Ⓑ Ⓒ Ⓓ
2 Ⓐ Ⓑ Ⓒ Ⓓ	6 Ⓐ Ⓑ Ⓒ Ⓓ	10 Ⓐ Ⓑ Ⓒ Ⓓ	14 Ⓐ Ⓑ Ⓒ Ⓓ	18 Ⓐ Ⓑ Ⓒ Ⓓ
3 Ⓐ Ⓑ Ⓒ Ⓓ	7 Ⓐ Ⓑ Ⓒ Ⓓ	11 Ⓐ Ⓑ Ⓒ Ⓓ	15 Ⓐ Ⓑ Ⓒ Ⓓ	
4 Ⓐ Ⓑ Ⓒ Ⓓ	8 Ⓐ Ⓑ Ⓒ Ⓓ	12 Ⓐ Ⓑ Ⓒ Ⓓ	16 Ⓐ Ⓑ Ⓒ Ⓓ	

Questions 1–5 are based on this passage

The United States National Park system is extensive, although most land dedicated to the park system is in the western states. This is no doubt the case because these lands are
(5) occupied by states most recently admitted to the union. I have some very happy personal memories about Yellowstone National Park, having visited there on several occasions. All of my visits came before the series of fires, which
(10) burned much of the park's forested areas. My most unusual recollection dates back a number of years when I was part of a group waiting for the Old Faithful geyser to erupt. A young child was standing about twenty yards away looking
(15) at something on the ground. The group gathered around where the child was standing. And while Old Faithful _____, we all watched a small, rusty water pipe leak onto the ground. I
(20) never understood what about the pipe drew everyone's interest. It must have to do with a child's wonder.

1. Which of the following best characterizes the preceding passage?
   (A) A person describes the American National Park System.
   (B) A person describes his childhood in Yellowstone National Park.
   (C) A person describes group behavior with an example from his or her own experience.
   (D) A person describes an unusual memory from Yellowstone Park.

2. Why does the writer discuss the Yellowstone fires in lines 9-11?
   (A) to discuss the destruction of the park
   (B) to give a time frame to the writer's visits
   (C) to warn against careless use of fire
   (D) to describe the burned areas

3. Which of the following words would be most appropriate to fill the blank space in line 18?
   (A) burned
   (B) gurgled
   (C) foamed
   (D) gushed

4. This passage is best characterized as
   (A) argumentation.
   (B) exposition.
   (C) narration.
   (D) reflection.

5. What is the subject of the sentence "My most unusual recollection dates back . . .," which begins at the end of line 10 and ends on line 13?
   (A) My
   (B) recollection
   (C) I
   (D) group

Questions 6–9 are based on the following passages.

   (A) The tires screeched, and the car spun uncontrollably. I gripped the wheel in fear as the car swung around again and again. My body was thrown against the side of the car—my heart pounded. A horn blared in my ear, and images of cars, buildings, and light poles went whizzing by. It seemed that I would careen into the car just ahead of me. Then everything stopped. I'm not going on that ride again.

   (B) A soft and silent breeze swept across the field carrying with it the sweet smell of blooming flowers, the delightful chirping of circling birds, and small bits of pollen and newly cut grass. The breeze softly passed unfelt by all but the few standing at the field's edge. Life is like that breeze in that field for all who will but stop to experience it.

   (C) The seat was hard, the room was crowded, and the perspiration flowed. All eyes were on the proctor who was handing out tests and on the air conditioner, which wasn't working. They all wanted to be teachers, and they were all ready to take the test, but they were not ready for the hottest day of the year and the stuffiest room imaginable. Someone sighed. What were they to do?

   (D) "I object your honor," called out the lawyer. "I object to the way that my rights and my client's rights have been systematically, outrageously, and impermissibly denied by this court, by the incredibly irresponsible reporting of the tawdry tabloid shows, and by the second-rate journalists who control the newspapers in this town."
"I guess the evidence is against that lawyer," thought the judge.

6. Which passage includes a metaphor for life?

7. Which passage describes a person's reaction to an amusement park ride?

8. Which passage includes a rhetorical question?

9. Which of the following choices describes a common element of these passages?
   (A) Each passage draws a conclusion.
   (B) Each passage describes a feeling.
   (C) Each passage includes dialogue.
   (D) Each passage is descriptive.

Questions 10–12 are based on the following reading.

I remember my childhood vacations at a bungalow colony near a lake. Always barefoot, my friend and I spent endless hours playing and enjoying our fantasies. We were
(5) pirates, rocket pilots, and detectives. Everyday objects were transformed into swords, ray guns, and two-way wrist radios. With a lake at hand, we swam, floated on our crude rafts made of old lumber, fished, and fell in. The
(10) adult world seemed so meaningless while our world seemed so full. Returning years later I saw the colony for what it was—tattered and torn. The lake was shallow and muddy. But the tree that had been our look-
(15) out was still there. And there was the house where the feared master spy hid from the FBI. There was the site of the launching pad for our imaginary rocket trips. The posts of the dock we had sailed from many times were
(20) still visible. But my fantasy play did not depend on this place. My child-mind would have been a buccaneer wherever it was.

10. Which of the following choices best characterizes this passage?
    (A) An adult describes disappointment at growing up.
    (B) A child describes the adult world through the child's eyes.
    (C) An adult discusses childhood viewed as a child and as an adult.
    (D) An adult discusses the meaning of fantasy play.

11. The sentence "The adult world seemed so meaningless while our world seemed so full" on lines 10 and 11 is used primarily to
    (A) emphasize the emptiness of most adult lives.
    (B) provide a transition from describing childhood to describing adulthood.
    (C) show how narcissistic children are.
    (D) describe the difficulty this child had relating to adults.

12. Which of the following best characterizes the last sentence in the passage?
    (A) The child would have been rebellious, no matter what.
    (B) Childhood is not a place but a state of mind.
    (C) We conform more as we grow older.
    (D) The writer will always feel rebellious.

Questions 13–16 are based on the following passages.
    (A) Swept along the gnarly road of life,
        Abounding with its traffic laden strife.
        Rest you now upon the yonder hill,
        Tis there that you'll finally be still.
        I am about the richest man there is,
    (B) 'Cause I was ever so great at biz.
        The biz that I was great at though,
        Was little more than blowing snow.
    (C) Birds in the meadow—
            chirp, chirp, chirp,
        Too full a tummy—
            burp, burp, burp,
        Cats at the milk saucer—
            slurp, slurp, slurp,
        Don't have another rhyme—
            gulp, gulp, gulp.
    (D) They say that fame and fortune
            comes,
        From starring in some fil-e-ums.
        But it seems to me that you end up,
        Just taking lots of pill-e-ums.

13. Which passage provides a contrast between two possible outcomes?

14. Which passage appears to be a metaphor for the end of life?

15. Which passage relates a person's success to obscuring or hiding?

16. Which of the following best explains why the author of selection (C) chose the words that appear at the end of each line?
    (A) For poetic effect
    (B) To have a particular number of beats in each line
    (C) To emphasize the *urp* sound
    (D) To conform to the rules for haiku

Questions 17–18 are based on the passages preceding them.

Japanese students have always been considered to be well-prepared for life in the world's business and engineering communities. The mathematics and science curricula of Japanese schools are considered to be superior to those in American schools. With the daily advancement of Japanese technological prowess, how can American children ever hope to compete with their Japanese counterparts?

17. Which of the following is the best descriptor of the author's tone in this passage?
    (A) disbelief
    (B) anger
    (C) pride
    (D) concern

The retired basketball player said that, while modern players were better athletes because there was so much emphasis on youth basketball and increased focus on training, he still believed that the players of his day were better because they were more committed to the game, better understood its nuances, and were more dedicated to team play.

18. The retired basketball player attributes the increased athletic prowess of today's basketball players to
    (A) better nutrition.
    (B) youth basketball programs.
    (C) salary caps.
    (D) more athletic scholarships.

Answers

1. **D**	5. **B**	9. **D**	13. **D**	17. **D**
2. **B**	6. **B**	10. **C**	14. **A**	18. **B**
3. **D**	7. **A**	11. **C**	15. **B**	
4. **D**	8. **C**	12. **B**	16. **A**	

PART IV

Reading in a Content Area

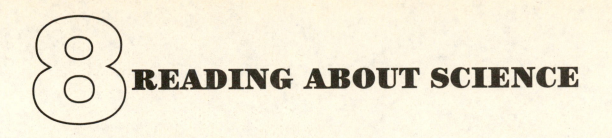

8 READING ABOUT SCIENCE

ANSWER SHEET

1 Ⓐ Ⓑ Ⓒ Ⓓ	4 Ⓐ Ⓑ Ⓒ Ⓓ	7 Ⓐ Ⓑ Ⓒ Ⓓ	10 Ⓐ Ⓑ Ⓒ Ⓓ	13 Ⓐ Ⓑ Ⓒ Ⓓ
2 Ⓐ Ⓑ Ⓒ Ⓓ	5 Ⓐ Ⓑ Ⓒ Ⓓ	8 Ⓐ Ⓑ Ⓒ Ⓓ	11 Ⓐ Ⓑ Ⓒ Ⓓ	14 Ⓐ Ⓑ Ⓒ Ⓓ
3 Ⓐ Ⓑ Ⓒ Ⓓ	6 Ⓐ Ⓑ Ⓒ Ⓓ	9 Ⓐ Ⓑ Ⓒ Ⓓ	12 Ⓐ Ⓑ Ⓒ Ⓓ	15 Ⓐ Ⓑ Ⓒ Ⓓ

16 Ⓐ Ⓑ Ⓒ Ⓓ	19 Ⓐ Ⓑ Ⓒ Ⓓ	22 Ⓐ Ⓑ Ⓒ Ⓓ	25 Ⓐ Ⓑ Ⓒ Ⓓ	28 Ⓐ Ⓑ Ⓒ Ⓓ
17 Ⓐ Ⓑ Ⓒ Ⓓ	20 Ⓐ Ⓑ Ⓒ Ⓓ	23 Ⓐ Ⓑ Ⓒ Ⓓ	26 Ⓐ Ⓑ Ⓒ Ⓓ	29 Ⓐ Ⓑ Ⓒ Ⓓ
18 Ⓐ Ⓑ Ⓒ Ⓓ	21 Ⓐ Ⓑ Ⓒ Ⓓ	24 Ⓐ Ⓑ Ⓒ Ⓓ	27 Ⓐ Ⓑ Ⓒ Ⓓ	30 Ⓐ Ⓑ Ⓒ Ⓓ

CELLS

The cell is the smallest unit of life that is capable of reproduction. There are two types of cells, prokaryotes and eukaryotes. Distribution outside the cell prokaryotes are bacteria, including cyanobacteria (previously called blue-green algae). Plant cells and animal cells are eukaryotes. In this overview we focus primarily on plant cells and animal cells.

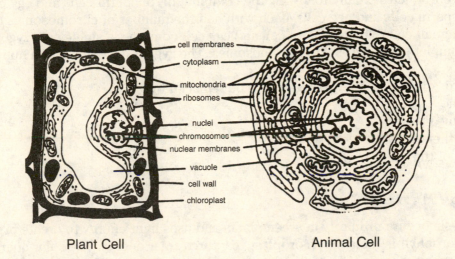

cell membranes
cytoplasm
mitochondria
ribosomes
nuclei
chromosomes
nuclear membranes
vacuole
cell wall
chloroplast

Plant Cell   Animal Cell

Plant cells and animal cells have many common components. Both types of cells have a membrane at the outer edge of the cell. The gel-like cytoplasm in the interior of the cell contains organelles (cell organs). A nucleus, the cell's "brain," is surrounded by a nuclear membrane. The nucleus contains genetic material. The golgi apparatus packages hormone and enzyme material for plant cells. They differ from animal cells in two primary ways: plant cells have a thick cell wall outside the membrane; plant cells contain plastids, which may include chloroplasts where photosynthesis takes place.

1. According to the passage, the cell wall
    (A) is narrower on animal cells than it is on plant cells.
    (B) occurs only on plant cells.
    (C) is one of the features found on all cells.
    (D) is thinner on plant cells than the cell wall on animal cells.

REPRODUCTION

Cells reproduce in five stages. Four of these stages are called mitosis. In mitosis, a cell duplicates its own set of chromosomes. The chromosomes migrate to opposite ends of the cell. Then the cell splits, making an exact copy of itself in cytokenesis.

Prophase	MITOSIS BEGINS as the cell begins to divide.
Metaphase	Chromosomes align around the equator of the cell.
Anaphase	Sister chromosomes are formed and move toward opposite ends of the cell.
Telophase	MITOSIS ENDS as two new nuclei are formed.
Cytokenesis	The cell splits into two daughter cells in the final stage of reproduction.

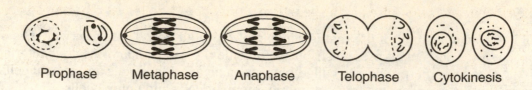

Prophase   Metaphase   Anaphase   Telophase   Cytokinesis

Humans reproduce sexually following the combination of sperm cells and egg cells. Meiosis creates sperm cells and egg cells, each with half the number of chromosomes (haploid) found in a human cell. When a sperm cell and egg cell combine, a single cell, zygote, is created with a complete (diploid) set of chromosomes. The zygote develops into a human.

2. The word "diploid" in the passage could be replaced by
   (A) all the
   (B) double the
   (C) half the
   (D) part of the

PHOTOSYNTHESIS

Photosynthesis occurs primarily in green plants and uses light energy to create organic compounds. Chlorophyll in a plant's chloroplasts captures solar energy. The solar energy combines with carbon dioxide (CO_2) from the atmosphere and water (H_2O) to produce glucose (sugar). Plant photosynthesis releases oxygen (O_2) into the atmosphere. Photosynthesis also occurs in some other organisms and some bacteria. Without photosynthesis we would not have breathable air.

3. Which of the following is NOT required for the process of photosynthesis?
   (A) water
   (B) sunlight
   (C) glucose
   (D) carbon dioxide

CELL ACTIVITIES

Cells convert food into usable energy through respiration. This process, which occurs in the mitochondria, can be either aerobic or anaerobic. Aerobic respiration is the oxidation of food, which takes place in the presence of oxygen. Anaerobic respiration is fermentation, which takes place without oxygen.

Ingestion	Take in food
Digestion	Break down food to usable forms
Secretion	Create and release useful substances
Excretion	Eliminate waste material
Homeostasis	Maintain the cell's equilibrium

A chromosome is a rodlike structure located in the cell nucleus. Each gene occupies a specific location on one of the chromosomes. Genes carry specific bits of genetic information.

Deoxyribonucleic acid (DNA) is the genetic material tightly coiled as a chromosome. DNA provides the genetic codes that determine many traits of an organism. There are very large quantities of noncoding DNA, which does not affect the makeup of an organism.

The DNA creates ribonucleic acid (RNA). The DNA cannot leave the nucleus; RNA serves as the messenger that carries the genetic code throughout the cell.

4. According to the passage
   (A) all DNA determines human traits.
   (B) genes occupy specific locations on RNA.
   (C) DNA carries genetic code throughout the cell.
   (D) a chromosome is made up of DNA.

BIOLOGY OF ORGANISMS AND EVOLUTION

There was very little oxygen in the earth's atmosphere about 3.5 billion years ago. Research has shown that atoms can combine spontaneously in this type of environment to form organic molecules. This is how life may have begun on earth about 3.4 billion years ago.

Eventually these molecules linked together in complex groupings to form organisms. These earliest organisms must have been able to ingest and live on nonorganic material. Over a period of time, these organisms adapted and began using the sun's energy. When photosynthesis released oxygen into the oceans and the atmosphere, the stage was set for more advanced life forms.

The first cells were prokaryotes (bacteria), which converted energy (respired) without oxygen (anaerobic). The next cells to develop were cyanobacteria (blue-green algae) prokaryotes, which were aerobic (created energy with oxygen) and used photosynthesis. Advanced eukaryotes developed from these primitive cells.

It took about 2.7 billion years for algae to develop. When this simple cell appeared 950 million years ago, it contained an enormous amount of DNA. This very slow process moved somewhat faster in the millennia that followed as animal and plant forms slowly emerged.

Animals developed into vertebrate (backbone) and invertebrate (no backbone) species. Mammals became the dominant vertebrate class, and insects became the dominant invertebrate class. As animals developed, they adapted to their environment. Those species that adapted best survived. This process is called natural selection. Entire species have vanished from the earth.

Mammals and dinosaurs coexisted for over 100 million years. During that time, dinosaurs were the dominant class. When dinosaurs became extinct 65 million years ago, mammals survived. Freed of dinosaurian dominance, mammals evolved into the dominant creatures they are today. Despite many years of study, it is not known what caused the dinosaurs to become extinct or why mammals survived.

Humans are in the primate (upright) family of mammals. Very primitive primates, along with other mammals, were found on earth before the dinosaurs became extinct. Modern humans demonstrate striking genetic similarities to other members of the primate group, particularly to African apes.

Scientists believe that early sapiens developed about 250,000 years ago and that modern *Homo sapiens* developed about 75,000 years ago.

5. Where did the earth's early oxygen supply come from?
   (A) It came from anaerobic cells.
   (B) Early molecules gave off oxygen.
   (C) It came from photosynthesis.
   (D) It came from aerobic cells.

Era	Period		Epoch	Approximate Beginning Date	Life Forms Originating
Cenozoic	Quaternary		Recent	10,000	Humans
			Pleistocene	2,500,000	
	Tertiary		Pilocene	12,000,000	Grazing and Meat-eating Mammals
			Miocene	26,000,000	
			Oligocene	38,000,000	
			Eocene	54,000,000	
			Paleocene	65,000,000	
Mesozoic	Cretaceous			136,000,000	Primates-Flowering Plants
	Jurassic			195,000,000	Birds
	Triassic			225,000,000	Dinosaurs-Mammals
Paleozoic	Permian			280,000,000	
	Carbonifurous	Pennsylvanian		320,000,000	Reptiles
		Mississippian		345,000,000	Ferns
	Devonian			395,000,000	Amphibians-Insects
	Silurian			430,000,000	Vascular Land Plants
	Ordovician			500,000,000	Fish-Chordates
	Cambrian			570,000,000	Shellfish-Trilobites
Precambrian				(700,000,000)	Algae
				(1,500,000,000)	Eukaryotic Cells
				(3,500,000,000)	Prokaryotic Cells

The History of Life

6. According to the chart
   (A) insects preceded reptiles.
   (B) birds preceded fish.
   (C) humans preceded grazing mammals.
   (D) primates preceded birds.

CELL CLASSIFICATION

Living things are generally classified into six kingdoms. Three kingdoms are dedicated to one-celled living things (prokaryote or eukaryote).There are three kingdoms of multicelled eukaryotes based on whether nutrition is obtained through absorption, photosynthesis, or ingestion.

The former Moneran kingdom is now two kingdoms—kingdom Archaea and kingdom Eubacteria. These two kingdoms include all prokaryotes. The organisms include bacteria and blue-green algae. These microscopic organisms are limited to respiration and reproduction.

The Protista kingdom includes all single-celled eukaryotes. These organisms include algae and protozoa. These cells have a fully functional organ system and some get their energy through photosynthesis.

The Fungi kingdom includes multicelled eukaryotes that gain their nutrition through absorption. These organisms include mushrooms and are rootlike with caps and filaments.

The Plantae kingdom includes multicelled eukaryotes that gain their energy through photosynthesis. These organisms have thicker cellulose cell walls.

The Animalae kingdom includes multicelled eukaryotes that gain their nutrition through ingestion. Most of these organisms are mobile at some time in their existence.

Bacteria are small, single-celled organisms (prokaryotes) found everywhere in the environment. As noted already, bacteria were the earliest organisms to develop. Bacteria are classified as bacilli (rod-shaped), cocci (circular or spherical), and spirilla (coiled). Bacteria that can move "swim" with flagella.

One type of bacteria live on dead animal and vegetable material. Without the decomposition these bacteria bring, the earth would quickly be covered with dead organic material. A second type of bacteria helps humans and is often needed for regular physiological processes. The third type, parasites, harm the organisms in which they live. About 200 types of bacteria cause diseases in humans.

A virus is a bit of genetic material surrounded by a protective coat of protein. The virus itself is lifeless, lacks the ability to reproduce by itself, and is not classified in one of the six kingdoms. Viruses cannot be seen in even the most powerful regular microscope. The smallest virus is about one millionth of a centimeter long.

Viruses are parasitic and remain a major challenge in battling infectious diseases. Once in a living cell, a virus can send its own genetic material into the cell, reproduce, and do significant damage to the host cell and the host organism.

7. Compared to cells, a virus is best characterized as
   (A) advanced.
   (B) parasitic.
   (C) primitive.
   (D) spirilla.

HUMAN BIOLOGY

Humans have 23 pairs of chromosomes. Females typically have 23 similar pairs including a pair of X chromosomes. Males typically have 22 similar pairs and one X and one Y chromosome.

Genes carry specific bits of genetic information. Each gene occupies a specific location on one of the chromosomes. Researchers today have identified and mapped the exact location of each gene. Scientists can even identify whether or not a person has certain hereditary traits. For example, scientists have identified a gene linked to hereditary breast cancer.

Diseases compromise the body's defense system. Most diseases can be recognized by symptoms that may include fever, aches and pains, fatigue, growths, changes in blood cell composition, and high blood pressure.

Many infectious diseases, including pneumonia and infections in cuts, are caused by bacteria. Other infectious diseases, including measles and influenza (flu), are caused by viruses. Environmental causes of disease include smoking, a high-fat diet, and pollution. Other diseases may result from genetic or occupational causes and abnormal cell growth. Many diseases are related to mental disorders or stress.

Acquired Immune Deficiency Syndrome (AIDS) is a disease caused by the HIV virus that attacks the body's immune system. There is no cure for the HIV virus or for AIDS. However, protease inhibitors have proven effective in blocking the spread of the HIV virus, and interfering with the development of AIDS. The HIV virus is transmitted through blood and bodily fluids, including those fluids associated with intimate sexual contact. Intravenous drug users who share needles may become infected with the virus by injecting small amounts of contaminated blood.

8. Intravenous (IV) drug users are at particular risk for acquiring the HIV virus because
   (A) the virus is transmitted through the injected drugs.
   (B) the virus is transmitted through blood.
   (C) the virus is transmitted through germs on the needle.
   (D) the virus is transmitted through intimate sexual contact.

HUMAN BODY SYSTEMS

Parts of the human body are made up of highly specialized cells. These cells combine to make tissue. Some tissues combine to form organs. Various organs combine in systems that enable the body to function.

$$\text{Cells} \rightarrow \text{Tissue} \rightarrow \text{Organ} \rightarrow \text{Organ System} \rightarrow \text{Body}$$

Food is usually taken in through the mouth. The teeth and tongue break the food down mechanically, and the saliva begins the digestive process. When food reaches the stomach, the stomach churns to mix the food while digestive enzymes break down the proteins. The semiliquid, digested food moves into the small intestine.

Nutrients are absorbed through the small intestine into the bloodstream. Waste and undigested food move into the large intestine. The large intestine carries the waste and undigested food to the rectum.

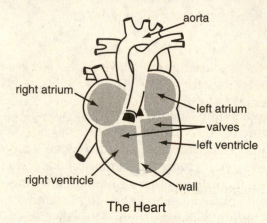

The Heart

The circulatory system carries oxygen and nutrients throughout the body. A four-chambered heart (see above) pumps blood through the circulatory system. Oxygenated blood is pumped from the heart's left side through arteries. Oxygen-poor blood flows back through veins to the heart's right side, and is pumped to the lungs to gain oxygen. Oxygenated blood enters the heart's left side.

The bones (about 200) and cartilage that make up the skeletal system provide form and rigidity to the human body. A series of joints throughout the skeleton provide flexibility. Bone is living, rigid tissue. Cartilage is found at bone joints, such as the knee, and makes up the nose and other rigid parts of the body.

The muscular system consists of skeletal (striated), smooth, and cardiac muscles. Most skeletal muscles are attached to the skeleton by tendons. These muscles are called voluntary muscles because they can be controlled consciously and make up most of human flesh. Smooth muscle is involuntary and is found in large blood vessels, internal organs, and the skin. Cardiac muscles are an involuntary muscle found only in the heart.

The nervous system receives stimuli, transmits electrochemical signals, and activates muscles. Receptors in the skin and elsewhere in the body receive stimuli. Nerve cells, called neurons, send signals to the central nervous system. Dendrites in the cell transmit signals, while axons receive stimuli.

The central and peripheral nervous systems form a single operating system. The central nervous system includes the brain and spinal cord. The peripheral nervous system connects the central nervous system to the rest of the body. The autonomic nervous system is connected to the central nervous system and controls circulation, respiration, digestion, and elimination.

9. Which of the following information can be found in the passage?

    I. The structure of the autonomic nervous system
    II. The types of muscles
    III. The path of blood flow.

    (A) I and II
    (B) II and III
    (C) I only
    (D) I, II, and III

OTHER BODY SYSTEMS

The excretory system consists of the kidney, bladder, and connecting tubes. Nephrons in the kidney collect liquid wastes. The liquid wastes are transferred to the bladder and leave the body as urine through the urethra.

Respiration delivers oxygen to the bloodstream. Nasal passages clean and warm the air on its way to the lungs through the trachea and bronchi. Air is collected in the alveoli, which transfers oxygen and other gases to the bloodstream.

The endocrine system is a complex system that produces and distributes hormones through the bloodstream. The system consists of glands that secrete hormones and other substances.

The **pituitary gland** is located near the brain and is the primary gland in the body. Hormones from this gland control the operation of other endocrine glands, sex glands, milk production, and pigmentation.

The **adrenal glands** are found near the kidney. Hormones from these glands affect heart rate, blood pressure, blood vessels, and blood sugar.

The **thyroid** is found in the neck. It regulates mental and physical alertness. The parathyroid glands are found near or inside the thyroid and regulate calcium in the blood.

The immune system resists the spread of disease by destroying disease-causing agents (antigens). This system is exceptionally complex and not fully understood. Normally, a combination of the following immune responses is needed to defeat an antigen.

The lymphatic system produces lymphocytes in bean-sized lymph glands located throughout the body. The lymphocytes are transported throughout bodily tissue by lymphatic capillaries. Lymphocytes control the immune system and kill antigens directly.

Granulocytes are very numerous. They ingest antigens already killed by cell enzymes. Monocytes exist in small numbers. They ingest and kill antigens and more importantly alter antigens in a way that makes it easier for lymphocytes to destroy them.

Immunoglobins (antibodies) combine with antigens to disable them. There are thousands of antibodies, each targeted for a specific antigen. Other proteins called cytokines complement proteins and aid the immune response.

10. Which of the following sentences could replace the first sentence of the last paragraph?
    (A) Antigens combine with antibodies to remove antibodies from the bloodstream.
    (B) Immunoglobins combine with antibodies to remove antigens from the bloodstream.
    (C) Immunoglobins combine with antigens to remove antibodies from the bloodstream.
    (D) Antibodies combine with antigens to remove antigens from the bloodstream.

ECOLOGY

Ecology refers to the relationship between organisms and their ecosystem (habitat). An ecosystem includes interdependent life forms and supports life through food, atmosphere, energy, and water. Organisms, including plants and animals, interact with and adapt to their ecosystem.

Earth is surrounded by a thin layer of atmosphere. Within that atmosphere lies earth's biosphere where life exists. The biosphere contains a number of biomes or living areas. Aquatic biomes include ocean, shallow water, and tidal marshes. Land biomes are classified by the predominant form of plant life and include forest, grassland, and desert.

Each organism in a biome occupies a place in the food web. Each organism, at some point in its life or death, is food for some other organism. In this way, energy is transferred among organisms in the biome.

A community refers to the interdependent populations of plants and animals. The dominance of one species in a community can affect the diversity (number of species and specie members). The community includes the habitat where a particular plant or animal lives and its niche (role).

Within a community, the primary interactions are predation, parasitism, competion, and cooperation. Predators and prey adapt and develop more effective ways of hunting or defense. Cooperation may develop due to the dependence of one organism on another.

Organisms may compete within their species or with other species for resources. Successful competitors survive and become dominant. Subdominant individuals either accept poorer habitats, give up the resources, migrate, or perish.

11. Which of the following questions could NOT be answered from this passage?
    (A) What may lead to cooperation among organisms?
    (B) What are the primary interactions within a community?
    (C) What does the earth's atmosphere consist of?
    (D) How are land biomes classified?

LIFE CYCLES

A number of essential life cycles take place on earth.

Most of the earth's water is salty, but humans need fresh water to survive. Fresh water is renewed through the water cycle. The cycle consists of three phases: evaporation, condensation, and precipitation.

Evaporation occurs when heat from the sun changes ocean water, and some water from other sources, into water vapor. Condensation follows when water vapor turns into water droplets, which form clouds. Precipitation occurs when the droplets become too heavy and water falls as rain, snow, sleet, or hail.

Humans and other animal organisms need oxygen to survive. Plants give off oxygen. An appropriate balance between plant photosynthesis and animal respiration ensures that enough oxygen is available.

Carbon is used by all living things. Plants need carbon dioxide for photosynthesis. Animals get the carbon from the plant and animal tissues they eat and exhale carbon dioxide as a by product of respiration. Here again, the balance between animal respiration and plant photosynthesis ensures that enough carbon will be available. In recent times, however, industrialization has added extra carbon to the atmosphere, jeopardizing the balance of this cycle.

Air, water, and soil pollution are serious environmental problems. Some lakes, rivers, and streams are so polluted they cannot be used by humans. Fish from many of these waters cannot be eaten. Air in some areas has been very polluted by factories and power plants, which use sulfur based fuels such as oil and coal. Land has been polluted by dumping hazardous wastes, including radioactive wastes. Pollution may lead to disease and premature death.

12. Which of the following words best describes the process of condensation in the second sentence of the second paragraph?
    (A) compression
    (B) contraction
    (C) shortening
    (D) expansion

SOLAR SYSTEM

Our solar system has one star (the sun), nine planets, some comets, and lots of satellites (moons), asteroids, and meteors. A diagram of the solar system is shown below. Only the planets are shown to rough scale in this diagram.

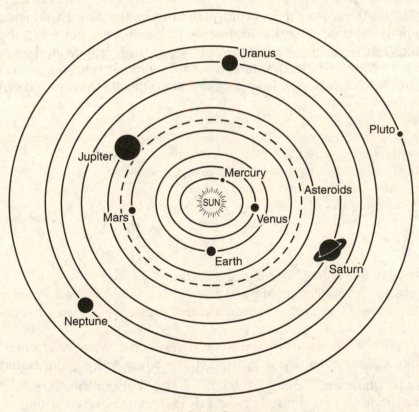

Our Solar System

Our sun is a star, a turbulent mass of incredibly hot gases exploding with repeated nuclear fusion reactions. Without the heat and light from the sun, our universe would not exist as we know it. About 1,000,000 earths could fit inside the sun. The sun's diameter is about 864,000 miles, and the surface temperature is over 10,000° Fahrenheit. Still, the sun is just average size by galactic standards.

The sun is at the center of our solar system, although this was not realized until the time of Copernicus in the 1500s. The most noticeable features of the sun's surface are the sunspots, cooler areas that move across the sun's surface. Sunspots appear in somewhat predictable cycles and are associated with interruptions in radio and television transmissions.

13. We can tell from the diagram that
    (A) asteroids are located between the earth and Jupiter.
    (B) the sun is approximately the same size as Jupiter.
    (C) the diameter of Jupiter's orbit is about the same size as the diameter of Saturn's orbit.
    (D) the radius of Saturn's orbit is about half the diameter of earth's orbit.

THE EARTH AND THE MOON

Earth is the name of our planet. The earth is the third planet from the sun. The earth's distance from the sun ranges from about 91,000,000 to 95,000,000 miles. It takes light about eight minutes to travel from the sun to earth. The earth's diameter is about 7,900 miles. The earth's rotation and revolution have a tremendous impact on life here.

Rotation. The earth *rotates* around its axis, which roughly runs through the geographic north and south poles. This rotation creates day and night as parts of the earth are turned toward and then away from the sun.

Revolution. The earth *revolves* in an orbit (path) around the sun. The earth's axis is tilted about 23° from perpendicular with the orbit around the sun. The tilting and revolving creates seasons as regions of the earth are tilted toward the sun and away from the sun.

The diagram here shows the earth's tilt and earth's relation to the sun at the beginning of each season in the Northern Hemisphere. Seasons are opposite in the Southern Hemisphere.

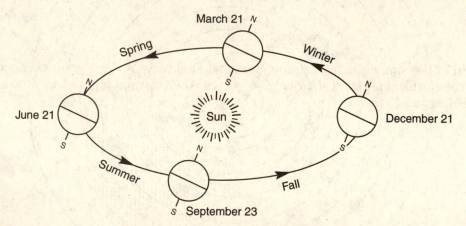

Seasons in the Northern Hemisphere

Moon is the name for the satellite that revolves around earth. The moon also rotates around its axis. The moon's diameter is about 2,100 miles and it is about 240,000 miles from the earth to the moon. The moon has no atmosphere and its surface is covered with craters from meteorites and from volcanoes.

The moon's rotation and revolution each take about 27½ days. These equal periods of rotation and revolution mean that the same part of the moon always faces the earth. It was not until lunar exploration in the 1970s that the other side of the moon was viewed and photographed.

14. Which of the following could replace "perpendicular" in the second sentence of the third paragraph?
    (A) horizontal
    (B) parallel
    (C) a right angle
    (D) an oval

15. Which of the following determines seasons on earth?
    (A) the earth's tilt
    (B) the earth's revolution
    (C) the earth's rotation
    (D) the earth's distance from the sun

TIDES AND ECLIPSES

The phases of the moon are also directly related to tides on earth. High tides occur on the parts of earth directly under the moon and on the other side of earth directly opposite this point. Low tides occur halfway between the two high tides. The tides move around the earth as the moon revolves around the earth, creating two high and two low tides each day at each place on earth.

The lowest and highest tides occur when the sun and the moon are in a straight line. These tides are called spring tides. The moon is either new or full during this direct alignment.

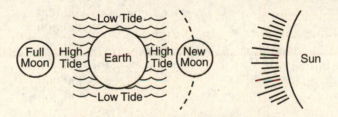

Alignment During Spring Tides

The position of the sun, earth, and moon can create eclipses. A lunar eclipse occurs when the moon is in the earth's shadow. A solar eclipse occurs when the sun is "hidden" behind the moon. Look at the diagrams below.

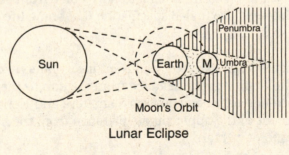

Lunar Eclipse

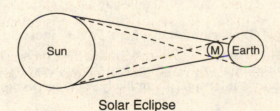

Solar Eclipse

16. According to the diagram, a solar eclipse occurs when
    (A) the moon hides the sun from some of the earth.
    (B) the moon hides some of the sun from the earth.
    (C) the moon covers the earth with a shadow.
    (D) the earth casts a shadow on the moon.

PLANETS AND ASTEROIDS

The word planet comes from the Latin word meaning traveler. Ancient observers were taken by the "lights" they saw traveling around the sky against a background of other "lights" that seemed stationary.

Today we know that nine planets including earth travel in orbits around the sun. Also in orbit around the sun are a belt of asteroids from 1 to 500 miles in diameter that may be the remains of an exploded planet. The table below gives some information about the planets and asteroids.

BODIES IN SOLAR ORBIT

Name	Approximate diameter in miles	Approximate distance from sun in miles	Revolution Period
Mercury	3,100	36,000,000	88 days
Venus	7,700	67,000,000	225 days
Earth	7,900	93,000,000	$365\frac{1}{4}$ days
Mars	4,200	142,000,000	687 days
Asteroids		161,000,000	
Jupiter	88,700	483,000,000	12 years
Saturn	75,000	886,000,000	$29\frac{1}{2}$ years
Uranus	32,000	1,783,000,000	84 years
Neptune	28,000	2,794,000,000	165 years
Pluto	1,420 (?)	3,670,000,000	248 years

Unmanned spacecraft and other observations reveal more about the planets each year. Recent discoveries of meteorites on earth thought to have come from Mars and evidence of ice and a former ocean bed on Mars have fueled speculation that some life forms might exist, or might have existed, on Mars.

17. The difference between earth's diameter and Neptune's diameter is closest to
    (A) one-millionth of the approximate distance from the sun to the planet Uranus.
    (B) a third of the difference between Jupiter's diameters and Neptune's diameter.
    (C) one tenth of a percent of the approximate distance from the sun to the planet Uranus.
    (D) four times the diameter of Mars.

METEOROLOGY

Meteorology is the study of the earth's atmosphere. We are most attentive to meteorologist's predictions about weather.

Weather observations are taken on the ground, in the upper atmosphere, and from satellites in space. All these observations inform us about likely weather events and add to our knowledge about the atmosphere.

The complex movement of air masses creates our weather. This movement begins because air around the equator is heated, causing it to rise, and air at the poles is cool. Air in the lower atmosphere moves toward the equator to replace the rising heated air, while upper air moves toward the poles. Added to this is the effect of Coriolis force, caused by the rotation of the planet. Coriolis force pulls air to the right in the Northern Hemisphere and to the left in the Southern Hemisphere.

Weather fronts move from west to east in the United States. High pressure systems are usually associated with good weather. Wind circulates to the right (left in the Southern Hemisphere) around a high pressure system. Low pressure systems are usually associated with bad weather. Wind circulates to the left (right in the Southern Hemisphere) around a low pressure system.

Humidity refers to the percent of water vapor in the air. Dew point is the temperature below which the air will become so humid that it is saturated with water. Humidity above 60 or 65 percent makes us more uncomfortable because perspiration evaporates slowly.

When condensed water or ice crystals become too dense for the air to support the precipitate, they fall toward the ground. *Rain* is water droplets that fall to the ground. *Snow* crystallizes from water droplets in clouds and falls to the earth. *Sleet* begins as rain and freezes or partially freezes as it falls to the earth. *Freezing rain* is rain that freezes when it strikes the surface. *Hail* is rain that freezes in cumulonimbus clouds and is blown up and falls only to be blown up again. This cycle is repeated many times, forming noticeable layers of ice in a hailstone.

Lightning is an instantaneous, high energy electrical discharge in the atmosphere. Lightning occurs when positive and negative charges are separated in the atmosphere. While this occurs most often in violent thunderstorms it can occur also in sandstorms or in clouds above volcanoes. Lightning can be from cloud to cloud, or from cloud to ground.

18. You're standing at the eastern end of Long Island in New York State. A high-pressure system is directly opposite you some miles offshore to the east. Where you are standing, the wind is most likely coming from which direction?
    (A) northwest
    (B) northeast
    (C) southwest
    (D) southeast

THE EARTH'S PARTS

The earth has five parts—atmosphere, crust, mantle, outer core, and inner core.

The atmosphere is the gaseous region that surrounds the earth; it consists of 78 percent nitrogen and 21 percent oxygen. The remaining 1 percent consists of carbon dioxide, argon, water vapor, and other gases. The atmosphere extends out about 650 miles. But air becomes thinner as you travel away from earth and only the bottom $3\frac{1}{2}$ miles or so of the atmosphere is habitable by humans without special equipment. The ozone layer, which protects earth from ultraviolet rays, is about 20 miles up.

The hydrosphere is the layer of water that covers about three-quarters of earth's surface. Ocean water, salt water, makes up about 95 percent of all earth's water. Oceans average about 12,400 feet deep. Below 100 feet, water temperature decreases rapidly. At 5,000 feet, the ocean temperature is near freezing.

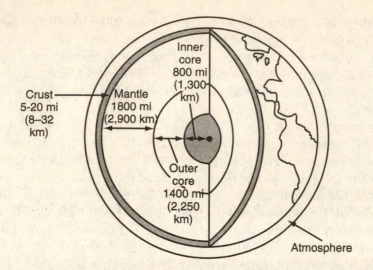

It is about 4,000 miles from the surface to the center of earth. Pressure and density increase with depth.

The lithosphere includes the rigid crust (20 miles thick) and upper mantle (40 miles thick) of the earth. The lithosphere is divided into a number of tectonic plates, which drift across earth's surface on the partially molten asthenosphere. The asthenosphere separates the lithosphere from the mantle.

The rigid mantle reaches to a depth of about 1,800 miles. The outer core is about 1,400 miles thick and consists of dense rigid materials. The inner core has a radius of about 800 miles and is very dense and hot with temperatures over 10,000° F. The heat generated in the inner core is transferred to the surface and provides the energy for continental drift and for molten rock, which erupts on land and in the ocean.

19. According to the passage, about how far is it from the ozone layer straight down to the dividing line between the inner core and the outer core?
    (A) about 4,500 miles
    (B) about 4,000 miles
    (C) about 3,800 miles
    (D) about 3,200 miles

ROCKS AND FOSSILS

Geologists study rocks. Three types of rocks are found in the earth's crust—sedimentary, igneous, and metamorphic. Sedimentary rocks form in water when sediments and remains of dead organisms harden. Igneous rocks form when molten rock, magma, crystallizes. Metamorphic rocks form when other rocks are subjected to extreme pressure. Sedimentary rocks are found near the surface of the earth while igneous and metamorphic rocks are usually found beneath the surface.

Fossils are evidence of living organisms. Geologists and other scientists use fossils to learn about earth's history. Fossils usually form when organisms die and are buried in the sediment that forms sedimentary rocks. Other fossils include footprints or tracks of animals. Fossils of animals help us date rocks and other layers of the earth. Rocks are dated through radioactive isotope dating, which helps date the fossils found in the rock layers.

20. Which of the following questions could NOT be answered from this passage?
    (A) What percentage of rocks are sedimentary?
    (B) What is one way of dating rocks? ·
    (C) What types of rocks are most likely found deep in the crust?
    (D) What type of rock develops from crystallization?

GEOLOGIC PROCESSES

As new rocks are being created, old ones are being destroyed, and earth's surface is being worn away. This process is called erosion.

Most erosion begins with weathering. Weathering disintegrates rocks physically and chemically. Physical weathering breaks up rocks and may be caused by intense heat or cold, by frost, or by the action of vines or the roots of plants. Chemical weathering changes the composition of the rocks. Rain water combines with small amounts of carbon dioxide in the atmosphere to form carbonic acid, which can dissolve or decompose minerals.

Streams, rivers, and wind erode rocks and carry away soil, while glaciers can gouge out huge grooves in rocks and in the soil. Beaches are the result of erosion from the pounding surf or oceans. Humans cause erosion. The dust bowl in the midwestern United States was caused by careless plowing, planting, and grazing.

The earth's interior is very hot. Holes drilled one mile into the earth can be 85° to 90° warmer at the bottom than on the surface. This is why geologists believe that the interior of the earth, which extends down almost 4,000 feet, is exceptionally hot. This belief is bolstered by the molten rock that erupts from volcanoes and by the boiling water in springs at the earth's surface.

New mountains and land are constantly being created. Hot magma comes to the surface, seeps out, and is cooled. Land masses also rise as the land is eroded and pushed up from below.

21. Which of the following words could be used in place of "pounding" in the second sentence of the third paragraph?
    (A) weighing
    (B) pulverizing
    (C) placating
    (D) grating

CHEMISTRY

Chemistry refers to the composition, properties, and interactions of matter. Organic chemistry is about living things. Inorganic chemistry deals with all other substances.

Matter consists of atoms, which are so small they have never been seen—not even with the most powerful microscope. Atoms contain three subatomic particles—protons, neutrons, and electrons. The nucleus contains positively charged protons and neutrons with a neutral charge. Negatively charged electrons revolve around the nucleus.

Elements are the building blocks of chemistry. They cannot be broken by chemical means into other elements. Over 100 chemical elements are known today. Some have been produced artificially and have not been found in nature. Atoms are the smallest piece of an element.

Each element is classified by its atomic number, which is the total number of protons in the nucleus. Every element has its own symbol. Therefore, every substance can be represented by symbols that show how many atoms of each element it contains.

Matter is anything that has mass and takes up space. Matter can exist as a solid, liquid, or gas. The form of matter may change. For example, water becomes solid below freezing, and lead can be heated to a liquid.

All matter is made up of atoms. The weight of matter is a measure of the force that gravity places on its mass. Matter is conserved. That is, it cannot be created or destroyed, but it can be converted into energy.

A compound is formed when two or more elements unite chemically. A molecule is the smallest part of a compound with the properties of that compound.

There are three important types of chemical compounds—acids, bases, and salt. Acids dissolved in water produce hydrogen. Bases dissolved in water produce hydroxide. When acids and bases are combined chemically, they form salts.

A solution is formed when element(s) or compound(s) are dissolved in another substance. Club soda is a solution with carbon dioxide dissolved in water. Lemonade is a solution of lemon juice and sugar dissolved in water.

22. Which of the following best summarizes the difference between matter and compounds?
    (A) Neither compounds nor atoms can be destroyed.
    (B) Both matter and compounds can be destroyed, but matter can be destroyed only by energy.
    (C) Matter can be converted, but compounds can be destroyed.
    (D) Compounds can be converted, but matter can be destroyed.

MATTER AND MASS

Mass is the amount of matter in a body and is a measure of the body's inertia (resistance to change of motion). Weight is a measure of the force of gravity on a body. Weight and mass are different. Mass at rest is the same everywhere, but mass increases as it approaches the speed of light. Weight varies depending on its location in a gravitational field.

The density (specific gravity) of matter describes how compact the matter is. Archimedes discovered density and is reputed to have shouted "Eureka" in the process. He found that, in similar weights of lead and gold, the gold displaced less water, showing that it was more dense.

23. You weigh a lump of clay on earth, and then weigh the same lump of clay on the moon. Which of the following accurately summarizes the result?
    (A) The weight and the mass both remain the same on the moon as on earth.
    (B) The mass is altered by its presence on the moon, so the clay will have a different weight on the moon than on earth.
    (C) The mass of the object remains the same on the moon as on earth, but the weight will be different on the moon than it is on earth.
    (D) The clay weight is different on a scale while on the moon than it was on earth, but the mass is the same on the moon as on earth, so the actual weight of the clay is the same on the moon as it is on earth.

MOTION

Physics is concerned with an object's response to force and the resulting movement. Force is energy that causes a change in an object's motion or shape. To explain force completely, you must describe both the magnitude and the direction. For example, two forces of the same magnitude pushing in the same direction are different from these same forces pushing at one another.

Velocity is described as magnitude (e.g., miles per hour) and direction (e.g., from 220 degrees). The magnitude portion of velocity is speed. The following formula describes the distance traveled for a constant velocity and a known time. For a time t and a constant velocity v the distance traveled d is:

$$d = vt$$

Newton's three laws of motion are still most important in everyday life. We must remember, though, that recent theories have shown that these laws do not apply to objects traveling near the speed of light or for very small subatomic particles.

Newton's First Law (Inertia). A body maintains its state of rest or uniform motion unless acted upon by an outside force.

Newton's Second Law (Constant Acceleration). As force is applied to an object, the object accelerates in the direction of the force. Both the mass and the force affect how the object accelerates. The more the mass the less the acceleration. The formula for this law follows:

$$F(\text{orce}) = M(\text{ass}) \times A(\text{cceleration}) \text{ or } A(\text{cceleration}) = \frac{F(\text{orce})}{M(\text{ass})}$$

Newton's Third Law (Conservation of Momentum). This law states that for every action there is an equal and opposite reaction. If two objects bump into each other, they are pushed away from each other with an equal force. The net effect of this event is 0, and the momentum is conserved.

24. An object travels at a constant speed over 90 feet in four minutes. What is the velocity?
    (A) 360 feet
    (B) 360 feet per minute
    (C) 22.5 feet
    (D) 22.5 feet per minute

25. Based on this passage, what conclusion can be reached.
    (A) As mass increases and force decreases, then acceleration decreases.
    (B) As acceleration decreases and mass increases, then force increases.
    (C) As mass stays constant and force increases, then acceleration increases.
    (D) As force increases and acceleration stays constant, then mass stays constant.

ENERGY, WORK, AND HEAT

Energy is the ability to do work. Energy can be mechanical, solar, thermal, chemical, electrical, or nuclear. Potential energy is stored energy or energy ready to be released. Kinetic energy is energy resulting from motion. Activation energy converts potential energy into kinetic energy.

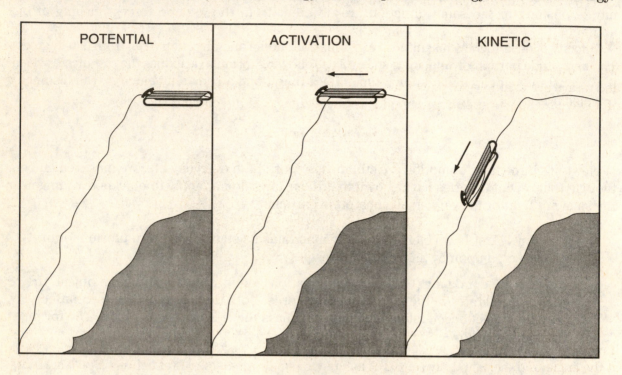

| POTENTIAL | ACTIVATION | KINETIC |

In one simple example, a sled at the top of a hill possesses potential energy. The push of the sledder is the activation energy needed to set the sled in motion. While in motion, the sled possesses kinetic energy.

In another example, the fuel in a rocket car has potential energy. This potential energy is activated by energy from a flame and transformed into the kinetic energy of the moving car.

Work is the movement of a body by a force. If there is no movement, there is no work. Work occurs when you pick up an object. Trying without success to move a heavy object or holding an object steady involves no work. It does not matter that a lot of effort was involved. The rate of work is power. Power is measured in foot-pounds. A foot-pound is the amount of work it takes to raise one pound, one foot at sea level.

In physics, heat is energy in motion. Heat transfers energy within a body or from one body to the other when there is a temperature difference. Heat moves from higher temperature to lower temperature, lowering the former and raising the latter. Heat is measured in calories.

Temperature measures how fast the molecules in a substance are moving. The faster the molecules move, the hotter the substance. Temperature is commonly measured on two scales, Fahrenheit (freezing 32 degrees, boiling [water] 212 degrees) and Celsius (freezing 0 degrees and boiling [water] 100 degrees). The Kelvin scale is used in science. Zero on the Kelvin scale is absolute zero—molecules are not moving at all—and is equal to $-273°C$ or $-460°F$.

Heat is transferred by conduction (physical contact), convection (from moving liquid or gas), and radiation (no physical contact). A heating pad *conducts* heat to your back. Moving hot water transfers heat to the radiator by *convection*. The sun *radiates* heat to the earth.

26. Based on this passage, which of the following statements is correct?
    (A) Where there's energy, there's work.
    (B) Where there's work, there's energy.
    (C) Where there's heat convection, there's heat conduction.
    (D) Where there's heat conduction, there's heat convection.

WAVE PHENOMENA

Waves transfer energy without transferring matter. Microwaves, radio waves, sound waves, and x-rays are examples of waves in action. Most waves resemble the one below. The frequency of a wave is the vibrations per second. The wavelength is the distance between crests.

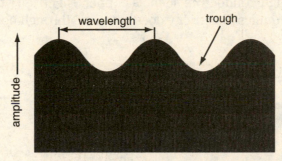

Most light is produced by heated electrons vibrating at high frequencies. Light makes it possible for us to see things and to observe colors. Plants need light to carry out photosynthesis.

Light travels in straight lines and spreads out as it travels. When light strikes a rough surface it may be absorbed or scattered. When light strikes a highly polished surface it is reflected away at the angle of the original ray (angle of incidence equals the angle of reflection). Black surfaces absorb all light, while white surfaces scatter all light. This is why white clothes are recommended for sunny, warm days.

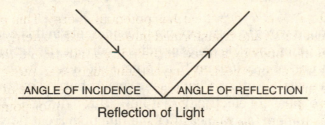

Reflection of Light

Sounds are waves. For the human ear to hear a sound it must travel through a medium—a gas, a solid, or a liquid. As the sound waves travel through the medium, molecules in the medium vibrate.

Sound travels more quickly through solid media because the molecules are more closely packed together. Sound travels through air at about 1,100 feet per second, through water at about 5,000 feet per second, and through stone at about 20,000 feet per second.

27. You are looking out the window and you see a single lightning flash. About 25 seconds later you hear the thunderclap. About how far away was the lightening bolt?
    (A) 1 mile
    (B) 3 miles
    (C) 5 miles
    (D) 7 miles

ELECTRICITY

Atoms are composed of protons (positive charge), electrons (negative charge), and neutrons (neutral charge). All things have either a positive (more protons), negative (more electrons), or neutral (balance of protons and electrons) charge.

Electricity is based on these charges and follows these rules. Like charges repel, unlike charges attract. Neutral charges are attracted by both positive and negative charges, but not as strongly as opposite charges.

In a static electricity experiment, the experimenter shows that the glass rod does not attract bits of paper. Then the glass rod is rubbed with a piece of silk. This process removes electrons from the rod, creating a negative charge. Then the rod attracts the neutral bits of paper.

Electricity speeds through conductors such as copper. Electricity moves slower through semiconductors such as ceramics. Electricity does not move through nonconductors or insulators such as rubber and glass.

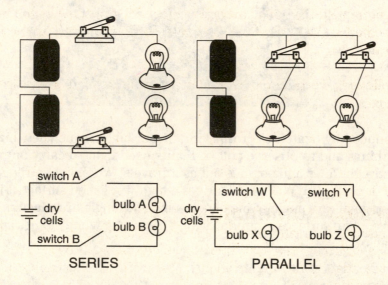

Electricity moves through wires to form circuits. Most circuits in this country use alternating current (AC). Circuits in other countries may use direct current (DC). Most circuits are wired parallel—if a light burns out, or a switch is off, all other switches or lights work. Some circuits are wired in series—if a switch is off or a light is missing or burned out, all lights go out.

Three units are used to measure electricity as it flows through wires. The volt measures the force of the current. The ampere (amp) measures the rate of current flow. The ohm tells the resistance in the wire to the flow of electricity.

Batteries are used to produce, store, and release electricity. Batteries used in a toy or flashlight are dry cell batteries. Car batteries are wet cell batteries.

28. Which of the following is most likely when you remove one light from a string of lights and all the lights go out?
    (A) A circuit breaker burned out.
    (B) All the other lights burned out when you removed the light.
    (C) The lights are wired in parallel.
    (D) The lights are wired in series.

Magnetism

Magnets occur naturally in magnetite, although most magnets are manufactured from iron. Magnetism is very similar to electricity, and electromagnets can be made from coils of wire. Magnets have a north and south pole—like poles repel, while opposite poles attract. The magnetic field is strongest around the poles.

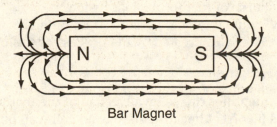

Bar Magnet

Earth has a magnetic field that aids navigation. Magnetic north is located in northeastern Canada. It is not located at the North Pole. Compass needles point to magnetic north, not to the geographic North Pole.

29. Which of the following words could be used in place of the word "poles" in the last sentence in the first paragraph?
    (A) ends
    (B) rods
    (C) stakes
    (D) pushes

MODERN PHYSICS AND RADIOACTIVITY

Modern physics studies very small particles of energy. Energy as very small, discrete quantities gives scientists a different view than energy as a continuous flow. Particle physics is particularly useful as scientists study atomic energy. For example, scientists study light as the transmission of tiny particles called photons. In fact, it is believed that energy is transmitted as both particles and waves.

Modern physics also studies the conversion of matter into energy and energy into matter. Einstein's famous equation quantifies the conversion between mass to energy.

$$E = mc^2$$

(E is energy, m is mass, and c is the speed of light, 186,000 miles per second.)

Calculations with this equation reveal that very small amounts of mass can create huge amounts of energy. Similarly, calculations reveal it would take huge amounts of energy to create a very small amount of mass.

Materials are radioactive when they have unstable nuclei. Uranium is an example of a naturally occurring radioactive substance. Radioactive materials decay, losing their radioactivity at a certain rate. The decay of radioactive materials is very useful for dating rocks and other materials.

Other radioactive material is created through nuclear fission in nuclear power plants. The energy from the reaction can be used as a power source.

Radioactive materials release energy including alpha, beta, and usually gamma radiation. Gamma rays penetrate living organisms very deeply and can destroy living cells and lead to the death of humans. The sun creates energy through fusion. Attempts are underway to create energy through nuclear fusion. Fusion creates much less radioactivity and could be fueled by deuterium, which is found in limitless quantities throughout the ocean.

30. Which of the following questions could be answered from the information in this passage?
    (A) At what rate do radioactive materials decay?
    (B) What is the main source of fuel for nuclear fusion?
    (C) How much energy would it take to create a gram of mass?
    (D) What radioactive material is created by the process of fission?

Explained Answers

1. **B** The last paragraph identifies the cell wall as one of the features found only on plant cells. Choice (D) is incorrect because there is no cell wall on animal cells.

2. **A** In the passage, "diploid" appears in parentheses following the word "complete," to show that diploid and complete mean the same in this context. The phrase "all the" is a reasonable synonym for complete, and so this is the correct answer. Diploid also means double the haploid number of chromosomes, but that meaning is not the most appropriate choice in this context.

3. **C** Glucose is produced by photosynthesis, but it is not needed for photosynthesis to take place.

4. **D** The passage explains that DNA is genetic material tightly coiled as a chromosome.

5. **C** The early supply came from photosynthesis. Refer to the last sentence in the second paragraph.

6. **A** Insects came before reptiles. If one event precedes another, the first event is closer to the bottom of the chart. As you go from bottom to top, you come to insects (Devonian Period) before you come to reptiles (Carboniferous Period).

7. **C** A virus is primitive in that it is simpler and less well developed than a cell. Answer (B) is incorrect because cells can also be parasitic.

8. **B** Intravenous (IV) drug users are at particular risk because sharing needles may transmit small quantities of infected blood.

9. **B** The third paragraph from the bottom describes the types of muscles. The paragraph under the heart diagram describes the blood flow path. The last paragraph describes the function of the autonomic nervous system, but it does not describe the structure.

10. **D** This sentence correctly restates the original sentence. The "them" in the original sentence refers to antigens.

11. **C** The passage does not describe what the atmosphere consists of.

12. **A** Compression; the water vapor is compressed into water droplets.

13. **A** The diagram shows that asteroids are located between the earth and Jupiter. They're also between Mars and Jupiter, but that's not one of the choices and choice (A) is absolutely correct. Choice (B) is incorrect because the diagram is not to scale and we can't tell anything about the comparative size of the sun and Jupiter. In fact, the sun's diameter is about ten times Jupiter's diameter.

14. **C** "Perpendicular" means at a right angle.

15. **A** The earth's tilt is the primary reason for seasons, as explained in the last sentence of the third paragraph.

16. **A** A solar eclipse occurs when the moon hides the sun from some of the earth. The moon casts a shadow on the earth, but the shadow does not cover the earth.

17. **B** Earth's diameter is about 7,900 miles, Neptune's diameter is about 28,000 miles. 28,000 − 7,900 = 20,100. That's about 20,000 miles.

    Jupiter's diameter is about 88,700 miles. Neptune's diameter is about 28,000 miles. Subtract: 88,700 − 28,000 = 60,700. 60,700 × 1/3 = 20,233. That's also about 20,000 miles.

18. **D** Southeast, because the wind travels clockwise around a high-pressure system in the Northern Hemisphere.

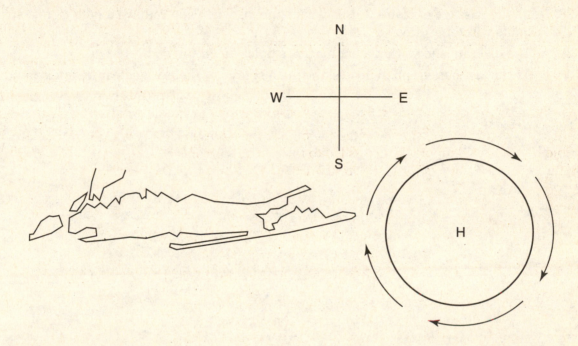

19. **D** 20 miles (distance from ozone layer to surface) + 20 miles (approximate thickness of crust) + 1,800 miles (mantle) + 1,400 miles (outer core) = 3,240. That's about 3,200 miles.

20. **A** The passage mentions that there are three types of rocks, but it does not say what percent are sedimentary.

21. **B** Pulverizing means the same thing as pounding, in this context.

22. **C** Matter can't be destroyed; it can only be converted to energy. A compound can be destroyed by breaking it down into elements.

23. **C** Weight measures the force of gravity on an object. Since gravity is lower on the moon, the clay will weigh less on the moon.

24. **D** The formula is $d = vt$.

    Divide both sides by t to get $v = d/t$.
    Then substitute 90 feet for d and 4 minutes for t.

    $v = 90$ feet/4 minutes
    $v = 22.5$ feet per minute

25. **C** $A(\text{cceleration}) = \dfrac{F(\text{orce})}{M(\text{ass})}$

    If the mass part of the fraction stays the same, and the force part increases, the value of the fraction increases. That means the acceleration increases.

26. **B** Work always involves energy; energy does not necessarily create work.

27. **C** In 25 seconds sound travels about $25 \times 1{,}100$ feet = 27,500 feet.
    Divide by the number of feet in a mile 27,500 = 5,280 feet = 5.2 miles.
    That's about 5 miles. You can estimate this answer.

28. **D** As the passage explains, this is what happens when you remove a bulb from a string of lights wired in series.

29. **A** The diagram shows that a bar magnet's poles are at the end.

30. **B** As the last paragraph indicates, the main source of fuel for nuclear fusion is deuterium.

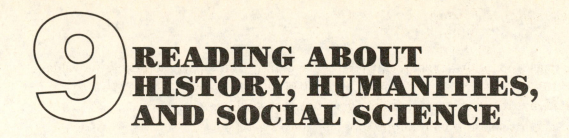

9 READING ABOUT HISTORY, HUMANITIES, AND SOCIAL SCIENCE

This chapter provides a practice for the multiple-choice reading comprehension items on the LAST. These passages may also strengthen your understanding of social studies.

There are 45 passages and 55 reading comprehension questions in History, Humanities, and Social Sciences. You should complete as many of the items as you need to sharpen your reading comprehension skills. You can always come back and complete more items later on.

On the real LAST you will have an average of two minutes to answer each question. Use that time limit on these practice items. For example, if you plan to answer 20 items, time yourself and finish all the items in 40 minutes or less.

Follow the steps for answering reading comprehension questions from pages 35–46.

Skim the passage.

Read the questions and answers.

Eliminate incorrect answers.

Scan the details to find the answer.

Choose the answer that is absolutely correct.

ANSWER SHEET

1 Ⓐ Ⓑ Ⓒ Ⓓ	6 Ⓐ Ⓑ Ⓒ Ⓓ	11 Ⓐ Ⓑ Ⓒ Ⓓ	16 Ⓐ Ⓑ Ⓒ Ⓓ
2 Ⓐ Ⓑ Ⓒ Ⓓ	7 Ⓐ Ⓑ Ⓒ Ⓓ	12 Ⓐ Ⓑ Ⓒ Ⓓ	17 Ⓐ Ⓑ Ⓒ Ⓓ
3 Ⓐ Ⓑ Ⓒ Ⓓ	8 Ⓐ Ⓑ Ⓒ Ⓓ	13 Ⓐ Ⓑ Ⓒ Ⓓ	18 Ⓐ Ⓑ Ⓒ Ⓓ
4 Ⓐ Ⓑ Ⓒ Ⓓ	9 Ⓐ Ⓑ Ⓒ Ⓓ	14 Ⓐ Ⓑ Ⓒ Ⓓ	19 Ⓐ Ⓑ Ⓒ Ⓓ
5 Ⓐ Ⓑ Ⓒ Ⓓ	10 Ⓐ Ⓑ Ⓒ Ⓓ	15 Ⓐ Ⓑ Ⓒ Ⓓ	20 Ⓐ Ⓑ Ⓒ Ⓓ

21 Ⓐ Ⓑ Ⓒ Ⓓ	26 Ⓐ Ⓑ Ⓒ Ⓓ	31 Ⓐ Ⓑ Ⓒ Ⓓ	36 Ⓐ Ⓑ Ⓒ Ⓓ
22 Ⓐ Ⓑ Ⓒ Ⓓ	27 Ⓐ Ⓑ Ⓒ Ⓓ	32 Ⓐ Ⓑ Ⓒ Ⓓ	37 Ⓐ Ⓑ Ⓒ Ⓓ
23 Ⓐ Ⓑ Ⓒ Ⓓ	28 Ⓐ Ⓑ Ⓒ Ⓓ	33 Ⓐ Ⓑ Ⓒ Ⓓ	38 Ⓐ Ⓑ Ⓒ Ⓓ
24 Ⓐ Ⓑ Ⓒ Ⓓ	29 Ⓐ Ⓑ Ⓒ Ⓓ	34 Ⓐ Ⓑ Ⓒ Ⓓ	39 Ⓐ Ⓑ Ⓒ Ⓓ
25 Ⓐ Ⓑ Ⓒ Ⓓ	30 Ⓐ Ⓑ Ⓒ Ⓓ	35 Ⓐ Ⓑ Ⓒ Ⓓ	40 Ⓐ Ⓑ Ⓒ Ⓓ

41 Ⓐ Ⓑ Ⓒ Ⓓ	46 Ⓐ Ⓑ Ⓒ Ⓓ	51 Ⓐ Ⓑ Ⓒ Ⓓ
42 Ⓐ Ⓑ Ⓒ Ⓓ	47 Ⓐ Ⓑ Ⓒ Ⓓ	52 Ⓐ Ⓑ Ⓒ Ⓓ
43 Ⓐ Ⓑ Ⓒ Ⓓ	48 Ⓐ Ⓑ Ⓒ Ⓓ	53 Ⓐ Ⓑ Ⓒ Ⓓ
44 Ⓐ Ⓑ Ⓒ Ⓓ	49 Ⓐ Ⓑ Ⓒ Ⓓ	54 Ⓐ Ⓑ Ⓒ Ⓓ
45 Ⓐ Ⓑ Ⓒ Ⓓ	50 Ⓐ Ⓑ Ⓒ Ⓓ	55 Ⓐ Ⓑ Ⓒ Ⓓ

NATIVE AMERICAN CIVILIZATIONS

Current scholarship indicates that Native Americans, "Indians," came to this continent about 30,000 years ago. They passed over a land bridge near what is now the Bering Strait between Siberia and Alaska. These Native Americans eventually spread throughout all of North, Central, and South America.

Even with a glacier covering Alaska, the Aleuts had established a culture on the Aleutian islands off southern Alaska by 5000 B.C. This hunting/fishing society has retained much of its ancient character.

Primitive northern woodland cultures developed in the northeastern United States about 3000 B.C. These cultures included the Algonquin-speaking tribes, such as the Shawnee, and the Iroquois Federation. There is evidence that Native Americans in the northern woodlands may have been exposed to outside contact five hundred years before the arrival of Europeans after Columbus.

Also at about 3000 B.C., civilizations developed in southeast North America, in and around what is now Florida and Georgia. These sophisticated cultures built cities with central plazas. The tribes of this area included the Cherokee, Choctaw, and Seminole. These tribes had highly organized governments and economic systems.

Once glaciers melted in the area, the Eskimo and Inuit Indians established a culture in northern Alaska about 1800 B.C. Their use of igloos, kayaks, and dogsleds in harsh conditions was a remarkable adaptation to their environment.

1. Which Native American group established a culture in Alaska about 7,000 years ago?
   (A) Aleuts
   (B) Algonquins
   (C) Eskimos
   (D) Inuits

RECENT CULTURES

In the Southwest United States, the Anasazi (Pueblo) culture developed by about 500 A.D. Pueblo and Hopi Indians built walled towns, some on the sides of inaccessible mountains or on mesas.

Around 600 A.D. a mound-building culture developed from the Mississippi River into Ohio. This culture probably built a town with a population of over 30,000 on the east side of the Mississippi River near St. Louis.

Starting about 750 A.D., a nomadic culture was established on the great plains of the United States. These Native American nomads lived in tepees as they followed and hunted herds of bison. These are probably the most popularized of Native Americans. Original tribes of this area include the Blackfoot.

Around 1400 A.D., Native Americans who became the Navajos and the Apaches migrated from Canada to the southwestern United States.

Other western tribes included the Ute and Shoshone. The Nez Pierce and Walla Walla tribes inhabited the northwestern United States. Each had advanced agricultural and cultural traditions.

By 1500 advanced Native American cultures existed across North America. However, these cultures did not rival the Aztec, Inca, and Mayan cultures of Central and South America. They were nonetheless sophisticated, organized cultures that lacked only the technological developments of Europe and Asia.

2. In what structure did plains Native Americans live?
 (A) mounds
 (B) pueblos
 (C) tepees
 (D) walled towns

EUROPEAN EXPLORATION AND COLONIZATION

A number of groups visited what is now the United States before Columbus sailed. Whether by accident or design, sailors from Iceland, Europe, and Africa came to this continent before 1000 A.D. It appears that Celtic and Norse settlements were established in North America between 1000 and 1300 A.D. These settlements were not maintained.

Notoriety greeted Columbus as he returned to Spain from the first of his four voyages. Columbus never reached the mainland of North America, but he landed throughout the Caribbean and established a settlement in what is now the Dominican Republic.

John Cabot reached the North American mainland in 1497 and claimed the land for England. In 1584 Sir Walter Raleigh established the "lost colony" on Roanoke Island just off the North Carolina coast. The settlement failed when all the settlers disappeared, leaving the word CROATION carved in a tree.

In 1607 the English established Jamestown, Virginia, under John Smith. Tobacco exports sustained the colony, and slaves from Africa were brought to Jamestown in 1619. In that same year, the House of Burgesses was formed in Virginia as the first elected governing body in America.

In 1620 Pilgrims left England on the *Mayflower* to escape religious persecution. The Pilgrims established a colony at Provincetown and then a second colony at Plymouth in December 1620. The Pilgrims drafted and received popular approval for the Mayflower Compact as a way of governing their colony.

3. What nonindigenous group established North American settlements before the voyage of Columbus?

 (A) Pilgrims
 (B) Africans
 (C) Spanish
 (D) Celts

OTHER EXPLORERS

Cortez conquered Mexico around 1520, and Pizarro conquered Peru around 1530. The Spaniards imported slaves from Africa at this time. Records of the native civilizations were destroyed, and natives were forced to convert to Catholicism. The Spanish also imported diseases, which effectively wiped out whole populations of natives. In North America the Spanish established a fort in St. Augustine, Florida, around 1565 and in Santa Fe, New Mexico, around 1610.

In the 1500s the French, through Cartier, explored the Great Lakes. The French city of Quebec was founded about 1609.

Henry Hudson, under Dutch contract, explored the East Coast and the Hudson River in the 1600s. The Dutch established settlements under Peter Minuit in Manhattan about 1624. The Dutch built the first road for wheeled vehicles in America around 1650.

Disease was the most devastating impact of European colonization. Native Americans did not have a natural immunity to measles, smallpox, typhoid, and influenza. These diseases decimated the Native American population. By the early 1700s there were more Europeans than Native Americans living in the Americas.

By 1740 there were 13 English colonies, all located along the eastern seaboard. These colonies grew in size and prosperity and developed diversified populations by the time of the Revolutionary War. The colonists were in an almost constant state of conflict with Native Americans, with Spanish colonists, and with the French in the French and Indian wars.

4. In 1740 why were the English colonies located along the eastern seaboard of what is now the United States?
   (A) Constant conflict with Native Americans and the French prevented colonists from moving west.
   (B) That seaboard is closest to England.
   (C) Spanish explorers were settling the West.
   (D) Colonists concentrated on developing the colonies' size and prosperity.

THE AMERICAN REVOLUTION AND THE FOUNDING OF AMERICA

This chronology details the causes up to the Revolutionary War. Note how cumulative the causes are and how a change in English policy might have averted the conflict.

After the English won the French and Indian War they signed the Proclamation of 1763, which forbade English colonial expansion west of the current colonies. The proclamation was designed to avoid unnecessary expenditures and to appease France. It angered many colonists.

The English government was in serious financial debt after the French and Indian War. The English government levied a sugar tax on the colonies to help pay for the war. Colonists protested this tax saying it was "taxation without representation."

In 1765 England passed a law called the Quartering Act. The act required colonial governments to pay for quarters and supplies for English troops and to quarter these troops in barracks and inns and taverns.

The Stamp Act required every legal piece of paper (college degrees, policies, licenses, etc.) to carry a tax stamp. The act was protested vehemently and eventually repealed by England.

These acts led to many colonial reactions. Patrick Henry spoke against the acts in the Virginia House of Burgesses. Revolutionary groups called Sons of Liberty were formed.

The Townshend Acts, named for Charles Townshend, British Chancellor of the Exchequer, were import duties on most things used by colonists. Colonists objected, and some tax officials in Boston were attacked. British troops were sent to Boston. Three years later, the British repealed all the Townshend duties except for the duties on tea!

British troops fired on colonial protesters, killing five including Crispus Attucks in the Boston Massacre. The English soldiers were defended in court by patriots including John Adams, leading to the acquittal of most of the soldiers by a Boston jury. Other tensions continued for the next three years.

To protest the remaining import tax on tea, men dressed as Indians boarded English ships in Boston Harbor. They dumped hundreds of chests of tea into Boston Harbor in what has come to be known as the Boston Tea Party. In retaliation Britain closed Boston Harbor and took more direct control of the colony.

In September, representatives from each colony except Georgia met at the First Continental Congress in Philadelphia. The Congress called on the colonies to boycott goods from England until the English repealed the tax on tea and opened Boston Harbor. Massachusetts minutemen armed themselves and were declared in rebellion by Parliament.

5. Which act led most directly to Britain taking more control of the colonies?
   (A) the Quartering Act
   (B) the Tea Act
   (C) the Sugar Act
   (D) the Townshend Act

WAR'S BEGINNINGS

On April 18, 1775, English General Gage left Boston to commandeer arms at Concord. Paul Revere and William Dawes rode out to alert the minutemen. The English troops first encountered minutemen in Lexington. The first shot was fired, but no one knows by whom. There were American and English dead. British troops destroyed supplies at Concord but were decimated by minuteman attacks on the march back to Boston. Hostilities had begun.

The Second Continental Congress named George Washington commander-in-chief. The Congress asked England for negotiations but was rebuked.

Gage attacked colonists on the top of Breeds Hill (Bunker Hill because of the bunker on top). The British won the battle but at a tremendous cost, establishing the fighting ability of colonial forces.

In 1776 Thomas Paine wrote his pamphlet *Common Sense*, which favored American independence. On July 4, 1776, the Continental Congress approved the Declaration of Independence authored by Thomas Jefferson.

The Declaration included four self-evident truths:

1. Equality of all persons.
2. Inalienable rights of life, liberty, and the pursuit of happiness.
3. Rights of the government come from the governed.
4. The right of the people to alter or abolish a destructive government.

6. Which of the following is NOT an example of a self-evident truth found in the Declaration of Independence?
   (A) being treated as equal to someone else
   (B) being free from taxation without representation
   (C) being able to have a say in the government
   (D) being able to change a government that is hurting society

REVOLUTIONARY WAR

The battles of Bunker Hill and Concord and Lexington took place in 1775. Fighting also broke out in Virginia.

In March 1776, Washington laid siege to Boston. The British sent forces to New York. Washington failed in his attempt to drive the British out of New York and withdrew across New Jersey to Pennsylvania. Washington led a successful surprise attack against the British in Trenton, New Jersey, in December 1776.

In January 1777, Washington followed up his Trenton victory with a successful attack at Princeton, New Jersey. Washington spent the remainder of the winter in camp at Morristown, New Jersey. The British, under Howe, attacked and occupied the American capital at Philadelphia. The fighting delayed Howe's planned move to Saratoga, New York. This action enabled American militia under Gates to defeat British troops invading from Canada at Saratoga.

The American victory at Saratoga and the British occupation of Philadelphia moved the French to recognize America. The French joined the war as allies in 1778. This action by France was the decisive moment in the Revolutionary War. Washington's forces spent the winter in Valley Forge, Pennsylvania.

American forces suffered through a harsh winter in Valley Forge, while British forces were much better accommodated in New York and Philadelphia. The forces from Philadelphia marched to New York under the new British general, Clinton. The British forces narrowly avoided defeat at the Battle of Monmouth in June 1778. Late that year, British forces conquered Georgia. Fighting took place primarily around the British main headquarters in New York. Late in 1779 Clinton took the British army south.

When Clinton captured Charleston, South Carolina, Cornwallis took over the southern army, while Clinton returned to New York. Cornwallis defeated American forces under Gates. Things were looking bleak for American forces, and American General Benedict Arnold became a traitor. Then American forces under George Rogers Clark won a battle in the northwest while frontiersmen defeated Cornwallis in North Carolina.

Cornwallis was beset by American guerrillas including Francis Marion, the swamp fox. Cornwallis moved into Virginia and maneuvered himself into a trap at Yorktown. Surrounded by American forces on the land and the French fleet in Chesapeake Bay, Cornwallis surrendered on October 17, 1781. England decided to withdraw from the colonies. In 1783 Britain and the United States signed the Treaty of Paris, which gave the United States lands east of the Mississippi.

7. According to the passage, what was the decisive moment in the Revolutionary War?
   (A) Cornwallis trapping himself at Yorktown
   (B) the actions of the swamp fox, Francis Marion
   (C) France entering the war
   (D) George Washington's superior generalship

8. Which general defeated British troops from Canada?
   (A) Clark
   (B) Clinton
   (C) Gates
   (D) Washington

GROWTH OF THE NEW REPUBLIC

In 1781 the Articles of Confederation, drawn up in 1777, were approved by Congress as the "first constitution" of the United States. The Land Ordinance of 1785 established surveys of the Northwest Territories. (These territories became states such as Ohio and Illinois.) The Northwest Ordinance detailed the way in which states would be carved out of these territories.

The Articles of Confederation proved too weak and a Constitutional Convention convened during 1787 in Philadelphia. A compromise Constitution was written with special efforts by James Madison. The Constitution was sent to Congress, which approved it and in turn submitted it to the states for ratification.

The state ratification process fostered a brisk debate. Alexander Hamilton, John Jay, and James Madison authored *The Federalist Papers* to support ratification. Anti-Federalists were concerned that the Constitution did not sufficiently protect individual rights.

Delaware was the first state to ratify the Constitution in 1787 and Rhode Island was the last to ratify in 1790. Many of the ratification votes were very close. Strict versus loose construction of the Constitution has been a contentious issue since its ratification.

New York City was chosen as the temporary capital. Once the required nine states had ratified the Constitution, George Washington was sworn in as the first president on April 30, 1789. John Adams was sworn in as vice president.

The concern of the Anti-Federalists was partially answered in 1791 when the first ten amendments to the Constitution were ratified. A summary of the Bill of Rights follows.

   I. Freedom of religion, speech, press, assembly, and petition
   II. Right to bear arms
   III. No troops can be quartered in homes without permission
   IV. Warrants and probable cause needed for search and seizure
   V. Rights of the accused are assured
   VI. Right to a speedy public trial and the right to a lawyer
   VII. Right to a jury trial
   VIII. Excessive bail, excessive fines, and cruel and unusual punishment are forbidden
   IX. Rights not spelled out are retained by the people
   X. Powers not specifically federal are retained by the states.

The issue of a stronger versus a weaker central government was an active debate then as it is now. Washington was elected without opposition for his second term, the differences between Jeffersonians (less government, Democrat-Republicans) and Hamiltonians (more government, Federalists) led to a two-party system. In 1796 Washington bade farewell as president with three gems of advice for the country:

1. Avoid political parties based on geographic boundaries.
2. Avoid permanent alliances with foreign powers.
3. Safeguard the ability of America to pay its national debts.

9. What was the first governing document for the United States?
   (A) the Declaration of Independence
   (B) the Articles of Confederation
   (C) the Constitution of the United States of America
   (D) the Bill of Rights

10. Which group at that time would be referred to as the more conservative group today?
   (A) Jeffersonians
   (B) Hamiltonians
   (C) Federalists
   (D) Washingtonians

ADAMS TO MADISON

In the 1796 presidential election, John Adams eked out a victory over Thomas Jefferson. In the controversial XYZ affair, France sought bribes from America. Concern about France led to the Alien and Sedition Acts. These acts put pressure on noncitizens and forbade writing that criticized the government.

Some western states opposed these acts and wanted to nullify the acts for their state. This Theory of Nullification, and the states' rights mentioned in the tenth amendment to the Constitution, raised issues still important today.

In 1800 Aaron Burr and Jefferson were tied for the presidency in the Electoral College. Alexander Hamilton supported Jefferson. Jefferson won the vote in the House of Representatives and went on to serve a second term. Four years later, Burr killed Hamilton in a duel.

Jefferson resisted the demands of Barbary pirates for tribute. In 1801 Tripoli declared war on the United States, and Jefferson successfully blockaded the Tripoli coast. Tribute continued to be paid to other Barbary states.

Jefferson also arranged the purchase of the Louisiana Territory from France, doubling the size of the country. In 1804 Jefferson sent Lewis and Clark to explore the territory and open it for settlement.

Madison was elected president in 1808 and again in 1812. For a number of years, British ships had been impressing American sailors at sea. In response to this practice, the war hawks pressed for war with Britain in 1811.

11. Which of the following best summarizes the nullification theory?
    (A) Individual states' rights are superior to federal government rights.
    (B) Individual states could nullify their statehood and leave the Union.
    (C) Individual states could decide which laws applied in their states.
    (D) Individual states could nullify treaties made with foreign governments.

WAR OF 1812

The War of 1812 began with a failed American invasion of Canada. The U.S.S. *Constitution* (Old Ironsides) and "We have met the enemy and they are ours" Admiral Perry were active in this conflict. The British sacked and burned Washington and unsuccessfully attacked Fort McHenry in Baltimore, Maryland. Francis Scott Key wrote "The Star Spangled Banner" while a prisoner on a British ship off Fort McHenry. After the war had been declared officially over, Andrew Jackson fought and defeated the British at the Battle of New Orleans.

Federalists had opposed the war and ceased to exist as a viable political party. In the wake of the Federalist collapse, Monroe was elected president in 1816 and again in 1820. In treaties with Spain and England, under the leadership of John Quincy Adams, the United States established borders with Canada, acquired Florida from Spain, and gave up any claims to Texas.

12. The battle of New Orleans was fought
    (A) after an armistice was declared.
    (B) while "The Star Spangled Banner" was being written.
    (C) near Fort McHenry.
    (D) mainly on ships with Admiral Perry in command.

1830–1850

The Missouri Compromise of 1820 was a response to rapid westward expansion and the slavery issue. It admitted Maine as a free state and Missouri as a slave state and excluded slavery in the northern part of the Louisiana Purchase. The compromise maintained the balance of free and slave states.

James Monroe and John Quincy Adams established the Monroe Doctrine in 1823. The doctrine said: (1) the Americas were off limits for further colonization, (2) the political system in the United States was different from Europe, (3) the United States would see danger if European states meddled in the United States, and (4) the United States would not interfere in the internal affairs of other states or their established colonies.

In 1824 Andrew Jackson entered the electoral college with more electoral votes than any other candidate, but not a majority. He still lost in the House of Representatives to J.Q. Adams. In 1828 Jackson was elected president. In this year, people voted directly for electors in all but 2 of 24 states. Jackson used a "kitchen cabinet" of friends to advise him on important issues. Jackson favored the removal of Native Americans to reservations and ignored Supreme Court decisions in favor of the Native Americans. This "trail of tears" is an uncomfortable American story. The age of Jackson marks a time of increased democracy in the United States.

Martin Van Buren was elected president in 1836. On the heels of the financial panic of 1837, Van Buren lost the presidency to William Harrison in 1840. Harrison died less than a month after his inauguration. John Tyler, the vice president, succeeded to the presidency.

James K. Polk was elected president in 1844. There had been conflict in Texas since 1836. Despite a loss at the Alamo, Texas became a sovereign country. After years of debate and infighting, Polk was able to obtain congressional approval, and Texas was admitted as a slave state in 1844.

Mexico objected to Texas statehood, and the Mexican-American War started in 1846. U.S. generals, including Robert E. Lee, led troops into Mexico and captured Mexico City. The Treaty of Guadeloupe Hidalgo ended the war, and the United States acquired Texas north of the Rio Grande as well as the California and New Mexico Territories. Much of the manifest destiny of the United States to stretch from sea to sea had been achieved under Polk.

Zachary Taylor, a general in the Mexican-American War, was elected president in 1848. Slavery remained a significant and contentious issue. In 1849 gold was discovered near Sutters Mill in California. The gold rush brought thousands of prospectors and settlers to California.

The Compromise of 1850 specified whether territories would be granted statehood as a free or slave state and contained a strict fugitive slave law. *Uncle Tom's Cabin* by Harriet Beecher Stowe was published in 1852.

Horace Mann and others established public schools and training schools for teachers. The women's movement, featuring an 1848 meeting in Seneca Falls, New York, did not achieve much success. Abolitionists were active. The Underground Railroad helped slaves escape to the North. The temperance movement reduced the consumption of alcohol. Transcendentalist writers, who believed in the sanctity and importance of individual experience, were active during this period. These writers included James Fenimore Cooper, Ralph Waldo Emerson, Henry David Thoreau, and Herman Melville.

Large groups of non-English, Catholic immigrants arrived in New York. In the 1840s there was regular steamship travel between Liverpool, England and New York City.

13. Which of the following is a result of the Missouri Compromise of 1820?
    (A) Slavery was excluded in the Louisiana Purchase region.
    (B) Westward expansion continued.
    (C) Slavery was abolished.
    (D) Maine and Missouri were admitted as states.

14. Just before Texas became a state it was a
    (A) part of Mexico.
    (B) territory.
    (C) nation.
    (D) part of the Louisiana Purchase.

THE ROAD TO CIVIL WAR

Franklin Pierce was elected president in 1852. There was bloody warfare in Kansas over whether Kansas should enter the union as a free or slave state. Another significant event was Commodore Perry's visit to Japan, opening Japan to the West.

James Buchanan was elected president in 1856. In 1857 the Supreme Court decided the *Dred Scott* case. They found that Dred Scott, a slave, was property, not a citizen, and had no standing in the court.

In 1859 an erratic John Brown launched an ill-prepared raid on the arsenal in Harpers Ferry, Virginia. Brown was tried, executed, and became a martyr in the abolitionist movement.

In 1860, and again in 1864, Abraham Lincoln was elected president. Southern states sought assurances about their right to hold slaves. Slaves were too important to the southern economy, and attempts at compromise failed. South Carolina seceded in December 1860. Alabama, Georgia, Florida, Louisiana, Mississippi, and Texas soon followed. In February 1861 the Confederate States of America (CSA) was formed with Jefferson Davis as its president.

15. John Brown was
    (A) from Virginia.
    (B) for slavery.
    (C) against slavery.
    (D) from Kansas.

THE CIVIL WAR

On April 12, 1861, Confederate forces attacked Fort Sumter in South Carolina. Arkansas, North Carolina, Tennessee, and Virginia seceded once hostilities began. The war pitted brother against brother, and one in every 30 Americans was killed or wounded. The North had a larger population and an industrialized economy. The South had an agrarian economy. Neither the English nor the French (who tried to conquer Mexico) supported the South. The English did build some Confederate ships. While Northern troops performed poorly in initial battles, the North was too strong and too populous for the South. Lee's generalship during the early war years sustained the South.

Northern ships blockaded Southern ports. This blockade effectively denied foreign goods to the South. The Confederate ironclad *Merrimac* sailed out to challenge blockading ships in 1862, sinking several Union ships. The *Merrimac* was challenged and repulsed by the Union ironclad *Monitor* in March 1862.

In 1862 Lincoln issued the Emancipation Proclamation. The proclamation freed all the slaves in Confederate states. The Union launched a successful attack on the South through Tennessee. New Orleans was captured in 1862. A final wedge was driven through the South with the capture of Vicksburg, Mississippi, in 1863. Atlanta fell in 1864. Sherman then launched his infamous march to the sea, which cut a 20-mile wide swath of destruction through the South. Sherman reached the Gulf of Mexico in December 1864.

Confederate forces did much better in and around Virginia, and there were draft riots in New York City during 1863. Lee brilliantly led his army and invaded Pennsylvania in 1863. The advance ended with Lee's questionable decision to launch Pickett's charge against the massed Union forces at Gettysburg. Four months after the battle, Lincoln delivered the Gettysburg Address at the dedication of the Union Cemetery near Gettysburg. The brief transcendent address ends "...government of the people, by the people, for the people shall not perish from the earth."

In 1864 Grant took command of the Union Army of the Potomac. He waged a war of attrition against Lee. Richmond fell on April 2, 1865. On April 9, 1865, Lee surrendered at Appomattox Court House, Virginia. Lincoln was assassinated five days later on April 15, 1865.

In 1862 the Homestead Act made public lands available to Western settlers. Public lands were granted to the Union Pacific and Central Pacific companies to build rail lines from Omaha to California. After the war, farmers and settlers moved west.

16. What was the effect of the Emancipation Proclamation?
    (A) It freed slaves in the United States.
    (B) It freed slaves in the Confederate states.
    (C) It freed slaves who escaped from Confederate states.
    (D) It freed slaves who served in the Union Army.

17. The Battle of Gettysburg was fought
    (A) before New Orleans was captured.
    (B) after the Gettysburg Address.
    (C) before Atlanta fell.
    (D) after Sherman reached the Gulf of Mexico.

RECONSTRUCTION

Three civil rights amendments were adopted between 1865 and 1870.

    XIII. Prohibited slavery (1865)
    XIV. Slaves given citizenship and rights (1868)
    XV. Voting rights for former slaves (1870)

Andrew Johnson became president after Lincoln was assassinated. During his administration, William Seward acquired Alaska (Seward's Folly) and occupied Midway Island. Johnson's dismissal of Secretary of War Stanton led to Johnson's impeachment (legislative indictment). Johnson survived the impeachment ballot by one vote.

Southern states slowly returned to the Union, but troops stayed in the South until 1877. During Reconstruction, former slaves gained some power in the South. This power did not last beyond 1877. Carpetbaggers from the North collaborated with white scalawags and former slaves to keep Confederates out of power. In turn, the Black Codes and the KKK emerged as ways to subjugate and terrorize former slaves. Grandfather clauses, which stated that you couldn't vote if your grandfather didn't, were used to deny former slaves the vote.

In 1868 and again in 1872, Ulysses S. Grant was elected president. Corruption was widespread in Grant's government. The "Whiskey Ring" involved members of Grant's administration in fraud. Boss Tweed and the Tweed Ring were looting the New York City treasury.

The Indian Wars continued. In 1876 Sioux chiefs Sitting Bull and Crazy Horse defeated Custer and his cavalry at the Little Big Horn River in Montana.

18. Which of the following is most accurate about Carpetbaggers?
    (A) Carpetbaggers worked indirectly with the KKK.
    (B) Carpetbaggers moved south to improve slaves' conditions.
    (C) Carpetbaggers helped fill a power vacuum.
    (D) Carpetbaggers joined with Confederates to repress slaves.

1877–1899

Individual presidents in the late 1800s were not notable, and this was the era of caretaker presidents. The highlights of this era were the growth of business, economic conditions, and other national events and issues. The presidents in this period were:

Rutherford B. Hayes	1876	Wins a close disputed election
James A. Garfield	1880	Shot and killed in 1881
Chester Arthur	1881	Succeeds Garfield
Grover Cleveland	1884, 1892	
William Henry Harrison	1888	
William McKinley	1896, 1900	Shot and killed in 1901

In 1877 Hayes directed the removal of troops from the South and southern whites reestablished their control over the South. Reconstruction was over.

During this period most of the military action against Native Americans was concluded. Until then the government moved Native Americans onto reserved areas (reservations). But in 1887, under the Dawes Severalty Act, the federal government tried to move Native Americans from reservations into society. The effort failed, and Native Americans continued to be treated poorly.

The unfenced frontier, which had produced most of American western folklore, was shrinking. By 1890 railroads, settlers, and farmers had brought it to a final end. The railroads brought other changes to American life. Chinese immigrants who came to work on the railroads were banned from immigration by 1890. Huge herds of buffalo were killed so that they could not interfere with train travel. Railroads stimulated the economy and created a unified United States.

Inventions during this period included the telephone (Alexander Graham Bell) and the light bulb (Thomas Alva Edison). But it was business and profits that ruled the time. John D. Rockefeller formed the Standard Oil Trust. A trust could control many companies and monopolize business. Business owners cut wages and hired new workers if there was a strike. Social Darwinism, popular during this time, stressed the survival of the fittest. Trusts grew so rapidly that the Sherman Anti-Trust Act was passed in 1890. Any trust "in restraint of trade" was illegal. Sewing machines and typewriters drew many women to the workforce. Clara Barton founded the Red Cross in 1881.

Unions tried to respond. In 1878 the Knights of Labor started to organize workers successfully. The union collapsed after the Chicago Haymarket Riot in 1888 when eight police officers died. The American Federation of Labor, under Samuel Gompers, successfully organized workers in 1886. The government intervened in several strike situations. In 1894 Grover Cleveland used troops to break the Pullman Strike. In 1902 Teddy Roosevelt sided with coal miners in the Anthracite Coal Strike. Another issue was hard versus cheap money. Hard money meant that currency was linked to something valuable (gold), limiting inflation. Cheap money removes the linkage, hastening inflation.

Immigration increased dramatically after 1880. The new immigrants to the United States now came from eastern and southern Europe. Many immigrants settled in urban areas in the eastern United States. Living conditions were difficult in tenements. Urban gangs and crime were common during this period.

The temperance movement was making steady progress to prohibition (enacted in 1919). Carrie Nation was famous for smashing liquor bottles with a hatchet. Elizabeth Cady Stanton and Susan B. Anthony led the women's suffrage movement. (Suffrage for women came with the Nineteenth Amendment in 1920, nearly 125 years after the U.S. Constitution was adopted.)

During Spanish suppression of a Cuban revolt in 1898, the battleship *Maine* was sunk in Havana Harbor. Popular reaction led to the Spanish-American War in Cuba and the Philippines. The war lasted eight months with most casualties coming from disease. The Battle of San Juan Hill took place during this conflict. The treaty ending the war gave the United States Puerto Rico, Guam, and the Philippines. In unrelated actions, the United States also annexed Wake Island and Hawaii.

19. Which president was reelected during this period?
    (A) Arthur
    (B) Cleveland
    (C) Harrison
    (D) McKinley

20. Which of the following brought women to the workforce?
    (A) increased immigration
    (B) typewriters
    (C) the influence of unions
    (D) telephones

1900–1916

In 1901 Teddy Roosevelt, credited with leading the charge up San Juan Hill, succeeded McKinley. Roosevelt was reelected in 1904. Roosevelt was a progressive opposed to monopolies. Roosevelt was particularly moved by the novel *The Jungle* (Upton Sinclair), which exposed abuses in the meat-packing industry and championed conservation. Roosevelt used "big stick diplomacy," and the United States started to become policeman of the world. Roosevelt earned the Nobel Peace Prize for arranging a cessation to the Russo-Japanese War.

William Howard Taft was elected president in 1908. Taft continued Roosevelt's campaign against monopolies and established the Bureau of Mines. Some of Taft's policies on conservation offended Teddy Roosevelt. Roosevelt established the Bull Moose Party for the 1912 election.

In 1912 Woodrow Wilson was elected president with about 40 percent of the vote in a three way race with Roosevelt and Taft. Wilson was a scholarly man who hated war. Wilson established the Federal Reserve Banking System in 1913. His Federal Trade Commission Act helped unions and forbade monopolies. The Mexican Revolution in 1910 led to the U.S. army's pursuit of Pancho Villa in Mexico in 1916.

21. What is the most appropriate reference to "jungle" in this passage?
    (A) slaughterhouses
    (B) Roosevelt's travels in Africa
    (C) politics in Washington D.C.
    (D) the pursuit of Pancho Villa in Mexico

WORLD WAR I: CAUSES AND CONSEQUENCES

Europe was ripe for war. The balance of power had been destroyed, and Germany had a military advantage. There was tremendous tension in and around the Slavic, Balkan area of southeastern Europe that was controlled by the German Austro-Hungarian Empire.

Then a single act occurred. Archduke Ferdinand of Austria was assassinated on June 28, 1914. The unrest that followed led to Germany declaring war on Russia on August 1, 1914. Woodrow Wilson declared U.S. neutrality. By 1915 the Central powers of Germany, Austria-Hungary,

Bulgaria, and Turkey were at war with the Allies of England, France, Japan, and Russia. (The United States joined the Allies in 1917.)

So began the war that was to claim more than 12,000,000 lives and decimate Europe. The war consisted of two fronts—Western (France, etc.) and Eastern (Russia, etc.). The war soon deteriorated into trench warfare, which led to a virtual stalemate for four destructive years. Airplanes, tanks, poison gas, and machine guns were all introduced during this conflict.

The Russian Revolution occurred in 1917 as World War I was underway. The Bolsheviks gained power. As they had promised, the Bolsheviks withdrew from the war, even though Russia gave up more than 1,000,000 square miles of land with more than 50,000,000 people in the peace settlement.

The sinking of the cruise liner *Lusitania* in 1915 with 139 Americans on board marked the beginning of American involvement in the war. Wilson was outraged when Germany started to use submarines and protested when the *Lusitania* was sunk. The Germans agreed to stop unrestricted submarine warfare. In 1917 the Germans resumed unrestricted submarine warfare, and the United States declared war on Germany. The American Expeditionary Force (AEF) arrived in France on June 25, 1917. The Allies fought back German attacks and launched their own offensive in 1918. Germany signed a very demanding armistice, and the war ended on the eleventh hour of the eleventh day of the eleventh month in 1918.

The Germans were forced to sign the Treaty of Versailles on June 28, 1919, which officially ended World War I. Japan and Italy (Allies) were not pleased with some of the terms of the Treaty of Versailles.

As the war was drawing to a close, Wilson presented his Fourteen Points. These points form a basis for the Treaty of Versailles, which ended the war, and for the League of Nations. The league was formed in 1919 and lasted until the 1940s. The forerunner of the United Nations was built on President Wilson's Fourteen Points. The United States' seat was never filled because the Senate did not ratify the Treaty of Versailles. The League of Nations sought to provide mechanisms for worldwide monetary control, conflict resolution, and humanitarian assistance.

22. What was the Bolsheviks' main impact on World War I?
    (A) They gave up more than 1,000,000 square miles of land.
    (B) They removed a German adversary.
    (C) They lost more than 50,000,000 citizens.
    (D) They won the Russian Revolution.

POST-WORLD WAR I AMERICA

Warren G. Harding was elected president in 1920. Calvin Coolidge became president in 1923 when Harding died. Coolidge was elected in 1924. Herbert Hoover was elected president in 1928. Prohibition dominated this period, and America entered the roaring twenties. Speakeasys had liquor for those who wanted in, and distilling became a huge underground industry. Gangsters such as Al Capone were prominent on the American scene. Sigmund Freud's views of sexuality had become well known, and the country entered the sexual revolution. In the "Monkey Trial," John Scopes was tried and convicted of teaching evolution in a Tennessee school.

In October 1929 the stock market crashed. People lost their investments and often their homes. Banks failed, and people lost their deposits. Excessive borrowing, greed, and ineffective regulations were all factors in the collapse. The Depression began and spread throughout the world. During the Depression, unemployment reached 25 percent. Some workers had no employment for years. Hoover took an ineffective hands-off approach. He did support the

Reconstruction Finance Corporation, which lent money to employers in the hope that it would "trickle down" to the unemployed.

In 1932 Franklin Delano Roosevelt (FDR) was elected president in a landslide victory with about 89 percent of the electoral vote. He was reelected in 1936, 1940, and 1944. Roosevelt's Democratic Party enjoyed an enormous margin in the Congress during this time. FDR offered the country a New Deal. He said, "the only thing we have to fear is fear itself," and held radio fireside chats that reassured the country. Some of the New Deal actions follow in a sort of governmental alphabet soup.

- The Civilian Conservation Corps (CCC) put unemployed young men to work building roads, stopping erosion, and reforesting the country.
- The Works Project Administration (WPA) gave other public service jobs.
- The Agricultural Adjustment Act provided subsidies to farmers for not growing crops.
- The Federal Deposit Insurance Corporation (FDIC) insured bank deposits.
- The Securities and Exchange Commission (SEC) oversaw the stock market.
- The Tennessee Valley Authority (TVA) built hydroelectric plants and controlled floods.

23. When it came to money, Hoover's approach is best described as
    (A) antiworker.
    (B) bottom up.
    (C) top down.
    (D) antiunion.

24. During this period, Prohibition dominated by prohibiting
    (A) speakeasys.
    (B) liquor.
    (C) smuggling.
    (D) gang activity.

THE ROAD TO WORLD WAR II

The Depression of the late 1920s ruined the German economy. Imports and exports fell while unemployment soared. Germany was also frustrated by what they saw as the harsh terms of the Treaty of Versailles.

Out of all this emerged Adolf Hitler, a would-be artist who had emerged from World War I as a decorated corporal. In 1921 he became the leader of the Nazi Party and put together a group of "brown shirts" to exert his will forcefully. With 50,000 or so followers he tried to take power in 1923 in the Beer Hall Putsch. He was arrested and jailed, where he dictated *Mein Kampf (My Struggle)* to Rudolf Hess.

Between 1930 and 1932 Hitler's Nazi Party got increasing vote counts. Hitler was made Chancellor, and then his party gained control of the legislature. In 1933 all political parties were outlawed except the Nazi Party. In that same year the Gestapo was established, and Hitler became Fuhrer on August 2, 1934.

Anti-Semitism was rampant in Germany, and Jews were declined civil service employment. The regime became a harsh dictatorship in which no dissent was tolerated. However, economic conditions improved dramatically under Hitler, and military manufacturing just about erased unemployment. Hitler was supported by the German people, and the world was moving toward war.

The United States proclaimed neutrality in 1935, 1936, and 1937. No belligerents were permitted to purchase arms from America. The United States also stayed neutral in the Spanish Civil War.

The Spanish Civil War (1936–1939) provided a testing ground for Hitler and his military leaders. The German Air Force fought on the side of the Fascist leader Francisco Franco, and the war united Hitler and the Italian dictator Benito Mussolini. In 1938 Hitler bullied and then captured Austria, and later annexed Czechoslovakia.

The Depression also caused great economic hardship in Japan, and military leaders gained more power. In 1931 Japan occupied Manchuria, and in 1937 war broke out between Japan and China. In 1938 Japan announced its intentions to establish a new order in Asia. In 1940 Japan signed a formal alliance with Germany and Italy.

25. What main factor led to Hitler's rise to power in Germany?
    (A) popular support
    (B) anti-Semitism
    (C) the Depression
    (D) American neutrality

WORLD WAR II BEFORE PEARL HARBOR

On September 1, 1939, Hitler invaded Poland without provocation. England and France declared war on Germany a few days later, and World War II began.

The Soviets signed a nonaggression pact with Germany, occupied Estonia, Latvia, and Lithuania, and forced concessions from Finland. The Allies included England, France, and eventually the United States. The Axis powers included Germany, Japan, and Italy.

German forces launched a major offensive against Belgium, France and the Netherlands and attacked Denmark and Norway. The Germans by-passed the fortified Maginot line armament by attacking through Luxembourg. About 400,000 British and French troops were trapped but managed to escape without their equipment from around Dunkirk.

Germany tried to conquer Britain from the air in the Battle of Britain. While devastating, this tactic was unsuccessful. The Germans considered and then abandoned a plan to invade England.

Just before this time, British Prime Minister Neville Chamberlain was replaced by Winston Churchill. Churchill had long warned of German intentions. Once the war began, the United States cooperated with England. The Lend-Lease Act of 1941 allowed the president to sell, lend, or transfer arms to countries vital to American defense. Roosevelt used this act to aid England.

Paris fell in June 1940, and France surrendered. The Vichy government of France followed a policy of collaboration. Only a few Frenchmen joined the Free French movement led from London by Charles DeGaulle.

In 1940 Charles Lindbergh, the first person to fly solo across the Atlantic (1927), supported Hitler's call for an expanded Germany. Roosevelt said the United States would not enter the war, and he was reelected. In 1941 Roosevelt met with Churchill off Newfoundland and signed the Atlantic Charter. The charter's postwar goals roughly incorporated Roosevelt's Four Freedoms: Freedom of Speech and Expression; Freedom of Religion; Freedom from Want; Freedom from Fear.

Hitler turned his attention to the Soviet Union in June 1941. He began Operation Barbarossa, an invasion of the Soviet Union with 3,000,000 Axis troops. The invasion was initially successful, and Axis troops actually entered the suburbs of Moscow in November 1941. A combination of the Soviet winter, very long supply lines, and a Soviet counterattack drove the Axis forces away from Moscow during the winter of 1941–1942. The German army attacked again and was stopped literally in the streets of Stalingrad. Hitler forbade a retreat, and German forces were surrounded and decimated. The German forces at Stalingrad surrendered in January 1943, and the Soviet forces moved to the offensive.

26. What were the Soviet Union's actions at the beginning of World War II?
    (A) to attack Germany
    (B) to defend Stalingrad
    (C) to counteract Axis forces
    (D) to occupy other countries

WORLD WAR II: PEARL HARBOR TO CONCLUSION

On December 7, 1941, Japan attacked the United States at Pearl Harbor. The attack brought the United States into war against Japan, Germany, and Italy. American involvement in the war ultimately led to the defeat of Axis forces.

The Italians and the Afrika Corps under German General Erwin Rommel controlled North Africa. Combined British and American forces launched a combined offensive that trapped Axis forces and led to their surrender in 1943.

During the early years of the war, German U-boats were winning the Battle of the Atlantic. Adequate supplies could not reach England and Europe. Improved ships, planes, and sonar reversed this trend, and by 1943 the Atlantic was an unsafe place for German submarines.

In January 1943 Churchill and Roosevelt met at Casablanca and planned the future conduct of the war. On June 6, 1944, after the successful invasion of Italy, the Allied forces under Dwight Eisenhower launched Operation Overlord, an invasion of France from England. It was the largest amphibious operation ever undertaken. The invasion was successful and by the end of 1944 all France had been recaptured and Allied forces were poised at German borders. Soviet forces had also been successful in their operations in Poland. Resistance to Hitler's leadership developed in Germany. On July 20, 1944, Hitler survived a bomb blast designed to kill him. His survival meant that there would be no truce.

American, British, Soviet, and other Allied forces attacked Germany simultaneously. Hitler committed suicide in his bunker, and the German army surrendered. Already, American and British leaders were questioning the results of their alliance with Stalin and the Soviet Union.

In February 1945, Churchill, Roosevelt, and the Soviet leader, Stalin, met at Yalta and agreements were reached about postwar political subdivisions. Many have criticized Roosevelt's participation in this meeting. In their view, Roosevelt made agreements too favorable to Stalin. In July 1945 Stalin and Churchill met at Potsdam with newly inaugurated President Truman (Roosevelt had died after the Yalta meeting). While at the conference, Churchill was defeated for prime minister.

Truman learned of the successful test of the atomic bomb (Manhattan Project) while at Potsdam. After deciding that there was no practical way to demonstrate the bomb's force, it was dropped twice on Japan. The cities of Hiroshima and Nagasaki were obliterated. A new era of warfare had begun and the Japanese surrendered immediately. The surrender was taken on the battleship *Missouri* in Tokyo Bay under the leadership of General Douglas MacArthur.

With about 12,000,000 Americans in the armed forces during World War II, unemployment was eliminated. New businesses were created, and many new workers, particularly women, entered the work force. "Rosie the Riveter" became the symbol of these new workers. The Office of Price Administration (OPA) issued ration books and set prices. Other government boards regulated business and labor. The only documented attack on the United States occurred when a Japanese submarine shelled a refinery in California. However, fear of Japanese Americans reached hysterical proportions. All Japanese Americans, most of them American citizens, were sent to internment camps. None were accused of wrongdoing. They were not released until the end of the war.

27. Which of the following statements best describes events at the Potsdam Conference?
    (A) Roosevelt died
    (B) Truman attended
    (C) Churchill didn't attend
    (D) Roosevelt too lenient

28. The attack on Pearl Harbor
    (A) led to the control of North Africa by Italian and German forces.
    (B) defeated the Axis powers.
    (C) was on Midway Island.
    (D) brought Italy into war with the United States.

1946–1949

The Cold War broke out immediately after World War II. Divisions appeared between Russia and the other Allies. Speaking in Fulton, Missouri in 1946, Churchill said that an Iron Curtain had descended across the Continent, describing Soviet isolation from the rest of the world.

Germany and Berlin were divided into four Occupation Zones—American, British, French, and Soviet. Berlin was inside the Soviet zone. The Soviets blockaded land access to Berlin, but the blockade was overcome by the Berlin Airlift.

After succeeding Roosevelt, Harry Truman won an upset victory over New York Governor Thomas Dewey in 1948 and served as president until 1952. Truman reacted to the Cold War and fear of communism by issuing the Truman Doctrine. The doctrine stipulated that the United States would help any free countries resisting armed minorities. The United States entered a period of Soviet containment designed to counter worldwide Soviet pressure. At home, Truman used the Smith Act, designed for use against World War II subversives, to jail domestic Communist leaders. A Loyalty Board and the House UnAmerican Activities Committee also investigated Communist infiltration into government.

The Marshall Plan helped rebuild Europe with West Germany reaping the greatest benefits. The United Nations was established with a Security Council consisting mainly of Allied countries. Stalin pushed for recovery at home while taking further control of Eastern Europe. Germany remained under Allied occupation.

The mass killings of Jews in concentration camps during Hitler's regime gained support for a Jewish State in Palestine. In 1948 Israel was established and a series of conflicts with Egypt and other Arab states began. Following the Berlin Airlift, the North Atlantic Treaty Organization was formed, which united the European allies in a military alliance. NATO was strengthened in the aftermath of the Korean War. The Cold War between the Western powers and Russia became a nuclear arms race.

29. Jailing suspected terrorists living in the United States is most compatible with which of the following?
    (A) the Cold War
    (B) the Truman Doctrine
    (C) the Smith Act
    (D) the Marshall Plan

1950–1953

Brooding and paranoid, Stalin died in 1953. Khrushchev and his successors Brezhnev, Andropov, and Gorbachev attacked his ruthlessness and relaxed the political climate. Gradually, countries occupied or controlled by the Soviet Union sought freedom or autonomy. These freedom movements, such as in Hungary, were usually thwarted by a Soviet military reaction.

Britain and Western Europe formed a Common Market designed to create a free trade zone and to stimulate commerce. Soviet Communist influence decreased markedly in the 1980s. Countries occupied by Russia sought and gained freedom. East and West Germany were reunited at a great cost to West Germany. Satellites of Russia, such as Cuba, stopped receiving aid. Provinces of Russia were in revolt and there was open warfare between the Russian President Yeltsin and the Russian parliament. Some concluded that the Cold War was over and that communism had fallen.

The undeclared war in Korea broke out with an invasion by North Korea in 1950. American troops were sent to fight on South Korea's side. Later the defense of South Korea was under United Nation auspices. As UN troops approached the Yalu River border with China, China entered the war and forced UN forces back to the 38th parallel, the original boundary between North and South Korea. In a notable act of the war, Truman dismissed Douglas MacArthur as Commander-in-Chief of American forces because MacArthur advocated the nuclear bombing of North Korea and mainland China.

30. According to this section, a satellite is a
    (A) country.
    (B) space vehicle.
    (C) province of Russia.
    (D) part of the United Nations.

1952–1959

In 1952 Dwight Eisenhower, former Allied supreme commander in Europe, was elected president. He was reelected in 1956. After his election, Eisenhower went to Korea. Shortly thereafter, an armistice was established at the 38th parallel. Under Secretary of State John Foster Dulles, the United States embarked on a campaign of "brinkmanship." The policy was designed to show American resolve and toughness. In 1957 Congress approved the Eisenhower Doctrine, which gave the president the right to use force against aggressive acts by any country under the control of communism.

Concurrent with the beginning of the Korean War, Senator Joseph McCarthy used the communist scare to propel himself to national prominence (McCarthyism). He accused many Americans of anti-American activities, and needlessly ruined many lives. Accusations against the army led to Army-McCarthy hearings and to McCarthy's censure by the Congress.

In 1954 the Supreme Court decided the landmark case of *Brown v. Board of Education*. The Court found that "separate but equal" schools were unconstitutional. In 1955 the Supreme Court ordered an end to school segregation. In Little Rock, Arkansas, the governor ordered the National Guard to prevent minority students from entering the high school. President Eisenhower sent troops, nationalized the Guard, and the Little Rock nine entered school. In subsequent years, many public schools were closed in the South and replaced by private academies to escape desegregation laws.

In 1955 Dr. Martin Luther King, Jr., led the Montgomery bus boycott. In 1956 the Supreme Court found that segregation on local buses was unconstitutional. Civil disobedience and nonviolent protest were used throughout the South to gain civil rights victories.

31. The ruling in the case of *Brown v. Board of Education* found that
    (A) school segregation was unconstitutional.
    (B) separate but equal schools were unconstitutional.
    (C) segregation in any form whatsoever was unconstitutional.
    (D) school boards had to provide equal schooling for all children in a district.

KENNEDY AND JOHNSON

John F. Kennedy was elected president in 1960. After his assassination in 1963, Lyndon Johnson succeeded him, and Johnson was elected in 1964.

John Kennedy proclaimed the "New Frontier" but was unsuccessful in moving legislation through Congress. He also began the vigorous exploration of space and established the Peace Corps.

Kennedy eventually ordered troops to ensure that James Meredith was enrolled as a student in the University of Alabama. During his term, there were civil rights sit-ins in Birmingham, Alabama, and a civil rights march of 250,000 on Washington, D.C. It was at this march that Dr. Martin Luther King, Jr. made his "I have a dream" speech.

In 1961 Kennedy supported the Bay of Pigs invasion of Cuba. The invasion was disastrous. Some months later, Soviet missiles were located in Cuba. Kennedy established a blockade of Cuba and entered into a confrontation with Soviet leader Khrushev. Eventually, the missiles were withdrawn, and Cuba maintained its sovereignty.

John Kennedy is the president best known for his assassination. On November 22, 1963, John Kennedy was killed while visiting Dallas, Texas. The Warren Commission was formed to investigate the assassination and found that Lee Harvey Oswald was the lone assassin. Many disagree with this finding.

Lyndon Johnson succeeded Kennedy. Johnson was very effective in getting Kennedy's, and his own, legislative proposals through Congress. He supported a number of laws designed to create the Great Society and to launch a War on Poverty.

The War on Poverty included the Job Corps and Project Head Start, Upward Bound for bright but poor high school students, and VISTA, the domestic version of the Peace Corps.

Other Great Society programs included:

- The Water Quality and Air Quality Acts
- The Elementary and Secondary Education Act
- The National Foundation for Arts and Humanities
- Medicare
- Cabinet-level department of Housing and Urban Development (HUD)

32. It is correct to infer from this passage that President Kennedy
    (A) did not make errors in decisions about Cuba.
    (B) did organize the civil rights march on Washington, D.C.
    (C) was not effective implementing New Frontier ideas.
    (D) was responsible for the majority of the Great Society programs.

VIETNAM WAR

The Vietnam War stretched across the 12 years of the Kennedy and Johnson presidencies and into the presidency of Richard Nixon. While the war officially began with Kennedy as president, its actual beginnings stretched back many years.

Before the war, Vietnam was called French Indochina. During World War II the United States supported Ho Chi Minh in Vietnam as he fought Japan. After the war, the United States supported the French over Ho Chi Minh as France sought to regain control of its former colony.

Fighting broke out between the French and Ho Chi Minh with support from Mao Tse-tung, the leader of mainland China. Even with substantial material aid from the United States, France could not defeat Vietnam. In 1950 the French were defeated at Dien Bien Phu.

Subsequent negotiations in Geneva divided Vietnam into North and South with Ho Chi Minh in control of the North. Ngo Dinh Diem was installed by the United States as a leader in the South. Diem never gained popular support in the South. Following a harsh crackdown by Diem, the Viet Cong organized to fight against him. During the Eisenhower administration, 2,000 American "advisors" were sent to South Vietnam.

When Kennedy came to office, he approved a CIA coup to overthrow Diem. When Johnson took office, he was not interested in compromise. In 1964 Johnson started a massive buildup of forces in Vietnam until the number reached more than 500,000. The Gulf of Tonkin Resolution, passed by Congress, gave Johnson discretion to pursue the war.

Living and fighting conditions were terrible. Although American forces had many successes, neither that nor the massive bombing of North Vietnam led to victory. In 1968 the Vietcong launched the Tet Offensive. While ground gained in the offensive was ultimately recaptured, the offensive shook the confidence of military leaders.

The war cost 350,000 American casualties. At home, there were deep divisions. War protests sprung up all over the United States. Half a million people protested in New York during 1967 and the tension between hawks and doves increased throughout the country.

33. When it comes to Vietnam, it is most reasonable to say that
    (A) Geneva negotiations put Ho Chi Minh in control of the country.
    (B) Ngo Dinh Diem eventually took control of the country.
    (C) the French took control after World War II.
    (D) the country received American support.

NIXON, FORD, CARTER

Richard Nixon was elected in 1970 in the midst of this turmoil. While vigorously pursuing the war, he and Secretary of State Henry Kissinger were holding secret negotiations with North Vietnam. In 1973 an agreement was finally drawn up to end the war. American prisoners were repatriated although there were still a number Missing in Action (MIA), and U.S. troops withdrew from Vietnam.

Nixon was elected again in 1972, only to resign on August 8, 1974, during the Watergate investigation. Richard Nixon was the only U.S. president in history to resign. Spiro Agnew, Nixon's vice president, had resigned before him in 1973.

The economy deteriorated during Nixon's administration. The expensive Great Society programs and the Vietnam War had increased the federal deficit. The OPEC oil embargo forced inflation up and worsened the economic situation.

Nixon's greatest diplomatic contributions were in China and the Middle East. He opened a dialogue with China and, through Henry Kissinger, arranged a peace settlement to the 1973 Yom Kippur War between Egypt/Syria and Israel.

Nixon is best known for the Watergate scandal and his resignation. The resignation was caused initially by an unnecessary break-in by Republican operatives into the Democratic campaign headquarters in the Watergate office complex. The Watergate story was covered by Bob Woodward and Carl Bernstein, reporters for the *Washington Post*. Nixon was later taped in his office as he ordered the FBI to call off their Watergate investigation. When the Supreme Court ordered that these tapes be made public, Nixon resigned. Gerald Ford was the first

American president not elected through the electoral college. Ford replaced Agnew as vice president after Agnew was forced to resign and succeeded to the presidency when Nixon resigned. Unemployment and interest rates grew dramatically under Ford. Responses to these problems were inadequate, and the country started to enter a recession.

In 1976 Jimmy Carter was elected president. Carter introduced no major programs. The economy worsened under Carter with interest rates over 21 percent and double-digit inflation. The federal deficit continued to grow, and domestic programs became more expensive.

REAGAN, BUSH, CLINTON, BUSH

Ronald Reagan was elected president in 1980 and again in 1984. Reagan was a conservative ideologue who believed in supply-side economics. Supply-side theory held that tax cuts would result in more investment, and, in turn, these investments would create more jobs.

Under Reagan, tax rates were cut drastically. The economy emerged from recession, and the interest rates were reduced. However, government revenues did not increase, and the federal deficit sky-rocketed. Homelessness grew to significant proportions and became a major urban problem.

Deregulation of the savings and loan organizations during Reagan's presidency led to abuses with a multibillion dollar bankruptcy of these groups. The cost of the bankruptcies was borne by taxpayers.

34. Gerald Ford was
    (A) elected vice president.
    (B) never elected.
    (C) not elected through the electoral college.
    (D) directly responsible for Nixon's decision to resign.

In 1988 George Bush was elected president. Bush continued Reagan's economic programs but was forced to raise taxes in 1990. This reversal of his promise "read my lips, no new taxes" probably led to his defeat in the 1992 election. S & Ls continued to fail, and the national debt continued to grow dramatically. The Communist bloc was disintegrating, and the Cold War was coming to a close.

Bill Clinton was elected president in 1992 and again in 1996. He was the first president impeached (legislative indictment) since Andrew Johnson. He was acquitted by the Senate. Health reform, deficit reduction, and crime were three major issues of his administration. Inflation was low and the stock market soared during most of Clinton's presidency.

George W. Bush, son of the earlier president, was elected president in 2000 in a hotly contested process decided in the Supreme Court. Terrorist attacks on September 11, 2001 set the agenda for his administration. Events resulting from these attacks included military engagements in Afghanistan and Iraq and action against terrorist organizations in the United States and abroad.

35. When we say supply-side economics, we mean
    (A) less taxes.
    (B) more supply.
    (C) more deficits.
    (D) less employment.

PREHISTORY AND THE DEVELOPMENT OF EARLY CIVILIZATIONS

World population grew steadily from 1 A.D. through 1650 A.D. After 1650 A.D., world population exploded. Rapid population growth has made it more difficult to provide for everyone. A table showing population growth follows.

1 A.D.	500	1000	1650	1850	1930	1975	2000
200 million	220 million	300 million	500 million	1 billion	2 billion	4 billion	6.1 billion

Current knowledge of human history stretches back about 8,000 years to 6000 B.C. The earliest established date is around 4200 B.C. Most historians agree that civilization began when writing was invented about 3500 B.C. This date separates prehistoric from historic times.

In prehistoric time, humans used calendars, invented and used the wheel, played flutes and harps, and alloyed copper. These humans also created pottery and colored ceramics. There was an active trade in the Mediterranean Sea with Cretan shipping most prominent. What follows is a brief summary of historic times.

The earliest recorded civilizations were in Mesopotamia. This region was centered near the Tigris and Euphrates Rivers in what is now Iraq and extended from the western Mediterranean to Palestine to the Persian Gulf. The Sumerians inhabited Mesopotamia from 4000 B.C. to 2000 B.C. and probably invented the first writing—wedge-shaped symbols called cuneiform.

The Old Babylonians (2000–1550 B.C.) inhabited this area and established a capital at Babylonia (hanging gardens). King Hammurabi, known for the justice code named after him, ruled during the middle of this period. The militaristic Assyrians ruled from 1000 to about 600 B.C. The Assyrians were followed by the New Babylonians under King Nebuchadnezzar from about 600 to 500 B.C. A defeat by the Persians in the fifth century B.C. led to a dissolution of Mesopotamia.

36. According to experts, about when did civilization begin?
    (A) 4200 B.C.
    (B) 4000 B.C.
    (C) 3500 B.C.
    (D) 2000 B.C.

CLASSICAL EGYPT AND GREECE

Egyptian history is usually divided into seven periods. Pharaohs became deities during the Old Kingdom (2685–2180 B.C.). Most pyramids were built during the Fourth Dynasty of the Old Kingdom (about 2600–2500 B.C.) Our common vision of Egyptians in horse-drawn chariots marked the Second Intermediate Period (1785–1560 B.C.). The Egyptians invaded Palestine and enslaved the Jews during the New Kingdom (1560–1085 B.C.). King Tutankhamen reigned during this period. In the first millennium B.C. Egypt was controlled by many groups and leaders, including Alexander the Great. In about 30 B.C., Egypt came under control of the Roman Empire.

Greece has always been linked to its nearby islands. One of these islands, Crete, was inhabited by the Minoans (about 2600–1250 B.C.). During this time the ancient city of Troy was built. The mainland, inhabited by the Myceneans since about 2000 B.C., eventually incorporated Crete and the Minoan Civilization about 1200 B.C.

Dorian invasions from the north around 1200 B.C. led to the defeat of the Myceneans and to the Greek Dark Ages from 1200 to 750 B.C. The Trojan War, which occurred during this period, was described by Homer in the *Iliad*.

Athens (founded 1000 B.C.) and Sparta (founded 750 B.C.) were famous Greek city-states. Draco was a harsh Athenian leader and democracy was established only in 527 B.C. During this period, the Parthenon was built in Athens. In Sparta, each male citizen became a lifetime soldier at the age of 7.

The Classic Age of Greece began about 500 B.C. when Athens defeated Persia Marathon and declined with the Peloponnesian War (430–404 B.C.) between Athens and Sparta.

The Classic Age was a time for the development of great literature and great thought. During this period, Socrates, Plato, and Aristotle taught and wrote in Greece. (Aristotle tutored Alexander the Great after Alexander conquered Greece. In this relatively brief period, Aeschylus wrote his *Orestea Trilogy* and Sophocles wrote *Oedipus Rex*. Also writing during this period were Aristophanes, Euripides, Herodotus, and Thucydides.

The Hellenistic Age begins with the death of Alexander the Great. Alexander lived for only 33 years (356–323 B.C.) but during his brief life he carved out a huge empire. His conquests led to the spread of Greek culture and thought to most of that region of the world. This age ended about 30 B.C. when Greece, like Egypt, was incorporated in the Roman Empire.

Epicurus and Zeno wrote during this time. The Hellenistic Age was a time of great scientific and mathematical development. Euclid wrote his *Elements* in the third century B.C. while Archimedes and Erasthotenes made important discoveries later in the period.

37. Which of the following is the most likely cause of the dispersion of Greek culture?
    (A) science
    (B) learning
    (C) literature
    (D) tutoring

38. Approximately how long was it from the beginning of the New Kingdom in Egypt to the end of the Old Kingdom?
    (A) 475 years
    (B) 620 years
    (C) 1,105 years
    (D) 1,600 years

ROME

Some say that Rome was founded between 700 and 800 B.C. The real founding of Rome may be closer to 500 B.C. The Roman Senate consisting of landowners was eventually replaced by the Plebeian Assembly about 300 B.C. as the governing body of Rome.

Rome acquired all of Italy by about 300 B.C., defeated Carthage (in North Africa) during a series of Punic Wars, and controlled both sides of the Mediterranean by about 150 B.C. The Roman victories were marked by one defeat at the hands of the Carthaginian general Hannibal. Julius Caesar and Pompeii were leaders in the first century B.C. and Spartacus led a rebellion by slaves. Caesar was assassinated on the Ides of March, 44 B.C. in a conspiracy led by Brutus ("et tu Brute") and Cassius. Octavius defeated Antony and Cleopatra at the Battle of Acton around 38 B.C. Following this, Octavius was crowned the first "God-Emperor." The 200 years of peace that followed, called the Pax Romana, is the longest period of peace in the Western World.

The birth of the Roman Empire coincided roughly with the beginning of the A.D. era. During the first century A.D., the Emperor Nero committed suicide. Jewish zealots also committed suicide at Masada following the destruction of their temple by the Romans. The empire reached its greatest size during this century. A code of law was established. Scientists Ptomely and Pliny the Elder were active, and the Colosseum was constructed.

Following the death of Emperor Marcus Aurelius, the Roman Empire began its decline. Civil war raged in the 200s A.D. and there were defeats of provinces by the Persians and the Goths. Constantine's attempts to stop the empire's decline were ultimately fruitless, and the Visigoths looted Rome in about 400 A.D.

39. How are the United States Senate and the Roman Senate most different?
    (A) United States senators do not have to own land.
    (B) United States senators do not have to be citizens.
    (C) Roman senators were often members the Plebian Assembly, which is similar to the United States House of Representatives.
    (D) Roman senators served about 2,300 years ago.

FEUDALISM IN JAPAN

The Japanese Islands had an early civilization by 3000 B.C. Throughout the whole B.C. period Japan remained a primitive society overrun by successive invasions of Mongols and Malays. Around the beginning of the A.D. period, Chinese writers referred to Japan as a backward nation.

The first religion in Japan was Shinto, a cult of nature and ancestor worship. Around 550 A.D., Buddhism was introduced in Japan and quickly spread throughout the country. Throughout this period Japan existed in the shadow of China. Chinese words are still found today in the Japanese language.

Japanese emperors had always been powerful, godlike figures. But around 1150 A.D., Shoguns were installed as the permanent leaders of Japan, leaving the emperor with only ceremonial duties. Until that time Shoguns had been only military leaders. In the following years a succession of Shoguns were ultimately unsuccessful in unifying Japan. Japan was reduced to a group of warring states.

Around 1600 the strong Tokugawa Shogunate was formed. This Shogunate ruled Japan until 1868. Japan was at peace for most of this period. Under this Shogunate, Christians were persecuted, and in 1639 foreign ships were forbidden in Japanese waters. This period of isolation lasted until American Commodore Perry forced Japan to sign a treaty in 1853, opening limited trade with the West.

The Menji period of Japan lasted from 1868 until 1912. Feudalism established under the Shogunates was outlawed, and Japan started to develop an industrial economy. As lords lost their feudal manors, the importance of the samurai (a lord's private soldiers) declined. In 1876 samurai were forbidden to wear their swords. Some 250,000 samurai rebelled in 1876 but were easily defeated by soldiers bearing modern weapons. Buddhism declined, and Shintoism enjoyed a rebirth during this period. Japan actively sought contact with Western nations and adopted a number of Western customs and institutions. In 1889 the first Diet or parliament was established.

In 1894 Japan entered into war with China (Sino-Japanese War) over a dispute about Korea. Japan defeated China, establishing Japan as a military power. In 1904 Japan entered into war with Russia (the Russo-Japanese War). Japan also emerged victorious in this war and established a new balance of power between East and West. This new balance of power set the stage for conflicts yet to come.

40. Which of the following was the basis for a rebellion in Japan?
    (A) Mongol invasions
    (B) Korean dispute
    (C) wearing swords
    (D) Buddhism's spread

FEUDALISM IN EUROPE

Charles Martel, a Frankish palace mayor who became known as Charlemagne, halted a Muslim advance in what is now France. Later he ruled the Frankish kingdom from about 770–815 A.D. He was named emperor of the Holy Roman Empire in 800 A.D. by Pope Leo III. Charlemagne's authority was also accepted in the East. After much fighting in Europe, the Normans, under William the Conqueror, defeated England at the Battle of Hastings in 1066.

The High Middle Ages lasted from the Battle of Hastings until about 1300. During this time the Roman road system was rebuilt, and Europe grew larger than the Muslim and Byzantine Empires.

In England a long series of battles with the Danes and Danish occupation preceded the Battle of Hastings. Henry II arranged for Archbishop Thomas Becket's murder in the late 1100s followed by the reign of Richard the Lionhearted and the signing of the Magna Carta in 1215.

There were at least seven crusades from 1100 to 1300 to dislodge "infidels" from the Holy Land. The third crusade was led by Richard the Lionhearted. Ultimately, these crusades were unsuccessful, and many Muslims and Jews were massacred. Jews were persecuted throughout Europe beginning with the first crusade. Hundreds of Jewish communities were destroyed in the area of present-day Germany alone.

Scholasticism, an attempt to bring together the Christian faith and logic, was active during this period with leaders such as St. Anselm, Thomas Aquinas, Albertus Magnus, and Peter Abelard.

41. Which of the following preceded the Battle of Hastings?
    (A) scholasticism
    (B) battles with Danes
    (C) the High Middle Ages
    (D) the Crusades

CHINA TO 1900

Early civilization developed near the Yellow River in ancient times. It appears that cities developed in China after they appeared in Egypt. The Shang Dynasty emerged in China about 1500 B.C. and lasted until about 1100 B.C. This dynasty is known for its works of art, particularly its fine bronze castings and walled cities. Life in this dynasty did not emphasize religion, a trait noted also in modern China. The Chou Dynasty ruled from about 1100 to 250 B.C. Jade carvings and Chinese calligraphy were developed during this time.

Confucius was born near the end of this dynasty around 550 B.C. He was a philosopher who was concerned with the way people acted. He emphasized regard for authority, self-control, conformity, and respectful behavior. Confucius had little impact during his lifetime. His disciples carried his thoughts and ideas throughout China. Eventually he came to be revered, and his ideas and sayings give a distinct shape and form to Chinese thought.

Following the Chou Dynasty were the Ch'in rulers, including the first emperor of China. During this time the Great Wall of China was expanded and built along the northern Chinese border. Confucian writings were destroyed by these leaders.

A successor in this period founded the Han Dynasty, which ruled China from about 200 B.C. to 220 A.D. During this period Confucius became a revered figure, and his writings were the objects of careful study.

Invaders from the north attacked China around 315 A.D. and controlled north China until about 560 A.D. The Chinese maintained their independence in the south, but China was divided into a number of states. Influence from India established Buddhism in China during this time.

China was reunited under the Sui Dynasty about 580 A.D. In 618 the Sui Dynasty was overthrown. The T'ang Dynasty that followed lasted until about 906 A.D. During this time Turkish incursions were halted, and Chinese influence grew to include Korea and northern Indochina. The T'angs developed a civil service testing apparatus, and the Chinese economy improved during this time. During the Sung Dynasty (960–1279 A.D.) gunpowder was used for weapons. The nation prospered during this time, and the standard of living rose to new heights.

The Mongols, under Genghis Kahn, invaded and controlled much of northern China by 1215. Kublai Khan followed, and his successors ruled China until 1368. During this time the Chinese launched a fleet to attack Japan. The fleet was destroyed in a typhoon. The Japanese refer to this typhoon as the divine wind—*kamikaze*.

In 1368 the Khan Dynasty was overthrown, and the Ming Dynasty was born. Rulers of the Ming Dynasty launched a campaign to stamp out any remnants of the Mongol occupation. Even though there were some contacts with the West, the rulers of this dynasty forbade sea travel to foreign lands. Beginning in 1433 Chinese isolation and suspicion of foreigners grew. The Ming Dynasty reigned until 1644 when it was overthrown by the Manchu Dynasty.

Contacts with the West increased under the Manchu Dynasty. However, in 1757 the Chinese government became offended by some Western traders. They allowed trade only through the port of Canton and under very strict regulations. At that time, opium was one of the few Chinese <u>imports</u>. The Chinese government objected to these imports, and this led to the Opium War of 1839, won by the British. Western intervention in China continued through 1900.

42. What was the cause of the Chinese-British Opium War?
   (A) The Chinese resisted importation of opium.
   (B) The British wanted to stop the exportation of opium from China.
   (C) The Chinese wanted to import opium only through Canton.
   (D) The Chinese and the British joined forces to fight against opium dealers.

43. Which group developed a way to place people in jobs?
   (A) The T'angs
   (B) The Chous
   (C) The Shangs
   (D) The Suis

INDIA TO 1900

Early, advanced civilizations developed in the Indus Valley. The inhabitants were called Dravidians. Around 2500 B.C., a series of floods and foreign invasions appears to have all but destroyed these civilizations. Between 2500 and 1500 B.C. the Dravidians were forced into southern India by a nomadic band with Greek and Persian roots.

The conquerors brought a less sophisticated civilization and it was this latter group that formed the Indian civilization. An early caste system was established with the Dravidians serving as slaves.

After a time the society developed around religious, nonsecular concerns. The Mahabarata became a verbal tradition around 1000 B.C. It describes a war hero Krishna. The Mahabarata's most significant impact was the frequent descriptions of correct conduct and belief. The Mahabarata also describes how the soul remains immortal through transmigration—the successive occupation of many bodies.

From about 1000 to 500 B.C. the caste system became fixed and it was almost impossible for people to move out of their caste. The priests, or Brahmans, were at the top of the caste system. Next were rulers and warriors and then farmers and tradesmen. Near the bottom were workers. Finally, there were those who had no caste at all—outcastes—who could not participate in society.

Buddha was born in India about 580 B.C. His teachings developed the Buddhist religion. Buddha preached nirvana—a rejection of worldly and material concerns and a surrender of individual consciousness. During his lifetime his ideas spread throughout India.

The Maurya Empire ruled India from about 320 to 185 B.C. During this time Buddhism was spread throughout Asia, China, and Southeast Asia. The Andhran Dynasty ruled India proper to 220 A.D. Buddhism became less popular in India during this period while Brahmans gained more prominence.

After disorder following the collapse of the Andhran Dynasty, the Gupta Dynasty ruled from about 320 to 500 A.D. Arts, literature, and mathematics flourished during this period. Indian mathematicians used the decimal system and probably introduced the concept of zero. Hinduism developed from earlier religions and became the dominant religion in India. Most people in India worshipped many gods including Brahma (creator), Vishnu (preserver), and Shiva (destroyer).

The Gupta Dynasty declined with the invasion of the Huns in the fifth century A.D. Successors of these invaders, called Rajputs, intermarried, joined Hindu society, and dominated northern India until 1200 A.D. Other kingdoms were established in central and southern India. By this time the caste system and the power of Brahman priests were dominant throughout India.

Around 1200 A.D. Muslims (Turks and Afghans) invaded India from the north. The invaders controlled all but the southern part of India by about 1320. The Delhi Sultanate lasted in a state of intrigue until about 1530. Muslim sultans oppressed Hindus while their supporters killed or converted many Hindus. Remnants of this strife between Muslims and Hindus can be seen to this day.

In 1530 the Mongols, also Muslims, invaded India and by 1600 controlled most of India. The Mongol leader Akbar assumed the throne about 1560. His reign featured religious tolerance, the development of arts and literature, and a massive building campaign. In 1756 the Mongol Dynasty was overthrown by internal strife and Hindu resistance. India became a divided state.

Into this void stepped the European powers, particularly England. The East India Company of England virtually ruled India through 1857. In 1857, sepoys, Indian soldiers in the British army, mutinied. The revolt was eventually put down after two years of savage fighting. The British government began to rule Indian directly. This form of British rule was superior to that provided by the East India Company. Indian troops fought with Britain in World War I.

44. According to the passage
    (A) Buddhism spread throughout Asia about 580 B.C.
    (B) Brahma was a priest.
    (C) Buddhism became more popular in India during the Andhran Dynasty.
    (D) Muslim sultans oppressed Hindus.

45. Which was best known for its descriptions of correct conduct?
    (A) the Guptas
    (B) the Mahabaratas
    (C) the Dravidians
    (D) the Mauryas

SUB-SAHARAN AFRICA

The Sudan, south of Egypt, developed a culture patterned after Egypt in about 1000 B.C. The Cush civilization of Sudan flourished in middle Africa and was dominant until about 250 A.D. The A.D. period marks the conquest of North Africa by the Roman Empire. Christian European influence was dominant until about 640 A.D.

Islam spread throughout Africa in the seventh century A.D. During this time Muslims conquered the area occupied by Egypt and the rest of North Africa, including Morocco and Libya. By about 1050 A.D. most of northern Africa was an Islamic land.

The earliest state in West Africa was probably Ghana (established about 700 A.D.). By 1050 Ghana was also a Muslim state. In about 1100 A.D., the Mali evolved from tribes near the headwaters of the Senegal and Niger Rivers. Around 1300 Mali became a Muslim state. Songhai emerged as the dominant state in West Africa about 1400 A.D. Islam became the dominant faith in Songhai around 1500 and the capital, Timbuktu, became a major center for trade and learning. Songhai was overrun by Morocco in 1591.

East African civilizations had an early exposure to Asian peoples. Most towns were established by Arab and Indonesian settlers. There was a great deal of intermarriage among natives and settlers. Mogadishu and Mombassa were among a number of smaller states, which emerged around 1250 A.D.

Civilizations in central Africa are shrouded in mystery. Bantu-speaking people apparently settled there around 700 A.D. In the fourteenth century the Kongo Kingdom was formed. The area around Lake Tanganyika was formed in the Luba Empire about the time Columbus made his first voyage. South Africa is best known for the Zulu people. They conquered most of South Africa between 1816 and 1850. European conquest and domination of Africa began in the late fifteenth century. Slave trade by Europeans began at this time. Most slaves were supplied by African kingdoms, which grew rich on the slave trade.

46. What role did African kingdoms play in the slave trade?
    (A) The kingdoms resisted the slave trade.
    (B) Citizens of African kingdoms were not taken as slaves.
    (C) The kingdoms supplied slaves.
    (D) The kingdoms ignored the slave trade.

CIVILIZATIONS OF THE AMERICAS

Before 1500 the inhabitants of the Americas were related to the Native Americans. This group had migrated over the land bridge from Siberia about 30,000 years before. About 90 percent of the tens of millions of ancestors of this migratory tribe were found in Latin America in 1500.

By 7000 B.C., primitive cultures existed throughout the Americas. Cultures developed more slowly in the jungle areas of South America. Primitive cultures still exist there today. Agriculture seems to have been widespread by about 2500 B.C.

The dominant civilization in Mexico until about 900 A.D. were the Mayans. They began to occupy the Yucatan peninsula of Mexico and surrounding areas about 1700 B.C. The Mayans probably developed the most sophisticated indigenous American culture. The Mayan civilization ended suddenly with the mysterious desertion of Mayan cities and migration of the Mayan population.

Striking Mayan cities, plazas, and pyramids survive to this day. Mayans had a written language and wrote books about astronomy. Their calendar was the most accurate in the world at that time. Many Mayan descendants live as peasants in Mexico and speak dialects of their ancient language.

From about 1500 to 600 B.C., the Olmec civilization was a sophisticated culture in eastern Mexico. About this time a culture centered in Teotihuacan, near Mexico City, also grew in prominence. This culture was to dominate central Mexico until about 900 A.D.

In about 900 A.D. the Aztecs began their rise to power in northern Mexico. Aztecs referred to themselves as Mexica. Aztecs were warlike and sacrificed humans. By about 1300 A.D. they established a capital city in a marsh, which is now the site of Mexico City.

The Spaniards, under Cortez, entered Mexico in 1519, duped the Aztec Emperor Montezuma II and easily defeated the Aztec confederation in 1521. Over a million descendants of the Aztecs still live in Mexico, mainly living a subsistence existence and speaking their ancient language.

The Incas were the dominant pre-Columbian civilization in South America. This culture existed in Peru by about 500 A.D. From about 1100 to about 1500 A.D. the Incas expanded their empire to most of the western coast of South America and included parts of Argentina.

The Incas had the best developed system of government in the Americas. They built extensive systems of stone roads and huge stone structures such as the Temple of the Sun. The Incas also built the fortress Machu Picchu high in the Andes. Machu Picchu may have been the last stronghold of the Incas after the Spaniard, Pizzaro, overcame the Incan empire in 1532 with about 200 troops and palace intrigue.

47. About how many years elapsed from the beginning of the Olmec civilization in Mexico to the end of Teotihuacan domination in northern Mexico?
    (A) 400
    (B) 500
    (C) 1,400
    (D) 2,400

RISE AND EXPANSION OF EUROPE

Renaissance (1300–1600) and the Reformation (1500–1600)

The Renaissance, which means the rebirth, arose in Italy and particularly in Florence. It was a time for the discovery and rediscovery of literature and art. Humanism, reading, and the ideas of Classical Greece were dominant during this period. Dante wrote the *Inferno* and the *Divine Comedy* early in the Renaissance and Machiavelli wrote *The Prince* near the end of the period. Leonardo DiVinci painted the Mona Lisa and designed many workable mechanical devices. Michelangelo painted the ceiling of the Sistine Chapel, among other accomplishments.

The abuses of the Catholic church, then monolithic in Europe, drew much criticism. The practice of selling indulgences (relief from punishment in purgatory) was considered particularly repugnant. Martin Luther drew particular attention to these abuses when, on October 31, 1517, he nailed his *95 Theses* to the Wittenburg Church door. Luther authored many books and wrote the most popular hymn of the time, *A Mighty Fortress Is Our God*. Since Luther's teachings *protested* church practice, his followers were called Protestants.

The reform movement spread beyond Luther in Germany to England and other parts of Europe. Henry VIII in England broke with the pope and formed the Church of England. Protestantism was effectively blocked in Spain and Italy and was the subject of warfare in France.

Most national boundaries were fixed at the end of the Reformation in 1560. The 90 years that followed were marked by religious strife. Gunpowder, available since the 1300s, was now used in cannons. Warfare became more regimented and more deadly. There were no fewer than seven civil wars in France. The St. Bartholomew's Day Massacre occurred in 1572, when Catherine DeMedici arranged the death of about 20,000 French Huguenots (Calvinist Protestants).

Mary I (Bloody Mary) of England killed many Protestants in her brief five-year reign (1553–1558). Her successor, Elizabeth I, was a Protestant and achieved some degree of religious peace in England. Later attempts were made to force England back to Catholicism.

By 1575 governments were in shambles, and many religious groups were discriminated against. In England the Puritans objected to what they saw as a pro-Catholic shift in the Church of England. Many Puritans escaped to the New World.

48. According to the passage
    (A) Mary I was a Protestant.
    (B) Henry VIII formed a Protestant church.
    (C) Catholics were murdered in the St. Bartholomew's Day Massacre.
    (D) Michelangelo painted the Sistine Chapel in protest against the Catholic Church.

SCIENTIFIC REVOLUTION (1550–1650) AND THE ENLIGHTENMENT (C. 1650–1790)

The scientific revolution took place toward the end of the Renaissance. Copernicus showed that the sun was at the center of the solar system. Kepler discovered the orbits of the planets. Galileo made significant discoveries in astronomy, mechanics, and surveying. He proved that all falling bodies fall at the same rate.

Francis Bacon championed inductive investigations in which data are gathered and used to form hypotheses. Rene Decartes (Cartesian coordinates) provided leadership in mathematics and championed the deductive, step-by-step method of proof.

In 1650 Europe consisted of 300 to 500 smaller states and a Germany devastated by the Thirty Years War. A series of treaties and wars brought a kind of order out of this chaos.

The Grand Alliance (1701)—A coalition of Spain and France against England led to the formation of the Grand Coalition (Holy Roman Empire, England, Holland, and Prussia).

Treaty of Utrecht (1742)—The Spanish Empire was partitioned. England received Gibraltar, Newfoundland, Hudson Bay, and Nova Scotia.

King William's War (1744–1748)—Prussia emerged as a world power.

Seven Years War (1756–1763)—Prussia fought Austria, France, and Russia. With help from England and the withdrawal of Russia from the conflict, Prussia held onto its lands.

Treaty of Paris (1763)—France, which had already given Spain all its western American lands, lost the rest of its North American possessions to England. England traded Cuba to Spain for Florida.

Treaty of Paris (1783)—Britain recognized the United States following the Revolutionary War, but no lands were given to France, even though France (Lafayette, Rochambeau) had aided the United States in the Revolutionary War.

Life was still difficult in the 1700s. In the early 1700s the average life expectancy was 30, and almost no one lived to see their grandchildren. Famine and disease (including smallpox, bubonic plague, and typhus) were rampant. But, slowly, the economies and social institutions of Europe began to change for the better.

Mercantilism, an emphasis on material wealth, became a leading force in Europe. In Holland and England productivity became important. As a result, these countries became leading economic powers.

In the early eighteenth century, technology provided a means for further economic development. Watt refined and developed the steam engine, while other inventors devised power-driven textile equipment.

The Enlightenment established intellect as distinct from God and sought to establish a rational basis for life. Descartes paused in his scientific work to proclaim, "I think; therefore, I am."

This period included the Baroque art movement. Baroque art featured grandeur and included the works of Rembrandt. Rubens, Bach, and Handel were great Baroque artists and composers.

The impact of the Enlightenment can be seen in the theories of Jean Jacques Rousseau who believed that common people should have a wider role in their own government. The centralized mercantilist theory was attacked by economist Adam Smith and others, who believed in free trade and the law of supply and demand.

49. In the Treaty of Paris (1783)
    (A) France gave the remainder of its North American possessions to the United States.
    (B) Britain recognized the United States and traded Cuba for Florida.
    (C) France received no lands but Britain recognized the United States.
    (D) England and Spain exchanged Cuba and Florida and recognized the United States.

ROMANOV RUSSIA

The Romanovs ruled Russia from about 1613 until 1917. From 1682 until 1725 the giant (7 feet tall), driven, and cruel Peter the Great ruled Russia. He used secret police to identify and punish those who opposed him. Despite his bizarre behavior, he spent time among the common people. He modernized and westernized Russia. He built St. Petersburg as a modern western city. Many of the companies begun during his reign were controlled by the state. After six short-lived emperors, Catherine the Great (1762–1796) continued the modernization of Russia.

50. The word "bizarre" in this passage most nearly means
    (A) mundane.
    (B) peculiar.
    (C) cruel.
    (D) lethal.

THE FRENCH REVOLUTION AND NAPOLEON

King Louis XVI was on the throne as France became bankrupt in the late 1780s. Food was in short supply and food prices were inflated as the Third Estate (commoners) asserted themselves and took over the national assembly. They forced recognition by the king.

Galvanized by food shortages, repression, and unemployment, Parisian workers armed themselves and stormed the fortress Bastille on July 14, 1789. The French Revolution was born. After two years of fighting and intrigue, the newly formed national assembly condemned and executed Louis XVI and Marie "let them eat cake" Antoinette in 1792.

Robespierre emerged to direct a Committee of Public Safety, which conducted the Reign of Terror from 1793–1794. During the Reign, thousands were summarily found guilty of real or imagined wrongs and guillotined. Robespierre was executed under orders from the National Convention on July 28, 1794.

Napoleon was born in 1769, and while in Paris in 1795, he helped put down a royalist uprising. He was also there to lead the overthrow of the government in 1799 and soon become the dictator (Consul for Life in 1801) of France. Napoleon was a brilliant, charismatic man and a true military genius. He led France on a 10-year quest for an expanded empire from 1805 to 1815.

However, he was unable to complete his militaristic expansion successfully. He was deposed and exiled to Elba only to return to "meet his Waterloo" at the battle of that name. He was exiled again and died on the island of St. Helena in 1821.

The Quadruple Alliance (Austria, England, Prussia, and Russia), who had defeated Napoleon, reached a settlement that encircled France. This settlement maintained a balance of power in Europe until Germany was unified 60 years later.

51. Which of the following statements is most likely to have caused the quote from Louis XVI's wife found in this passage?
    (A) "This phrase can be used to describe any failed situation."
    (B) "The people are hungry."
    (C) "It happened after Elba."
    (D) "There is no bread."

THE INDUSTRIAL REVOLUTION (1750–1850) AND ROMANTICISM (1790–1850)

Increased population, cheap labor, available capital, raw materials, and industrial skill led to the beginning of the Industrial Revolution in England about 1750. Textiles and metal industries were the first to develop. These industries were helped along by the steamboat and the locomotive. During the early 1800s this industrialism moved to the continent.

The Industrial Revolution produced a new class of factory workers. These workers did not benefit from the Industrial Revolution until late in the 1800s. Until then, work had centered around the family, but all that changed. Generally speaking, men worked outside the home, and women worked in the home.

Romanticism had its biggest impact from the late 1700s through 1850. This movement stressed personal freedom and humanitarianism. The names of many Romantic writers, painters, and composers are familiar to us. Some writers were Balzac, Burns, Browning, Byron, Coleridge, Cooper, Dostoyevsky, Dumas, Emerson, Longfellow, Poe, and Thoreau. Painters included Goya and Delacorte. Composers of the era were Brahms, Chopin, and Schubert.

Romanticism broadened thought and led to a number of different philosophies and approaches to living. Liberalism celebrated the individual and proclaimed that individuals have certain natural rights. Conservatism proposed that some people were better prepared to rule and lead than others. Nationalism stressed loyalty to a group or country rather than the individual. Socialism expressed the view that all should receive their share of a nation's wealth. Marxism developed by Marx and Engels was a popular form of socialism. Marxism is described in *Das Kapital* and *Communist Manifesto*. A series of revolutions swept Europe in 1820, 1825, and 1830, culminating in 1848. Italy and Germany were unified as an aftermath of these revolutions.

52. A system that distributes taxes from wealthier individuals to poorer individuals is an example of
    (A) conservatism.
    (B) liberalism.
    (C) nationalism.
    (D) socialism.

EUROPEAN DEVELOPMENTS

The year 1854 found Great Britain and France allied with the Turks against Russia in the Crimean War. It was this war that sparked the writing of "The Charge of the Light Brigade" and featured the nursing work of Florence Nightingale and her disciples. The war ended in 1856 with the Peace of Paris.

Following the revolutions of 1848, capitalism and communism competed for economic supremacy in Europe. Anarchists believed that there should be no authority. They used violent means to further their ends.

Beginning about 1870, Europe was producing more goods than it could consume. So European powers began to vie for colonies. Much of the early activity focused on Africa. By 1914 Belgium, Britain, France, Germany, Italy, Portugal, and Spain controlled about 90 percent of Africa, with Britain and then France controlling the most territory.

During this time the German Empire developed under Bismarck. Great Britain's move to democratic government ended in 1911 when the House of Commons usurped the power of the House of Lords. The Third French Republic survived infighting and socialist challenges and solidified support of the majority of the French populace.

This period also saw the emergence of new and revolutionary ideas. Freud established psychoanalytic psychology, Einstein presented his theory of relativity, and Darwin wrote the *Origin of the Species*.

53. Which of the following were African colonizers that did NOT control the most territory?
    (A) Britain
    (B) France
    (C) Portugal
    (D) Russia

ANTHROPOLOGY

Anthropology is a holistic study of humans. Anthropologists study the biology, culture, and development of human species and communities. Anthropologists rely on field work, fossils, and observation in their work.

Physical anthropology is concerned with the evolution of primates and humans. Physical anthropologists are seeking to trace the evolution of humans through human fossils. Louis Leakey is probably the most famous physical anthropologist. He discovered the three-million-year-old remains of "Lucy" at the Olduvai gorge in Africa.

Biological anthropologists study the genetic development of primates and humans. They seek to identify the cause of human diseases such as high blood pressure. Other biological anthropologists such as Jane Goodall study the behavior of apes and other primates. These anthropologists have found that primates can use tools and communicate.

Cultural anthropology is concerned with the social systems, customs, languages, and religion of existing cultures. Cultural anthropologists classify cultures as patrilineal, matrilineal, or bilateral depending on whether the family roots are traced through the father, mother, or both father and mother.

The simplest cultures are associated with nomadic hunter-gatherers. About 13,000 years ago, humans began domesticating livestock and raising crops. More stable communities developed as cultures became more stationary. Then these communities became linked together to form tribes with a shared tradition (religion). Political systems developed, and leaders or chiefs of these tribes appeared. Some of these tribes developed unevenly into kingdoms with a shared language. Occasionally a kingdom would develop into a civilization with different hierarchies of individuals. More advanced cultures featured complex religious systems, important priests, and codified religious rules. Early cultures typically had a single religious system. Until recently there was a close relationship between religion and government. Most cultural anthropologists agree that the primary determinants of culture are the material conditions of life—food, energy sources, and technology. Geography and climate have a tremendous influence on these factors. Ideas, movements, and personalities also have a significant impact on a culture.

54. Which of the following statements would be most likely associated with a cultural anthropologist?
    (A) The primary determinants of culture are ideas, movements, and personalities.
    (B) The primary determinants of culture are the material conditions of life.
    (C) The primary determinants of culture are the family roots.
    (D) The primary determinants of culture are social systems, customs, languages, and religions.

UNITED STATES GOVERNMENT

The United States government is based on the Constitution of the United States. The Constitution can be amended by a two-thirds vote of Congress with concurrence of three-fourths of the state legislatures. The first ten amendments to the Constitution are called the Bill of Rights. Other important amendments provided protection by due process of law, abolished slavery, and gave women the right to vote. The Constitution established a federal form of government. States have rights and hold all power not expressly granted to the federal government. The federal government of the United States has three branches: legislative, executive, and judicial. The framers of the Constitution established these as three complementary, overlapping branches to provide checks and balances in the governmental process.

The Congress of the United States consists of the Senate and the House of Representatives. The 100 senators, two from each state, serve for six years with one-third standing for election every two years. The 435 representatives in the House are partitioned among the states according to population. Every state must have at least one representative. All representatives stand for election every two years.

Measures passed by a majority of Congress present and voting are sent to the president as a bill. The president may sign the bill into law or veto it. If the bill is vetoed, the Congress may still make the bill law by a two-thirds vote of each body.

The president and the vice president are the elected heads of the federal government. Their election takes place through a cumbersome process in which electors are chosen from each state by popular vote. These electors then gather in an Electoral College to cast votes for the president and vice president.

The president is Commander-in-Chief of the Armed Forces, but only Congress has the power to declare war. The president also has the right to negotiate treaties. Two-thirds of the Senate must vote to ratify any treaties. Treaties are null and void without this ratification.

The Constitution established the Supreme Court as the final arbiter of whether a law adhered to the Constitution. Other federal courts established by Congress can also rule on a law's constitutionality.

Supreme Court justices are nominated by the president. A majority of the Senate must consent to any Supreme Court nomination.

55. Which choice below best characterizes the federal government?
    (A) States have all powers not constitutionally assigned to the federal government.
    (B) A bill vetoed by the president can become law by a two-thirds vote of the House of Representatives.
    (C) The Supreme Court of the United States can overturn laws when a majority of the justices disagree about that law.
    (D) The Constitution of the United States of America can be amended upon a vote of three-fourths of the state legislatures.

Explained Answers

1. **A** The Aleuts founded a civilization in Alaska around 5000 B.C, or about 7,000 years ago. The Eskimos and Inuits also established cultures in Alaska, but about 3,800 years ago.

2. **C** The third paragraph indicates that the nomadic plains Indians lived in tepees.

3. **D** The Celts established settlements hundreds of years before Columbus sailed. While African sailors reached North America at least 500 years before Columbus, the passage does not indicate that the African sailors established settlements.

4. **B** The obvious answer is the correct answer—the east coast is closest to England. All the other answers are mentioned in the reading, but not as reasons why the colonies were along the eastern seaboard.

5. **D** The Townshend Act tax on tea led to the Boston Tea Party, which in turn caused Britain to take more direct control of the colonies. There was no Tea Act.

6. **B** Choices (A), (C), and (D) are specifically referred to as self-evident truths. Even though freedom from taxation without representation was a basis for the Revolutionary War, the Declaration of Independence does not include it as a self-evident truth.

7. **C** The fourth paragraph includes the statement "This action by France [entering the war] was the decisive moment in the Revolutionary War."

8. **C** General Gates had command during this action, as explained at the end of the third paragraph.

9. **B** The passage indicates the Articles of Confederation were the "first Constitution" of the United States. The Articles of Confederation were too weak, and so they were replaced by the Constitution, which was the second governing document of the United States.

10. **A** Conservative political parties are generally associated with less government involvement, as championed by the Jeffersonians and described in the last paragraph.

11. **C** You'll find the answer in the first line of the second paragraph—states wanted to "nullify acts" (laws) for their state.

12. **A** The Battle of New Orleans was fought after the war was officially over, as noted in the last line of the first paragraph.

13. **D** Maine and Missouri were admitted as states, one as a free state and one as a slave state. This answer is correct even though it omits the fact that Maine was admitted as a free state and Missouri was admitted as a slave state.

14. **C** Texas was a sovereign nation before becoming a state. See the fifth paragraph for confirmation of this answer.

15. **C** As an abolitionist, John Brown was against slavery. The passage does not mention where he was from, which was Torrington, Connecticut.

16. **B** The Emancipation Proclamation freed slaves only in Confederate states, as you can see from the second sentence in the third paragraph.

17. **C** As we can see from the passage, the Battle of Gettysburg was in 1863, before Atlanta fell in 1864. New Orleans was captured in 1862 and Sherman reached the Gulf of Mexico in 1864.

18. **C** Carpetbaggers, along with white scalawags and former slaves, filled a power vacuum during reconstruction, as explained in the second full paragraph.

19. **D** McKinley was reelected. Cleveland was elected twice, but was never reelected. Reelected means elected to consecutive terms.

20. **B** According to the passage, typewriters and sewing machines brought women to the workforce. Sewing machines are not given as a choice here; typewriters is the correct answer.

21. **A** The reference to jungle in this passage is the book *The Jungle*, by Upton Sinclair, which exposed abuses in the meat-packing industry (slaughterhouses).

22. **B** When the Bolsheviks gained power they withdrew Russia from World War I and removed a German adversary. The other answer choices are true, but none of them had a main impact on World War I.

23. **C** Hoover used a top-down approach—lend money to employers and hope that the money moved down to workers. You'll find confirmation of this answer near the end of the second paragraph.

24. **B** You can infer this answer from the sentence that indicates that distilling was a huge underground industry, meaning that liquor, the product of distilling, must have been prohibited

25. **C** The second paragraph indicates that Hitler emerged "out of all this," referring primarily to the Depression mentioned in the first paragraph.

26. **D** According to the second paragraph, the Soviet Union occupied Estonia, Latvia, and Lithuania. The other answer choices do not refer to Soviet actions at the beginning of World War II.

27. **B** Truman attended the Potsdam Conference, but not the Yalta Conference. The other statements are false.

28. **D** This attack brought Italy into war with the United States, as the first paragraph details.

29. **C** The Smith Act was used to jail subversives in the United States during World War II. Refer to the second half of the third paragraph.

30. **A** The passage refers to Cuba, a country, as a satellite of Russia. Satellite has other meanings, but in this context it means country.

31. **B** The Supreme Court ruled on that relatively narrow issue—that separate but equal schools were not constitutional—as indicated at the beginning of the third paragraph.

32. **C** President Kennedy was not effective at implementing his New Frontier ideas because he could not move legislation through Congress. You will find confirmation in the second paragraph.

33. **D** The second paragraph indicates that the United States supported a Vietnamese leader during World War II. None of the other answer choices are supported by the paragraphs.

34. **C** President Ford was never elected to the presidency or vice presidency through the electoral college. He was elected to Congress. You will find confirmation near the end of the next-to-last paragraph.

35. **A** Supply-side economics supports the position that tax cuts create investments, as explained in the first paragraph.

36. **C** Civilization began about 3500 B.C. when writing was invented.

37. **D** Aristotle tutored Alexander the Great, and Alexander subsequently spread Greek culture to most of that region of the world.

38. **B** The New Kingdom dates are 1560 B.C. to 1085 B.C. The Old Kingdom dates are from 2685 B.C. to 2180 B.C. To find the answer subtract: 2180–1560 = 620.

39. **A** Roman senators were landowners but you don't have to own land to be a United States senator.

40. **C** The only rebellion mentioned in the passage was the rebellion of samuri after they were forbidden to wear their swords.

41. **B** The third paragraph in the passage indicates that battles with Danes preceded the Battle of Hastings. All the other events mentioned in the answer choices occurred after the Battle of Hastings.

42. **A** The last paragraph explains that the Chinese government's objection to opium imports led to the Opium War.

43. **A** The T'angs developed a civil service testing program, as explained in the sixth paragraph.

44. **D** The third paragraph from the end of the passage confirms that the Muslim sultans oppressed Hindus.

45. **B** The third paragraph indicates that the Mahabarata's most significant impact was a description of correct conduct.

46. **C** The last paragraph in the passage explains that African kingdoms provided most slaves.

47. **D** The fifth paragraph mentions that the Olmec civilization began about 1500 B.C. and the Teotihuacan domination ended about 900 A.D. Dating that uses A.D. and B.C. is like negative and positive numbers; 1500 B.C. is like –1500 and 900 A.D. is like + 900. It's about 2,400 years from 1500 B.C. to 900 A.D.

48. **B** In the third paragraph we read that Henry VIII broke with the pope (Catholic) and formed the Church of England, which had to be Protestant.

49. **C** This answer correctly describes the 1783 Treaty of Paris.

50. **B** The word "peculiar" is a reasonable synonym for "bizarre." The other choices have completely different meanings than bizarre.

51. **D** The context shows that there were food shortages during the reign of Louis XVI when his wife, Marie Antoinette, is reported to have said "let them eat cake." This response is more likely to be caused by a specific report that there was no bread, rather than the general report that the people were hungry.

52. **D** The socialist philosophy holds that all should receive their share of a nation's wealth. You will find confirmation of this answer in the last paragraph.

53. **C** The passage indicates that Britain and France controlled the most territory in Africa. Russia is not mentioned as an African colonizer. That leaves Portugal.

54. **B** This answer is a direct quote from the last paragraph in the passage.

55. **A** The first paragraph confirms that the states have rights and hold all powers not expressly granted to the federal government.

PART V

ATS-W Review

10 ASSESSMENT OF TEACHING SKILLS-WRITTEN

TEST INFO BOX

This chapter helps you prepare for the ATS-W. It includes a review of the topics on the ATS-W.

Test takers agree that teaching experience may be the most useful preparation for the ATS-W.

MULTIPLE-CHOICE TEST

The ATS-W has 80 multiple-choice items. The items are about the practical aspects of teaching.

WRITTEN ASSIGNMENT

The ATS-W includes a written assignment. You may be asked to respond to a classroom situation, or some other education-related situation. The written assignment must be clear enough to be understood, but the readers do not evaluate your writing ability. However, a well-written assignment always makes the best impression. The written assignment is rated 0–3 by two readers based on the appropriateness of your response. The final written assignment score of 0–6 is the sum of these two scores.

USING THIS CHAPTER

This chapter helps you prepare to take the ATS-W. Choose one of these approaches.

I want a quick ATS-W review. (BEST FOR MOST PEOPLE)

❏ Take and correct the ATS-W Review Quiz on page 216.

I want a thorough ATS-W review.

❏ Take the ATS-W Review Quiz on page 216.
❏ Correct the Review Quiz and read the indicated parts of the review.

ATS-W REVIEW QUIZ

This Review Quiz tests your knowledge of topics included on the ATS-W. The quiz will help you refresh your memory about these topics.

This quiz is not like the ATS-W. It does not use a multiple-choice format. The idea here is to find out what you know and what you don't know. So don't guess answers on this Review Quiz.

This short-answer quiz will also be more difficult than the questions on the actual ATS-W. It is not important to answer all of these questions and don't be concerned if you miss many of them.

The answers are found immediately after the quiz. It is to your advantage not to look at them until you complete the quiz. Once you complete and correct the quiz, you can use the answer checklist to decide which sections to study.

Write the answers in the space provided or on a separate sheet of paper.

---

1. At about what age do boys and girls enter adolescence? Boys _12_ Girls _10_

2. Who provided an experimental basis for behaviorism?
   Rnoget Pavolv – dogs

3. Give Piaget's four stages of cognitive development along with the approximate ages and one characteristic of each stage.
   Sensorimotor   0-18months
   Preoperational 18m-7yrs
   operational 7-12yrs
   concrete 12-↑

4. According to Eriksen, what is the primary emotional crisis experienced by children in grades 6–9?
   Identity vs. Iden Confusion

5. Generally speaking, what moral behavior do children exhibit in Kohlberg's stage of Preconventional Morality?
   no clear morality

6. What do social learning theorists mean when they talk about modeling?
   acting how you want others to act

7. Which has the most significant impact on human development, nature or nurture?
   both

8. About what percent of American families have children, a mother at home, and a father at work?

9. About when would we expect the school population in America to be evenly divided between Caucasian and minority students?

10. To what country do most Hispanic Americans trace their origin?
    Mexico

11. Which ethnic group in America has the highest suicide rate and alcoholism rate?

_____

_____

12. About what percent of those who commit serious crimes are caught?

_____

_____

13. What is the most used and abused drug?

_____

_____

14. How is the HIV virus transmitted?

_____

_____

15. The New York Learning Standards are presented in which six categories?

_____

_____

16. Planning for instruction begins with what first step?

_____

_____

17. What is the highest order of thinking in cognitive domain?

_____

_____

18. What types of diversity might require modification of objectives?

_____

_____

19. What should an objective describe?

_____

_____

20. What are prerequisite competencies?

_____

_____

21. According to Madeline Hunter, what is an anticipatory set?

_____

_____

22. Describe formative evaluation.

_____

_____

23. What is the most common error made when reading standardized test reports?

_____

_____

24. What is content validity?

_____

_____

25. What is authentic assessment?

_____

_____

26. What factor correlates most highly with normed scores?

_____

_____

27. What is extrinsic motivation?

_____

_____

28. Do students learn more when they are being taught or when they are working independently?

_____

_____

29. Lectures and explanations are most effective when they begin with what first step?

_____

_____

30. Using Bloom's Taxonomy, what level of questions should be asked in classrooms?

_____

_____

31. About how long should a teacher wait for a student to respond to a question?

_____

_____

32. What types of questions do teachers ask in a student-centered classroom?

_____

_____

33. What important aspects characterize active learning?

_____

_____

34. What is the last step in inquiry learning?

_____

_____

35. How would you adapt instruction for learning disabled students?

_____

_____

36. Overall, what factor correlates most highly with school achievement?

_____

_____

37. Where do most seventh and eighth graders typically turn for leadership?

_____

_____

38. List three characteristics of successful teachers.

_____

_____

39. Initially, how should the teacher arrange classroom seating?

_____

_____

40. Kounin's approach of with-it-ness has been shown to be an effective disciplinary technique. What is with-it-ness?

_____

_____

41. Under the approach recommended by Canter and Canter, how should a teacher respond when students break rules during class?

_____

_____

42. What are nonverbal cues?

_____

_____

43. How can modeling change student behavior?

_____

_____

44. How can negative reinforcement change student behavior?

_____

_____

45. Which groups or entities in the United States are legally responsible for education?

_____

_____

46. What New York regional organization provides services to local school districts?

_____

_____

47. How has the acculturation of ethnic groups changed during the last 40 years?

_____

_____

48. What federal document establishes responsibility for education?

_____

_____

49. When in the process of hiring and dismissing teachers may "reverse discrimination" be legal?

_____

_____

50. What limits have the courts placed on the free speech rights of teachers?

_____

_____

51. How may students publish a paper not subject to review and editing by school officials?

_____

_____

52. About when and where did formal education begin?

_____

_____

53. What educator is credited with establishing the kindergarten?

_____

_____

54. Where did dame schools offer classes?

_____

_____

55. What was the primary teaching device during the American colonial period?

_____

_____

56. What was the main feature of Dewey's progressive schools?

_____

_____

57. How did PL 94-142 impact American education?

_____

_____

ANSWER CHECKLIST

The answers are organized by review section. Check your answers. If you miss any question in a section, check the box and review that section.

Knowledge of the Learner
❑ *Human Development, page 221*
1. Boys about 12, girls about 10

2. Pavlov with his experiments on dogs

3. *Sensorimotor* (Birth–18 months) Children develop the idea of object permanence, out of sight not out of mind, during this stage.
Preoperational (18 months–7 years) Children develop language and are able to solve some problems. Students' thinking is egocentric and they have difficulty developing concepts such as the conservation of number task.
Concrete Operational (7 years to 12 years) During this period, students' thinking becomes operational. This means that concepts become organized and logical, as long as they are working with or around concrete materials or images. Students master the conservation tasks.
Formal Operational (12 years–) Children develop and demonstrate concepts without concrete materials or images. Students think fully in symbolic terms about concepts. Children become able to reason effectively, abstractly, and theoretically.

4. Identity vs. Identity confusion

5. No conscience, no clear morality

6. Acting in a way you want others to act

7. The issue remains unresolved.

❑ *Diversity, page 226*
8. About 10 percent

9. By about 2020. (Count your answer correct if you were within 10 years.)

10. Mexico

11. Native Americans

12. About 30 percent

13. Alcohol

14. Exchange of blood and bodily fluids (Intravenous drug users can acquire AIDS when they share needles and inject small quantities of infected blood.)

Instructional Planning and Assessment
❑ *New York Learning Standards, page 230*
15. - The Arts
    - Mathematics, Science and Technology
    - English/Language Arts
    - Social Studies
    - Languages Other than English
    - Health, Physical Education/Home Economics

❑ *Objectives, page 235*
   16. Write an objective

❑ *Taxonomy of Objectives, page 235*
   17. Evaluation

❑ *Choosing and Modifying Objectives, page 235*
   18. Academic, Cultural, Linguistic

❑ *Writing Objectives, page 236*
   19. What a student should know or be able to do *after* instruction

❑ *Planning to Teach the Lesson, page 237*
   20. What a student should know or be able to do *before* instruction

   21. Anticipatory set—something that is said or done to focus students on the lesson.

❑ *Evaluating Instruction, page 245*
   22. Formative is used to plan instruction.

   23. Looking at a single score instead of a range of scores.

   24. Content validity describes the extent to which a test measures the material being taught.

   25. Students are evaluated as they demonstrate knowledge or a skill in a real life setting.

   26. Socioeconomic status (SES)

❑ *Motivation, page 248*
   27. External rewards to improve student performance

❑ *Successful Learning, page 248*
   28. Students learn more when they are being taught.

❑ *Classroom Approaches, page 250*
   29. Motivation

   30. Questions should be asked at all levels.

   31. 4 to 5 seconds

   32. More open-ended questions

33. Group work, active learning, full participation, democratic structure

34. Metacognition—that is, students analyze their thought processes.

❑ *Adapting Instruction, page 253*

   35. Provide structured brief assignments, manipulative activities, and auditory learning

❑ *Cultural and Linguistic Diversity, page 253*
   36. Socioeconomic status (SES)

Instructional Delivery
❑ *Managing the Instructional Environment, page 255*
   37. They turn to their peer group

   38. Any three of the following:
   - Accept children within a teacher-student relationship.
   - Set firm and clear but flexible limits.
   - Enforce rules clearly and consistently.
   - Have positive, realistic expectations about student's achievement.
   - Have clear reasons for expectations about students.
   - Practice what they preach (model acceptable behavior).
   - Don't take it personally. Students usually misbehave or act out because of who they are, not because of who you are.

   39. So that they can see the faces of all the students

❑ *Specific Management Techniques, page 257*
   40. With-it-ness means that the teacher is constantly monitoring and aware of what is happening in the classroom.

   41. Write the names of the students on the board.
   One violation—no action
   Two violations—conference
   Three violations—parental conference

   42. A silent gesture or signal to alert students to a transition or to gain attention

❏ *Changing Behavior, page 258*

43. Students who observe a person behaving a particular way often emulate that person.

44. Negative reinforcement means showing students how to avoid undesirable consequences by doing acceptable work.

The Professional Environment

❏ *The Schools in Society, page 240*

45. Boards of Cooperative Educational Services (BOCES)

46. The states

47. Recent immigrants have been less acculturated and have maintained more of their cultural identity and language.

❏ *Legal, Legislative, and Political Influences, page 00*

48. Constitution of the United States

49. May be legal for hiring, but not for dismissal

50. Teachers cannot disrupt the curriculum or the schools.

51. Publish it with private funds off school property.

❏ *Historical and Philosophical Foundations, page 243*

52. About 2000 B.C. in Northern Africa and China. Formal education that led to our system began about 500 B.C. in Athens, Greece

53. Herbart

54. In the houses of the female teachers

55. The Horn Book

56. Student centered education

57. It mandated an appropriate education in the least restrictive environment for handicapped Americans aged 3–21.

ATS-W REVIEW

KNOWLEDGE OF THE LEARNER

Physical Development

Adequate nutrition in mothers is essential for proper fetal development. Adequate nutrition and exercise are essential for a child's physical growth. Inadequate nutrition can hamper growth and lead to inattentiveness and other problems that interfere with learning.

Alcohol and drug abuse by mothers can cause irreparable brain damage to unborn children. Children of drug-and-alcohol-abusing mothers tend to have lower birth weights. Low birth weight is associated with health, emotional, and learning problems. Alcohol and drug addiction, smoking, stress, and adverse environmental factors are among the other causes of abnormal physical and emotional development.

During the first 12 months after birth, the body weight of infants triples and brain size doubles. Infants crawl by about 7 months, eat with their hands at about 8 months, sit up by about 9 months, stand up by about 11 months, and walk by about 1 year.

From 12–15 months to 2.5 years, children are called toddlers. During this period, children become expert walkers, feed themselves, evidence self control, and spend a great deal of their time playing. This period is characterized by the word *no* and is also when children begin bowel training.

The preschool years span the time from the end of toddlerhood to entry into kindergarten. Children start to look more like adults with longer legs and a shorter torso. Play continues but becomes more sophisticated.

The elementary school years refer to ages 6–10 in girls but 6–12 in boys. During this period children enter a period of steady growth. Most children double their body weight and increase their height by one-half. Play continues but involves more sophisticated games and physical activities, often involving groups or teams of other children.

Adolescence begins at about age 10 for girls but at about age 12 for boys. The growth rate spurt begins during this time. Because this period begins earlier for girls than for boys, girls are more mature than boys for a number of years. Sexual and secondary sex characteristics appear during this time. Most adolescents rely heavily on peer group approval and respond to peer pressure.

Behavioral Development

Behaviorism was the first significant theory of development. Behaviorism is concerned with observable, measurable behavior and with those events that stimulate or reinforce the behavior.

Watson

John Watson originated the behaviorist movement during the early 1900s. His theoretical ideas centered around conditioned responses in children. Conditioned response means that a child was "taught" to respond in a particular way to a stimulus that would not naturally elicit that response. Watson's experiment to condition a child to fear a white rat that the child initially liked is most quoted in texts. Many claim that the success of the experiment was overstated.

Pavlov

Many trace the experimental basis for behaviorism to the Russian psychologist Pavlov who, in the 1920s, conducted classical conditioning experiments with dogs. Dogs naturally salivate in an unconditioned response to the unconditioned stimulus of food. Pavlov showed that dogs would salivate in response to any neutral stimulus. The neutral stimulus is called a conditioned stimulus, and the salivation that occurs is called a conditioned response.

Thorndike

Also in the early 1900s Edward Thorndike developed his own form of behaviorism called instrumental conditioning. Thorndike's work with animals led him to two significant conclusions:

- The law of exercise—a conditioned response can be strengthened by repeating the response (practice).
- The law of effect—rewarded responses are strengthened while punished responses are weakened.

Skinner

Skinner was the most influential behaviorist. Skinner referred to his approach as operant conditioning, which studied how voluntary behavior could be shaped. Operant conditioning relies on these basic mechanisms.

- Reward or positive reinforcement—Students are rewarded for repeating desired responses.

- Negative reinforcement—Students escape punishment by repeating desired responses.

- Extinction—Undesired responses are not reinforced.

- Punishment—Undesired responses are punished.

Skinner showed that he could condition very complex behaviors in animals. He believed that students learned when teachers gave immediate positive feedback for a desired behavior and used extinction or punishment for undesirable behaviors.

Cognitive Development

Jean Piaget

Jean Piaget is the most prominent of cognitive psychologists who believe that students develop concepts through a series of stages. Stage theory is currently the most popular form of child development.

According to Piaget, children proceed through a fixed but uneven series of stages of cognitive development. His stages help us understand the general way in which students learn and develop concepts.

Action and logic versus perception are at the center of Piaget's theory. He believed that children learn through an active involvement with their environment. He also believed that students have developed a concept when their logical understanding overcomes their perceptual misunderstanding of the concept.

His conservation experiments explain this last point. In conservation of number, students are shown two matched rows of checkers. The child confirms that there are the same number of checkers in each row. Then one row of checkers is spread out and the child is asked if there are still the same number of checkers. Children who believe there are more checkers in one of

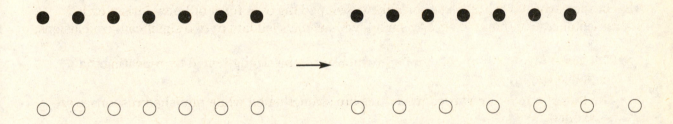

the rows do not understand the concept of number because their perception holds sway over their logic.

Piaget presents these four stages of cognitive development.

- Sensorimotor (birth to 18 months)—Children exhibit poor verbal and cognitive development. Children develop the idea of object permanence (out of sight not out of mind) during this stage.

- Preoperational (18 months to 7 years)—Children develop language and are able to solve some problems. Students' thinking is egocentric, and they have difficulty developing concepts. For example, students in this stage may not be able to complete the conservation of number task shown above.

- Concrete operational (7–12 years)—Students' thinking becomes operational. This means that concepts become organized and logical, as long as they are working with or around concrete materials or images. During this stage, students master the number conservation and other conservation tasks, but most students do not understand symbolic concepts.

- Formal operational (12+ years)—Children develop and demonstrate concepts without concrete materials or images. In this stage, students think fully in symbolic terms about concepts. Children become able to reason effectively, abstractly, and theoretically. Full development of this stage may depend on the extent to which children have had a full range of active manipulative experiences in the concrete operational stage.

Personality Development

Freud's psychoanalytic theories have profoundly affected modern thought about psychological and personality development. He believed that humans pass through four stages of psychosexual development: oral, anal, phallic, and genital. The personality itself consists of the id, ego, and superego. According to Freud, an integrated personality develops from the gratification experienced at each of these stages.

Psychosocial Development

Eriksen built on Freud's work and partitioned the life span into eight psychosocial stages. An emotional crisis at each stage can lead to a positive or negative result. The result achieved at each stage determines the development pattern for the next stage. Four of these stages fall within the school years.

Stage	Characteristic	Description
Kindergarten	Initiative vs. Guilt	Children accepted and treated warmly tend to feel more comfortable about trying out new ideas. Rejected children tend to become inhibited and guilty.
Elementary grades	Industry vs. Inferiority	Students who are accepted by their peer group and do well in school, and those who believe they are accepted and do well, are more successful than those who do not feel good about themselves.
Grades 6–9	Identity vs. Identity Confusion	Students who establish an identity and a sense of direction and who develop gender, social, and occupational roles experience an easier transition into adulthood than those students who do not establish these roles.
Grades 10–12	Intimacy vs. Isolation	Students who have passed successfully through the other stages will find it easier to establish a relationship with a member of the opposite sex. Those students who are unsuccessful at this stage may face an extremely difficult transition into adult life.

Moral Development

Kohlberg built on Piaget's original work to develop stages of moral development. Kohlberg proposed three levels of moral development with two stages at each level. His stages provide a reasonable approach to understanding moral development. Not everyone moves through all stages.

Preconventional Morality (preschool and primary grades)

Stage 1   Children do not demonstrate a conscience but do react to fear of punishment. Children are very egocentric.

Stage 2   Children still have no clear morality. Children concentrate on their own egocentric needs and let others do the same. Children may not be willing to help others meet their needs even though it would help them meet their own needs.

[Some children and antisocial adults may not pass this stage.]

Conventional Morality (middle grades through high school)

Stage 3   These children want to be good. They associate themselves with parents and other adult authority figures. They show concern for others and evidence a number of virtues and try to live up to expectations.

Stage 4   These children shift from wanting to please authority figures to a more generalized sense of respect for rules and expectations. These children see their responsibility to maintain society through a strict enforcement of society's laws.

[Many adults do not progress beyond this stage of development.]

Postconventional Morality (high school and beyond)

Stage 5   People at this stage differentiate between legality and morality. They have a more flexible view of right and wrong and realize that societal needs often take precedence over individual needs.

Stage 6   Very few people reach this stage. Those at stage six have pure, cosmic understanding of justice and dignity. These principles always take precedence when they conflict with what is considered legal or socially acceptable.

Social Learning Theory

Social learning theory is a fairly new field. Social learning theorists seek to combine behavioral and cognitive learning theories along with other types of learning.

Albert Bandura is the leading social learning theorist. He believes that a great deal of learning can take place through modeling. That is, students often act the way they see others act, or they learn vicariously by observing others. Bandura believes that verbal explanations and reinforcement are also important and that students become socialized through systematic modeling of appropriate behavior. Students can also develop cognitive skills by observing a problem-solving process and learn procedures by observing these procedures in action.

Nature Versus Nurture

The relative affects of nature (heredity and genes) and nurture (environment and experience) on growth and development is still not resolved. Certain traits, sex, eye color, some forms of mental retardation, and susceptibility to some mental illnesses such as schizophrenia are linked to genes and heredity. However, other developmental questions are not clear, and even studies of twins separated at birth has not yielded the kind of conclusive results needed to draw conclusions.

DIVERSITY

Society and Culture

America is a multiethnic and multicultural society. Consequently, the culture of the community and the culture of the school varies widely depending on the school's geographic location, socioeconomic setting, and local norms. To understand schools, we must understand society and culture.

Anthropology and sociology provide a scientific basis for studying society and culture. Anthropology is the formal study of culture and the development of society. Much of the early anthropological work dealt with primitive cultures. However, in recent years anthropologists have turned their attention to communities and schools. Sociology is the study of how people behave in a group. Sociology can help us understand how students behave in school, how teachers function on a faculty, and how citizens interact in the community.

Culture is directly affected by the ethnicity of the community. Each ethnic group brings its own culture, its own language, and its own customs to this country.

Until recently, most immigrant groups have been acculturated. That is, they have largely adopted the dominant language and culture of the United States. Lately there has been a shift toward cultural pluralism in which immigrants maintain their cultural, and occasionally linguistic, identity.

Under cultural pluralism, the challenge is to provide equal educational opportunity while also providing for these cultural differences among students. There is little prospect, however, that non-English speakers will realize their full potential in the United States.

Socioeconomic status has a direct affect on culture and on the schools. As noted earlier, there is a strong correlation between SES and academic achievement. In the United States, groups, communities, and schools are stratified by social class. Social stratification often occurs within schools. Unlike many other countries, individuals are able to move among social classes, usually in an upward direction.

The Family

The family remains the predominant influence in the early lives of children. However, the nature of the American family has changed, and for the worse.

Divorce rates are very high and some say that a majority of Americans under 40 will be divorced. American families are fragmented with about 30 percent of children living with a stepparent. About one-quarter of children are raised in one-parent families, and about two-thirds of these children live below the poverty level.

An increasing number of children, called latchkey children, return from school with no parents at home. School programs developed for these students cannot replace effective parenting.

In many respects, the school, social or religious institutions, peer groups, and gangs have replaced parents. This means that parents and families have less influence on children's values and beliefs.

The pressures of economic needs have drastically changed the American family. Less than 10 percent of American families have children, a mother at home, and a father at work. Over 30 percent of married couples have no children, and over 70 percent of mothers with children are working mothers.

Ethnicity

In 1990 the population of the United States was about 78 percent Caucasian, 12 percent African American, 9 percent Hispanic, 3 percent Asian, and 1 percent Indian or Eskimo. Hispanics are the fastest growing ethnic group. By the year 2000 we expect about 67 percent of the population to be white, 15 percent Hispanic, 12 percent African American, 5 percent Asian, and 1 percent Native American. By the year 2020 America's school population will be about evenly divided between white and minority students.

About 15 percent of the families in the United States live below the poverty level. Some 30 percent of African American and Hispanic families do so, and an astonishing 65 percent of Native American families also live below the poverty level.

Hispanics

Hispanics come predominantly from Mexico and from other countries in Central and South America and the Caribbean. Many Mexican American families have been in this country for more than 100 years. Puerto Ricans form another large Hispanic group.

Language is the primary difficulty faced by this ethnic group. About half of the Hispanics in this country speak Spanish as their first language.

The nature of the Hispanic population varies by region. Most Hispanics in California or their forbearers are from Mexico. Many Hispanics living in and around New York City are from Puerto Rico or the Dominican Republic, while many Hispanics in Florida trace their ancestry to Cuba.

Hispanic students have more school problems than white students. Hispanics are disproportionately poor and low achieving.

African Americans

African Americans have been in this country for centuries, but they began their lives here as slaves. There is not a recent history of large-scale African immigration to the United States.

Their status as slaves and second-class citizens denied African Americans the education, experience, and self-sufficiency needed for upward social mobility. Even when African Americans developed these qualities, they were frequently discriminated against just because of their race. It took almost 200 years from the founding of this country for the Supreme Court to rule that overt school segregation was unconstitutional. Of course, de facto segregation continues to exist.

Many African Americans have achieved middle class status. However, the overwhelming proportion of poor in urban areas are African Americans. The unemployment rate of young African Americans can be near 50 percent in some areas.

Native Americans

Groups of Eskimos and other Native Americans have lived on the North American continent for over 25,000 years. Most Native Americans living today are descendents of tribes conquered and put on reservations about 100 years ago.

During this time of conquest, treaties made with tribes were frequently broken. Native Americans lost their lands and their way of life. They were made dependent on the federal government for subsidies and were not able to develop the education, experience, or self-sufficiency needed for upward mobility.

Native Americans have the largest family size and fastest growth rate of any ethnic group. They also have among the highest suicide and alcoholism rates of any ethnic group.

Native Americans are disproportionally poor and disenfranchised. They live in poverty on reservations and are often alienated when they move off reservations to metropolitan areas.

Asian Americans

Asian Americans are predominately Chinese and Japanese together with recent immigrants from Korea and Southeast Asia. Asian Americans represent a countertrend among American minorities. Their achievement and success tend to be above the national average.

Many recent immigrants do not have the educational background of other Asian Americans. They tend to be more ghettoized and to attain a lower SES than other Asian Americans.

However, overall, Asian students perform better on American standardized tests than non-Asian students. This finding holds also for those Asian Americans who immigrated to this country unable to speak, read, or understand English.

Some researchers have said that a particular work ethic currently found in Asian countries together with a strong family structure are responsible for these trends.

Societal Problems

This decade finds our society beset with unprecedented problems of crime and violence, alcohol and drug abuse, sex, AIDS, high dropout rates, and child abuse. Many of these problems can be traced directly to poverty. Schools are a part of society so that they too are affected by these problems.

Crime and Violence

The number of serious crimes in the United States is at the highest level in memory. Students bring guns to school, and large urban areas report dozens of deaths each year from violent acts in school. Murder is the leading cause of death among African American teens. More than 70 percent of those who commit serious crimes are never caught. We live in a society where crime is rampant and crime pays.

Crime in school presents a particular problem for teachers. Some estimate that 3 to 7 percent of all students bring a gun with them to school. Students attack teachers every day in America. While this behavior is not defensible, attention to the principles of classroom management mentioned earlier can help in averting some of these incidents.

Alcohol and Drug Abuse

Alcohol is the most used and abused drug. Even though it is legal, there are serious short- and long-term consequences of alcohol use. Alcoholism is the most widespread drug addiction and untreated alcoholism can lead to death.

Tobacco is the next most widely used and abused substance. Some efforts are being made to declare tobacco a drug. Irrefutable evidence shows that tobacco use is a causative factor in hundreds of thousands of deaths each year.

Other drugs including marijuana, cocaine, heroin, and various drugs in pill form carry with them serious health, addiction, and emotional problems. The widespread illicit availability of these drugs creates additional problems. Many students engage in crimes to get money to pay for drugs. Others may commit crimes while under the influence of drugs. Still others may commit crimes by selling drugs to make money.

More than 90 percent of students have used alcohol by the time they leave high school. About 70 percent of high school graduates have used other illegal drugs. Awareness programs that focus on drug use can have some positive effects. However, most drug and alcohol abuse and addiction has other underlying causes. These causes must be addressed for any program to be effective.

Sex

Many teens, and preteens, are sexually active. While many of these children profess to know about sex, they do not. It is in this environment that we find increases in teenage pregnancies, abortions, dropouts, and ruined lives. Sex spreads disease. So we also note increases in syphilis, gonorrhea, and other sexually transmitted diseases.

About 10 percent of teenage girls will become pregnant. Teenage pregnancy is the primary reason why girls drop out of high school. These girls seldom receive appropriate help from the child's father and are often destined for a life of poverty and dependence.

AIDS

AIDS stands for Acquired Immune Deficiency Syndrome. AIDS is a breakdown in the body's immune system caused by a virus called HIV. This virus can be detected with blood tests. People with the HIV virus may take 10 years or longer to develop AIDS. Those who develop AIDS die.

The HIV virus is transmitted by infected blood and other bodily fluids. Sexual relations and contact with infected blood, including blood injected with shared hypodermic needles, are all examples of ways that AIDS can be transmitted. Some 2 to 5 percent of the teens in some urban areas may be HIV positive.

Students can try to avoid becoming HIV positive by reducing their risk factors. Abstinence from sex and never injecting drugs will virtually eliminate the likelihood that a teenager will become HIV positive. Less effective measures can be taken to help sexually active students reduce the likelihood of becoming HIV positive. Girls run a higher risk than boys of becoming HIV positive through sexual activity.

Acquiring the HIV virus is associated with drug and alcohol use. Even when students know the risks, and how to avoid them, alcohol and drug use can lower inhibitions and lead to unsafe practices.

Dropouts

About 10 percent of white students, 15 percent of African American students, and 30 percent of Hispanic students drop out of school. Dropout rates are worst in urban areas, with over half the students dropping out of some schools. High school dropouts are usually headed for a life of lower wages and poorer living conditions.

Many of these students feel alienated from society or school and need support or alternative learning environments. Intervention, counseling, and alternative programs such as therapeutic high schools, vocational high schools, and other special learning arrangements can help prevent a student from dropping out.

Child Abuse

Child abuse is the secret destroyer of children's lives. Some estimate that between two and three million children are abused each year. Child abuse is a primary cause of violent youth, runaways, and drug abusers.

Physical and sexual abuse are the most destructive of the abuses heaped upon children. Contrary to popular belief, most child abuse is perpetrated by family members, relatives, and friends. Younger children are often incapable of talking about their abuse and may not reveal it even when asked.

In many states, teachers are required to report suspected child abuse. When child abuse is suspected, a teacher should follow the guidelines given by the school, the district, or the state.

INSTRUCTIONAL PLANNING AND ASSESSMENT

New York Learning Standards

Those at the New York State Education Department recently developed 28 preliminary Learning Standards in broad curricular areas. These final standards will form the basis for instruction in New York State schools. Elementary school, middle school, and high school assessments will be based on these broad standards. The standards are summarized below.

The Arts—Dance, Music, Theater, and Visual Arts
1. **Creating, Performing, and Participating in the Arts**
   Students will actively engage in the processes that constitute creation and performance in the arts (dance, music, theater, and visual arts) and participate in various roles in the arts.

2. Knowing and Using Arts Materials and Resources

Students will be knowledgeable about and make use of the materials and resources available for participating in the arts in various roles.

3. Responding to and Analyzing Works of Art

Students will respond critically to a variety of works in the arts, connecting the individual work to many other works and to other aspects of human endeavor and thought.

4. Understanding the Cultural Dimensions and Contributions of the Arts

Students will develop an understanding of the personal and cultural forces that shape artistic communication and how the arts in turn shape the diverse cultures of past and present society.

Mathematics, Science, and Technology

1. Analysis, Inquiry, and Design

Students will use mathematical analysis, scientific inquiry, and engineering design, as appropriate, to pose questions, seek answers, and develop solutions.

2. Information Systems

Students will access, generate, process, and transfer information using appropriate technologies.

3. Mathematics

Students will understand mathematics and become mathematically confident by communicating and reasoning mathematically, by applying mathematics in real-world settings, and by solving problems through the integrated study of number systems, geometry, algebra, data analysis, probability and trigonometry.

4. Science

Students will understand and apply scientific concepts, principles, and theories pertaining to the physical setting and living environment and recognize the historical development of ideas in science.

5. Technology

Students will apply technological knowledge and skills to design, construct, use, and evaluate products and systems to satisfy human and environmental needs.

6. Interconnectedness: Common Themes

Students will understand the relationships and common themes that connect mathematics, science, and technology and apply the themes to these and other areas of learning.

7. Interdisciplinary Problem Solving

Students will apply the knowledge and thinking skills of mathematics, science, and technology to address real-life problems and make informed decisions.

English Language Arts

1. Language for Information and Understanding

Students will listen, speak, read, and write for information and understanding. As listeners and readers, students will collect data, facts, and ideas, discover relationships, concepts, and generalizations; and use knowledge generated from oral, written, and electronically produced texts. As speakers and writers they will use oral and written language to acquire, interpret, apply, and transmit information.

2. Language for Literary Response and Expression

Students will listen, speak, read, and write for literary response and expression. Students will listen to oral, written, and electronically produced texts and performances, relate texts and performances to their own lives, and develop an understanding of the diverse social, historical, and cultural dimensions the texts and performances represent. As speakers and writers, students will use oral and written language for self-expression and artistic creation.

3. Language for Critical Analysis and Evaluation

Students will listen, speak, read, and write for critical analysis and evaluation. As listeners and readers, students will collect and analyze experiences, ideas, information, and issues presented by others using a variety of established criteria. As speakers and writers, they will present, in oral and written language and form, a variety of perspectives and opinions.

4. Language for Social Interaction

Students will use oral and written language for effective social communication with a wide variety of people. As readers and listeners, they will use the social communications of others to enrich their understanding of people and their views.

Social Studies

1. History of the United States and New York

Students will use a variety of intellectual skills to demonstrate their understanding of major ideas, eras, themes, developments, and turning points in the history of the United States and New York.

2. World History

Students will use a variety of intellectual skills to demonstrate their understanding of major ideas, eras, themes, developments, and turning points in world history and examine the broad sweep of history from a variety of perspectives.

3. Geography

Students will use a variety of intellectual skills to demonstrate their understanding of the geography of the independent worlds in which we live—local, national, and global —including the distribution of people, places, and environments over the earth's surface.

4. Economic Systems

Students will use a variety of intellectual skills to demonstrate their understanding of how the United States and other societies develop economic systems and associated institutions to allocate scarce resources. Students will also use these skills to understand how major decision making units function in the United States and other national economies, and how an economy solves the scarcity problem through market and nonmarket mechanisms.

5. Civics, Citizenship, and Government

Students will use a variety of intellectual skills to demonstrate their understanding of the necessity for establishing governments; the governmental system of the United States and other nations, the United States Constitution, the basic civil values of American constitutional democracy; and the roles, rights, and responsibilities of citizenship, including avenues of participation.

Languages Other Than English

1. Communication Skills

Students will be able to use a language other than English for communication.

2. Cultural Understanding

Students will develop cross-cultural skills and understandings.

Health, Physical Education, and Home Economics

1. Personal Health and Fitness

Students will have the necessary knowledge and skills to establish and maintain physical fitness, participate in physical activity, and maintain personal health.

2. A Safe and Healthy Environment

Students will acquire the knowledge and ability necessary to create and maintain a healthy environment.

3. Resource Management

Students will understand and be able to manage their personal and community resources.

Career Development and Occupational Studies

1. Career Development

Students will be knowledgeable about the world of work, explore career options, and relate personal skills, aptitudes, and abilities to future career decisions.

2. Integrated Learning

Students will demonstrate how academic knowledge and skills are applied in the workplace and other settings.

3a. Universal Foundation Skills

Students will demonstrate mastery of the foundation skills and competencies essential for success in the workplace.

3b. Career Options

Students who choose a career major will acquire the career-specific technical knowledge/skills necessary to progress toward gainful employment, career advancement, and success in post-secondary programs.

Thematic Unit Plans and Interdisciplinary, Integrated Approaches to Instruction

Contemporary instructional units are built around themes. Within these themes many different subject areas are taught in an integrated way. For example:

Consider a thematic unit about weather. Weather seems to be a unit about science and yet this unit can be used to teach almost every subject area in an integrated way. Look at the following examples.

Art—Students draw or paint clouds and create weather maps.

Reading—Students read books and articles about weather.

Technology—Students gather information about weather, including weather forecasts on the Internet.

Writing/Language Arts—Students write reports about their research on weather. Students write original short stories or poems about weather.

Social Studies—Students learn about the effects of local climates on the lives and about the impact of climates worldwide.

Science—Students learn about the mechanics of cloud building, such as the forces that create cumulonimbus storm clouds.

Thematic units such as the one outlined here provide a basis for teaching needed skills and concepts in all subject areas while emphasizing the interrelatedness of these topics.

Objectives

All useful instruction has some purpose. Planning for instruction begins with choosing an objective that expresses this purpose. Objectives usually refer to outcomes, while goals usually refer to more general purposes of instruction. The terms *aim, competency, outcome,* and *behavioral objective* are also used to refer to an objective. Each New York Learning Standard is accompanied by an extensive set of objectives.

Objectives are also established by national or state organizations. The national or state English, mathematics, and science professional organizations may recommend objectives for their subject. The national or state organizations for speech, primary education, elementary education, preschool education, and special education may recommend objectives for specific grades or specialties.

Most school texts contain objectives, usually given for each text unit or lesson. These objectives are also reflected in national, state, and local achievement tests.

School districts usually have their own written objectives. There may be a scope and sequence chart that outlines the objectives for each subject and grade. The district may also have a comprehensive set of objectives for each subject and grade level.

Taxonomy of Objectives and Critical Thinking

Benjamin Bloom and others described three domains of learning: cognitive, affective, and psychomotor. The cognitive domain refers to knowledge, intellectual ability, and the other things we associate with school learning. The affective domain refers to values, interests, attitudes, and the other things we associate with feelings. The psychomotor domain refers to motor skills and other things we associate with movement.

Each domain describes various levels of objectives. The six levels on the cognitive domain, noted below, are most useful in classifying objectives. Students should be exposed to objectives at all levels of the taxonomy, particularly analysis, synthesis, and evaluation, which foster critical thinking.

1. Knowledge—Remembering specifics, recalling terms and theories.
2. Comprehension—Understanding or using an idea but not relating it to other ideas.
3. Application—Using concepts or abstractions in actual situations.
4. Analysis—Breaking down a statement to relate ideas in the statement.
5. Synthesis—Bringing or putting together parts to make a whole or find a pattern.
6. Evaluation—Judging value, comparing work or product to a criteria.

Choosing and Modifying Objectives

Initially, you will identify an objective from the Learning Standards or one of the sources noted previously. Consider these criteria when choosing and sequencing objectives.

- The objective should meet the intent of the New York Learning Standards and overall goals of the school district.
- The objective should be appropriate for the achievement and maturation level of students in the class.
- The objective should be generally accepted by appropriate national, regional, or state professional organizations.

The objective you select may not exactly describe the lesson or unit you are going to teach. Modify the objective to meet your needs. You also may need to select or modify objectives and other plans to meet the needs of diverse student populations.

Your class may be academically diverse. You may teach special-needs students or you may have special-needs students in your class under the inclusion model. When you select and modify objectives for academically diverse students, consider the different achievement levels or learning styles of these students.

Your class may be culturally diverse. When you select and modify objectives for a culturally diverse class, consider the range of experiences and backgrounds found among the class. Do not reduce the difficulty of the objective.

Your class may be linguistically diverse. You may have limited English proficiency (LEP) students in your class. For a linguistically diverse class, take into account the limits that language places on learning. You may have to select or modify objectives to help these students learn English.

Writing Objectives

An objective should answer the question: "What are students expected to do once instruction is complete?" Objectives should not describe what the teacher does during the lesson. Objectives should not be overly specific, involved, or complicated.

Whenever possible, objectives should begin with a verb. Here are some examples.

Not an objective:	I will teach students how to pronounce words with a silent *e*. [This is a statement of what the teacher will do.]
Not an objective:	While in the reading group, looking at the reading book, students will pronounce words with a silent *e*. [This statement is overly specific.]
Objective:	Sounds out words with a silent *e*. [This is an objective. It tells what the student is expected to do.]
Objective:	States what he or she liked about the trip to the zoo.
Objective:	Reads a book from the story shelf.
Objective:	Serves a tennis ball successfully twice in a row.

Do not limit objectives to skills or tiny bits of strictly observable behavior. Specific objectives are not limited objectives. Objectives can include statements that students will appreciate or participate in some activity. Objectives should include integrating subject matter, applying concepts, problem solving, decision making, writing essays, researching projects, preparing reports, exploring, observing, appreciating, experimenting, and constructing and making art work and other projects.

Special Education Classification and IEPs

Students are generally classified as special education students by the district Committee on Special Education (CSE) with the approval of the student's parents. The classification process includes thorough testing along with observations and reports by the social worker, the psychologist, the teacher, the occupational therapist, and other education evaluators.

Once students are classified, each receives an Individualized Education Plan (IEP). The IEP is a complete education plan for that student. The plan includes test scores and reports prepared as a part of the classification process.

The IEP prominently contains the goals and objectives for the student in all applicable academic and nonacademic areas and their placement in classes. This listing is extensive. Also included are the modifications to be made for this student. Some typical modifications are listed here.

- extra test time
- hearing aid
- preferential class seating
- extra homework help
- writing aid
- test exemptions
- sessions with a psychologist or a social worker

The final version of the IEP is discussed and agreed to at a CSE meeting with the teacher, psychologist, social worker, parent advocate, and child's parent(s) in attendance. Once enacted the district must provide the services and arrange for the modifications described in the IEP.

Planning to Teach the Lesson

Once you have decided what to teach, you must plan how to teach it. Consider these factors as you plan the lesson or unit.

- Determine the prerequisite competencies. This is the knowledge and skills students must possess before they can learn the objective. Draw up a plan that ensures students will demonstrate prerequisite competencies before you teach the lesson.

- Determine the resources you need to help students reach the objective. The resources could include books, manipulatives, overhead transparencies, and other materials for you or the students to use. The resources could also include technological resources including computers or computer software and human resources including teacher aides, students, or outside presenters.

- Devise a plan to help students reach the objective. In addition to the factors discussed previously, the plan will usually include motivation and procedures.

Madeline Hunter posited the following important stages for effective lessons.

- Anticipatory set—Something that is said or done to prepare students and focus the students on the lesson.

- Objective and purpose—The teacher should state the objective of the lesson, and the students should be aware of the objective.

- Input—New information is presented during this stage.

- Modeling—The skills or procedures being taught or demonstrated.

- Checking for understanding—Following the instructional components in the previous two stages, the teacher should ensure that students understand the concept before moving to the next phases of the lesson.

- Guided practice—Students are given the opportunity to practice or use the concept or skill with the teacher's guidance.

- Independent practice—Students practice or use the concept on their own.

A sample lesson plan format follows.

SAMPLE LESSON PLAN FORMAT

Name _____   Date _____

Class _____

Objective: The objective answers the question "What do I expect students to be able to do once instruction is complete?"

Integration: Indicate which, if any, topics are "integrated" in this lesson.

Resources: The materials and the technological and human resources needed to teach the lesson.

Motivation: An introduction that interests the students and focuses their attention on the lesson.

Procedures

Review (Warm-up)
Review the prerequisite competencies. Reteach these competencies if students have forgotten them.

Preview
Fully inform students about the lesson objective and the way they will learn the objective.

Teach
The actual procedures, approaches, and methods for teaching the lesson.

Assessment
Use interaction, observation of students, tests, or other means to determine if the objective has been reached.

Practice
Students practice the skill or concept embodied in the objective.

Independent Work (Seatwork-Homework)
Assign up to fifteen minutes of work for students to do on their own.

THE PROFESSIONAL ENVIRONMENT

The School in Society

The school is a part of society. It reflects the society and socializes students. To that end, the schools prepare students to function in society. Students are taught, directly and indirectly, acceptable social values and behavior.

The academic curriculum reflects society's expectations. Students are taught a generally accepted body of knowledge. Students are also prepared for society by being exposed to potential careers as a part of the school curriculum.

Every society has a culture. The culture combines the history of the society and the society's current norms. The culture includes customs, values, ethical and moral structures, religions and beliefs, laws, and a hierarchy of most valued contributions by members of society.

The School as a Society

The school is a society in itself. The school society consists of a complex interrelationship of teachers, students, administrators, parents, and others. Each school has its own character, practices, and informal hierarchy. Generally speaking, new teachers must find a niche in the school's society to be successful. The school has a formal decision-making hierarchy of teachers, supervisors, principals, superintendents, and school boards. The new teacher must usually gain acceptance at each level of this hierarchy to experience success.

Each state in the United States has its own system of education. States are legally responsible for education. Locally elected or appointed school boards usually have the most direct legal impact on the schools. Within state and federal laws, school boards pay for the schools from tax receipts and other funds, hire teachers and administrators, approve curricula, and set school policy.

Many of the decisions made by school boards are affected by the amount of money available to the schools. Generally speaking, wealthier districts have more money to spend on schools. The difference in the funds available may create a difference in the quality of schooling.

LEGAL, LEGISLATIVE, AND POLITICAL INFLUENCES

Structure and Organization of the New York Education System

The Constitution of the United States does not assign the responsibility for education to the federal government, leaving this responsibility to each state. The state government, including the governor, the legislature, and the courts have the ultimate responsibility for public education. The Board of Regents of the State University of New York (SUNY) has overall responsibility for all educational activities in New York State. The Board of Regents was established on May 1, 1784. The State University of New York includes all elementary, secondary, and postsecondary institutions, both public and private, offering education in New York. The board acts primarily as a policy making body.

The Board of Regents appoints the New York State Commissioner of Education who is also president of the State University of New York, chief executive officer for the board, and head of the New York State Education Department.

The New York State Education Department supervises all educational institutions in New York State. Among these responsibilities, the Education Department charters all schools in the state, develops and approves school curricula and assessments, and supervises teacher certification.

There are 38 Boards of Cooperative Educational Services (BOCES) located throughout New York State. Each BOCES superintendent reports directly to the New York State Commissioner of Education and serves as the commissioner's local representative. Every public school system in New York is affiliated in some way with a BOCES that offers vocational and special education programs as well as administrative services to member districts.

Local or regional boards of education are directly responsible for operating schools in their district or town. In most cases, these boards are elected. A local or regional superintendent of schools reports to the board and, along with other administrators and support staff, has the daily responsibility for operating the schools.

Building principals report to the superintendent and are responsible for the daily operations of their school building. Teachers have the responsibility for teaching their students and carrying out district and state education policies.

It's the Law

A complex set of federal, state, and local laws govern education. Court cases are changing the interpretation of these laws each day. Here is a brief summary of legal rights they may apply to schools, teachers, and students. This summary should not be used to make any decisions related to school law. Any specific interest in legal issues should be referred to a competent attorney.

Schools

- Schools may not discriminate against students, teachers, or others because of their race, sex, ethnicity, or religion. "Reverse discrimination" *may* be legal when hiring teachers, but it is not legal when dismissing teachers.

- Prayer is not permitted in schools. In all other ways, schools may not embrace or support religion.

- Schools must make children's school records available to parents and legal guardians.

- Schools may remove books from the school library. However, a book may not be removed from the library just because a school board member or other school official does not agree with its content.

Teachers

- Teachers do not have to provide information unrelated to employment on an employment form or to an interviewer. You do not have to give your age, your marital status, sexual orientation, or any other unrelated information.

- Nontenured teachers usually have very limited rights to reappointment. Generally speaking, schools may not rehire a nontenured teacher for any reason. For example, the schools may simply say that they want to find someone better, that the teacher doesn't fit in, or that they just don't want to renew the contract.

- Teachers cannot be fired for behavior that does not disrupt or interfere with their effectiveness as teachers. However, even personal behavior away from school, which significantly reduces teaching effectiveness, might be grounds for dismissal.

- Pregnant teachers may not be forced to take a maternity leave. Decades ago, pregnant teachers were often forced to resign.

- Teachers may be dismissed or suspended for not doing their job. Any such action must follow a due process procedure.

- Teachers may be sued and be liable for negligence. Successful suits and actions against teachers have occurred when the evidence showed that the teacher could have reasonably foreseen what was going to happen or that the teacher acted differently than a reasonable teacher would have acted in that same situation.

- Teachers have the right to associate freely during off-school hours with whomever they wish. They may belong to any political party, religious group, or other group even if the group is not supported in the community or is disapproved of by board members, administrators, or others.

- Teachers have freedom of speech. Teachers have the same free speech rights as other citizens. They may comment publicly on all issues, including decisions of the school administrators or the school board. However, a teacher may not disclose confidential information or be malicious, and the statements can't interfere with teaching performance. Teachers do not have unlimited academic freedom or freedom of speech in the classroom or elsewhere in the school. Teachers are not permitted to disrupt the school or the school curriculum.

- Corporal punishment is not unconstitutional. However, corporal punishment is generally not permitted in New York. Teachers should never strike children in anger and should administer corporal punishment if permitted only as a part of a due process procedure.

Students

- Handicapped students from ages 3 to 21 are entitled to a free and appropriate public education as a matter of federal law. This education should take place in the least restrictive environment available.

- Students have limited freedom of the press. Student newspapers supported by school funds may be reviewed and edited by school officials. However, papers paid for and produced by students off school property may not be censored by school officials.

- Students are entitled to due process. In particular, students have a right to a hearing and an opportunity to present a defense before being suspended. Students who pose a threat to others in the school are not entitled to this due process.

- Students have freedom of speech unless it causes a significant disruption in the school. They may display messages or symbols on their persons, and refuse to participate in the pledge of allegiance. However, they may not use speech considered vulgar or offensive.

HISTORICAL AND PHILOSOPHICAL FOUNDATIONS OF EDUCATION

Development of Formal Education

Education is a fairly recent development. Formal education has existed for only a fraction of the time that humans have been on earth. Many events in the history of education led to the structure of our education system today.

The first formal education probably began about 2000 B.C. in northern Africa and China. It was about 500 B.C. when the formal education that led to our system was instituted in Athens, Greece. Boys were educated in schools, and girls were educated at home.

Three philosopher-intellects of this time—Socrates, Plato and Aristotle—left an indelible mark on education. Socrates developed the Socratic or inquiry method of teaching. Plato believed that an education should help a person fully develop body and soul. Aristotle introduced a scientific and practical approach to education. Plato and Aristotle both believed in the superiority of the ruling classes and the inferiority of women and slaves.

Formal Roman education began about 50 B.C., after Rome had conquered Greece. The grammiacticus schools, developed in Rome, taught such subjects as Latin, history, mathematics, and music and were like our high schools.

Around 70 A.D. Quintilian wrote a series of twelve books that described current and preferred Roman educational practices. These books may have been the first educational methods and psychology texts.

Education continued to develop and began to bring a unified language and thought throughout the known world. Then the Dark Ages (400 to 1000 A.D.) began. Enormous amounts of learning were lost during this period, and schooling was set back. The revival of learning following the Dark Ages was led by religious leaders such as St. Thomas Aquinas, who devised scholasticism (the formal study of knowledge).

During the Renaissance and the Reformation (1300–1700 A.D.), schooling was freed from control by the church. Church groups, particularly the Jesuits and the Christian Brothers, established religious schools.

Beginning around 1700, thought and schooling focused more on reason and logic. During this time, the "common man" in Europe sought a better life and better education. Great educators emerged from this period. Jean Jacques Rousseau, who wrote *Emile* in 1762, held a positive view of children and believed that education should be a natural process. Pestalozzi established schools that incorporated Rousseau's ideas. The schools featured understanding and patience for children and methods that enabled students to develop concepts through manipulative materials.

Herbart was Pestalozzi's student. In the early 1800s, Herbart formalized the approach to education. He presented some steps for teaching including presentation, generalization, and application. These steps bear a remarkable similarity to the stages from the taxonomy of educational objectives presented earlier.

Froebel was another educator influenced by Rousseau and Pestalozzi. Froebel established the first kindergarten with emphasis on social development and learning through experience. Kindergarten means child's garden.

American Education

In the 1600s American children were educated at home by their parents. Later that century, Dame schools began in the East. Classes were offered in a woman's home and often amounted to no more than child care. Secondary education consisted of Latin grammar schools, which provided a classical education.

In the mid-1600s laws were introduced in Massachusetts requiring education. Some localities provided schooling, and this form of local school lasted into the 1800s. Private schools also offered an education during this period. Admission to these schools was limited to those who could afford to pay.

In rural America there were not enough students in one locality to form a school. In these areas schooling was provided by tutors through the 1700s and by itinerant teachers through the 1900s.

English grammar schools and academies began operation as secondary schools during the 1700s. English grammar schools prepared students for careers while academies combined the features of Latin and English grammar schools.

Common schools provided free, public education for all students beginning in the 1800s. About that same time high schools were established to provide free, public secondary education. Junior high schools were introduced in the early 1900s, and middle schools were introduced in the 1950s.

Horn books, the alphabet covered by a transparent horn, were the predominant teaching device of the colonial period. The New England primer was the first substantial text and was used as a reading text until the late 1700s. The American spelling book, written by Noah Webster, contained stories and the alphabet along with lists of spelling words and was the most popular school book in the early 1800s. McGuffey's readers were reading books geared for different grade levels and were the main education materials for Americans from around 1840 to 1920.

American schools from the early 1800s through the early 1900s were based on the teachings of Pestalozzi and Herbart. These schools showed both the compassion suggested by Pestalozzi and the severe formalism based on Herbart's ideas.

Maria Montessori established her school, Casa Bambini, in 1908. She believed that students thrive in an environment that naturally holds their interest and that offers specially prepared materials. Schools following a modified version of her approach are found throughout the United States today.

Around 1900 John Dewey established the first "progressive" school. Progressive schools sought to build a curriculum around the child rather than around the subject matter. Progressive schools were very popular through the 1930s, and the progressive education movement continued into the 1950s.

The essentialist movement has a view opposite to progressivism. Educators associated with this movement favor a teacher-centered classroom. They believe in a more challenging, subject-oriented curriculum, and have a heavy reliance on achievement test results. Most school practices today primarily reflect the essentialist approach.

With the Depression of the 1930s, the federal government took a more active role in the schools. This active role increased through 1960 with programs designed to improve mathematics and science programs to bolster the national defense. In the 1960s and 1970s federal government focused on social issues as they relate to the schools, such as desegregation and equal educational opportunity.

Public Law 94-142 marked the federal government's first direct intervention in school instruction. This law and Public Law 99-457 mandate an appropriate public education in the least restrictive environment for handicapped Americans aged 3–21. Public Law 98-199 mandates transitional services for high school students. The federal government remains a vital force in American education today.

Jerome Bruner, B. F. Skinner, and Jean Piaget had an impact on American schools in the last half of this century.

In the *Process of Education*, Bruner urged the student's active involvement in the learning process. He called for more problem solving and believed that any topic could be taught in some significant way to children of any age.

B. F. Skinner took a different view than Bruner. He thought that material to be learned should be broken down into small manageable steps. Then students should be taught step by step and rewarded for success. Skinner's approach, behaviorism, built on the work of the Russian scientist Pavlov. Token reinforcement is an example of the behaviorist approach. Behaviorism is characterized by many as too limiting and controlling for regular classrooms.

Jean Piaget posited that students go though a series of stages—sensorimotor, preoperational, concrete operational, and formal operational—as they develop concepts. He believed that students need to work individually, based on their stage of development, and that movement through the stages for a concept could not be accelerated. Piaget's work indicates that more concrete and pictorial materials should be used in the schools and that students should be actively involved in the learning process.

ASSESSMENT

Assessment Program

Every teacher evaluates instruction. The assessment program and the assessment instruments should measure mastery and understanding of important topics. The assessment program should also be used as a teaching tool. That is, the program should be used to help students learn and to improve instruction. The program should include authentic assessment of students' work as well as teacher-made and standardized tests.

Formative assessment information is usually gathered before or during teaching. Formative information is used to help you prepare appropriate lessons and assist students. Formative evaluations help teachers decide which objectives to teach, which instructional techniques to use, and which special help or services to provide to individual students.

Summative assessment information is usually gathered once instruction is complete. Summative evaluation is used to make judgments about student achievement and the effectiveness of the instructional programs. Summative evaluations lead to grades, to reports about a student's relative level of accomplishment, and to alterations of instructional programs.

Assessment information may be used for both purposes. For example, you may give a test to determine grades for a marking period or unit. You may then use the information from this test to plan further instruction and arrange individual help for students.

You may informally gather formative and summative information. Just walking around the room observing students' work can yield a lot of useful information. You can frequently discern the additional work that students need and identify different levels of student achievement.

Assessment Instruments

Tests have long been used to determine what students have learned and to compare students. Every test is imperfect. Many tests are so imperfect that they are useless. It is important to realize how this imperfection affects test results.

Some students are poor test takers. Every test assumes that the test taker has the opportunity to demonstrate what they know. A student may know something but be unable to demonstrate it on a particular test. We must also consider alternative assessment strategies for these students.

Familiarize yourself with these basic assessment concepts.

- Errors of Measurement—Every test contains errors of measurement. In other words, no one test accurately measures a student's achievement or ability. Carefully designed standardized tests may have measurement errors of 5 percent or 10 percent. Teacher-designed tests typically have large errors of measurement.

A test result shows that a student falls into a range of scores and not just the single reported score. Focusing on a single score and ignoring the score range is among the most serious of score-reporting errors.

- Reliability—A reliable test is consistent. That is, a reliable test will give similar results when given to the same person in a short time span. You can't count on unreliable tests to give you useful scores. Use only very reliable standardized tests and be very aware of how important reliability is when you make up your own tests.

- Validity—Valid tests measure what they are supposed to measure. There are two important types of validity: content validity and criterion validity.

   A test with high content validity measures the material covered in the curriculum or unit being tested. Tests that lack high content validity are unfair. When you make up a test it should have complete content validity. This does not mean that the test has to be unchallenging. It does mean that the questions should refer to the subject matter covered.

   A test with high criterion validity successfully predicts the ability to do other work. For example a test to be an automobile mechanic with high criterion validity will successfully predict who will be a good mechanic.

Norm-Referenced and Criterion-Referenced Tests

Norm-referenced tests are designed to compare students. Intelligence tests are probably the best-known norm-referenced tests. These tests yield a number that purports to show how one person's intelligence compares to everyone else's. The average IQ score is 100.

Standardized achievement tests yield grade-level equivalent scores. These tests purport to show how student achievement compares to the achievement of all other students of the same grade level.

A fifth grader who earns a grade level equivalent of 5.5 might be thought of as average. A second-grade student with the same grade equivalent score would be thought of as above average. About half of all the students taking these tests will be below average.

Standardized tests also yield percentile scores. Percentile scores are reported as a number from 0 through 100. A percentile of 50 indicates that the student did as well as or better than 50 percent of the students at that grade level who took the test. The higher the percentile, the better the relative performance.

Criterion-referenced tests are designed to determine the degree to which an objective has been reached. Teacher-made tests and tests found in teachers' editions of texts are usually criterion referenced tests. Criterion referenced tests have very high content validity.

Authentic Assessment

Standardized and teacher-made tests have significant drawbacks. These types of tests do not evaluate a student's ability to perform a task or demonstrate a skill in a real-life situation. These tests do not evaluate a student's ability to work cooperatively or consistently.

In authentic assessment, students are asked to demonstrate the skill or knowledge in a real-life setting. The teacher and students collaborate in the learning assessment process and discuss how learning is progressing and how to facilitate that learning. The idea is to get an authentic picture of the student's work and progress.

The student has an opportunity to demonstrate what they know or can do in a variety of settings. Students can also demonstrate their ability to work independently or as part of a group.

Portfolio assessment is another name for authentic assessment. Students evaluated through a system of authentic assessment frequently keep a portfolio of their work.

Authentic assessment might include the following approaches.

- The student might be observed by the teacher, or occasionally by other students. The observer takes notes and discusses the observation later with the students.

- Students establish portfolios that contain samples of their work. Students are told which work samples they must include in their portfolios. The students place their best work for each requirement in the portfolio. Portfolios are evaluated periodically during a conference between the teacher and the student.

- Students maintain journals and logs containing written descriptions, sketches, and other notes that chronicle their work and the process they went through while learning. The journals and logs are reviewed periodically during a conference between the teacher and the student.

Grading and Interpreting Test Scores

The grade level at which you are teaching determines the approach you will take to grading. In the primary grades, you are often asked to check off a list of criteria to show how a student is progressing. Starting in intermediate grades, you will usually issue letter grades.

You should develop a consistent, fair, and varied approach to grading. Students should understand the basis for their grades. You should give students an opportunity to demonstrate what they have learned in a variety of ways.

It is not necessary to adopt a rigid grading system in the elementary grades. Remember, the purpose of a grading system should be to help students learn better, not just to compare them to other students.

Beginning about sixth or seventh grade, the grade should reflect how students are doing relative to other students in the class. By this age, students need to be exposed to the grading system they will experience through high school and college. The grading system should always be fair, consistent, and offer students a variety of ways to demonstrate their mastery.

You will need to interpret normed scores. These scores may be reported as grade equivalents or as percentiles. You may receive these results normed for different groups. For example, one normed score may show performance relative to all students who took the test. Another normed score may show performance relative to students from school districts that have the same socioeconomic status (SES) as your school district.

When interpreting normed scores for parents, point out that the student's performance falls into a range of scores. A student's score that varies significantly from the average score from schools with a similar SES requires attention followed by remediation or enriched instruction.

When interpreting district-wide normed scores, remember that these scores correlate highly with SES.

INSTRUCTIONAL DELIVERY

Planning instruction and implementing instruction are intertwined. Many of the points discussed here will have been considered during the planning process.

Classrooms are dynamic places. Students and teachers interact to further a student's learning and development. Follow these guidelines to establish a successful classroom and teach successful lessons.

Motivation

Most good lessons begin with a motivation. The motivation interests the learner and focuses their attention on the lesson. It is also important to maintain students' motivation for the duration of the lesson.

The motivation for a lesson may be intrinsic or extrinsic. Intrinsic motivation refers to topics that students like or enjoy. Effective intrinsic motivations are based on a knowledge of what is popular or interesting to students of a particular age.

For example, you might introduce a lesson about the French and Indian War to older students by discussing the book and movie *Last of the Mohicans*. You might introduce a lesson on patterns to young children by picking out patterns in children's clothes. You might introduce a lesson on fractions to middle school students with a discussion about the stock market.

Extrinsic motivation focuses on external rewards for good work or goal attainment. Extrinsic rewards are most successful when used in conjunction with more routine work. Extrinsic motivations may offer an appropriate reward for completing an assignment or for other acceptable performance. Establish rewards for activities that most students can achieve and take care to eliminate unnecessary competition.

For example, you might grant a period of free time to students who successfully complete a routine but necessary assignment. You might offer the whole class a trip or a party when a class project is successfully completed. Special education programs feature token reinforcement in which students receive or lose points or small plastic tokens for appropriate or inappropriate activity.

Motivation needs to be maintained during the lesson itself. Follow these guidelines for teaching lessons in which the students remain motivated. Lessons will be more motivating if you have clear and unambiguous objectives, give the students stimulating tasks at an appropriate level, get and hold the students' attention, and allow students some choices. Students will be most motivated if they like the topic or activities, believe that the lesson has to do with them, believe that they will succeed, and have a positive reaction to your efforts to motivate them.

Individual work gives a further opportunity to use intrinsic motivation. Use the interests and likes of individual students to spark and maintain their motivation.

The extrinsic motivation of praise can be used effectively during a lesson. For praise to be successful, it must be given for a specific accomplishment, including effort, and focus on the student's own behavior. It does not compare behavior with other students nor establish competitive situations.

Successful Learning

Research indicates that the following factors are likely to lead to successful learning.

- Students who are engaged in the learning process tend to be more successful learners, particularly when they are engaged in activities at the appropriate level of difficulty.

- Students learn most successfully when they are being taught or supervised as opposed to working independently.

- Students who are exposed to more material at the appropriate level of difficulty are more successful learners.

- Students are successful learners when their teachers expect them to master the curriculum and use available instructional time for learning activities.

- Students who are in a positive, uncritical classroom environment are more successful learners than students who are in a negative, critical classroom environment. This does not mean that students cannot be corrected or criticized but that students learn best when the corrections are done positively and when the criticisms are constructive.

- Students generally develop positive attitudes to teachers who appear warm, have a student orientation, praise students, listen to students, accept student ideas, and interact with them.

Classroom Interaction

Flander's interaction analysis gives a way to understand how teachers teach. His scheme focuses on the kind of teacher talk and student talk in a classroom. In Flander's work, one of the codes below was assigned to every three seconds of classroom instruction. This kind of frequent coding and the numbers or precise names of the categories are not important. However, the coding system can help you understand how to structure successful learning experiences.

Indirect Teacher Talk

1. Accepts feelings—Teacher acknowledges and accepts students' feelings.

2. Praises and encourages—Teacher praises students' contributions and encourages students to continue their contributions.

3. Accepts or uses students' ideas—Teacher helps students develop their own ideas and uses students' own ideas in the lesson.

4. Asks questions—Teacher asks questions about lesson content or solicits students' opinions. Rhetorical questions and questions not related to the lesson content are not included in this category.

Direct Teacher Talk

5. Lectures, explains, or demonstrates—Teacher presents facts, opinions, or demonstrations related to the lesson topic.

6. Gives directions—Teacher gives directions to which students are expected to comply.

7. Criticizes or justifies authority—Teacher responds negatively to students, criticizes, or justifies authority.

Student Talk

8. Student talk (response)—Student responds to a teacher's question. The correct answer is predictable and anticipated by the teacher.

9. Student talk (initiation)—Student initiates response that is not predictable. The response may follow an open-ended or indirect question from the teacher.

10. Silence or confusion—The classroom is silent or you can't make out what is being said.

Classroom Approaches

Effective classrooms are characterized by a variety of teaching approaches. The approaches should be tailored to the ability of the learner and the lesson objectives.

Teacher-Centered Approaches

Teacher-centered approaches are characterized by teacher presentation, a factual question, and a knowledge-based response from the student.

Lecture or Explanation

You can present material through a lecture or an explanation. A lecture is a fairly long verbal presentation of material. Explanation refers to a shorter presentation. Lecture and explanation are efficient ways to present information that must be arranged and structured in a particular way. However, lecture and explanation may place learners in too passive a role.

Lecture and explanation work best under the following circumstances: (1) the lesson begins with a motivation, (2) the teacher maintains eye contact, (3) the teacher supplies accentuating gestures but without extraneous movements, (4) the presentation is limited to about 5–40 minutes depending on the age of the student, and (5) the objective is clear and the presentation is easy to follow and at an appropriate level.

Demonstrations

Demonstrations are lectures or explanations in which you model what you want students to learn. That is, you exhibit a behavior, show a technique, or demonstrate a skill to help students reach the objective. Demonstrations should follow the same general rules as lectures and the actual demonstration should be clear and easy to follow.

Teacher Questions

Teachers frequently ask questions during class. The following guidelines describe successful questions.

- Formulate questions so that they are clear, purposeful, brief, and at an appropriate level for the class.

- Address the vast majority of questions to the entire class. Individually addressed questions are appropriate to prepare "shy" students to answer the question.

- Avoid rhetorical questions.

- Use both higher and lower level questions on Bloom's taxonomy (knowledge, comprehension, application, analysis, synthesis, evaluation). All types of questions have their place.

- Avoid question-and-answer drills. A consistent pattern of teacher questions that call for responses at the first level of Bloom's taxonomy is too limiting for most classrooms.

- Pause before you call on a student to answer the question, giving students an opportunity to formulate their responses.

- Call on a wide range of students to answer. Do not pick students just because they are either likely or unlikely to respond correctly.

- Wait 4 or 5 seconds for an answer. Don't cut off students who are struggling with an answer.

- Rephrase a question if it seems unclear or vague.

- Set a target for about 70 percent or so of questions to be answered correctly.

Student-Centered Approaches—Active Learning

In a student-centered or active learning environment, the teacher ceases to be the prime presenter of information. The teacher's questions are more open-ended and indirect. Students will be encouraged to be more active participants in the class. This type of instruction is characterized by student-initiated comments, praise from the teacher, and the teacher's use of students' ideas.

Just because there is student involvement does not mean that the teacher is using a student-centered or active approach. For example, the pattern of questions and answers referred to as drill is not a student-centered approach.

Cooperative Learning

Students involved in cooperative learning work together in groups to learn a concept or skill or to complete a project. Students, in groups of two to six, are assigned or choose a specific learning task or project presented by the teacher. The group consults with the teacher and devises a plan for working together.

Students use many resources, including the teacher, to help and teach one another and to accept responsibilities for tasks as they complete their work. The students summarize their efforts and, typically, make a presentation to the entire class or the teacher.

Cooperative learning is characterized by active learning, full participation, and democracy within a clearly established structure. Cooperative learning also engages students in learning how to establish personal relationships and a cooperative working style.

Inquiry Learning

Inquiry learning uses students' own thought processes to help them learn a concept, solve a problem, or discover a relationship. This kind of instruction has also been referred to as Socratic. Inquiry learning often requires the most structure and preparation by the teacher. The teacher must know that the situation under study will yield useful results.

The teacher begins by explaining inquiry procedures to students, usually through examples. Next the teacher presents the problem to be solved or the situation that will lead to the concept or relationship. Students gather information and ask questions of the teacher to gain additional information. The teacher supports students as they make predictions and provide tentative solutions or results. Once the process is complete, the teacher asks students to think over and describe the process they used to arrive at the solution. This last step is referred to as a metacognition.

Resources for Instruction

You may have to assemble a number of resources for instruction. It often helps to jot down the resources you will need to teach a lesson or a unit. The materials you select should help the students meet the lesson objectives and match the teaching-learning approach you will use. The resources may include textual, manipulative, technological, and human resources.

Be sure to assemble in advance the materials you need to teach a lesson. The materials may include texts, workbooks, teacher-made handouts, or other printed materials. Check the materials to ensure that they are intact and in appropriate condition.

You may use manipulative materials to teach a lesson. Be sure that the materials are assembled and complete. Any laboratory materials should be tested and safe. Be sure that the materials are at an appropriate level for the students.

You may use technological resources, such as a computer, during your lesson. Be sure that the computer will be available during your lesson. Try the computer out and be sure that it is working. Be sure that any software you will use is at an appropriate grade and interest level and matches the objectives of the lesson.

You will frequently use human resources in your lesson. You may decide to cooperatively teach a lesson or unit with another teacher. This approach requires advanced planning and regular communication. You may need to arrange for a guest speaker to speak to the class about a particular topic.

Special education teachers frequently teach in consultative or collaborative roles. That is, they work in classrooms with regular education teachers. In this arrangement, teachers must coordinate their activities and agree on how they will interact during the lesson.

INCLUSION

Inclusion means that special needs students are included in a regular school setting and placed in more restrictive environments only when needed. This does not mean that every special education student will be in a regular classroom all day. It does mean that students will be given every opportunity to function in a regular environment.

For some students, inclusion means attending a local special education school instead of a residential school. For other students it may mean attending a neighborhood school instead of a special education school. For still other students it means spending the maximum amount of time in regular classrooms.

Inclusion may mean placing students in regular education class and then switching them to special education settings as needed during the day. Inclusion may mean that a special education teacher goes into a regular education classroom to work with special education students in the class during the regular class periods. Teams of regular education and special education teachers frequently work together with students moving easily from regular education to special education settings.

It is impossible to include all students. Some students with severe physical disabilities require a special setting. Other students with severe mental handicaps will not be able to function effectively in a regular setting. Other students with severe emotional disorders or who are extremely disruptive will have to be educated in a self-contained special education class.

Parental Involvement

The key to a successful special education program is parental involvement. Parents are naturally concerned about their child's special education classification. They need to be constructively involved in their child's program. Keep parents abreast of the child's progress on a regular basis. If there are issues or concerns about the child, notify the parents immediately. Help parents understand the academic gains their child is making.

ADAPTING INSTRUCTION

Adapt instruction for the following factors, types of learners, and students.

Age—Primary students should have more structure, short lessons, less explanation, more public praise, more small group and individual instruction, and more experiences with manipulatives and pictures. Older students should have less structure, increasingly longer lessons, more explanation, less public praise, more whole-class instruction, more independent work, and less work with manipulatives.

Academically Diverse

Aptitude—Students exhibit different abilities to learn. You can provide differentiated assignments to enable students at different aptitude levels to maximize their potential.

Reading Level—Ensure that a student is capable of understanding the reading material. Do not ask students to learn from material that is too difficult. Identify materials at an appropriate reading level or with an alternative learning mode (tapes, material read to student). Remember that a low reading level does not mean that a student cannot learn a difficult concept.

Learning Disabled—Learning-disabled students evidence at least a 2-year discrepancy between measures of ability and performance. Learning-disabled students should be given structured, brief assignments, manipulative experiences, and many opportunities for auditory learning.

Visually Impaired—Place the visually impaired student where he or she can most easily see the instruction. Use large learning aids and large print books. Use a multisensory approach.

Hearing Impaired—Ensure that students are wearing an appropriate hearing aid. Students with less than 50 percent hearing loss will probably be able to hear you if you stand about 3 to 5 feet away.

Mildly Handicapped—Focus on a few, highly relevant skills, more learning time, and lots of practice. Provide students with concrete experiences. Do not do for students what they can do for themselves, even if it takes these students an extended time.

Gifted—Gifted students have above average ability, creativity, and a high degree of task commitment. Provide these students with enriched or differentiated units. Permit them to test out of required units. Do not isolate these students from the rest of the class.

Cultural and Linguistic Diversity

SES (Socioeconomic Status)—Socioeconomic status and school achievement are highly correlated. Overall, students with higher SES will have higher achievement scores. In America, SES differences are typically associated with differences in race and ethnicity. However, the achievement differences are not caused by and are not a function of these differences in race or ethnicity. Rather, achievement differences are typically caused by differences in home environment, opportunity for enriched experiences, and parental expectations.

Teachers frequently have a higher SES than their students. These students often behave differently than teachers expect. The crushing problems of poor and homeless children may produce an overlay of acting out and attention problems. All this frequently leads the teacher to erroneously conclude that these students are less capable of learning. In turn, the teacher may erroneously lower learning expectations. This leads to lower school performance and a compounding of students' difficulty.

A teacher must consciously and forcibly remind herself or himself that lower SES students are capable learners. These teachers must also actively guard against reducing learning expectations for lower SES students.

There are appropriate ways of adapting instruction for students with different SES levels. For high SES students, minimize competitiveness, provide less structure, and present more material. For low SES students, be more encouraging, guard against feelings of failure or low self-esteem, and provide more structure. Do not lower learning expectations, but do present less material and emphasize mastery of the material.

Culturally Diverse—Almost every class will have students from diverse cultural backgrounds. Use the values embedded in these cultures to motivate individual learners.

Language Diverse—The first language for many students is not English. In addition, a number of American students speak local variants of the English language. Teachers frequently, and erroneously, lower their learning expectations for these students. There are a number of useful strategies for adapting instruction for these students.

A number of students are referred to as Limited English Proficiency (LEP) who need English as a second language (ESL) instruction. Teaching English as a second language can be accomplished in the classroom, but often requires a specialist who works with students in "pull-out programs." When teaching these students, use simpler words and expressions, use context clues to help students identify word meaning, clearly draw students' attention to your speech, and actively involve students in the learning process.

Multiple Intelligences and Learning Styles

Multiple intelligences means there are many different ways students can demonstrate their ability. It follows that students have different learning styles. This approach is in sharp contrast to the current approach of measuring ability on a single scale, usually with an IQ test.

Howard Gardner of Harvard is credited with originating this approach to understanding intelligence. According to Gardner, there are seven ways to be smart. These seven intelligences are listed below.

1- verbal/linguistic
2- logical/mathematical
3- visual/spatial
4- bodily/kinesthetic
5- musical/rhythmic
6- interpersonal
7- the naturalist

Gardner also says that if students are smart in different ways then they learn in different ways. Children will have a learning style that matches their particular intelligence or intelligences. The idea is to use instructional approaches that match the learner's style. For example, use art to teach visual learners and use music to reach musical learners.

MANAGING THE INSTRUCTIONAL ENVIRONMENT

Classroom management is a more encompassing idea than discipline or classroom control. Classroom management deals with all the things a classroom teacher can do to help students become productive learners. The best management system for any classroom will establish an effective learning environment with the least restrictions.

Teachers who are proactive and take charge stand the best chance of establishing an effective learning environment. Classroom management is designed to prevent problems, not react to them.

Classroom management begins with understanding the characteristics of students in your class.

Characteristics of Students

We can make some general statements about the students in a class. We know that 3–7 percent of girls and 12–18 percent of boys will have some substantial adjustment problems. Prepare yourself for these predictable sex differences.

Boys are more physically active and younger children have shorter attention spans. Respond to this situation by scheduling activities when students are most likely to be able to complete them.

A teacher's management role is different at different grade levels. Prepare for these predictable differences in student reaction to teacher authority.

In the primary grades, students see teachers as authority figures and respond well to instruction and directions about how they should act in school. In the middle grades, students have learned how to act in school and still react well to the teacher's instruction.

In seventh through tenth grade, students turn to their peer group for leadership and resist the teacher's authority. The teacher must spend more time fostering appropriate behavior among students. By the last two years of high school, students are somewhat less resistant and the teacher's role is more academic.

We know that many adolescents resent being touched and that teachers may anger adolescents by taking something from them. Avoid this problem by not confronting adolescent students.

We know that there will be cultural differences among students. Many minority students, and other students, may be accustomed to harsh, authoritarian treatment. Respond to these students with warmth, acceptance, and structure. Many minority students will feel completely out of place in school. These students also need to be treated warmly and also with the positive expectation that they will succeed in school.

Many other students may be too distracted to study effectively in school. These students may need quiet places to work and the opportunity to schedule some of their own work time.

Other factors, such as low self-esteem, anxiety, and tension, can also cause students to have difficulty in school.

Classroom Management Techniques

The following guidelines for effective classroom management include techniques for dealing with student misbehavior.

Teacher's Role

Teachers who are good classroom managers understand their dual role as an authority figure and as someone who helps children adapt to school and to life. Teachers are authority figures. Students expect the teacher to be an authority figure and expect teachers to establish a clear and consistent classroom structure.

Teachers must also help students learn how to fit into the classroom and how to get along with others. Teachers fare better in their role as authority figures than they do in this latter role. But teachers who have realistic expectations and know how to respond to problems can have some success.

Characteristics of Successful Teachers

In general effective teachers have these general characteristics.

* Accept children within a teacher-student relationship.
* Set firm and clear but flexible limits.
* Enforce rules clearly and consistently.
* Have positive, realistic expectations about students' achievements and adaptations.
* Have clear reasons for expectations about students.
* Practice what they preach (model acceptable behavior).
* Don't take students' actions personally. Students usually misbehave or act out because of who they are, not because of who the teacher is.

Establishing an Effective Climate for Management

Classroom Physical Layout

There are several general rules to follow for a successful classroom layout. Set up the initial layout of the room so that you can see the faces of all the students. Rearrange the desks for individual and group work. Ensure that heavily used areas are free of all obstacles. Arrange the room so students do not have to stand in line, by having books and supplies available at several locations.

Classroom Leadership

Research indicates that the following factors are most important in establishing effective classroom leadership. Develop a cohesive class by promoting cooperative experiences and minimizing competition among class members. Identify and gain the confidence of peer leaders, particularly in grades 7–10. Establish an authoritative, but not authoritarian, leadership style.

Depending on the grade level, set three to six reasonable, adaptable rules that describe the overall nature of acceptable and unacceptable behavior. The expectations that accompany these rules should be stated clearly. The rules should be posted for students to see.

Much of the first two weeks of school should be spent establishing these rules, which may be stated by the teacher and/or developed through class discussion. Once the rules are established and the expectations are understood, the teacher should follow through. Student misbehavior should be handled immediately and appropriately but without causing a confrontation or alienating the student from the class.

Effective classroom managers take steps to ensure that the majority of class time is spent on instruction. They also take steps to ensure that students use their seat work and other in-class study time to complete assignments.

Specific Management Techniques

There are some specific management techniques that a teacher can apply to all classes. These techniques are summarized here.

Kounin

Kounin is a well-known expert on classroom management. Research results show that a number of Kounin's management techniques are effective. The following techniques have the most research support:

Kounin noted that teacher with-it-ness is an important aspect of classroom management. In other words, teachers who are constantly monitoring and aware of what is happening in the classroom are better managers.

Kounin also showed that effective managers' lessons have smoothness and momentum. By this he meant that these lessons are free of teacher behavior that interrupts the flow of activities or slows down lesson pacing.

Finally, Kounin showed that group alerting was an effective technique. In group alerting, the teacher keeps bringing uninvolved students back into the lesson by calling their attention to what is happening and forewarning them of future events.

Canter and Canter

Canter and Canter developed an approach called assertive discipline. Their approach is popular but lacks the research support of the approach recommended by Kounin.

The Canters recommend a direct and assertive approach to problem children. They point out that passive and hostile reactions to student misbehavior are not effective. Among other approaches, they recommend that the teacher and students establish rules and post those rules in the classroom. During each class session, the teacher writes and then marks the names of students who have violated rules. One rule violation in a session requires no action. Two rule violations, and the student meets with the teacher after school. Three violations requires a parental visit to the school.

Cueing

Cues are words, gestures, or other signals that alert students to a coming transition or that gain their attention. A cue may be spoken, such as "We'll be leaving for art in about 5 minutes. Take this time to get ready." Another cue might be, "Your group has about 15 minutes to complete your project."

Other cues are nonverbal. You may glance at a student or make eye contact to re-engage them in the lesson. You may raise your arm or hold your hand in a particular way to gain attention. You may flick the classroom lights quickly to indicate that groups should stop working and return to whole-class instruction.

Other Effective Techniques for Maintaining Attention During a Lesson

The techniques listed below have proven effective in classrooms.

- Stand where you can scan and see the entire class.

- Ask questions of the whole class and then call on individuals for a response.

- Involve all students in the question-and-answer sessions and don't call on students just to catch them in a wrong answer or because they will give the correct answer.

- Gain attention through eye contact or a gesture.

- If a comment is required, make it very brief.

- Ensure that the material being taught is at an appropriate level.

- Base seat work or group work on an established system that is monitored closely and positively.

Changing Behavior

Students may act so unacceptably that their behavior must be changed. Here are some suggestions for changing behavior.

Modeling

Students learn how to behave from observing others. In the classroom the teacher is the authority figure and the one whom students may model their behaviors after. The following teacher behaviors can have a positive impact on student behaviors. In general, teachers should act as they expect their students to act.

- Listen carefully to what students say.

- Act after thoughtful consideration, not in anger or on an impulse.

- Treat students with respect.

- Do not be sarcastic or hostile with students.

- Respond to difficulty or criticism carefully. Don't take it personally.

Reinforcement

All teachers use positive reinforcement, whether through grades, praise, tokens, or other means. Teachers also use negative reinforcement by showing students how to avoid an undesirable consequence (poor grade) by doing acceptable work. Negative reinforcement is not punishment.

In the classroom you should increase the duration or quality of the desired behavior before reinforcing. Reach explicit agreements with students about the level of performance that will yield rewards (positive reinforcement). Praise is often an ineffective reinforcer.

Contracts and Logs

You may be able to help children change behavior by using contracts or by asking students to maintain logs. These approaches cause students to think about their behavior and both have been proven effective.

When writing a contract, work with a student to establish desired learning goals or classroom behavior. The contract, signed by the teacher and the student, sets short-term goals for classroom conduct and academic achievement. A teacher may also ask students to maintain a log of their classroom behavior. A brief daily review of the log may improve behavior.

Punishment

Punishment is a temporary measure. It should be administered to improve student performance, not to make the teacher feel better. Limited punishment given for a specific reason when students are emotionally stable can be effective. Other punishments, such as extra work, punishment of the entire class, and corporal punishment, are usually not effective.

Effective punishment should be reasonable, deliberate, and unemotional. The punishment should also be short and somewhat unpleasant. The reason for the punishment should be clear, and the punishment should be accompanied by examples of appropriate behavior.

PART VI

Two Complete LASTs with Explained Answers

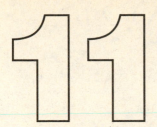 # PRACTICE LAST I

This practice test contains the types of items you will encounter on the real test. The distribution of items varies from one test administration to another.

Take this test in a realistic, timed setting.

The setting will be most realistic if another person times the test and ensures that the test rules are followed exactly. But remember that many people do better on a practice test than on the real test. If another person is acting as test supervisor, he or she should review these instructions with you and say "Start" when you should begin and "Stop" when time has expired.

You have 4 hours to complete the 80 multiple-choice questions and the written assignment. Keep the time limit in mind as you work.

Each multiple-choice question or statement in the test has four answer choices. Exactly one of these choices is correct. Mark your choice on the answer sheet provided for this test.

Use a pencil to mark the answer sheet. The actual test will be machine scored so completely darken in the answer space.

Once the test is complete, review the answers and explanations for each item.

When instructed, turn the page and begin.

ANSWER SHEET PRACTICE LAST I

1	Ⓐ Ⓑ Ⓒ Ⓓ	21	Ⓐ Ⓑ Ⓒ Ⓓ	41	Ⓐ Ⓑ Ⓒ Ⓓ	61	Ⓐ Ⓑ Ⓒ Ⓓ
2	Ⓐ Ⓑ Ⓒ Ⓓ	22	Ⓐ Ⓑ Ⓒ Ⓓ	42	Ⓐ Ⓑ Ⓒ Ⓓ	62	Ⓐ Ⓑ Ⓒ Ⓓ
3	Ⓐ Ⓑ Ⓒ Ⓓ	23	Ⓐ Ⓑ Ⓒ Ⓓ	43	Ⓐ Ⓑ Ⓒ Ⓓ	63	Ⓐ Ⓑ Ⓒ Ⓓ
4	Ⓐ Ⓑ Ⓒ Ⓓ	24	Ⓐ Ⓑ Ⓒ Ⓓ	44	Ⓐ Ⓑ Ⓒ Ⓓ	64	Ⓐ Ⓑ Ⓒ Ⓓ
5	Ⓐ Ⓑ Ⓒ Ⓓ	25	Ⓐ Ⓑ Ⓒ Ⓓ	45	Ⓐ Ⓑ Ⓒ Ⓓ	65	Ⓐ Ⓑ Ⓒ Ⓓ

6	Ⓐ Ⓑ Ⓒ Ⓓ	26	Ⓐ Ⓑ Ⓒ Ⓓ	46	Ⓐ Ⓑ Ⓒ Ⓓ	66	Ⓐ Ⓑ Ⓒ Ⓓ
7	Ⓐ Ⓑ Ⓒ Ⓓ	27	Ⓐ Ⓑ Ⓒ Ⓓ	47	Ⓐ Ⓑ Ⓒ Ⓓ	67	Ⓐ Ⓑ Ⓒ Ⓓ
8	Ⓐ Ⓑ Ⓒ Ⓓ	28	Ⓐ Ⓑ Ⓒ Ⓓ	48	Ⓐ Ⓑ Ⓒ Ⓓ	68	Ⓐ Ⓑ Ⓒ Ⓓ
9	Ⓐ Ⓑ Ⓒ Ⓓ	29	Ⓐ Ⓑ Ⓒ Ⓓ	49	Ⓐ Ⓑ Ⓒ Ⓓ	69	Ⓐ Ⓑ Ⓒ Ⓓ
10	Ⓐ Ⓑ Ⓒ Ⓓ	30	Ⓐ Ⓑ Ⓒ Ⓓ	50	Ⓐ Ⓑ Ⓒ Ⓓ	70	Ⓐ Ⓑ Ⓒ Ⓓ

11	Ⓐ Ⓑ Ⓒ Ⓓ	31	Ⓐ Ⓑ Ⓒ Ⓓ	51	Ⓐ Ⓑ Ⓒ Ⓓ	71	Ⓐ Ⓑ Ⓒ Ⓓ
12	Ⓐ Ⓑ Ⓒ Ⓓ	32	Ⓐ Ⓑ Ⓒ Ⓓ	52	Ⓐ Ⓑ Ⓒ Ⓓ	72	Ⓐ Ⓑ Ⓒ Ⓓ
13	Ⓐ Ⓑ Ⓒ Ⓓ	33	Ⓐ Ⓑ Ⓒ Ⓓ	53	Ⓐ Ⓑ Ⓒ Ⓓ	73	Ⓐ Ⓑ Ⓒ Ⓓ
14	Ⓐ Ⓑ Ⓒ Ⓓ	34	Ⓐ Ⓑ Ⓒ Ⓓ	54	Ⓐ Ⓑ Ⓒ Ⓓ	74	Ⓐ Ⓑ Ⓒ Ⓓ
15	Ⓐ Ⓑ Ⓒ Ⓓ	35	Ⓐ Ⓑ Ⓒ Ⓓ	55	Ⓐ Ⓑ Ⓒ Ⓓ	75	Ⓐ Ⓑ Ⓒ Ⓓ

16	Ⓐ Ⓑ Ⓒ Ⓓ	36	Ⓐ Ⓑ Ⓒ Ⓓ	56	Ⓐ Ⓑ Ⓒ Ⓓ	76	Ⓐ Ⓑ Ⓒ Ⓓ
17	Ⓐ Ⓑ Ⓒ Ⓓ	37	Ⓐ Ⓑ Ⓒ Ⓓ	57	Ⓐ Ⓑ Ⓒ Ⓓ	77	Ⓐ Ⓑ Ⓒ Ⓓ
18	Ⓐ Ⓑ Ⓒ Ⓓ	38	Ⓐ Ⓑ Ⓒ Ⓓ	58	Ⓐ Ⓑ Ⓒ Ⓓ	78	Ⓐ Ⓑ Ⓒ Ⓓ
19	Ⓐ Ⓑ Ⓒ Ⓓ	39	Ⓐ Ⓑ Ⓒ Ⓓ	59	Ⓐ Ⓑ Ⓒ Ⓓ	79	Ⓐ Ⓑ Ⓒ Ⓓ
20	Ⓐ Ⓑ Ⓒ Ⓓ	40	Ⓐ Ⓑ Ⓒ Ⓓ	60	Ⓐ Ⓑ Ⓒ Ⓓ	80	Ⓐ Ⓑ Ⓒ Ⓓ

Each item on this test includes four answer choices. Select the best choice for each item and mark that letter on the answer sheet.

The space vehicle verification program is designed to show that the vehicle meets all design and performance specifications. The verification program also seeks to ensure that all hazards and sources of failure have been either eliminated or reduced to acceptable levels. The specific spacecraft verification is based on a series of carefully monitored testing protocols. The verification tests are conducted under the strictest controls including temperature and stress levels. Full-scale hull models are used to verify the drawn specifications.

To date, seven full-stress tests have been completed. The tests evaluated the redesigned hull and the hull-to-motor nozzle connectors. The temperature is closely controlled in these tests, as are the internal hull pressures. Both temperature and hull pressures are critical factors in hull integrity. These tests showed that the parts of the hull that were strongest had the most potential for being weak. The tests also revealed that the hull-to-motor nozzle connectors were stronger that the connectors found in earlier versions on the hull. Additional full-stress tests are expected to further clarify the full impact of redesign efforts on the strength of the hull and the hull-to-motor nozzle connectors.

There have been eight full-static tests of engine performance to evaluate the impact of engine motor thrust on hull integrity. Before the tests were begun, specific test objectives were established, including parameters for acceptable performance. The test included a thorough evaluation of all engine attitudes—engine up, engine down and engine nominal. The tests showed that the engines performed within acceptable parameters at each attitude. But further tests are planned to determine if engines need to be strengthened at the points at which they are most likely to show weakness.

There have been six tests of the hull strength where it interfaces with the payload. These portions of the hull are often subjected to additional stress during payload detachment. The tests involved dynamic models that included maximum payload weights combined with maximum thrust and maximum torque. The tests showed that a further evaluation is needed to determine the maximum payload weight that is appropriate for the hull strength and hull characteristics at the point of interface. This evaluation will be based on the tests conducted to date and the tests planned for the next phase.

Another phase of tests are planned to determine the effectiveness of hull integrity with a new version of rocket motor—the PL-12. The PL-12 has more thrust than previous engines and may subject the hull to more stress requiring that potential hull weakness be fully evaluated. These tests will begin after a formal report on previous tests is prepared and new test guidelines and outcome expectations have been established.

1. Which of the following can be inferred from the statement above?
   (A) The parts of the hull that are potentially strongest do not receive as much attention from engineers as those that are potentially weakest.
   (B) The potentially weaker parts of the hull appear stronger in models than the potentially stronger parts of the hull.
   (C) Being potentially weaker, these parts of the hull appear relatively stronger in a model.
   (D) Potentially weaker parts of the hull have the most potential for being stronger.

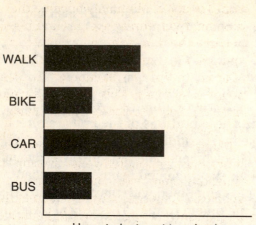

How students got to school.
MONDAY

School officials were trying to decide how students arrived to school each morning. This information was important because those at the school had to decide how many bike stands to have and how much space to set aside for parents to drop off their children at school.

At first they estimated the percent of students who walked to school and those who arrived by bike, car or bus. Their original estimates were that 60 percent of students walked to school or rode a bike to school, while 40 percent of students arrived by car or by bus. But then they realized that these estimates were not accurate enough. So they conducted a survey to gather this information directly from the students.

On Monday, the principal visited each class and found out how they arrived at school that morning. The principal tabulated the results and recorded them on the graph shown above. The principal also took the survey on each day that week. That was because the principal realized that students might not arrive the same way each day.

On Tuesday, the graph for walking shrank by half, while the graph for biking doubled. On Wednesday the results for walking and biking stayed the same as Monday, but the numbers for car and bus were reversed. On Thursday it rained and all but twenty percent of the students arrived by bus or by car. The results on Friday were almost the same as the results for Monday.

A committee reviewed the results and realized that the results were always going to be affected by the weather. So the committee decided to take another approach to plan for the different ways that students arrive at school. They posted a request for suggestions to answer this question.

2. Which of the following statements accurately describes the graph on that Wednesday
   (A) There were about twice as many walkers as bikers.
   (B) There were about three times as many car riders as bus riders.
   (C) There were about three times as many car riders as bikers.
   (D) There were about half as many car riders as bike riders.

We use language, including gestures and sounds, to communicate. Humans first used gestures but it was spoken language that opened the vistas for human communication. Language consists of two things. First we have the thoughts that language conveys and then the physical sounds, writing and structure of the language itself.

Human speech organs (mouth, tongue, lips, and the like) were not developed to make sounds, but they uniquely determined the sounds and words humans could produce. Human speech gradually came to be loosely bound together by unique rules for grammar.

Many believe that humans developed their unique ability to speak with the development of a specialized area of the brain called Broca's area. If this is so, human speech and language probably developed in the past 100,000 years.

3. What is the main idea of this passage?
   (A) Language consists of thoughts and physical sounds.
   (B) Human communication includes gestures.
   (C) Human speech and language slowly developed through the years.
   (D) Broca's area of the brain controls speech.

4. What is the first component of language development?
   (A) gestures
   (B) thoughts
   (C) sound
   (D) writing

5. What power of 10 would you multiply times 3.74 to get 374,000,000?
   (A) 10^6
   (B) 10^7
   (C) 10^8
   (D) 10^9

There was very little oxygen in the earth's atmosphere about 3.5 billion years ago. We know that molecules (much smaller than a cell) can develop spontaneously in this type of environment. This is how life probably began on earth about 3.4 billion years ago.

Eventually these molecules linked together to form complex groupings of molecules. These earliest organisms must have been able to ingest and live on nonorganic compounds. Over a period of time, these organisms adapted and began using the sun's energy. The organisms began to use photosynthesis, which released oxygen into the oceans and the atmosphere. The stage was set for more advanced life forms.

The first cells were prokaryotes (bacteria), which created energy (respired) without oxygen (anaerobic). Next these cells developed into blue-green algae prokaryotes, which were aerobic (creating energy with oxygen) and used photosynthesis. The advanced eukaryotes were developed from these primitive cells.

Algae developed about 750 million years ago. Even this simple cell contained an enormous amount of DNA and hereditary information. It took about 2.7 billion years to develop life to this primitive form. This very slow process moved somewhat faster in the millennia that followed as animal and plant forms slowly emerged.

Animals developed into vertebrate (backbone) and invertebrate (no backbone) species. Mammals became the dominant vertebrate species and insects became the dominant invertebrate species. As animals developed, they adapted to their environment. The best adapted survived. This process is called natural selection. Entire species have vanished from earth.

Mammals and dinosaurs coexisted for more than 100 million years. During that time, dinosaurs were the dominant species. When dinosaurs became extinct 65 million years ago, mammals survived. Freed of dinosaurian dominance, mammals evolved into the dominant creatures they are today. Despite many years of study, it is not known what caused the dinosaurs to become extinct or why mammals survived.

6. This passage suggests
   (A) that mammals were the more intelligent species.
   (B) how life evolved on earth.
   (C) that mammals and dinosaurs were natural enemies.
   (D) the environment did not affect evolution.

7. The author's purpose for writing this passage is to
   (A) entertain.
   (B) narrate.
   (C) persuade.
   (D) inform.

8. The tone of this passage is best described as
   (A) objective.
   (B) depressed.
   (C) nostalgic.
   (D) cynical.

9. The main idea of the second paragraph is
   (A) Molecules can only ingest nonorganic compounds.
   (B) Evolution is based on adaptation.
   (C) Photosynthesis allowed organisms to exist without the need of sunlight.
   (D) Oxygen is more important to life than the sun's energy.

Many anthropologists believe the first inhabitants of South America crossed over the Bering Strait land bridge. These native South Americans traveled down the west coast of what is now Canada, the United States, Mexico, and Central America to South America.

The crossing may have begun 15,000 to 20,000 years ago, and continued for thousands of years. Some of these Native South Americans reached the Islands of Terra del Fuego off the tip of South America about 8,000 years ago. Two major native civilizations developed in South America. The Incan empire developed in the highlands near the Andes mountains, while the Chibcha empire became dominant in what is now Columbia. Other native civilizations developed throughout South America.

These native groups were the only human inhabitants of South America until Europeans arrived following the voyage of Columbus in 1492. At the beginning of the sixteenth century, there may have been 30,000,000 inhabitants of South America. But Europeans brought cruelty and disease that decimated the native population. At the beginning of the seventeenth century the native population in South America was most likely less than 7,500,000.

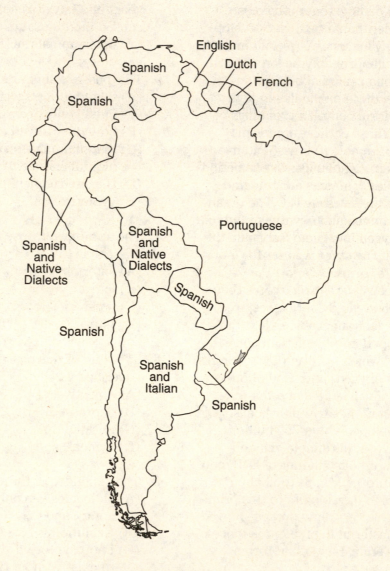

Languages of
South American Countries

European colonizing nations introduced African slaves into South America, primarily into northeastern Brazil and into the Caribbean Islands. Most slaves were forced into labor on sugar plantations. Historians believe that the number of slaves brought to these regions may be 25 times the 500,000 African slaves brought into the United States.

The importation of slaves stopped before 1850 and European immigration increased about this same time. Most Europeans came to the east coast of South America, primarily to southern Brazil and to Argentina. By 1950 about 8,000,000 Europeans had immigrated to South America.

Population experts estimate that there may by 300 million inhabitants in South America. About 7 percent of the inhabitants speak native languages, and pockets of native civilizations can still be found in the countryside. Most South Americans with European origins trace their roots to Portugal, Spain, and Italy.

10. The non-Spanish languages spoken in western South America result from
   (A) early Incan influence.
   (B) the primitive nature of the countries.
   (C) immigration by Mayan Indians.
   (D) proximity to Central America.

11. What accounts for the use of Italian as an official language in southeastern South America?
   (A) The voyages of Christopher Columbus
   (B) The exploration of the Americas by Amerigo Vespucci
   (C) Italian and German immigration following World War II
   (D) Italian and German immigration in the eighteenth century

12. The only French-speaking South American nation is associated with
   (A) the French government in exile during World War II.
   (B) exiles from French-speaking Quebec.
   (C) the revolt of the Foreign Legion during the Algerian crisis.
   (D) the French penal colony Devil's Island.

13. According to the map, about what percent of South American countries have Spanish as an official language?
   (A) 80 percent
   (B) 70 percent
   (C) 50 percent
   (D) 40 percent

Items 14–19.

The War of 1812 is one of the least understood conflicts in American history. However, many events associated with the war are among the best remembered from (5) American History. The war began when the United States invaded British colonies in Canada. The invasion failed, and the United States was quickly put on the defensive. Most Americans are not aware (10) of how the conflict began. During the war, the *USS Constitution* (Old Ironsides) was active against British ships in the Atlantic. Captain William Perry, sailing on Lake Erie, was famous for his yelling to his (15) shipmates, "Don't give up the ship." Most Americans remember Perry, and his famous plea but not where, or in which war, he was engaged.

Most notably, British troops sacked and (20) burned Washington, D.C. during this conflict. Subsequent British attacks on Fort McHenry near Baltimore were repulsed by American forces. It was during this battle that Francis Scott Key wrote the "Star-(25) Spangled Banner" while a prisoner on a British ship. The "rockets' red glare, bombs bursting in air" referred to ordinance used by the British to attack the fort. Many Americans mistakenly believe that the (30) "Star-Spangled Banner" was written during or shortly after the Revolutionary War.

Uncle Sam is one of the most popular fictional representatives of the United States. Historians attribute the fictional (35) Uncle Sam to "Uncle Sam" Wilson, a meat packer who supplied meat to the American army during the War of 1812. Reports have it that he stamped U. S. on the sides of his packing cases. People (40) often assume that Uncle Sam was "born" during the first or second world war when "I Want You" recruiting posters featured an image of Uncle Sam.

Many are not aware that the War of (45) 1812 created a secessionist movement. In this case, it was the New England states that considered withdrawing from the Union. New England was threatened most by British troops in Canada, and (50) the war had devastated trade from New England. Representatives of New England states met at the Hartford Convention in Connecticut to discuss creating their own country. In the end, the repre-(55) sentatives decided not to leave the Union.

The British defeat of Napoleon posed a further threat to the United States. The British were then able to transfer a large (60) number of troops and ships to the conflict. Most of these troops were sent to Canada and to New Orleans. It is not unusual to be unaware of the historical relationship between Britain's conflict (65) with France and the War of 1812.

The name Thomas MacDough is unfamiliar to most Americans, yet the forces under his command were likely responsible for preserving the United States of (70) America. In the fall of 1814, a large force of British troops entered the United States from Canada. The American force arrayed before them was almost certainly too weak to halt the British advance. (75) But on September 14, 1814 MacDough's naval forces destroyed the British fleet in the Battle of Lake Champlain, also called the battle of Plattsburg Bay. Almost inexplicably, the British were concerned (80) about the loss of a line of communication and the British forces withdrew into Canada.

American and British negotiators were in Europe discussing terms to end the (85) war. When word of the failed attack reached the British negotiators, they decided to end the war without any concessions from the United States. The treaty of Ghent was signed by both war-(90) ring powers on December 24, 1814 and that should have ended hostilities.

However, communication across the Atlantic was slow, and in January 1815 the British forces in New Orleans attacked as planned. But American forces (95) under the leadership of General Andrew Jackson won a complete victory over the British forces. Most Americans associate the ending of the War of 1812 with Jackson's success at New Orleans and were (100) convinced that the war ended in victory for the United States.

14. All the following statements can be implied from the passage EXCEPT
    (A) The British did not start the war.
    (B) Francis Scott Key was not at Fort McHenry when he wrote the "Star-Spangled Banner."
    (C) The rockets referred to in the "Star-Spangled Banner" were part of a celebration.
    (D) The British army entered Washington, D.C., during the war.

15. Which of the following words is the most appropriate replacement for "sacked" in line 19?
    (A) entered
    (B) ravished
    (C) invaded
    (D) enclosed

16. Which of the following statements best summarizes the difference referred to in the passage between Perry's involvement in the War of 1812 and the way many Americans remember his involvement.
    (A) Perry was a drafter of the Constitution and later served on the *Constitution* in the Atlantic, although many Americans don't remember that.
    (B) Perry served in the Great Lakes, but many Americans don't remember that.
    (C) Perry served in the Great Lakes, and many Americans remember that.
    (D) Perry served on the *Constitution* at Fort McHenry during the writing of the "Star-Spangled Banner," although many Americans do not remember that.

17. What can be inferred about Francis Scott Key from lines 24–26 of the passage?
    (A) He was killed in the battle.
    (B) All his papers were confiscated by the British after the battle.
    (C) He was released by or escaped from the British after the battle.
    (D) He returned to Britain where he settled down.

18. What main point is the author making in this passage?
    (A) The Americans fought the British in the War of 1812.
    (B) The Revolutionary War continued into the 1800s.
    (C) The British renewed the Revolutionary War during the 1800s.
    (D) Many Americans are unaware of events associated with the War of 1812.

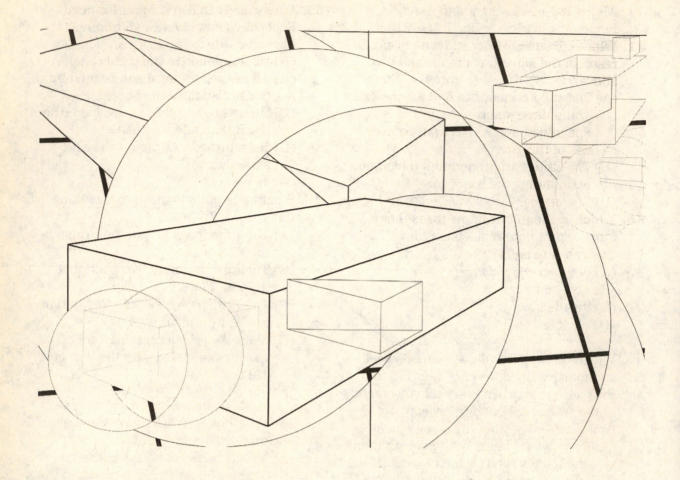

[Mercury Zone III. The Metropolitan Museum of Art, George A. Hearn Fund, 1976. (1976.21)]

19. This painting incorporates which of the following techniques?

(A) It uses three-dimensional space.

(B) It uses only regular geometric shapes.

(C) The curved lines of the three-dimensional figures contrast with the straight lines of the two-dimensional figures.

(D) It uses two-dimensional space to represent two- and three-dimensional figures.

20. A scientist cuts in half a just fallen hailstone and finds a series of rings much like tree rings. What could be found from counting the approximate number of rings?

(A) how long the hailstone was in the atmosphere before falling to earth

(B) how far from the surface the hailstone was before it started falling

(C) how much precipitation fell during the hailstorm

(D) how many times the hailstone was blown above the freezing level

$$(123 + 186 + 177) \div (3) =$$

21. Which of the following statements could result in the number sentence given above?
(A) The athlete wanted to find the median of the three jumps.
(B) The athlete wanted to find the average of the three jumps.
(C) The athlete wanted to find the quotient of the product of three jumps.
(D) The athlete wanted to find the sum of the quotients of the three jumps.

Use this graph to answer item 22.

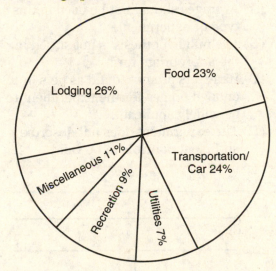

Jane's Monthly Budget

22. Jane spends $2,600 in May. She needs $858 that month for transportation/car expenses, which is more than the budget allows. Any needed money will come from miscellaneous. When she recalculates her budget chart, what percent is left for miscellaneous?
(A) 2 percent
(B) 6 percent
(C) 9 percent
(D) 11 percent

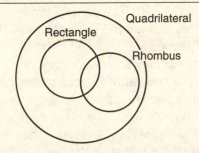

23. The above diagram shows the relationship among quadrilaterals, rectangles, and rhombuses. What conclusion can we draw from this diagram?
(A) All quadrilaterals are rhombuses.
(B) All quadrilaterals are rectangles.
(C) All rectangles are not rhombuses.
(D) Some rhombuses are not rectangles.

An experiment usually tries to test the effect of one thing on something else. The thing the experiment is testing the effect *of* is the independent variable. The thing the experiment is testing the effect *on* is the dependent variable. For example, the experimenter may test the effect of a particular hamster food. In that experiment, the independent variable is the type of food. The dependent variable is the growth of the hamster.

An experimental design should include both experimental and control groups. The experimental group consists of hamsters that get the new food—HF2. The control group consists of hamsters that get the current food—HF1

The experimental and control groups must be very similar. You don't want one of the groups to grow more because the hamsters in that group are healthier, younger or more likely to grow for some other reason.

You can take some steps to ensure that the two groups of hamsters will be as identical as possible. One way is to randomly assign hamsters to the two groups. Random assignment means that the experimenter has no role in assigning the hamsters, and ensures that hamsters are assigned to either the experimental group or the control group in an unbiased way.

Some experiments establish a correlation. Correlation is a way of showing how strongly two variables are related. But correlation does not mean cause and effect. For example, a correlation of 1 between two variables means they are perfectly related. However, this correlation does not mean that one necessarily causes the other. For example, economists report that there is a high positive correlation between the amount of snowfall in Colorado and the size of the state budget. The snowfall does not cause the higher state budget. But there is a strong correlation between the two.

AVERAGE OUNCES GAINED PER ANIMAL

Week #	HF1	HF2
1	4	9
2	3	4
3	2	3
4	1	2
5	1	2
6	1	1

24. An experiment is set up to determine the effects of a new hamster food HF2 as compared to the effects of a current hamster food HF1. Each group receives the same quantity of food and the same attention. From the above data choose the best conclusion for the experiment.
    (A) HF2 group gained more weight.
    (B) HF1 group lived longer.
    (C) HF2 group got more protein.
    (D) HF1 group got better nutrition.

25. What appropriate criticism might a scientist have of the experiment in the previous question?
    (A) Averages should not be used in this type of experiment.
    (B) The null hypothesis is not stated in the appropriate form.
    (C) Hamsters are not found as pets in enough homes for the experiment to be widely applicable.
    (D) The experiment does not describe sufficient controls to be valid.

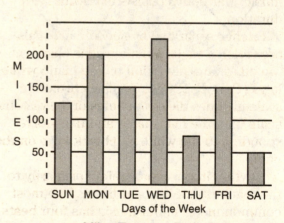

Miles Traveled Each Day
on a Family Camping Trip

26. In total, how many miles were traveled Wednesday through Friday?
    (A) 150
    (B) 225
    (C) 300
    (D) 450

Items 27 and 28 refer to this passage.

Good evening, my name is Max Drea. Before our host and our quartet come out, I want to talk to you a little bit about music.

Music can be thought of as organized sounds. Our culture has many different types of music and there are various types of music for cultures all over the world. We usually classify our music in three categories. (1) Popular music is professionally composed, recorded or performed live and represents the type of music of most current interest to the public. (2) Classical music was composed in the past and, while it is also recorded for sale, is usually performed by large orchestras in "symphony" halls (3) Folk music usually has a rural origin, is usually not composed professionally, and is often transmitted by oral tradition.

Music consists of pitch, the actual frequency or sound of a note, and duration. A tone has a specific pitch and duration. Different tones occurring simultaneously are called chords. A melody is the tones that produce the distinctive "sound" of the music. Harmony consists of chords with duration.

Pitches separated by specific intervals are called a scale. Most music is based on the diatonic scale found on the piano white keys (C, D, E, F, G, A, B). The chromatic scale includes the seven notes of the diatonic scale with the five sharps and flats corresponding to the white and black keys on the piano.

Rhythm in our music refers primarily to the regularity of beats or meter. The most common meter in our music has four beats with an emphasis on the first beat.

Think of the piano. The piano represents the chromatic scale with groups of seven white keys and five black keys. Music is played using tones from this scale for varying durations. Usually the melody consists of one note at a time and is played with the right hand. Harmony usually consists of chords and is played with the left hand. The rhythm of the music reflects the meter and the arrangements and duration of notes.

Our musical notation uses a staff to represent notes. A time signature is written at the beginning of each staff. The top number shows how many beats per measure and the bottom number shows which note gets a beat. A typical staff showing G and bass clefs is shown below. The clef placed at the beginning of the staff determines the pitches for each line and space on the staff. Notes are written on the staff using the notation shown below. A flat lowers the note a half-tone while a sharp raises the note a halftone. Rests indicate a time when no music is played. A note followed by a dot is increased in value by half. The staff is partitioned into measures. The sum of the values of the notes in a measure equals one. A key signature of sharps or flats can be written at the beginning of a staff to change these notes throughout the piece. The natural cancels a flat or sharp.

And now, on with the show.

Ladies and gentlemen, welcome to the Glow Room of the Rabrons Hotel. We are here tonight to bring you some enjoyable music for your listening pleasure. First let me introduce our musicians. On the piano, Mr. Ryan Bert. On the saxophone, Mr. Chad Ekred. That's Ms. Blaire Nan on the bass fiddle and Ms. Liz Mans on the drums. I'm your host Mr. Bob Mans. Take a bow everyone. Now we're going to play one of our favorites in three-quarter time.

27. What type of instrument is Mr. Ryan Bert playing?
(A) percussion
(B) string
(C) reed
(D) woodwind

28. In the music the group is about to play,
(A) the quarter note gets two beats.
(B) there are four beats per measure.
(C) the dotted quarter note gets one beat.
(D) there are three beats per measure.

29.
> ah autumn coolness
> hand in hand paring away

Which of the following could be the third line in the haiku poem above?
(A) in the wetness
(B) branches and leaves
(C) eggplants cucumbers
(D) til the end of day

Items 30 and 31 refer to the following poem.

> My love falls on silence nigh
> I am alone in knowing the good-bye
> For while a lost love has its day
> A love unknown is a sadder way

30. The word *nigh* in line 1 means
(A) clear.
(B) complete.
(C) near.
(D) not.

31. This passage describes
(A) loving someone and being rebuffed.
(B) being loved by someone you do not love.
(C) loving someone who loves another person.
(D) loving someone without acknowledgment.

An Internet advertising company renovated a deserted warehouse near the Canadian border to hold their offices. The offices themselves occupied about 5,000 square
(5) feet, and there was a lunchroom and other common areas that took up about another 750 square feet. Just about everyone in the company was a skier, so the location made a lot of sense. Of course it did not make
(10) any difference where the offices were—no clients ever came to visit. All the work was done over the Internet, or on the phone.

The advertising company placed advertisements on web pages. Most of their ads
(15) were banner ads. That means when the page came up the ad appeared. The number of pixels they occupied on a web page identified the banner ad's size. There are three banner ad sizes. Size A is 463 pixels
(20) by 70 pixels. Size B is 130 pixels by 220 pixels. Size C is 130 by 145 pixels.

Advertising representatives like to sell the largest ads because this size costs the most and the representatives get a higher com
(25) mission. The average representative sells nine to ten size A banner ads each day. The advertising company has a way to count the number of times that a web page is accessed. They base their advertising rates
(30) on the number of times the ad appears in a month. For example, an A banner ad costs $85 per thousand appearances up to 100,000 appearances, and $75 per thousand for each thousand over 100,000 appear-
(35) ances. The smallest banner is about half the price of the largest banner ad, and the average representative sells about fifteen to twenty of these ads each day. This size ad is good for a few high impact words.
(40) Of course, the agency offers other types of Internet ads as well. One type is where the advertiser pays a fee each time the on line user pushes a button that takes the user to the advertiser's home page. This
(45) type of ad costs more than other ads, but it is used less frequently. The average representative sells six to ten of these ads each day, while the average representative sells twelve to fourteen middle-size ban-
(50) ner ads. This advertising agency also has contracts with Internet search engine companies and the agency can arrange for an ad to appear when a particular search term is entered. These ads are the most
(55) expensive, and the average representative sells two to four of these ads each day.

32. What is the total maximum and minimum of banner ads that the average representative sells each day?
(A) 9 and 20
(B) 9 and 15
(C) 15 and 20
(D) 36 and 44

Items 33–38 refer to this passage.

Computer-based word processing programs have spelling checkers and even a thesaurus to find synonyms for highlighted words. To use the thesaurus, the student just types in the word, and a series of synonyms and antonyms appears on the computer screen. The program can also show recommended spellings for misspelled words. I like having a computer program that performs these mechanical aspects of writing. However, these programs do not teach about spelling or word meanings. A person could type in a word, get a synonym and have not the slightest idea what either meant.

Relying on this mindless way of checking spelling and finding synonyms, students will be completely unfamiliar with the meanings of the words they use. In fact, one of the most common misuses is to include a word that is spelled correctly but used incorrectly in the sentence.

It may be true that a strictly mechanical approach to spelling is used by some teachers. There certainly is a place for students who already understand word meanings to use a computer program that relieves the drudgery of checking spelling and finding synonyms. But these computer programs should never and can never replace the teacher. Understanding words—their uses and meanings—should precede this more mechanistic approach.

33. What is the main idea of this passage?
(A) Mechanical spell checking is one part of the initial learning about spelling.
(B) Programs are not effective for initially teaching about spelling and synonyms.
(C) Teachers should use word processing programs as one part of instruction.
(D) Students who use these programs won't learn about spelling.

34. Which of the following information is found in the passage?
I. The type of computer that runs the word processor
II. The two main outputs of spell-checking and thesaurus programs
III. An explanation of how to use the word-processing program to teach about spelling and synonyms
(A) I only
(B) II only
(C) I and II only
(D) II and III only

35. Which aspect of spell-checking and thesaurus programs does the author like?
(A) That you just have to type in the word
(B) That the synonyms and alternative spellings are done very quickly
(C) That the difficult mechanical aspects are performed
(D) That you don't have to know how to spell to use them

36. Which of the following questions could be answered from the information in the passage?
(A) When is it appropriate to use spell-checking and thesaurus programs?
(B) How does the program come up with recommended spellings?
(C) What type of spelling learning experiences should students have?
(D) Why do schools buy these word processing programs?

37. Which of the following statements could be used in place of the first sentence of the last paragraph?
(A) It may be true that some strict teachers use a mechanical approach.
(B) It may be true that a stringently mechanical approach is used by some teachers.
(C) It may be true that inflexible mechanical approaches are used by some teachers.
(D) It may be true that some teachers use only a mechanical approach.

38. According to this passage, what could be the result of a student's unfamiliarity with the meanings of words or synonyms?
(A) using a program to display the alternative spellings
(B) relying on mindless ways of checking spelling and finding synonyms
(C) strictly mechanical approaches
(D) using microcomputers to find synonyms for highlighted words

Use this map to answer items 39 and 40.

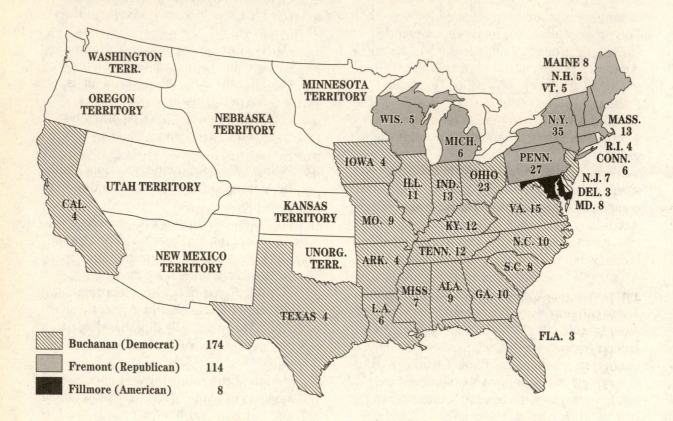

WASHINGTON TERR.

OREGON TERRITORY

MINNESOTA TERRITORY

NEBRASKA TERRITORY

MAINE 8
N.H. 5
VT. 5

WIS. 5

N.Y. 35

MASS. 13
R.I. 4
CONN. 6

UTAH TERRITORY

CAL. 4

IOWA 4

MICH. 6

PENN. 27

N.J. 7
DEL. 3
MD. 8

KANSAS TERRITORY

NEW MEXICO TERRITORY

UNORG. TERR.

ILL. 11

IND. 13

OHIO 23

VA. 15

MO. 9

KY. 12

N.C. 10

ARK. 4

TENN. 12

S.C. 8

TEXAS 4

L.A. 6

MISS. 7

ALA. 9

GA. 10

FLA. 3

▨ Buchanan (Democrat)   174

▨ Fremont (Republican)   114

■ Fillmore (American)   8

Presidential Election of 1856

39. The numbers in each state on this map show
(A) the number of counties in each state.
(B) the number of representatives from each state.
(C) the electoral votes in each state.
(D) the number of representatives won by the victorious party in each state.

40. What conclusion might you reasonably draw from this map?
(A) Were it not for Texas and California, Fremont would have won the election.
(B) Buchanan supported the rebel cause.
(C) Fremont was favored by the northernmost states.
(D) Fremont was favored by the states that fought on the Union side in the Civil War.

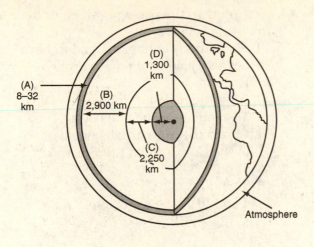

The Earth

41. In the diagram, what letter labels the mantle?
(A) A
(B) B
(C) C
(D) D

Items 42–44 refer to this passage.

Most of the world's religions emerged in Africa and Asia. About two billion people follow some Christian religion, and one billion Christians are Roman Catholics. There are about one billion Muslims, 800 million Hindus and 350 million Buddhists. There are fewer who follow tribal religions or who are Sikhs, Jews, Shamanists, Confucians, and followers of other religions. About one billion people are nonreligious and about 250 million people are atheists.

Hinduism emerged in India about 2500 B.C. Hindu beliefs are a mixture of the religious beliefs of invaders of India and the religious beliefs of native Indians. Hinduism embraces a caste system with religious services conducted by members of the priestly caste. Most Hindus worship one of the gods Vishnu and Shiva, and the goddess Shakti.

Hindus believe that a person's *karma*, the purity or impurity of past deeds, determines a person's ultimate fate. A karma can be improved through pure acts, deeds, and devotion.

Judaism developed from the beliefs of the Hebrew tribes located in and around Israel before 1300 B.C. From about 1000 B.C. to 150 B.C. a number of different authors wrote a series of books describing the religion, laws, and customs which are now known as the Old Testament of the Bible. The Old Testament describes a single just God. Judaism is an important world religion because elements of Judaism can be found in both Islam and Christianity.

Hebrews trace their ancestry to Abraham and his grandson Jacob, whose 12 sons are said to have founded the 12 tribes of Israel. About 1000 B.C. David is believed to have united these 12 tribes into a single religious state. Modern Jews refer to the Talmud, a book of Jewish law and tradition written around 400 A.D.

Buddhism was founded around 525 B.C. in India. The religion was founded by Buddha, Siddhartha Gautama, who lived from about 560 B.C. to about 480 B.C. The Triptika contains Buddha's teachings. A large number of *Sutras* contains a great body of Buddhist beliefs and teachings. Monastic life provides the main organizational and administrative structure for modern-day Buddhism.

It is said that Buddha achieved his enlightenment through meditation, and meditation is an important Buddhist practice. Buddhism holds that life is essentially meaningless and without reality. Buddhists seek to achieve Nirvana, a great void of perfection, through meditation and just acts.

Jesus was probably born about 5 B.C. He acquired a small following of Jews who believed he was the Messiah. Later this belief was developed into a worldwide religion known as Christianity. Christianity was generally tolerated in Rome, although there were periods of persecution. The Emperor Constantine converted to Christianity about 300 A.D. In the mid-300s Christianity was decreed the state religion of Rome. Augustine (St. Augustine) converted to Christianity in the late 300s.

In the Byzantine Era, starting after the Visigoths looted Rome, there was an Eastern and Western emperor. Constantinople was the capital in the East. This division led in 1054 to the great schism of the Catholic church, which survives to this day. The Crusaders captured Constantinople and defeated the Eastern Byzantines in 1204. In 1453 Constantinople was captured by the Turks and renamed Istanbul.

Mohammed was born in 570 A.D. and went into Mecca in 630 and founded Islam. The Koran contains the 114 chapters of Islamic religion and law. Around 640 A.D. the Omar, religious leader, established an Islamic empire with Damascus as the capital. The capital was eventually moved to Baghdad. The Muslims enjoyed a prosperous economy, and in the late days of the empire Omar Khayyam wrote the *Rubaiyat*.

Muslim armies conquered Spain and much of France by about 730. A series of Caliphs ruled from 750 until 1250 when an army originally led by Ghengis Kahn sacked Baghdad and killed the last caliph.

42. According to the passage, a Sutra would be best described as which of the following?
    (A) It contains just teachings.
    (B) It contains just a list of tribes.
    (C) It contains both beliefs and teachings.
    (D) It contains both law and tradition.

43. According to the passage, which of the following is correct?
    I. Siddhartha Gautama is said to have achieved enlightenment through karma.
    II. Jews today do not rely on the Old Testament for religious law.
    III. Christians were usually persecuted in the Holy Roman Empire.
    (A) II only
    (B) II and III
    (C) I and III
    (D) I, II, and III

44. Which of the following best paraphrases the first sentence in the fourth paragraph?
    (A) Judaism led to beliefs of the Hebrew tribes located near Israel before 1300 B.C.
    (B) The beliefs of Hebrew tribes located near Israel before 1300 provided the basis for Judaism.
    (C) Hebrew tribes in and around Israel before 1300 developed their beliefs from Judaism.
    (D) The area in and around Israel before 1300 had Hebrew tribes with Judaic beliefs.

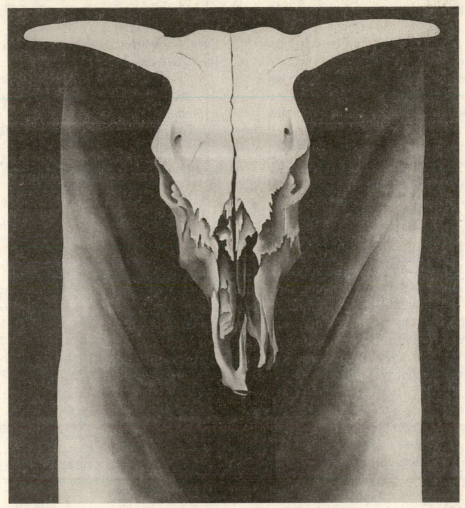

[The Metropolitan Museum of Art, The Alfred Stieglitz Collection, 1952. (52.203)]

45. This picture could be best described by saying
  (A) it is an abstract figure on a rectangular background.
  (B) the nearly symmetrical shape of the figure suggests that its completion is expected.
  (C) the Rorschach-like image suggests an underlying psychological theme.
  (D) the real life object has an abstract quality.

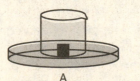
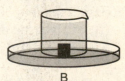

A   B

46. Identical beakers (above) were filled with water. Overflow was caused by the different solid objects placed in the beakers. The size of the objects cannot be determined. What is the most likely explanation of the differing amounts of overflow?
  (A) The object in beaker A is heavier.
  (B) The object in beaker B is heavier.
  (C) The object in beaker A has more mass.
  (D) The object in beaker B has more mass.

Cellular phones, once used by the very rich, are now available to almost everyone. With one of these phones, you can call just about anywhere from just about anywhere. Since the use of these phones will increase, we need to find legal and effective ways for law enforcement agencies to monitor calls.

47. Which of the following choices is the best summary of this passage?
    (A) Criminals are taking advantage of cellular phones to avoid legal wire-taps.
    (B) The ability to use a cellular phone to call from just about anywhere makes it harder to find people who are using the phones.
    (C) The increase in cellular phone use means that we will have to find legal ways to monitor cellular calls.
    (D) Cellular phones are like regular phones with a very long extension cord.

Occasionally, college students will confuse correlation with cause and effect. Correlation just describes the degree of relationship between two factors. For example, there is a positive correlation between poor handwriting and intelligence. However, writing more poorly will not make you more intelligent.

48. The authors main reason for writing this passage is to
    (A) explain the difference between cor-relation and cause and effect.
    (B) encourage improved penmanship.
    (C) explain how college students can improve their intelligence.
    (D) make those with poor penmanship feel more comfortable.

The way I look at it, Robert E. Lee was the worst general in the Civil War—he was the South's commanding general, and the South lost the war.

49. What assumption does the writer of this statement make?
    (A) War is horrible and should not be glorified.
    (B) Pickett's charge at Gettysburg was a terrible mistake.
    (C) A general should be judged by whether he wins or loses.
    (D) The South should have won the Civil War.

1	②	③	4	⑤	6	⑦	8	9	10
11	12	13	14	15	16	17	18	19	20
21	22	23	24	25	26	27	28	29	30
31	32	33	34	35	36	37	38	39	40
41	42	43	44	45	46	47	48	49	50
51	52	53	54	55	56	57	58	59	60
61	62	63	64	65	66	67	68	69	70
71	72	73	74	75	76	77	78	79	80
81	82	83	84	85	86	87	88	89	90
91	92	93	94	95	96	97	98	99	100

50. Cross off the multiples of 2, 3, 5, and 7 that are greater than these numbers in the above hundreds square. Which numbers in the 80s are not crossed off?
    (A) 83, 87
    (B) 81, 89
    (C) 83, 89
    (D) 81, 87

Use this graph to answer items 51 and 52.

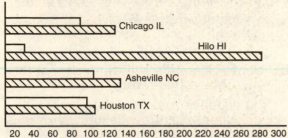

Clear Days
Days with Precipitation

51. A correct interpretation of this graph is, on average,
(A) most days in Houston have precipitation.
(B) less than 10 percent of the days in Hilo have no precipitation.
(C) most days in Asheville have no precipitation.
(D) most days in Chicago have precipitation.

52. A business may be moved to one of the four cities on the graph. What conclusion can be drawn from the graph to help make the final decision?
(A) On average, most precipitation in Hilo is from brief afternoon thundershowers.
(B) On average, Asheville, North Carolina, gets only a few inches of snow.
(C) On average, Asheville and Chicago receive about the same amount of precipitation.
(D) On average, Houston has the most days without precipitaton.

53. You add the first 5 odd numbers (1, 3, 5, 7, 9) and find that the answer is 25. What is the sum of the first 90 odd numbers?
(A) 450
(B) 8,100
(C) 179
(D) 4,500

54. The steplike appearance of the buildings in this photograph is created by
(A) the setbacks that occur every three or four stories.
(B) the photographer's position when the picture was taken.
(C) the proximity of the buildings to the street.
(D) the relationship between the symmetric appearance of the windows and the horizontal lines indicating new floors.

The computers in the college dormitories are actually more sophisticated than the computers in the college computer labs, and they cost less. It seems that the person who bought the dormitory computers looked around until she found powerful computers at a low price. The person who runs the labs just got the computers offered by the regular supplier.

55. The best statement of the main idea of this paragraph is
    (A) it is better to use the computers in the dorms.
    (B) it is better to avoid the computers in the labs.
    (C) the computers in the dorms are always in use so, for most purposes, it is better to use the computers in the labs.
    (D) it is better to shop around before you buy.

The college sororities are "interviewed" by students during rush week. Rush week is a time when students get to know about the different sororities and decide which ones they want to join. Each student can pledge only one sorority. Once students have chosen the three they are most interested in, the intrigue begins. The sororities then choose from among the students who have chosen them.

56. Which of the following strategies will help assure a student that she will be chosen for at least one sorority and preferably get into a sorority she likes?
    I.   Choose at least one sorority she is sure will choose her
    II. Choose two sororities she wants to get into
    III. Choose her three favorite sororities
    IV. Choose three sororities she knows will choose her
    (A) I and II
    (B) I and III
    (C) I only
    (D) III only

In response to my opponent's question about my record on environmental issues, I want to say that the real problem in this election is not my record. Rather the problem is the influence of my opponent's rich friends in the record industry. I hope you will turn your back on his rich supporters and vote for me.

57. Which of the following statements best illustrates the author's primary purpose?
    (A) clearing the author's name
    (B) describing the problems of running for office
    (C) informing the public of wrongdoing
    (D) convincing the voting populous

58. A boat costs $5 more than half the price of a canoe. Which of the following expressions shows this relationship?
    (A) B + $5 = C/2
    (B) B = 1/2C + $5
    (C) B + $5 = 2C
    (D) B + $5 > C/2

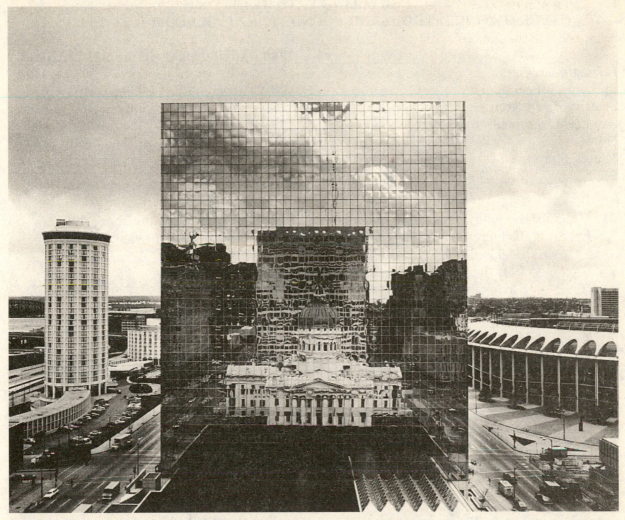

["Reflection, Old St. Louis County Courthouse, 1976." © William Clift 1976 The Metropolitan Museum of Art, Purchase, Gift of various donors and matching funds from NEA, 1981. 1981.1044.1]

59. The primary function of the central building in this photograph is to
(A) contrast with the cloudy sky.
(B) emphasize the symmetry of the roadways on either side.
(C) complete a collection of geometric shapes with the other structures shown to the left and right.
(D) serve as a reflective surface.

60. All the following items in this photograph suggest symmetry EXCEPT
(A) the clouds.
(B) the central building.
(C) the main building on the left part of the picture.
(D) the structure on the right part of the picture.

RECYCLING RATE BY CITY
(PER HUNDRED THOUSAND POUNDS PER YEAR FROM 1988–1993)

	1988	1989	1990	1991	1992	1993
Chicago, Illinois	*	52	67	120	302	485
St. Louis, Missouri	20	80	175	360	420	650
Seattle, Washington	15	70	98	136	243	358
San Francisco, California	*	23	75	124	285	402
New York, New York	*	10	56	250	370	590
Miami, Florida	*	25	98	145	290	370

* The recycling rate is less than one per hundred thousand pounds.

61. Which of the following statements is supported by the data given in the above table?
 (A) St. Louis increased the capabilities of its recycling plants by 50 percent during the years 1990 and 1991.
 (B) Since 1991 the recycling rate increased significantly in each city.
 (C) People living in Miami are not recycling as they should be.
 (D) The population of all these cities has increased significantly since 1988.

Items 62–64 refer to these three paragraphs.

I

(1) Of course, I have never gotten too involved in my children's sports. (2) I have never yelled at an umpire at any of my kid's games. (3) I have never even—_____, I didn't mean it.

II

(4) Before long, the umpire's mother was on the field. (5) There the two parents stood, toe to toe. (6) The players and the other umpires formed a ring around them and looked on in awe.

III

(7) Sometimes parents are more involved in little league games than their children. (8) I remember seeing a game in which a player's parent came on the field to argue with the umpire. (9) The umpire was not that much older than the player.

62. Which of the following shows the correct order for these three paragraphs?
 (A) I, II, III
 (B) I, III, II
 (C) II, I, III
 (D) III, II, I

63. Which of the following best fits in the blank in sentence 3?
 (A) Well
 (B) Being a parent
 (C) How come I
 (D) Repeat after me

64. What other "sporting" event is the author trying to recreate in paragraph II?
 (A) bullfight
 (B) wrestling match
 (C) boxing match
 (D) football game

Use this excerpt from Washington Irving's *The Legend of Sleepy Hollow* to answer items 65–67.

About two hundred yards from the tree a small brook crossed the road and ran into a marshy and thickly wooded glen, known by the name of Wiley's swamp. A few rough logs, laid side by side, served for a bridge over this stream. On that side of the road where the brook entered the wood, a group of oaks and chestnuts, matted thick with wild grapevines, threw a cavernous gloom over it. To pass this bridge was the severest trial. It was at this identical spot that the unfortunate Andre was captured, and under the covert of those chestnuts and vines were the sturdy yeomen concealed who surprised him. This has ever since been considered a haunted stream, and fearful are the feelings of the schoolboy who has to pass it alone after dark.

As he approached the stream his heart began to thump; he summoned up, however, all his resolution, gave his horse half a score of kicks in the ribs, and attempted to dash briskly across the bridge; but instead of starting forward, the perverse old animal made a lateral movement and ran broadside against the fence. Ichabod, whose fears increased with the delay, jerked the reins on the other side, and kicked lustily with the contrary foot; it was all in vain; his steed started, it is true, but it was only to plunge to the opposite side of the road into a thicket of brambles and alder bushes.

The schoolmaster now bestowed both whip and heel upon the starveling ribs of old Gunpowder, who dashed forward, snuffling and snorting, but came to a stand just by the bridge with a suddenness that had nearly sent his rider sprawling over his head. Just at this moment a plashy tramp by the side of the bridge caught the sensitive ear of Ichabod. In the dark shadow of the grove, on the margin of the brook, he beheld something huge, misshapen, black and towering. It stirred not, but seemed gathered up in the gloom, like some gigantic monster ready to spring upon the traveler.

65. Which of the following is discussed in the first paragraph?
   (A) the thing that frightened Ichabod
   (B) how trees affected the road
   (C) the sounds a horse makes
   (D) Ichabod nearly being thrown from a horse

66. What is the best replacement for the word "steed" in the second sentence of the second paragraph?
   (A) adversary
   (B) legs
   (C) shadow
   (D) nag

67. Which of the following is NOT associated with a description of Ichabod's horse?
   (A) plashy
   (B) jerked the reins
   (C) into a thicket
   (D) lateral movement

Items 68–69.

I think women are discriminated against; however, I think men are discriminated against just as much as women. It's just a different type of discrimination. Consider these two facts: Men die about 6 years earlier than women, and men are the only people who can be drafted into the armed forces. That's discrimination!

68. What is the author's main point in writing this passage?
   (A) Men are discriminated against more than women are.
   (B) Both sexes are discriminated against.
   (C) Women are not discriminated against.
   (D) On average, men die earlier than women.

69. Which of the following could be substituted for the word *drafted* in the second to last sentence?
   (A) inducted against their will
   (B) signed up
   (C) pushed in by society
   (D) drawn in by peer pressure

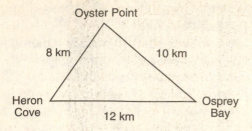

70. The diagram shows three towns, the roads connecting them, and the distance between each town. Which of the following is the shortest distance?
(A) Osprey Bay to Heron Cove to Oyster Point and then halfway to Osprey Bay
(B) Halfway between Oyster Point and Heron Cove, to Heron Cove to Osprey Bay to Oyster Point
(C) Quarter-way from Heron Cove to Osprey Bay, to Osprey Bay to Oyster Point to Heron Cove
(D) Heron Cove to Oyster Point to Osprey Bay, then halfway to Heron Cove

["The Veteran in a New Field" by Winslow Homer. The Metropolitan Museum of Art, Bequest of Miss Adelaide Milton de Groot (1876–1967), 1967]

71. Which of the following best describes how this picture shows the results of effort?
(A) The determination in the reaper's stance
(B) The fallen stalks of wheat
(C) The curved scythe handle
(D) The solitude of the reaper

The moon takes about 28 days to complete a cycle around the earth. Months, 28 days long, grew out of this cycle. Twelve of these months made up a year. But ancient astronomers realized that it took the earth about 365 days to make one revolution of the sun. Extra days were added to some months and the current calendar was born.

72. The passage indicates that the current calendar
(A) describes the moon's movement around the earth.
(B) is based on the sun's position.
(C) is based on the earth's rotation and position of the moon.
(D) combines features of the moons cycle and the earth's revolution.

Items 73–74.

Confederate Major General W. H. C. Whiting was recuperating in a prisoner-of-war camp in New York. Not long before, Whiting had been in charge of the Confederate forces in Wilmington, North Carolina. In the later years of the Civil War, Wilmington had become the gateway to the Confederacy. After Charleston, South Carolina, was captured by Union forces, Wilmington was the only southern port left open for blockade runners. These fast, sleek ships carried cotton to Bermuda, Nassau, and Nova Scotia and returned from these ports with arms, munitions, and commercial goods. Whiting knew that the capture of Wilmington closed the south's last supply pipeline. He said, "I do not know now that there is another place, excepting perhaps Richmond, we should not sooner see lost than this." Whiting died unexpectedly of his wounds in the prison camp.

Blockade runners coming to Wilmington traveled over the ocean, past Cape Fear into the Cape Fear River, and up the river to Wilmington. The most dangerous part of the journey was when ships entered the Cape Fear River. At the southern part of Cape Fear was Smith Island, now called Bald Head Island. This island and the barrier islands to the north form what looks like a huge check mark. The old inlet took ships one way around Smith Island into the Cape Fear River, while the new inlet took ships another way around the island and then into the river. Blockading Union ships waited outside the inlets. Some authorities report over a hundred blockade runners were captured or run aground in the Cape Fear region.

Whichever inlet that arriving blockade runners took, they passed by Fort Fisher. Fort Fisher was the key to protecting these ships, and the key to defending Wilmington. Blockade runners were just about immune from Union attack once they came under the fort's protection. No fewer than ten other fortifications protected the Cape Fear River.

Fort Holmes was on Smith Island, which was west across the new inlet from Fort Fisher. Fort Caswell was west across the Old Inlet from Fort Holmes, and Fort Johnson was across the Cape Fear River from Fort Fisher. Fort Fisher had extensive fortifications, both on the sea face and on the land face. But on January 12, 1865, Union forces attacked the first with what may have been the fiercest naval bombardment of the Civil War. Federal ships bombarded the fort's land face and sea face. On January 15, more than 3,000 Union infantry troops assaulted the land face. After vicious hand-to-hand fighting, Union forces troops captured the fort. Union forces captured Wilmington, and the Civil War soon ended near Cape Fear.

73. A blockade runner approached Wilmington with goods from Nova Scotia. As the blockade runner passed through the new inlet, Fort Fisher was generally to the
(A) east of Fort Holmes
(B) west of Fort Caswell
(C) west of Fort Holmes
(D) east of Fort Caswell

74. In the next to last sentence of the first paragraph, Whiting means
(A) I do not know which city is more important to the Confederacy, Richmond or Wilmington.
(B) The only place more important to the Confederacy than Richmond was Wilmington.
(C) Richmond is the most important city in the Confederacy and I do not know how important Wilmington is.
(D) I do not know if losing Richmond will be worse than losing the supply line between Wilmington and Bermuda, Nassau, and Nova Scotia.

Items 75–76.

The Sullen Sky

I see the sullen sky;
Dark, foreboding sky.
Swept by dank and dripping clouds;
Like ominous shrouds.

A sky should be bright,
Or clear and crisp at night.
But it hasn't been that way;
Oh, a dungenous day.

That has been my life,
And that has been my strife.
I wish the clouds would leave;
Ah, a sweet reprieve.

75. Which of the following best describes the author's message?
(A) The author doesn't like rainy, cloudy weather.
(B) The author wants people to be free of worry.
(C) The author is hoping his life will get better.
(D) The author lives in an area where it is often cloudy and rainy.

76. The last two lines in the first stanza reflect which of the following?
(A) simile
(B) hyperbole
(C) metaphor
(D) euphemism

77. The school is planning a class trip. They will go by bus. There will be 328 people going on the trip, and each bus holds 31 people. How many buses will be needed for the trip?
(A) 9
(B) 10
(C) 11
(D) 18

Items 78–79.

Using percentages to report growth patterns can be deceptive. If there are 100 new users for a cereal currently used by 100 other people, the growth rate is 100 percent. However if there are 50,000 new users for a cereal currently used by 5,000,000 people, the growth rate is 1 percent. It seems obvious that the growth rate of 1 percent is preferable to the growth rate of 100 percent. So while percentages do provide a useful way to report growth patterns, we must know the initial number the growth percentage is based on before we make any conclusions.

78. According to this passage,
(A) lower growth rates mean higher actual growth.
(B) higher growth rates mean higher actual growth.
(C) the growth rate depends on the starting point.
(D) the growth rate does not depend on the starting point.

79. Which of the following can be implied from this passage?
   (A) Don't believe any advertisements.
   (B) Question any percentage growth rate.
   (C) Percentages should never be used.
   (D) Any growth rate over 50 percent is invalid.

80. Say that Company A and Company B try to raise money by selling bonds to the public. Which of the following could cause the interest rate for Company A's bonds to be much higher than the rates for Company B's bonds?
   (A) The bonds for Company A have a higher risk.
   (B) The bonds for Company B have a higher risk.
   (C) The management of Company A wants to reward its investors.
   (D) The management of Company B wants to reward its investors.

WRITTEN ASSIGNMENT

Write an essay on the topic below. Use the lined pages that follow. Write your essay on this topic only. An essay on another topic will be rated Unscorable (U).

Was it better to have a maximum speed limit of 55 miles per hour, or is it better to have speed limits as high as 70 mph?

The maximum 55 mph speed limit was better. The national speed limit was set at 55 mph for two reasons: to conserve gasoline and to reduce accidents. These reasons are just as important today as they were when this speed limit was established. Why risk a single life so that people can go 10 or 15 miles per hour faster. If you have 60 miles to drive, then going 65 mph instead of 55 mph, you'll arrive ten minutes sooner—ten minutes; even if its 360 miles you'll arrive just 60 minutes sooner. Ten minutes or 60 does not justify losing a single life.

Speed limits as high as 70 mph are better. First it's important to note that speed limits as high as 70 mph does not mean there's a 70 mph speed limit everywhere. In fact, in most places the speed limit is 55 mph or less. But there are stretches of Interstate highways in rural areas where it does not make sense to limit the speed to 55 mph. Many people drive 500 or 600 miles a day on an Interstate trip and driving 70 mph instead of 55 shortens the trip by almost three hours. That means people will be less tired and less likely to be involved in an accident.

Was it better to have a maximum speed limit of 55 miles per hour, or is it better to have speed limits as high as 70 mph?

Review and evaluate the opposing positions presented above.

Choose one of these positions.

Write an essay that supports your position following the guidelines presented above.

PRACTICE LAST I

Explained Answers

1. **A** The item asks for an inference, which (A) provides. (B), (C), and (D) are true but they just restate the information in the paragraph. These choices do not include an inference from the passage.

2. **A** The graphs for walkers and bikers remained unchanged from Monday to Wednesday, so this statement is true for both Monday's graph and Wednesday's graph. (C) and (D) are incorrect because they are only true for Monday's graph. (D) is incorrect because there were approximately the same number of car and bike rides.

3. **C** The author gradually traces the evolution of speech and language. That is the main idea. (A) is false. The passage does not indicate that language consists of thoughts. (B) and (D) are true, but they are details and do not reflect the main idea of the passage.

4. **B** The author clearly states in the first paragraph that thought precedes speech as language develops. (A) gestures, (C) sound, and (D) writing are all language, but not the first component of language, according to the passage.

5. **C** To multiply by a positive power of 10, move the decimal point the right the number of places shown in the power.

   (A) $3.74 \times 10^6 = 3,740,000$

   (B) $3.74 \times 10^7 = 37,400,000$

   (C) $3.74 \times 10^8 = 374,000,000$

   Stop here—this is the correct answer.

   (D) $3.74 \times 10^9 = 3,740,000,000$

6. **B** The passage does not explicitly describe how life evolved, but it does suggest a chain of evolution. (A) is incorrect because the passage says mammals survived after dinosaurs became extinct, not that mammals were more intelligent. (C) is incorrect because there is no mention in the passage about conflict between dinosaurs and mammals. (D) is incorrect because the first paragraph indicates that the earliest stages of evolution happened because of the particular environment that existed on earth billions of years ago.

7. **D** The passage states facts, clarifies, and explains and the author's intent is to inform. (A) is incorrect because the author is not trying to entertain us. (B) is incorrect because the author does not intend to tell a story. A passage about a day in the life of a dinosaur might be a narration if the main purpose was to tell the story, not convey the facts. (C) is incorrect because the author is not trying to convince us of a particular point of view. This passage contains facts.

8. **A** The author's purpose for writing the passage dictates the tone. The author objectively states information that (B) is incorrect because the author displays no particular emotion. (C) is incorrect because, while the author is describing things from the past, he or she shows no interest in returning to these "good old days." (D) is incorrect because the passage is objective, and the author displays no particular emotion.

9. **B** The entire paragraph describes ways in which animals adapted to the environment. The other choices are generally too detailed to be the main idea. Besides, the other choices are false. (A) is false; the second paragraph says groupings of molecules "must have been able" to ingest nonorganic compounds. (C) and (D) are also false. The third paragraph mentions photosynthesis and that it releases oxygen into the atmosphere. However, the paragraph never mentions that photosynthesis allows plants to exist without sunlight nor that oxygen is more important to life than the sun's energy.

10. **A** The passage indicates that the Incas had an early culture near the Andes mountains on the west coast of South America, which is where the native dialects are shown on the map. (B) is incorrect because there is nothing about the primitive nature of a country that would explain the presence of a language. (C) is incorrect because the Mayans were primarily located on the east coast of Mexico. (D) is incorrect because Central America is several countries away and just being near Central America would not account for the languages.

11. **D** You can eliminate (A) and (B) because Columbus and Vespucci never reached South America. (C) and (D) are the only choices remaining, and it is just more reasonable that immigration 200 years ago would have more impact on a spoken language than immigration 55 years ago.

12. **D** The French penal colony of Devil's Island was located off the coast of French Guyana. (A) is incorrect because this French exile government was located in England. (B) is incorrect because there were no exiles from French-speaking Quebec. (C) is incorrect because Algeria is located in north Africa, not in South America.

13. **B** Nine of thirteen South American countries have Spanish as a language.

    $9 \div 13 = 0.69$, which is about $0.7 = 70\%$.

    Another approach is to work from the answers.

    (A) $80\% = 0.8 \times 13 = 10.4$

    (B) $70\% = 0.7 \times 13 = 9.1$ We can stop here—this is the correct answer.

    (C) 50%

    (D) 40%

14. **C** (C) *cannot* be implied from the passage. Lines 26–28 state that rockets refer to ordinance or weapons used by the British. You might also be struck that this is an unlikely answer. (A) can be implied from lines 5–7, which mention that the war started with an American invasion of Canada. (B) can be implied from lines 24–26, which mentions that

Francis Scott Key was a prisoner on a British ship. (D) can be implied from the passage because lines 19–20 state that the British troops sacked and burned Washington.

15. **B** You can tell from the context that damage is being done. In this context, sacked means looting a city. Ravished is the best choice and describes what happens when a town is sacked. The words in (A) and (D) have entirely different meanings than sacked. (C), "invaded," is incorrect because a city is sacked after it is invaded.

16. **B** The last sentence in the first paragraph says that most Americans remember Perry, but not where he served. (A) is incorrect because the ship *U.S.S. Constitution* and the Constitution of the United States are different. (C) is incorrect because the passage indicates that most Americans don't remember that he served in the Great Lakes. (D) is incorrect because Perry was not at Fort McHenry.

17. **C** Francis Scott Key was able to distribute his "Star-Spangled Banner" in America, so he must have been released by or escaped from the British. (A) and (B) are incorrect because the "Star-Spangled Banner" would not have been published if these choices were true. (D) is incorrect because there is nothing in the passage to indicate that Key returned to Britain, nor that he came from Britain for that matter.

18. **D** The author signals in the first sentence this main point of unawareness of events associated with the War of 1812. (A) is incorrect because, while this statement is true, it is not the main idea of this paragraph. (B) is incorrect because the Revolutionary War ended 25 years earlier. (C) is incorrect because, according to the passage, the British did not start the conflict.

19. **D** The painting uses only two dimensions, but it represents both two and three dimensions. (A) is incorrect because the painting is two-dimensional. (B) is incorrect because many of the shapes are irregular (have sides of differing lengths). (C) is incorrect because there are no three-dimensional figures.

20. **D** A new layer of water is added below the freezing level of the atmosphere and then the layer is frozen when the hailstone is blown above the freezing level. (A), (B), and (C) are incorrect because, while these events might impact the size of the hailstone, none of them would produce rings.

21. **B** The number sentence corresponds to finding an average. To find an average, you add the scores and divide by the number of scores. (A) is incorrect because the median is the middle number after the numbers are arranged in order. (C) is incorrect because the number sentence shows a "sum," not a "product." (D) is incorrect because the number sentence shows the "quotient of the sum," not the sum of the quotients.

22. **A** Divide to find the percent for transportation.

    $858 \div \$2600 = 0.33 = 33\%$

    Subtract the current transportation percentage from 33% to find the percent to be taken from miscellaneous

    $33\% - 24\% = 9\%$.

    Subtract to find the percent left for miscellaneous.

    $11\% - 9\% = 2\%$

    (B), (C), and (D) are incorrect because they do not result from the calculation shown above.

23. **D** The overlap of the rhombus and the rectangle rings shows that some (not all) rhombuses are rectangles. This means that some rhombuses are not rectangles. (A) is incorrect because the quadrilateral ring is not inside the rhombus ring. (B) is incorrect because the quadrilateral ring is not inside the rectangle ring. (C) is incorrect because the rhombus and rectangle rings overlap.

24. **A** The table shows that each animal in the HF2 group gained more weight each week than the HF1 group and more weight overall. (B), (C), and (D) are incorrect because there are no experimental results about which group lived longer, got more protein, or got better nutrition.

25. **D** The experiment does not describe how the experimenters ensured that group HF2 did not receive special attention, nor does it describe any other experimental controls. (A) is incorrect because averages are fine for this type of comparison. (B) is incorrect because the form of the hypothesis does not affect the validity of the experiment. (C) is incorrect because the statement is obviously false, and even if it were true, it is not an appropriate criticism of the experiment itself.

26. **D** Add 225 (W), 75 (TH), and 150 (F): $225 + 75 + 150 = 450$. (A) is incorrect because this is just the distance on Friday. (B) is incorrect because this is just the distance on Wednesday. (C) is incorrect because this is the sum of the Wednesday and Thursday distances.

27. **A** The last paragraph indicates that Ryan is playing the piano. The piano is a percussion instrument. Fingers strike the keys causing little "hammers" to strike strings. (B) is incorrect because the piano is not a string instrument like the guitar. (C) is incorrect because the piano is not a reed instrument such as the clarinet or saxophone. (D) is incorrect because the piano is not a woodwind such as the flute or clarinet.

28. **D** The 3 in ¾ time indicates that there are three beats per measure. The "quarter" indicates that the quarter note gets one beat. (A) and (C) are incorrect because the dotted quarter note in ¾ time gets 1½ beats. (B) is incorrect because there are three beats per measure.

29. **C** In general, haiku follows a 5-7-5 syllabic scheme with *no* rhyming. (C) alone meets these criteria. (A) and (B) are incorrect because they each include lines with four syllables, not the required five. (D) is incorrect because the last word "day" rhymes with the word "away."

30. **C** The word *nigh* means near in space or time. (A) is incorrect because "clear" means obvious or transparent. (B) is incorrect because "complete" means finished or total. (D) is incorrect because "not" is a modifier that means opposite.

31. **D** The passage indicates that love falls on silence and that love unknown is sad. This leads to the conclusion that the passage is about loving without acknowledgment. (A) is incorrect because rebuffed means rejected and there is no mention of rejection in the passage. (B) is incorrect because there is no indication of love from another person. (C) is incorrect because there is no mention of a third person.

32. **D** The information you need to answer this question is given in words and not in numerals. Add the three smaller numbers, and then add the three larger numbers. You must carefully scan the passage to find these words. You must also be careful to avoid information about ads that are not banner ads.

    Line 26 indicates that 9 to 10
    A banner ads are sold each day.
    Lines 37–38 indicate that 15–20
    C banner ads are sold each day.
    Lines 49–50 indicate that 12–14
    B banner ads are sold each day.

    Add the smaller number for each ad:
    9 + 15 + 12 = 36 minimum number.
    Add the larger number for each ad:
    10 + 20 + 14 = 44 maximum number.

33. **B** The next to the last sentence in the first paragraph indicates that these programs do not teach about spelling or word meanings. (A) is incorrect because this statement is contrary to the last sentence in the passage. (C) is incorrect; while true, it is not the main idea of this passage. (D) is incorrect because the passage never makes this claim.

34. **B** The types of computers used and teaching methods are not mentioned in the passage. To answer Roman numeral items, decide first which of the Roman numeral statements are true. Then find the answer that matches.

    I. Incorrect. The type of computer is never mentioned in the passage.
    II. Correct. The main outputs—spelling suggestions and synonyms—are in the passage.
    III. Incorrect. These approaches are specifically omitted.

    Only II is correct—(B).

35. **C** The fourth sentence in the first paragraph explains that the author likes having a program to perform the mechanical aspects. (A), (B), and (D) are incorrect because, while they are mentioned in the passage, they are not mentioned as something the author likes.

36. **A** This question can be answered from the information in the passage's last paragraph. (B), (C), and (D) are never directly addressed in the passage.

37. **D** This choice paraphrases the first sentence in the last paragraph. In that sentence the word "strictly" means exclusively or only. The word "only" appears in this choice. (A) is incorrect because there is no synonym for "strictly," and strict teachers may not strictly use this approach. (B) is incorrect because "stringently" means severe or harsh and it is not a synonym for "strictly." (C) is incorrect because "inflexible" means rigid and is not a synonym for "strictly."

38. **B** This choice paraphrases the first sentence in the second paragraph. (A), (C), and (D) are incorrect because these could not *result from* "unfamiliarity with meanings . . . ."

39. **C** Presidential elections are decided by electoral votes, and the caption clearly indicates that the map shows the results of a presidential election. (A), (B), and (D) are incorrect because the map clearly shows presidential election results, and not the number of representatives or the number of counties.

40. **C** Refer to the map shading, which shows that Fremont won all northernmost states. (A) is incorrect because Buchanan would have lost the 8 votes that Fremont gained, leaving a winning margin of 42 votes for Buchanan. (B) and (D) are incorrect because these conclusions are not supported by the shading patterns in the map. Just because a candidate won most of the Southern states does not *guarantee* that the candidate supported the rebel cause.

41. **B** The earth's mantle is the first part of the earth beneath the earth's surface. (A) indicates the earth's crust, (C) indicates the earth's outer core, (D) indicates the earth's inner core.

42. **C** This choice is the best answer because the third paragraph describes Sutras as containing beliefs and teachings. (A) is incorrect because the passage describes the Triptika as containing teachings. (B) is incorrect because the passage does not identify anything as containing just religious tribes. (D) is incorrect because the passage identifies the Talmud as containing both law and tradition.

43. **A** Consider each Roman numeral choice and then choose your answer.

   I. Incorrect. The passage indicates that Siddhartha Gautama (Buddha) is said to have achieved enlightenment through meditation.
   II. Correct. Jews today do not rely on the Old Testament for religious law; they rely on the Talmud.
   III. Incorrect. The passage indicates Christianity was generally tolerated in Rome.

   Only II is correct—(A).

44. **B** This sentence correctly reflects the essential point that Judaism developed from the beliefs of these tribes. (A) and (C) are incorrect because these choices make it seem that the tribes developed their beliefs *from* Judaism. (D) is incorrect because it makes it seem that the tribes already had Judaic beliefs.

45. **D** The title of this painting by Georgia O'Keeffe is "Cow's Skull." (A) and (B) might be reasonably correct answers, were it not for the most correct answer in (D). (C) is incorrect because the figure does not resemble a Rorschach inkblot.

46. **C** More mass means there is more of the object, that is, it takes up more space. Diagram A shows the most overflow, indicating that the object in that beaker has more mass. (A) and (B) are incorrect because a heavier object would not necessarily take up more space. For example, two ounces of gold would take up less space than one ounce of iron. (D) is incorrect because the overflow in Diagram B is less than the overflow in Diagram A.

47. **C** This choice paraphrases the conclusion found in the last sentence of the passage. (A) and (B) are incorrect because, while a person may draw this conclusion, it is not in the paragraph and would not be in the summary. (D) is incorrect because the passage does not contain this information.

48. **A** The author explains the difference between correlation and cause and effect with an explanation and an example. Choices (B), (C), and (D) are incorrect because they are not in the passage.

49. **C** The writer believes that generals should be judged by results. Even if you do not agree, that is the view of this writer. (A), (B), and (D) are incorrect because the writer does not base the paragraph on any of these statements.

50. **C** This process crosses all the numbers but the prime numbers. The numbers in (C) are the prime numbers in the 80s. (A), (B), and (D) are incorrect because they contain multiples of 3.

   81 is a multiple of $3 - 3 \times 17 = 81$

   87 is a multiple of $3 - 3 \times 19 = 87$

51. **C** On average, Asheville has 235 days without precipitation. Note that the graph does not show days that are cloudy and have no precipitation. (A) is incorrect because Houston has only 100 out of 365 days with precipitation. (B) is incorrect because Hilo has 285 days with precipitation, which leaves 85 days without precipitation. That's about 25 percent of the days without precipitation. (D) is incorrect because only about one-third of the days in Chicago have precipitation.

52. **D** On average, Houston has 259 days without precipitation. Notice this item is different from the previous one because this correct choice is the one city that has the most days without precipitation. (A) and (B) are incorrect because this information is not included in the graph. (C) is incorrect because the days with precipitation are not the same as the amount of precipitation.

53. **B** Investigate the pattern to find that the sum of the first n numbers is n^2. The sum of the first 90 odd numbers is 90^2 or 8,100. (A) is incorrect because it follows the incorrect pattern of multiplying 90 by 5. (C) is incorrect because it is too small to be the sum of the first 90 odd numbers. (D) is incorrect

because it follows the incorrect pattern of multiplying 90 by 50.

54. **A** The setbacks create the steplike appearance. (B), (C), and (D) are incorrect because none of these choices *creates* the steplike appearance.

55. **D** The paragraph describes how careful shopping can result in lower prices. (A), (B), and (C) are all conclusions that could be drawn from the passage, but none of them is the main idea.

56. **A** Consider each Roman numeral choice and then choose your answer.

> I. Yes. This choice guarantees that she will be accepted to at least one sorority.
> II. Yes. This choice means she will preferably get into a sorority she wants.
> III. No. This choice eliminates the guarantee that she will be chosen for at least one sorority.
> IV. No. This choice makes it unlikely she will be chosen for a sorority she likes.

Strategies I and II guarantee she will be chosen by at least one sorority and preferably the sorority that she likes—Choice (A).

57. **D** The author is denying one accusation, making another and trying to convince others. (A) is incorrect because the author never tries to clear his or her name. (B) is incorrect because the problems of running for office are not discussed. (C) is incorrect because the reference to "rich supporters" is not an accusation of wrongdoing.

58. **B** This expression correctly shows the relationship.

<u>Boat</u> <u>costs</u> <u>$5</u> <u>more than</u> <u>half the price</u> <u>of</u> <u>a canoe</u>
  B = $5 + ½ × c

B = ½ c + 5

(A) and (C) are incorrect because they do not correctly show the equality. (D) is incorrect because it is an inequality.

59. **D** The central building serves as a reflective surface for the courthouse. (A) is incorrect because the contrast with the clouds is insignificant compared to (D). (B) is incorrect because the building

does not emphasize the symmetry of the roads. (C) is incorrect because the building does not complete a collection of geometric shapes.

60. **A** The clouds do not suggest symmetry. (B), the rectangular central building, (C) and (D) the geometric buildings to the left and right, and the placement of the geometric buildings all suggest symmetry.

61. **B** The recycling amounts in the table increase for each city after 1991. (A) is incorrect because there is no data in the table to support recycling capability. (C) is incorrect because there is no basis for knowing how much recycling should be going on in Miami. (D) is incorrect because, while certainly true, it is not supported by data in the table.

62. **D** The paragraphs are most naturally ordered as shown in (D). III is the introductory passage, II follows directly from the last sentence in III, I follows directly from II.

63. **A** The author is saying, "You caught me or I caught myself. I'm guilty, but I didn't mean it." (B) and (C) make no sense in this context. (D) makes sense in this context but it is not as good a fit as (A).

64. **C** Boxers stand toe to toe in a boxing match. (A) is incorrect because a bullfight involves an animal and a person. (B) is incorrect because a wrestling match does not feature toe-to-toe action. (D) is incorrect because a football game involves teams.

65. **B** The third sentence tells us that "oaks and chestnuts [trees] . . . threw a cavernous gloom over it [the road]." (A) is incorrect because we don't learn of Ichabod's fears until the second paragraph. The "sturdy yeomen" described in the first paragraph were waiting for Andre. (C) and (D) are incorrect because these descriptions appear in the second paragraph.

66. **D** The context of the sentence shows that the word "steed" refers to Ichabod's horse. The word nag means a horse not in the best of condition. The word "steed" does not refer to (A), his adversary waiting in the dark, (B) his legs, or (C), a shadow.

67. **A** A good way to answer a "not" question is to eliminate answers. The terms "jerked the reins," "into a thicket," and "lateral movement" all appear in the second paragraph, in some way associated with Ichabod's horse. (A), plashy, is used to describe the "tramp by the side of the bridge."

68. **B** The author says that men are discriminated against just as much as women and gives an example to support his view. (A) is incorrect because the passage reads "discriminated against just as much." (C) is incorrect because the passage indicates that women are discriminated against. (D) is incorrect because, while true, this is a fact the author uses to support the main point, not the main point itself.

69. **A** Drafted, in the sense used here, means to be inducted into the armed forces against your will. (B) is incorrect because it does not show the lack of agreement that drafting carries with it. (C) is incorrect because society itself does not push someone into a draft. (D) is incorrect because peers do not draw a person into being drafted.

70. **D** Add to find the distances. The totals for each answer choice are as follows:

    A. 25

    B. 26

    C. 27

    D. 24

    (D) is the shortest.

71. **B** The *results* of the farmer's effort can be seen only in the stalks of wheat already cut. (A), (C), and (D) are incorrect because neither determination, nor the shape of the handle, nor the reaper's solitude shows results.

72. **B** The passage identifies both the moon's cycle and the earth's revolution as factors contributing to the development of the current calendar. (A) is incorrect because, while it describes how long it takes for the moon to travel around the earth, it does not describe the movement. (C) is incorrect because the current calendar is not based on the position of the moon. (D) is incorrect because the passage does not indicate that the current calendar is based on the earth's revolution.

73. **A** The first sentence in the fourth paragraph reads, "Fort Holmes was on Smith Island, which was west across the New Inlet from Fort Fisher." This means that Fort Fisher must be on the east side of the new inlet.

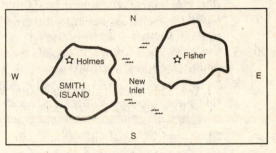

74. **B** General Whiting's words are a little convoluted, but this choice is what he meant. You can eliminate answers to confirm this choice. (A) is incorrect because Whiting thinks Richmond is more important. (C) is incorrect because Whiting thinks Wilmington is second in importance to Richmond. (D) is incorrect because, while Whiting does not want to lose the supply line, he is specifically discussing the loss of Wilmington.

75. **C** This poem is not to be taken literally. The poet is describing his or her life and expressing the hope that his or her life will improve. (A) and (D) are incorrect because these are literal interpretations. (B) is incorrect because the poet does not express concern about other people's lives.

76. **A** The last two lines in the first stanza compare clouds to shrouds. The comparison shows that the figure of speech must be a metaphor or a simile. The poem uses the word "like," so the figure of speech must be a simile. (B) is incorrect because a hyperbole is a drastic overstatement. (C) is incorrect because a metaphor is a comparison in which the word "like" is not used. (D) is incorrect because a euphemism is an inoffensive term substituted for an offensive term.

77. **C** Divide 328 ÷ 31 = 10 R 18. You will need ten buses and another bus for the 18 remaining people. That is a total of 11

buses. (A) and (B) are incorrect because 9 or 10 buses are not enough. (D) is incorrect because 18 are more buses than you need.

78. **C** The rate, alone, does not provide enough information. You must know the starting point. (A) and (B) are incorrect because the passage gives examples that directly contradict each of these choices. (D) is incorrect because the growth rate does depend on the starting point.

79. **B** You should question any growth rate when only the percentage is given. (A) is incorrect because the word "any" makes this answer too general. (C) is incorrect because this general statement is not supported by the paragraph. (D) is incorrect because nothing in the paragraph sets over 50 percent growth rate as invalid.

80. **A** The main reason a company pays a much higher rate than another company is because that company's bonds are riskier. (B) is incorrect because riskier bonds for Company B means the rates for those bonds would be higher. (C) is incorrect because a company may pay higher rates to attract investors, but the main reason a company pays a much higher rate than another company is because that company's bonds are riskier. (D) is incorrect because that would make the interest rates higher for Company B's bonds.

WRITTEN ASSIGNMENT

Show your essay to an English professor or a high school English teacher. Ask them to rate your essay 0–3 using this scale.

3   A well developed, complete written assignment.
Shows a thorough response to all parts of the topic.
Clear explanations that are well supported.
An assignment that is free of significant grammatical, punctuation, or spelling errors.

2   A fairly well developed, complete written assignment.
It may not thoroughly respond to all parts of the topic.
Fairly clear explanations that may not be well supported.
It may contain some significant grammatical, punctuation, or spelling errors.

1   A poorly developed, incomplete written assignment.
It does not thoroughly respond to most parts of the topic.
Contains many poor explanations that are not well supported.
It may contain some significant grammatical, punctuation, or spelling errors.

0   A very poorly developed, incomplete written assignment.
It does not thoroughly respond to the topic.
Contains only poor, unsupported explanations.
Contains numerous significant grammatical, punctuation, or spelling errors.

12 PRACTICE LAST II

This practice test contains the types of items you will encounter on the real test. The distribution of items varies from one test administration to another.

Take this test in a realistic, timed setting.

The setting will be most realistic if another person times the test and ensures that the test rules are followed exactly. But remember that many people do better on a practice test than on the real test. If another person is acting as test supervisor, he or she should review these instructions with you and say "Start" when you should begin and "Stop" when time has expired.

You have 4 hours to complete the 80 multiple-choice questions and the written assignment. Keep the time limit in mind as you work.

Each multiple-choice question or statement in the test has four answer choices. Exactly one of these choices is correct. Mark your choice on the answer sheet provided for this test.

Use a pencil to mark the answer sheet. The actual test will be machine scored so completely darken in the answer space.

Once the test is complete, review the answers and explanations for each item.

When instructed, turn the page and begin.

ANSWER SHEET PRACTICE LAST II

1 Ⓐ Ⓑ Ⓒ Ⓓ
2 Ⓐ Ⓑ Ⓒ Ⓓ
3 Ⓐ Ⓑ Ⓒ Ⓓ
4 Ⓐ Ⓑ Ⓒ Ⓓ
5 Ⓐ Ⓑ Ⓒ Ⓓ

21 Ⓐ Ⓑ Ⓒ Ⓓ
22 Ⓐ Ⓑ Ⓒ Ⓓ
23 Ⓐ Ⓑ Ⓒ Ⓓ
24 Ⓐ Ⓑ Ⓒ Ⓓ
25 Ⓐ Ⓑ Ⓒ Ⓓ

41 Ⓐ Ⓑ Ⓒ Ⓓ
42 Ⓐ Ⓑ Ⓒ Ⓓ
43 Ⓐ Ⓑ Ⓒ Ⓓ
44 Ⓐ Ⓑ Ⓒ Ⓓ
45 Ⓐ Ⓑ Ⓒ Ⓓ

61 Ⓐ Ⓑ Ⓒ Ⓓ
62 Ⓐ Ⓑ Ⓒ Ⓓ
63 Ⓐ Ⓑ Ⓒ Ⓓ
64 Ⓐ Ⓑ Ⓒ Ⓓ
65 Ⓐ Ⓑ Ⓒ Ⓓ

6 Ⓐ Ⓑ Ⓒ Ⓓ
7 Ⓐ Ⓑ Ⓒ Ⓓ
8 Ⓐ Ⓑ Ⓒ Ⓓ
9 Ⓐ Ⓑ Ⓒ Ⓓ
10 Ⓐ Ⓑ Ⓒ Ⓓ

26 Ⓐ Ⓑ Ⓒ Ⓓ
27 Ⓐ Ⓑ Ⓒ Ⓓ
28 Ⓐ Ⓑ Ⓒ Ⓓ
29 Ⓐ Ⓑ Ⓒ Ⓓ
30 Ⓐ Ⓑ Ⓒ Ⓓ

46 Ⓐ Ⓑ Ⓒ Ⓓ
47 Ⓐ Ⓑ Ⓒ Ⓓ
48 Ⓐ Ⓑ Ⓒ Ⓓ
49 Ⓐ Ⓑ Ⓒ Ⓓ
50 Ⓐ Ⓑ Ⓒ Ⓓ

66 Ⓐ Ⓑ Ⓒ Ⓓ
67 Ⓐ Ⓑ Ⓒ Ⓓ
68 Ⓐ Ⓑ Ⓒ Ⓓ
69 Ⓐ Ⓑ Ⓒ Ⓓ
70 Ⓐ Ⓑ Ⓒ Ⓓ

11 Ⓐ Ⓑ Ⓒ Ⓓ
12 Ⓐ Ⓑ Ⓒ Ⓓ
13 Ⓐ Ⓑ Ⓒ Ⓓ
14 Ⓐ Ⓑ Ⓒ Ⓓ
15 Ⓐ Ⓑ Ⓒ Ⓓ

31 Ⓐ Ⓑ Ⓒ Ⓓ
32 Ⓐ Ⓑ Ⓒ Ⓓ
33 Ⓐ Ⓑ Ⓒ Ⓓ
34 Ⓐ Ⓑ Ⓒ Ⓓ
35 Ⓐ Ⓑ Ⓒ Ⓓ

51 Ⓐ Ⓑ Ⓒ Ⓓ
52 Ⓐ Ⓑ Ⓒ Ⓓ
53 Ⓐ Ⓑ Ⓒ Ⓓ
54 Ⓐ Ⓑ Ⓒ Ⓓ
55 Ⓐ Ⓑ Ⓒ Ⓓ

71 Ⓐ Ⓑ Ⓒ Ⓓ
72 Ⓐ Ⓑ Ⓒ Ⓓ
73 Ⓐ Ⓑ Ⓒ Ⓓ
74 Ⓐ Ⓑ Ⓒ Ⓓ
75 Ⓐ Ⓑ Ⓒ Ⓓ

16 Ⓐ Ⓑ Ⓒ Ⓓ
17 Ⓐ Ⓑ Ⓒ Ⓓ
18 Ⓐ Ⓑ Ⓒ Ⓓ
19 Ⓐ Ⓑ Ⓒ Ⓓ
20 Ⓐ Ⓑ Ⓒ Ⓓ

36 Ⓐ Ⓑ Ⓒ Ⓓ
37 Ⓐ Ⓑ Ⓒ Ⓓ
38 Ⓐ Ⓑ Ⓒ Ⓓ
39 Ⓐ Ⓑ Ⓒ Ⓓ
40 Ⓐ Ⓑ Ⓒ Ⓓ

56 Ⓐ Ⓑ Ⓒ Ⓓ
57 Ⓐ Ⓑ Ⓒ Ⓓ
58 Ⓐ Ⓑ Ⓒ Ⓓ
59 Ⓐ Ⓑ Ⓒ Ⓓ
60 Ⓐ Ⓑ Ⓒ Ⓓ

76 Ⓐ Ⓑ Ⓒ Ⓓ
77 Ⓐ Ⓑ Ⓒ Ⓓ
78 Ⓐ Ⓑ Ⓒ Ⓓ
79 Ⓐ Ⓑ Ⓒ Ⓓ
80 Ⓐ Ⓑ Ⓒ Ⓓ

Each item on this test includes four answer choices. Select the best choice for each item and mark that letter on the answer sheet.

Lyndon Johnson was born in a farmhouse in central Texas in 1908. He grew up in poverty and had to work his way through college. He was elected to the
(5) U. S. House of Representatives in 1937, and served in the U. S. Navy during World War II. Following 12 years in the House of Representatives, he was elected to the U. S. Senate, where he became the
(10) youngest person chosen by any party to be their Senate leader.

In 1964, Johnson won the presidential election with 61 percent of the vote. He won the election by more than 15 million
(15) popular votes, the widest margin in the history of American presidential elections. But some historians report that the escalation of the Vietnam war made Johnson depressed almost to the point where he
(20) was unable to make decisions effectively. In 1968 Johnson announced that he would not be a candidate for president, even though he gained acceptance for programs suggested by his predecessor but never
(25) implemented. Robert Kennedy was assassinated before he had the chance to succeed Johnson as president. It appears that Johnson tried to reverse his decision to withdraw from the 1968 presidential campaign.
(30) His plans were thwarted when he did not get support from southern governors and because of the riots at the Chicago Democratic convention.

Johnson championed many Great
(35) Society programs including low-income housing; project Head Start, and Medicare. Historians suggest he supported Great Society programs because he experienced poverty as a child. To many, this made
(40) Johnson a better president than Kennedy.

But always it was the Vietnam war that preoccupied Johnson. He came to realize that American policy in Vietnam was a failed policy. He could scarcely accept that
(45) he had participated in a losing effort that cost 30,000 American lives during his presidency. Near the end of his presidency, he allegedly had wiretaps placed on the phones of friends and foes alike, including

(50) his party's standard bearer, Hubert Humphrey. He did not even try to help Hubert Humphrey in the 1968 campaign until he came to believe that Nixon had made a separate arrangement with the
(55) North Vietnamese not to negotiate so that Nixon would have a better chance of winning the election. Lyndon Baines Johnson died at his Texas ranch in 1973.

1. Based on this passage, Johnson
(A) was a better president than Kennedy.
(B) gained approval for programs proposed by Kennedy.
(C) was a member of a Great Society.
(D) was president before Kennedy.

---

2. Deena finished the school run in 52.8 seconds. Lisa's time was 1.3 seconds faster.

What was Lisa's time?
(A) 51.5 seconds
(B) 54.1 seconds
(C) 53.11 seconds
(D) 65.8 seconds

[The Metropolitan Museum of Art, Purchase, Edith Perry Chapman Fund, 1975. (1975.205)]

3. The pendant pictured above shows
(A) evidence of pain.
(B) evidence of ancient alien visitors.
(C) a strange animal with legs attached to one another.
(D) a close relationship between horse and rider.

Items 4–6.

The Black Plague—bubonic plague—was pandemic in Europe during a 200-year period in the middle of the twentieth century. The plague was a severe infection caused by bacteria that was untreatable until antibiotics were available. At its height, the plague killed two million people a year. AIDS has already claimed more than ten million lives, and AIDS in Africa is at the same pandemic levels as the Black Plague was in the Middle Ages. In some African nations more than 10 percent of the population, already infected with AIDS, will die from the disease. These deaths will create millions of orphans that will shatter the social fabric of the continent.

The AIDS rate may be highest in Zimbabwe where a culture of promiscuity fosters spread of the disease. In this country, women are victimized by a culture that virtually forces women to have sex with any man. In fact, women may be beaten or humiliated if they refuse a man's demand for sex. Other more subtle pressures present in the United States and other countries may compel both men and women to make unwise decisions about sexual partners. Freedom from pressure to engage in sex may be one of the most important tools for helping eradicate the AIDS epidemic.

Researchers were not sure at first what caused AIDS or how it was transmitted. They did know early on that everyone who developed AIDS died. Then researchers began to understand that the disease is caused by the HIV virus, which could be transmitted through blood and blood products. Even after knowing this, some blood companies resisted testing blood for the HIV virus. Today we know that the HIV virus is transmitted through blood and other bodily fluids. Women may be more susceptible than men, and the prognosis hasn't changed.

4. The main intent of this passage is to
   (A) show that blood companies can't be trusted.
   (B) detail the history of AIDS research.
   (C) detail the causes and consequences of AIDS.
   (D) raise awareness about AIDS.

5. Which of the following questions could be answered from this passage?
   (A) How do intravenous drug users acquire AIDS?
   (B) Is AIDS caused by blood transfusions?
   (C) Through what mediums is AIDS transmitted?
   (D) How do blood companies test for AIDS?

6. Which of the following would be the best concluding summary sentence for this passage?
   (A) AIDS research continues to be underfunded in the United States.
   (B) Sexual activity and intravenous drug use continue to be the two primary ways that AIDS is transmitted.
   (C) People develop AIDS after being HIV positive.
   (D) Our understanding of AIDS has increased significantly over the past several years, but we are no closer to a cure.

Items 7–9.

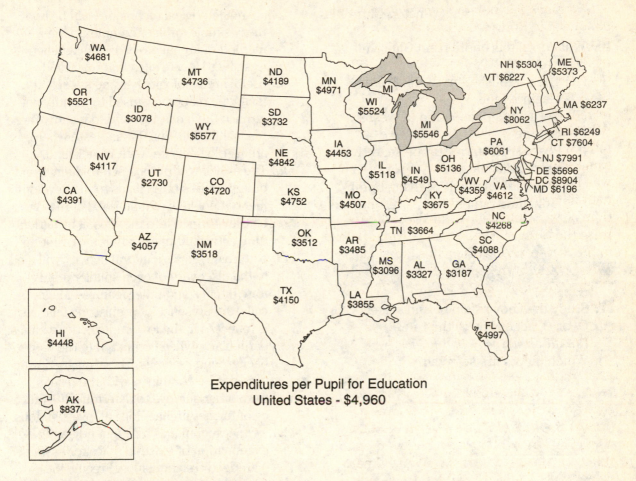

Expenditures per Pupil for Education
United States - $4,960

7. You can deduce from the map that teachers' salaries are probably lowest in
- (A) Georgia, Alabama, and Idaho.
- (B) South Dakota, Tennessee, and Oklahoma.
- (C) Kentucky, Louisiana, and New Mexico.
- (D) Florida, Hawaii, and Iowa.

8. You can deduce from the map that school taxes are probably highest in
- (A) the southeastern states.
- (B) the northeastern states.
- (C) the northwestern states.
- (D) the southwestern states.

9. Based on the information on this map, which of these states would be in the second quartile of per pupil expenditures?
- (A) Alaska
- (B) Alabama
- (C) Idaho
- (D) Arizona

An iron curtain has fallen across the continent.

Winston Churchill

10. What does this quote from Churchill refer to?
(A) The establishment of the French Maginot Line
(B) Germany's occupation of Western Europe
(C) Postwar Eastern Europe secretiveness and isolation
(D) The establishment of flying bomb launching ramps across Europe

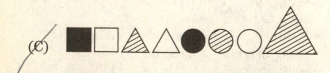

11. Study the above shapes, and select A, B, C, or D, according to the rule:
(small or striped) and large.
Which pieces are selected?

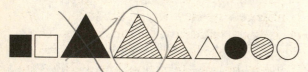

(A)

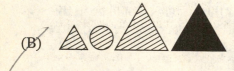

(B)

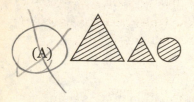

(C)

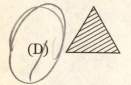

(D)

Items 12–14.

Archaeological techniques can be relatively simple, or very complex. One method of archaeology uses magnetic imaging to locate sites that may yield
(5) useful archaeological artifacts. Topsoil magnetic mapping is used to identify patterns in the landscape and to identify these resonance patterns that indicate where archaeological site work is indicated.
(10) The movement of topsoil into ditches and other features often leads to the development of pockets of material that may later be transformed into the topsoil by agricultural activity. It may be that the resulting
(15) patterns from agricultural activity will lead to the discovery of even smaller prehistoric ditches and other features. Magnetically, the presence of prehistoric features is reflected in the lower magnetic readings,
(20) particularly when compared to the higher background readings. These magnetic surveys can be combined with the results from other surveys to determine the efficacy of further archaeological investigations.
(25) Other techniques may just rely on the examination of existing relics for sustained patterns or relationships. Frequently, advanced numeric methods are useful for a full analysis of these patterns. In other
(30) cases, informed observation alone may reveal striking cultural information. But still, the success of these informed observations may presuppose a knowledge of mathematics or physics.

12. According to the passage, as a general rule, prehistoric features
(A) have to be compared with higher background readings.
(B) require advanced numerical analysis.
(C) must rely on the examination of existing relics.
(D) have lower magnetic readings.

13. Which of the following words could be used in place of the word "efficacy" in the last two lines of the first paragraph?
    (A) placement
    (B) usefulness
    (C) results
    (D) relationship

14. According to this passage, the resulting patterns from agricultural activity
    (A) may later be transformed into topsoil.
    (B) offer a great deal of assistance to archaeologists.
    (C) require a knowledge of mathematics or physics.
    (D) may lead to the discovery of prehistoric ditches.

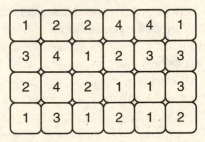

15. A ball is dropped randomly into the container shown above. What is the probability that the ball will land in a hole labeled "1"?
    (A) 8/12
    (B) 1/2
    (C) 1/3
    (D) 1/4

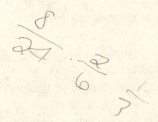

Items 16–17.

County highway officials have to submit all road construction plans to the state highway department for approval. The state highway department must approve all plans, but officials are most attentive to plans for new construction, and less concerned about plans for work on existing roads. A state highway inspector visits every site for a limited access highway. The department also uses a computer-simulation analysis to determine the traffic-flow impact of these roads. The state highway department may require a county to identify a similar road configuration elsewhere in the state to fully determine traffic-flow characteristics. The department is also very cautious about roads that may be used by school buses. The state highway department has found that there are more accidents on narrow, rural roads and they have taken planning steps to ensure that roads of this type are not built.

The state highway department has sets of regulations for the number of lanes a highway can have and how these lanes are to be used. A summary of these regulations follows.

- All highways must be five lanes wide and either three or four of these lanes must be set aside for passenger cars only.
- If four lanes are set aside for passenger cars, then one of these lanes must be set aside for cars with three or more passengers, with a second lane of the four passenger lanes also usable by school vehicles such as buses, vans, and cars.
- If three lanes are set aside for passenger cars, then one of these lanes must be set aside for cars with two or more passengers, except that school buses, vans, and cars may also use this lane.

16. Officials in one county submit a plan for a five-lane highway, with three lanes set aside for passenger cars and school buses able to use the lane set aside for cars with two or more passengers. Based on their regulations, which of the following is most likely to be the state highway department's response to this plan?

    (A) Your plan is approved because you have five lanes with three set aside for passenger cars and one set aside for passenger cars with two or more passengers.

    (B) Your plan is approved because you permitted school buses to use the passenger lanes.

    (C) Your plan is disapproved because you don't include school vans and school cars among the vehicles that can use the lane for cars with two or more passengers.

    (D) Your plan is disapproved because you include school buses in the lane for passenger cars with two or more passengers.

17. County officials send a list of three possible highway plans to the state highway department. Using their regulations, which of the following plans would the state highway department approve?

    I. 5 lanes—3 for passenger cars, 1 passenger lane for cars with 3 or more passengers, school buses and vans can also use the passenger lane for 3 or more people

    II. 5 lanes—4 for passenger cars, 1 passenger lane for cars with 3 or more passengers, 1 of the 4 passenger lanes can be used by school buses, vans, and cars

    III. 5 lanes—3 for passenger cars, 1 passenger lane for cars with 2 or more passengers, school vehicles can also use the passenger lane for 2 or more passengers

    (A) I only

    (B) II only

    (C) III only

    (D) I and II only

Items 18–20.

(A)

["Photograph: After the San Francisco Earthquake" by Arnold Genther. The Metropolitan Museum of Art, The Alfred Stieglitz Collection, 1933. (33.43.223)]

(C)

["Near Union Square-Looking up Park Avenue" by Fairfield Porter. The Metropolitan Museum of Art, Gift of Mrs. Fairfield Porter, 1978. (1978.224)]

(B)

["The Plantation." The Metropolitan Museum of Art, Gift of Edgar William and Bernice Chrysler Garbisch, 1963. (63.210.3)]

(D)

["Illustration from 'Interesting Events in the History of the U.S.': New Hampshire-Stamp Master in Effigy," Wood Engraving. The Metropolitan Museum of Art, Bequest of Charles Allen Munn, 1924. (24.90.1566a)]

18. Which of these pictures most likely involves dissent?

19. Which picture appears to have the least realistic representation of dimensionality?

20. Which realistic picture does not portray people?

The Board of Adjustment can exempt a person from the requirements of a particular land use ordinance. Several cases have come before the board concerning three ordinances. One ordinance states that religious and other organizations cannot build places of worship or meeting halls in residential zones. A second ordinance states that any garage must be less than 25 percent of the size of a house on the same lot, while a third ordinance restricts a person's right to convert a one-family house to a two-family house. It is interesting to note how a person can be in favor of an exemption in one case but opposed to exemption in another. For example, one homeowner applied to build a garage 45 percent of the size of her house but was opposed to a neighbor converting his house from a one-family to a two-family house. This second homeowner was opposed to a church being built in his neighborhood. The woman opposed to his proposal was all for the church construction project. The pressure on Board of Adjustment members who also live in the community is tremendous. It must sometimes seem to them that any decision is the wrong one. But that is what Boards of Adjustment are for, and we can only hope that this example of America in action will best serve the community and those who live there.

21. Which of the following sentences is the author of the passage most likely to DISAGREE with?
(A) These boards serve a useful purpose.
(B) No exemptions should be granted to any zoning ordinance.
(C) People can be very fickle when it comes to the exemptions they favor.
(D) Some people may try to influence Board of Adjustment members.

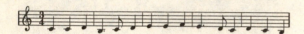

22. Which of the following songs begins with the four bars shown above?
(A) "My Country 'Tis of Thee"
(B) "Appalachian Spring"
(C) "I Fall to Pieces"
(D) "Star-Spangled Banner"

23. Which diagram shows object • to have the most potential energy?

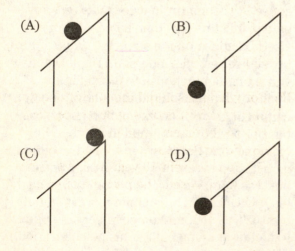

An archaeologist was investigating the books of an old civilization. She found the following table, which showed the number of hunters on top and the number of people they could feed on the bottom. For example, 3 hunters could feed 12 people. The archaeologist found a pattern in the table.

Hunters	1	2	3	4	5	6	7
Eaters	2	6	12	20	30		

24. Look for the pattern. How many eaters can 6 hunters feed?
(A) 42
(B) 40
(C) 30
(D) 36

25. What is the formula for the pattern:
H stands for hunters and
E stands for eaters?
(A) $E = 3 \times H$
(B) $E = 4 \times H$
(C) $E = H^2 + H$
(D) $E = 3 \times (H + 1)$

Following a concert, a fan asked a popular singer why the songs sounded so different in person than on the recording. The singer responded, "I didn't record my emotions!"

26. Which of the following statements is suggested by this passage?
(A) The singer was probably not in a good mood during that performance.
(B) The fan was being intrusive, and the performer was "brushing them off."
(C) The performance was outdoors where sound quality is different.
(D) The performance may vary depending on the mood of the performer.

27. Which of the following diagrams represents a situation that could result in a solar eclipse?

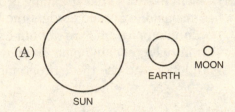

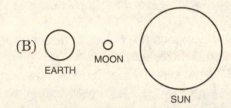

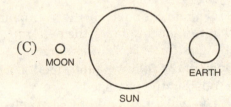

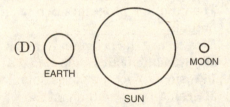

Items 28–29.

In response to my opponent's question about my record on environmental issues, I want to say that the real problem in this election is not my record. Rather the problem is the influence of my opponent's rich friends in the record industry. I hope you will turn your back on his rich supporters and vote for me.

28. What type of rhetorical argument does this passage reflect?
(A) narration
(B) reflection
(C) argumentation
(D) exposition

29. What type of fallacious reasoning is found in the passage?
(A) ad hominem
(B) non sequitur
(C) false analogy
(D) bandwagon

Items 30–33.

(1) The choice of educational practices sometimes seems like choosing fashions. (2) Fashion is driven by the whims, tastes, and zeitgeist of the current day. (3) The education system should not be driven by these same forces. (4) But consider, for example, the way mathematics is taught. (5) Three decades ago, teachers were told to use manipulative materials to teach mathematics. (6) In the intervening years, the emphasis was on drill and practice. (7) Now teachers are being told again to use manipulative materials. (8) This cycle is more akin to _____ than to sound professional practice.

30. Which of these sentences contains a simile?
(A) (1)
(B) (2)
(C) (5)
(D) (6)

31. Which of the following sentences contains an opinion?
(A) (4)
(B) (5)
(C) (6)
(D) (8)

32. For what reason did the author use the phrase *three decades* in sentence 5?
(A) To represent 30 years
(B) For emphasis
(C) To represent 10-year intervals
(D) To represent the passage of years

33. Which of the following choices best fits in the blank in sentence 8?
(A) Unsound practice
(B) A fashion designer's dream
(C) The movement of hemlines
(D) A fashion show

Items 34–37.

Computer graphing programs are capable of graphing almost any equations, including advanced equations from calculus. The student just types in the equation and the graph appears on the computer screen. The graphing program can also show the numerical solution for any entered equation. I like having a computer program that performs the mechanical aspects of these difficult calculations. However, these programs do not teach about graphing or mathematics because the computer does not "explain" what is going on. A person could type in an equation, get an answer, and have not the slightest idea what either meant.

Relying on this mindless kind of graphing and calculation, students will be completely unfamiliar with the meaning of the equations they write or the results they get. They will not be able to understand how to create a graph from an equation or to understand the basis for the more complicated calculations.

It may be true that a strictly mechanical approach is used by some teachers. There certainly is a place for students who already understand equations and graphing to have a computer program that relieves the drudgery. But these computer programs should never and can never replace the teacher. Mathematical competence assumes that understanding precedes rote calculation.

34. What is the main idea of this passage?
(A) Mechanical calculation is one part of learning about mathematics.
(B) Teachers should use graphing programs as one part of instruction.
(C) Graphing programs are not effective for initially teaching mathematics.
(D) Students who use these programs won't learn mathematics.

35. Which of the following questions could be answered from the information in the passage?
(A) How does the program do integration and differentiation?
(B) What type of mathematics learning experiences should students have?
(C) When is it appropriate to use graphing programs?
(D) Why do schools buy these graphing programs?

36. Which of the following information can be found in the passage?
I. The type of computer that graphs the equation
II. The graphing program's two main outputs
III. How to use the program to teach about mathematics
(A) I only
(B) II only
(C) I and II only
(D) II and III only

37. Which aspect of graphing programs does the author of the passage like?
(A) That you just have to type in the equation
(B) That the difficult mechanical operations are performed
(C) That the calculations and graphing are done very quickly
(D) That you don't have to know math to use them

Items 38–40.

The Vietnam war stretched across the twelve years of the Kennedy and Johnson administrations and into the presidency of Richard Nixon. While the war officially began with Kennedy as president, its actual beginnings stretch back many years.

Before the war, Vietnam was called French Indochina. During World War II, the United States supported Ho Chi Minh in Vietnam as he attacked Japan. After the war, the United States supported the French instead of Ho Chi Minh, as France sought to regain control of its former colony.

Fighting broke out between the French and Ho Chi Minh with support from Mao Zedong (Mao Tse-tung), the leader of mainland China. Even with substantial material aid from the United States, France could not defeat Vietnam. In 1950 the French were defeated at Dien Bien Phu.

Subsequent negotiations in Geneva divided Vietnam into North and South with Ho Chi Minh in control of the North. Ngo Dinh Diem was installed by the United States as a leader in the South. Diem never gained popular support in the South. Following a harsh crackdown by Diem, the Vietcong organized to fight against him. During the Eisenhower administration, 2000 American "advisors" were sent to South Vietnam.

When Kennedy came to office, he approved a CIA coup to overthrow Diem. When Johnson took office he was not interested in compromise. In 1964 Johnson started a massive buildup of forces in Vietnam until the number ultimately reached more than 500,000. The Gulf of Tonkin Resolution, passed by Congress, gave Johnson discretion in pursuing the war.

Living and fighting conditions were terrible. Although American forces had many victories, neither that nor the massive bombing of North Vietnam led to victory. In 1968, the Vietcong launched the Tet Offensive. While ground gained in the offensive was ultimately recaptured, the offensive shook the confidence of military leaders.

At home, there were deep divisions. War protests sprang up all over the United States. Half a million people protested in New York during 1967, while the tension between hawks and doves increased throughout the country.

Richard Nixon was elected in 1970 in the midst of this turmoil. While vigorously prosecuting the war, he and Secretary of State Henry Kissinger were holding secret negotiations with North Vietnam. In 1973 an agreement was finally drawn up to end the war. American prisoners were repatriated although there were still many missing in action (MIA), and U.S. troops withdrew from Vietnam.

The war cost 350,000 American casualties. The $175 billion spent on the war could have been used for Johnson's Great Society programs.

38. The tone of this passage is best described as
    (A) compassionate
    (B) reverent
    (C) serious
    (D) nostalgic

39. In this passage, the author expresses bias against
    (A) the Eisenhower administration
    (B) the French people
    (C) the military
    (D) hawks

40. The passage implies which of the following?
    (A) The Vietnam War was a glorious war.
    (B) Kennedy laid the foundation for this war.
    (C) The United States paid a great price for this war.
    (D) The United States people gave united support for the war effort.

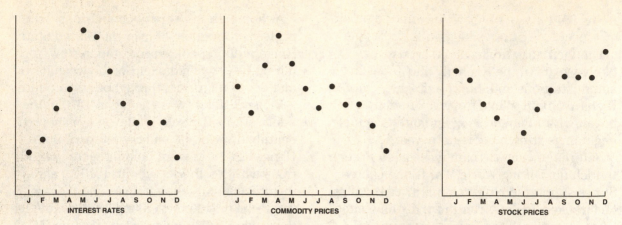

Graphs of Three Economic Indicators for the Same 12-month Period

41. Which of the following conclusions can be drawn from the information on the three graphs shown above?
(A) Higher interest rates cause lower stock prices.
(B) Interest rates and stock prices are inversely related.
(C) Commodity prices and interest rates are not related to one another.
(D) Commodity prices and stock prices are directly related.

Items 42–44.

As a child he read the *Hardy Boys* series of books and was in awe of the author Franklin Dixon. As an adult, he read a book entitled the *Ghost of the Hardy Boys*, which revealed that there was no Franklin Dixon and that ghost writers had authored the books. The authors were apparently working for a large publishing syndicate.

42. Which of the following is the likely intent of the author of this passage?
(A) To describe a book-publishing practice
(B) To contrast fiction and fact
(C) To contrast childhood and adulthood
(D) To correct the record

43. Which of the following does the word *syndicate* in the last sentence most likely refer to?
(A) A business group
(B) An illegal enterprise
(C) An illegal activity
(D) A large building

44. What does the word *Ghost* in the title of the second mentioned book refer to?
(A) A person who has died or was dead at the time the book was published
(B) A person who writes books without credit
(C) A person who influences the way a book is written
(D) The mystical images of the mind that affect the way any author writes

"The cause of liberty becomes a mockery if the price to be paid is the wholesale destruction of those who are to enjoy it."

45. The quote above from Mohandas Gandhi is best reflected in which of the following statements about the American civil rights movement?
(A) Bus boycotts are not effective because boycotters are punished.
(B) Nonviolence and civil disobedience are the best approach to protest.
(C) Desegregation laws were a direct result of freedom marches.
(D) America will never be free as long as minorities are oppressed.

Empty halls and silent walls greeted me. A summer day seemed like a good time for me to take a look at the school in which I would student teach. I tiptoed from classroom door to classroom door—looking. Suddenly the custodian appeared behind me and said, "Help you?" "No sir," I said. At that moment she may have been Plato or Homer for all I knew.

46. Which of the following best describes the main character in the paragraph above?
(A) timid and afraid
(B) confident and optimistic
(C) pessimistic and unsure
(D) curious and respectful

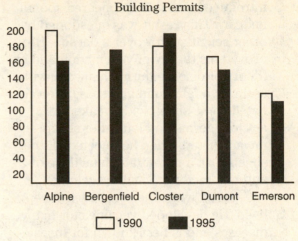

Building Permits

☐ 1990   ■ 1995

47. This graph best demonstrates which of the following?
(A) The town with the most building permits every year is Closter.
(B) Alpine has the biggest difference in permits between 1990 and 1995.
(C) The town with the fewest permits every year is Emerson.
(D) Bergenfield had more building permits in 1990 than Dumont had in 1995.

Items 48–51.

Europeans had started to devote significant resources to medicine when Louis Pasteur was born December 7, 1822. By the time he died in the fall of 1895, he had
(5) made enormous contributions to science and founded microbiology. At 32, he was named professor and dean at a French university dedicated to supporting the production of alcoholic beverages.
(10) Pasteur immediately began work on yeast and fermentation. He found that he could kill harmful bacteria in the initial brewing process by subjecting the liquid to high temperatures. This
(15) finding was extended to milk in the process called pasteurization. This work led him to the conclusion that human disease could be caused by germs. In Pasteur's time, there was a widely held
(20) belief that germs were spontaneously generated. Pasteur conducted experiments that proved germs were always

introduced and never appeared spontaneously. This result was questioned by
(25) other scientists for over a decade. He
proved his theory of vaccination and his
theory of disease during his work with
anthrax, a fatal animal disease. He vaccinated some sheep with weakened
(30) anthrax germs and left other sheep
unvaccinated. Then he injected all the
sheep with a potentially fatal dose of
anthrax bacteria. The unvaccinated
sheep died while the vaccinated sheep
(35) lived. He developed vaccines for many
diseases and is best known for his vaccine for rabies. According to some
accounts, the rabies vaccine was first
tried on a human when a young boy,
(40) badly bitten by a rabid dog, arrived at
Pasteur's laboratory. The treatment of
the boy was successful.

48. What does the process of pasteurization
involve?
(A) inoculating
(B) experimenting
(C) hydrating
(D) heating

49. Which of the following statements could
most reasonably be inferred from this
passage?
(A) The myth of spontaneous generation
was dispelled immediately following
Pasteur's experiments on the subject.
(B) The pasteurization of milk can aid in
the treatment of anthrax.
(C) Pasteur's discoveries were mainly
luck.
(D) Even scientists don't think scientifically all the time.

50. Which of the following choices best
characterizes the reason for Pasteur's
early work?
(A) to cure humans
(B) to cure animals
(C) to help the French economy
(D) to study germs

51. According to this passage, the rabies
vaccine
(A) was developed after Pasteur had
watched a young boy bitten by a
rabid dog.
(B) was developed from the blood of a
rabid dog, which had bitten a young
boy.
(C) was developed from the blood of a
young boy bitten by a rabid dog.
(D) was developed in addition to the
vaccines for other diseases.

Items 52–55.

The Iroquois were present in upstate New
York about 500 years before the Europeans
arrived. According to Iroquois oral history,
this Indian nation was once a single tribe,
subject to the rule of the Adirondack Indians. This tribe was located in the valley of
the St. Lawrence River, but they left and
moved south to be free from Adirondack
control. According to reports from French
explorers, there were still Iroquoian villages
around the St. Lawrence between Quebec
and Montreal in the early 1500s. But when
explorers returned around 1600, these villages had disappeared. It was about this
time that the Iroquois launched a fifty-year
war against the Adirondacks. When the
French reached Montreal around 1609, they
found a vast deserted area along the St.
Lawrence because Adirondack, and other
Indian tribes avoided the river for fear of
attacks from Iroquois raiding parties. The
French sided with the local tribes and
fought against the Iroquois, using firearms,
which caused the Iroquois to give up mass
formations and to replace wooden body
armor with the tactic of falling to the
ground just before the muskets were dis-
charged. The Iroquois were engaged in
many conflicts until the Revolutionary war,
when the Iroquois sided with the British.
The Iroquois were defeated and their lands
were taken.

The Iroquois nation consisted of five main
tribes—Cayuga, Mohawk, Oneida, Onondaga,
and Seneca. Called the Five Nations or the

League of Five Nations, these tribes occupied much of New York State. Since the tribes were arranged from east to west, the region they occupied was called the long house of the Iroquois.

The Iroquois economy was based mainly on agriculture. The main crop was corn, but they also grew pumpkins, beans, and fruit. The Iroquois used wampum (hollow beads) for money, and records were woven into wampum belts.

The Iroquois nation had a remarkable democratic structure, spoke a common Algonquin language, and were adept at fighting. These factors had made the Iroquois a dominant power by the early American Colonial period. In the period just before the Revolutionary War, Iroquoian conquest had overcome most other Indian tribes in the northeastern United States as far west as the Mississippi River.

During the Revolutionary War, most Iroquoian tribes sided with the British. At the end of the Revolutionary War the tribes scattered, with some migrating to Canada. Only remnants of the Seneca and Onondaga tribes remained in their tribal lands.

52. Which of these statements best explains why the Iroquois were so successful at conquest?
    (A) The Iroquois had the support of the British.
    (B) The Iroquois had a cohesive society and were good fighters.
    (C) All the other tribes in the area were too weak.
    (D) There were five tribes, more than the other Indian nations.

53. Which of the following best describes the geographic location of the five Iroquoian tribes?
    (A) the northeastern United States as far west as the Mississippi River
    (B) southern Canada
    (C) Cayuga
    (D) New York State

54. Which of the following best describes why the area occupied by the Iroquois was called the long house of the Iroquois?
    (A) The tribes were arranged as though they occupied different sections of a long house.
    (B) The Iroquois lived in structures called long houses.
    (C) The close political ties among tribes made it seem that they were all living in one house.
    (D) The Iroquois had expanded their original tribal lands through conquest.

55. According to the passage, which of the following best describes the economic basis for the Iroquoian economy?
    (a) wampum
    (B) corn
    (C) agriculture
    (D) conquest

Items 56–57.

I believe that there is extraterrestrial life—probably in some other galaxy. It is particularly human to believe that our solar system is the only one that can support intelligent life. But our solar system is only an infinitesimal dot in the infinity of the cosmos and it is just not believable that there is not life out there—somewhere.

56. What is the author of this passage proposing?
    (A) There is other life in the universe.
    (B) That there is no life on earth.
    (C) That humans live on other planets.
    (D) That the sun is a very small star.

57. The words *infinitesimal* and *infinite* are best characterized by which pair of words below?
    (A) small and large
    (B) very small and very large
    (C) very small and limitless
    (D) large and limitless

Items 58–60.

It is striking how uninformed today's youth are about Acquired Immune Deficiency Syndrome. Because of their youth and ignorance, many young adults engage in high-risk behavior. Many of these young people do not realize that the disease can be contracted through almost any contact with an infected person's blood and bodily fluids. Some do not realize that symptoms of the disease may not appear for ten years or more. Others do not realize that the danger in sharing needles to inject intravenous drugs comes from the small amounts of other's blood injected during this process. A massive education campaign is needed to fully inform today's youth about AIDS.

58. The main idea of this passage is
   (A) previous education campaigns have failed.
   (B) AIDS develops from the HIV virus.
   (C) the general public is not fully informed about AIDS.
   (D) young people are not adequately informed about AIDS.

59. Which of the following is the best summary of the statement about what young people don't realize about how AIDS can be contracted?
   (A) The symptoms may not appear for ten years or more.
   (B) AIDS is contracted because of ignorance.
   (C) AIDS is contracted from intravenous needles.
   (D) AIDS is contracted through contact with infected blood or bodily fluids.

60. Which of the following best describes how the author views young people and their knowledge of AIDS?
   (A) Stupid
   (B) Unaware
   (C) Dumb
   (D) Unintelligible

Items 61–63.

In humans, as in other higher organisms, a DNA molecule consists of two strands that wrap around each other to resemble a twisted ladder whose sides,
(5) made of sugar and rungs of nitrogen-containing chemicals called bases, connect phosphate molecules. Each strand is a linear arrangement of repeating similar units called nucleotides, which
(10) are each composed of one sugar, one phosphate, and a nitrogenous base. Four different bases are present in DNA: adenine (A), thymine (T), cytosine (C), and guanine (G). The particular
(15) order of the bases arranged along the sugar-phosphate backbone is called the DNA sequence; the sequence specifies the exact genetic instructions required to create a particular organism with its
(20) own unique traits.
   The two DNA strands are held together by weak bonds between the bases on each strand, forming base pairs (bp). Genome size is usually stated as the
(25) total number of base pairs; the human genome contains roughly three billion bp. Each time a cell divides into two daughter cells, its full genome is duplicated; for humans and other complex
(30) organisms, this duplication occurs in the nucleus. During cell division the DNA molecule unwinds and the weak bonds between the base pairs break, allowing the strands to separate. Each
(35) strand directs the synthesis of a complementary new strand, with free nucleotides matching up with their complementary bases on each of the separated strands. Strict base-pairing
(40) rules are adhered to; adenine will pair only with thymine (an A-T pair) and cytosine with guanine (a C-G pair). Each daughter cell receives one old and one new DNA strand. The cells'
(45) adherence to these base-pairing rules

ensures that the new strand is an exact copy of the old one. This minimizes the incidence of errors (mutations) that may greatly affect the resulting
(50) organism or its offspring.

Each DNA molecule contains many genes—the basic physical and functional units of heredity. A gene is a specific sequence of nucleotide bases whose
(55) sequences carry the information required for constructing proteins, which provide the structural components of cells and tissues as well as enzymes for essential biochemical
(60) reactions. The human genome is estimated to consist of approximately 80,000–100,000 genes. Human genes vary widely in length, often extending over thousands of bases, but only about
(65) 10 percent of the genome is known to include the protein-coding sequences (exons) of genes. Interspersed with many genes are intron sequences, which have no coding function. The balance of
(70) the genome is thought to consist of other noncoding regions (such as control sequences and intergenic regions), whose functions are obscure.

61. What is the guaranteed outcome of base pairing rules?
(A) Adenine will pair only with thymine.
(B) New strands exactly replicate old strands.
(C) DNA strands are held together by weak bonds between the bases on each strand.
(D) Sequences carry the information required for constructing proteins.

62. When it comes to coding,
(A) four different bases are present in DNA.
(B) the functions of many regions on the genome are obscure.
(C) the DNA molecule unwinds and the weak bonds between the base pairs break.
(D) the two DNA strands are held together by weak bonds on each strand, forming a base pair.

63. According to the passage, what does a nucleotide consist of?
(A) phosphate, sugar, nitrogenous base
(B) adenine, thymine, cytosine, guanine
(C) sugar, bases, phosphate molecules
(D) protein-coding sequences, intron sequences

64. This poster depicts
(A) the horrors of animal cruelty in early U.S. history.
(B) the break up of the United States leading to the Civil War.
(C) the need for the colonies to ratify the Constitution.
(D) the need for the colonies to unite against England.

Items 65–66.

Alice in Wonderland, written by Charles Dodgson under the pen name Lewis Carroll, is full of symbolism, so much so that a book titled *Understanding Alice* was written containing the original text with marginal notes explaining the symbolic meanings.

65. By symbolism, the author of the passage above meant that much of Alice in Wonderland
  (A) was written in a foreign language.
  (B) contained many mathematical symbols.
  (C) contained no pictures.
  (D) had a figurative meaning.

66. What does the author mean by the phrase "marginal notes" found in the last sentence?
  (A) Explanations of the musical meaning of the text
  (B) Notes that may not have been completely correct
  (C) Notes written next to the main text
  (D) Notes written by Carroll but not included in the original book

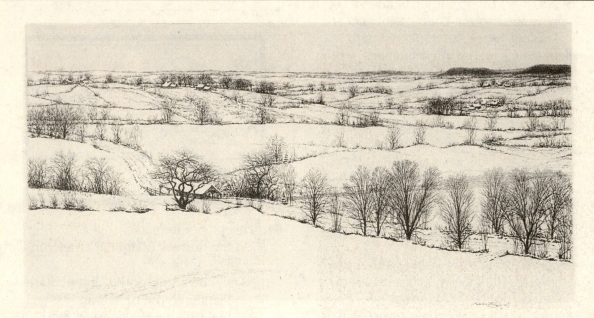

["A Connecticut Valley." The Metropolitan Museum of Art, Harris Brisbain Fund, 1940. (40.87.1)]

67. This picture best expresses
  (A) action and warmth.
  (B) isolation and cold.
  (C) fluctuation and flatness.
  (D) concern and denseness.

68. It is Monday at 6 P.M. near the coast of California when you call your friend who lives near the coast of New Jersey. It takes you 5 ½ hours to get through. What time is it in New Jersey when you get through?
  (A) 8:30 P.M. Monday
  (B) 9:30 P.M. Monday
  (C) 2:30 P.M. Tuesday
  (D) 3:30 P.M. Tuesday

During a Stage 4 alert, workers in an energy plant must wear protective pants, a protective shirt, and a helmet except that protective coveralls can be worn in place of protective pants and shirt. When there is a Stage 5 alert, workers must also wear filter masks in addition to the requirements for the Stage 4 alert.

69. During a Stage 5 alert, which of the following could be worn?
   I. masks, pants, shirt
   II. coveralls, helmet, mask
   III. coveralls, mask
   (A) I only
   (B) II only
   (C) III only
   (D) I and II only

Time	8 A.M.	9 A.M.	10 A.M.	11 A.M.	12 NOON
Temp	45°	55°	60°	60°	70°
Time	1 P.M.	2 P.M.	3 P.M.	4 P.M.	
Temp	75°	75°	70°	65°	
Time	5 P.M.	6 P.M.	7 P.M.	8 P.M.	
Temp	55°	50°	50°	45°	

70. The accompanying table shows the temperature tracked for a 12-hour period of time. Which graph best illustrates this information?

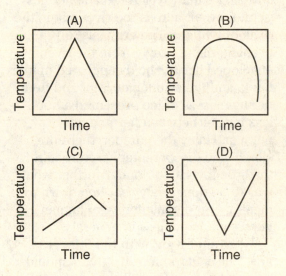

71. Which feature of this sculpture enables the viewer to perceive several different images?
   (A) The light color of the sculpture (against the dark background)
   (B) Mounting the sculpture at eye level
   (C) The sculpture's dimensionality
   (D) The alternating curvature of the sculpture's boundary

["Sevil-Configurations" (Threshold Configuration) by Jean Arp. The Metropolitan Museum of Art, Gift of Arthur and Madelaine Lejwa to The Museum to Honor the Citizens of New York, 1971. (1971.279)]

72. *C* is 5 more than half of *B*. Which of the following expressions states this relationship?

(A) $C + 5 = B/2$

(B) $C = \frac{1}{2}B + 5$

(C) $C + 5 = 2B$

(D) $C + 5 > B/2$

Base your answers to 73–76 on this passage from *Uncle Tom's Cabin* by Harriett Beecher Stowe.

Eliza, a runaway slave, made her desperate retreat across the river just in the dusk of twilight. The gray mist of evening, rising slowly from the river,
(5) enveloped her as she disappeared up the bank, and the swollen current and floundering masses of ice presented a hopeless barrier between her and her pursuer. Haley the pursuer, therefore
(10) slowly and discontentedly returned to the little tavern, to ponder further what was to be done. Haley sat him down to meditate on the instability of human hopes and happiness in general.
(15) "What did I want with the little cuss, now," he said to himself, "that I should have got myself treed like a coon, as I am, this yer say?" He was startled by the loud and dissonant voice of a man who
(20) was apparently dismounting at the door. He hurried to the window. "By the land! if this yer an't the nearest, now, to what I've heard folks call Providence," said Haley, "I do b'lieve that ar's Tom Loker."
(25) Haley hastened out. Standing by the bar, in the corner of the room, was a brawny; muscular man, full six feet in height and broad in proportion. In the head and face every organ and
(30) lineament expressive of brutal and unhesitating violence was in a state of the highest possible development. Indeed, could our readers fancy a bull-dog come into man's estate, and walking
(35) about in a hat and coat, they would have no unapt idea of the general style and effect of his physique. He was accompanied by a traveling companion, in many respects an exact contrast to himself.

(40) The large man poured out a big tumbler half full of raw spirits, and gulped it down without a word. The little man stood tiptoe, and putting his head first to one side and then to the other, and
(45) snuffing considerately in the directions of the various bottles, ordered at last a mint julep, in a thin and quivering voice, and with an air of great circumspection. "Wall, now, who'd a thought this yer
(50) luck 'ad come to me? Why, Loker, how are ye?" said Haley, coming forward, and extending his hand to the big man. "The devil" was the civil reply. "What brought you here, Haley?" The mousing
(55) man, who bore the name of Marks, instantly stopped his sipping. "I say, Tom, this yer's the luckiest thing in the world. I'm in a devil of a hobble, and you must help me out." Haley began a
(60) pathetic recital of his peculiar troubles. Loker shut up his mouth, and listened to him with gruff and surly attention. "This yer young-un business makes lots of trouble in the slave trade," said
(65) Haley dolefully. (Haley is referring to the fact that slave mothers were often separated from their children. The mothers, naturally, did their best to keep their children, thus causing what Haley calls
(70) "lots of trouble in the slave trade.")

73. Which of the following events occurs between the time when the brawny man is standing at the bar and when the last mint julep was ordered?

(A) Haley hastens out.

(B) The little man stood tiptoe.

(C) Gray mist rises.

(D) Tom Loker is recognized.

74. Based on the passage, which of the following is true about Haley?

(A) He looked like a bulldog.

(B) He was startled by a dissonant voice.

(C) He was himself a little man.

(D) He drank mint juleps in the Southern tradition.

75. Which of the following statements is true, according to the passage?
 (A) The runaway slave crossed the river just before sunrise.
 (B) The runaway slave was brought back to the tavern.
 (C) The runaway slave disappeared into the river.
 (D) The runaway slave was not captured.

76. Which of the following statements is the most accurate about Tom Loker?
 (A) Tom Loker stood by the bar in the corner of the room.
 (B) Haley saw him through the tavern window.
 (C) Haley met Tom Loker outside the tavern.
 (D) Tom Loker's real name was not Loker; it was Marks.

---

77. A person throws a black cloth over a pile of snow to make the snow melt faster. Why is that?
 (A) Cloth will make snow melt faster.
 (B) The black material absorbs more sunlight and more heat.
 (C) The black material holds the heat in.
 (D) The black cloth reflects light better and so absorbs more heat.

Advances in astronomy and space exploration during the past twenty-five years have been significant, and we now know more answers to questions about the universe than ever before, but we still cannot answer the ultimate question, "How did our universe originate?"

78. Which of the following best characterizes the author's view of how the advances in astronomy and space exploration affect our eventual ability to answer the ultimate question?
 (A) We now know more answers than ever before.
 (B) All the questions have not been answered.
 (C) Eventually we will probably find out.
 (D) The question can't be answered.

The sunrise in the desert sky was accompanied by a strange and eerie glow. Normally the sun shone big and bright and yellow. Now all eyes squinted to see the cause. Suddently, as if out of the sun itself, horsemen thundered into our midst. They spared no one the wrath of the guns which they held in their hands. I hid as I could among some baskets and then, as fast as they had come, the horsemen galloped away. I looked out and saw that almost none were moving and listened as the sound of horses faded in the distance.

79. The glow in the sky was probably caused by
 (A) an especially hot day.
 (B) the sun shining through dust from the horses.
 (C) the glint from the rider's guns.
 (D) an emotional reaction on the part of the observers.

80. You flip a fair coin three times and it comes up heads each time. What is the probability that the fourth flip will be a head?
 (A) 1/16
 (B) 1/4
 (C) 1/2
 (D) 1/3

WRITTEN ASSIGNMENT

Write an essay on the topic below. Use the lined pages that follow. Write your essay on this topic only. An essay on another topic will be rated Unscorable (U).

Is it better to group students homogeneously or heterogeneously?

It is better to group students homogeneously. Homogeneous grouping means that students with similar ability or similar achievement are grouped together. This is the correct way to group because students work more comfortably when they are around other similar students. The teacher can concentrate on a narrower range of objectives and does not have to worry about students who are surging ahead or lagging behind. This homogeneous approach offers the best opportunity for student learning.

It is better to group students heterogeneously. Heterogeneous grouping means that students with varying ability and achievement are grouped together. The first point to note is that homogeneous grouping for, say, reading does not produce heterogeneous grouping for mathematics. So no matter how you group, students will be heterogeneously grouped in most classes. But heterogeneous grouping is the best choice anyhow. There is no research to show that homogeneously grouped students do better, but there are studies that indicate that students who act as peer tutors do better, and this peer tutoring is most likely to occur in heterogeneous groupings.

Is it better to group students homogeneously or heterogeneously?

Review and evaluate the opposing positions presented above.

Choose one of these two positions.

Write an essay that supports your position following the guidelines presented above.

PRACTICE LAST II

Explained Answers

1. **B** This choice paraphrases the fourth sentence in the second paragraph. Choice (A) is incorrect because, even though the passage states that to many Johnson's Great Society programs made him "a better president than Kennedy," the passage does not affirm that view. (C) is incorrect because even while Johnson championed programs called Great Society programs, there was no real Great Society and he was not a member of it. (D) is incorrect because the passage indicates that his predecessor was Kennedy.

2. **A** Faster times are represented by smaller numbers. Subtract $52.8 - 1.3 = 51.5$ to find Lisa's time. (B) is incorrect because this is 1.3 seconds slower than Lisa's time. (C) is incorrect because this incorrectly adds $52.8 + 1.3$ without renaming. (D) is incorrect because this is the answer to $52.8 + 13$.

3. **D** This primitive African pendant clearly shows a close relationship between horse and rider. (A) is incorrect because even though there appears to be something sticking into the horse, there is no evidence of pain. (B) is incorrect because choice (D) is a much more likely answer. (C) is incorrect because the animal is not strange and the legs are not attached to one another.

4. **D** The author is trying to raise AIDS awareness by presenting a wide range of information about AIDS. The remaining choices are incorrect for the following reasons: (A) There are statements in the passage that might lead a person to believe that drug companies can't be trusted, but that is not the main idea of the passage. (B) The passage does not focus on the history of AIDS research. (C) There is information about the causes and consequences of AIDS, but that is not the main idea.

5. **C** The passage explains that AIDS is transmitted through blood and other bodily fluids. (A) is incorrect because the passage does not explain how IV drug users acquire AIDS. (B) is incorrect because AIDS is not caused by blood transfusions. (D) is incorrect because the passage does not describe how blood companies tests for AIDS.

6. **D** The combination of increased awareness, but no cure, sums up this passage. (A) This statement may be true, but this is not discussed in the passage and it is not a reasonable conclusion. (B) is incorrect because the passage does not mention intravenous drug use. (C) is incorrect because the paragraph does not mention that people develop AIDS after they become HIV positive.

7. **A** These states have the lowest per pupil expenditures ($3,187, $3,327, $3,078). The states in (B), (C), and (D) all have higher per pupil expenditures than the states in choice (A).

8. **B** Just a quick scan shows that all northeastern states have per pupil expenditures above $5,000, with many above $6,000. Only a few states in the remaining choices have per pupil expenditures above $5,000, and only Alaska in these other regions has per pupil expenditures above $6,000.

9. **D** The second quartile is the second one-fourth of per pupil expenditures ranked from highest to lowest. That's the 14th through the 26th highest expenditures. Arizona is the 14th score at the top of the second quartile. You can answer this question best by eliminating answers. (A) is incorrect because Alaska's expenditures are near the very top in the first quartile. (B) and (C) are incorrect because Alabama's and Idaho's expenditures are at the very bottom in the fourth quartile. That leaves (D), Arizona, as the only possible answer.

10. **C** This famous quote from Churchill referred to the isolation of Communist Bloc countries. You would have to be familiar with a little history to know what this Churchill quote refers to, and

that (A), (B), and (D) are incorrect. Questions like this do pop up on the LAST from time to time.

11. **D** First find all the pieces that are either small or striped and cross out the pieces that don't meet one of these rules. Then find all the pieces not crossed out that are "and large," and circle these pieces. The circled piece below shows the correct answer.

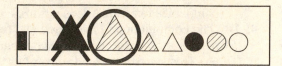

12. **D** Lines 18 and 19 state that as a general rule "the presence of prehistoric features is reflected in the lower magnetic readings." The remaining choices are found in the passage but do not answer the question. (A) This is how to tell that the magnetic readings are lower. (B) The passage indicates that advanced numerical readings may be useful for a full analysis of prehistoric patterns. (C) The passage notes that some techniques rely on the examination of existing relics.

13. **B** Usefulness is a synonym for efficacy. The placements (A) and the relationships (D) of features are the results (C) used to determine the efficacy of further investigations.

14. **D** Lines 14–17 explain that "the resulting patterns from agricultural activity will lead to the discovery of even smaller prehistoric ditches and other features." (A) is incorrect because the passage says "pockets of material [not patterns of agricultural activity] may later be transformed into the topsoil by agricultural activity." (B) is incorrect because the passage does not mention offering assistance to archaeologists. (C) is incorrect because the passage indicates that advanced numerical methods may presuppose a knowledge of mathematics or physics.

15. **C** There are 24 holes altogether, and 8 of them are labeled "1." So the probability of landing on a "1" is 8/24 or 1/3. (A) and (B) are incorrect because less than half the holes are labeled "1." (D) is incorrect because more than one in four holes are labeled "1."

16. **C** The plan must be disapproved because the third regulation states that if three lanes are set aside for passenger cars, then school buses, school vans, and school cars can all use the lane for cars with two or more passengers. (A) is incorrect because the extra provisions of the third regulation apply to this situation. (B) is incorrect because both the first and third regulation apply also to the situation described in this item. (D) is incorrect because the reason given conflicts with the third regulation.

17. **B** Consider each Roman numeral in turn and then choose your answer.

 I. Disapproved. It sets aside lanes for passenger cars with three passengers, not the two or more passengers required by the third regulation.
 II. Approved. It meets the requirements in the second regulation for when four lanes are set aside for passenger cars.
 III. Disapproved. It does not meet the requirements of the third regulation for when three lanes are set aside for passenger cars.

Only Plan II would be approved—(B).

18. **D** Dissent involves people, and only pictures (A) and (D) involve people. A closer look at (D) reveals a crowd throwing things at some figure and thus shows dissent. It turns out that this wood engraving shows a tax agent being stoned in effigy. Picture (A) shows people gathering after the San Francisco earthquake. (B) and (C) do not show dissent because there are no people.

19. **B** This painting from 1825 appears almost two dimensional. Sizes are not represented proportionally. The other pictures represent things three-dimensionally.

20. **C** Pictures (A), (C), and (D) are realistic. Of these three pictures, only (C) does not portray people.

21. **B** This statement puts the author at odds with the Board of Adjustment, but the author never questions or attacks the board or its responsibilities. The remaining choices paraphrase the author's statements in the passage.

22. **A** These notes show the distinctive beginning of "My Country 'Tis of Thee," to the exception of choices (B), (C), and (D).

23. **C** The ball at the top of the ramp has the furthest to roll and that means it has the most potential to create energy. Diagrams (A), (B), and (D) show that some of that potential energy has been used. Diagram (D) shows the least potential energy.

24. **A** The correct answer is 42. The number of "eaters" increases by 4, 6, 8, 10, and then 12. 30 + 12 = 42. Choices (B), (C), and (D) do not continue that pattern.

25. **C** To get the number of "eaters," multiply the number of hunters and one more than the number of hunters. This gives the formula: $H \times (H + 1) = H^2 + H$. This is the formula shown in (C). You can also find the answer to this question by just trying out "1" for the number of hunters. (A) is incorrect because $3 (1) = 3$, but the number of eaters for one hunter is 2. (B) is incorrect because $4 (1) = 4$, but the number of eaters for one hunter is 2. (D) is incorrect because $3 (1 + 1) = 6$, but the number of eaters for one hunter is 2.

26. **D** Music is more than just notes and varies with the mood of the performer. (A) is incorrect because there is nothing to indicate that the songs sounded worse in person. (B) is incorrect because there is nothing dismissive about what the performer has to say. (C) is incorrect because there is nothing to indicate that the concert was outdoors.

27. **B** In a solar eclipse, the moon blocks the sun's light from reaching earth. The moon must be between the sun and the earth for a solar eclipse to occur. (A) is incorrect because this situation could result in a lunar eclipse, in which the earth casts a shadow on the moon. (C) and (D) are incorrect because these diagrams show the sun between the earth and the moon, which is not possible.

28. **C** The speaker is making an argument to convince the audience of his or her position. An argument is an attempt to be persuasive, and is not the same as being argumentative. (A) is incorrect because a narration presents a fictional or factual story. (B) is incorrect because reflective passages describe a scene, person, or emotion. (D) is incorrect because expository passages simply explain.

29. **A** The speaker is making an "ad hominem" argument because he or she seeks to discredit the person rather than respond to the position in the question. (B) is incorrect because a "non sequitur" means presenting a conclusion that does not flow logically from the facts. (C) is incorrect because "false analogy" means using an analogy that does not match the situation under discussion. (D) is incorrect because "bandwagon" means arguing for a position because of its popularity.

30. **A** The first sentence contains the simile "choice of educational practices . . . like choosing fashions." A simile is a figure of speech that compares two things and usually uses the words "like" or "as." (B), (C), and (D) are incorrect because none of these sentences contains a comparison.

31. **D** Only sentence (8) contains an opinion among the sentences listed. (A) is incorrect because sentence (4) contains a statement that seems to be leading up to an opinion, but it is not an opinion itself. (B) and (C) are incorrect because sentences (5) and (6) contain statements of fact.

32. **B** The author is being a little dramatic to emphasize the length of time. The other choices do not capture the reason the author chose the phrase.

33. **C** Hemlines move without apparent reason, which is the author's point about educational practices. (A) is incorrect because nothing in the passage suggests this is unsound practice. (B) and (D) are incorrect because nothing about the passage is about fashion.

34. **C** The main point is that the author objects to using these programs with students who don't know mathematics. (A) and (B) are incorrect because they include information found in the passage, but it is not the author's main point. (D) is incorrect because the author never makes the claim that students who use these programs won't learn mathematics.

35. **C** This is the only question that can be answered from information in the

passage. The answer is found in the third paragraph, "There certainly is a place for students who already understand equations and graphing to have a computer program that relieves drudgery." (A) is incorrect because the passage never mentions how the program does anything. (B) is incorrect because the passage does not detail the kinds of mathematics learning experiences students should have. (D) is incorrect because the passage never mentions schools' purchasing practices.

36. **B** Consider each Roman numeral in turn.

    I. Incorrect. The passage never mentions the type of computer that graphs the equations.
    II. Correct. The first paragraph mentions graphs and numerical solutions as the two main outputs.
    III. Incorrect. The passage never mentions how to use the program to teach mathematics.

    Only II is correct—(B).

37. **B** The middle of the first paragraph mentions that the author likes the fact that the difficult mechanical operations are performed. (A), (C), and (D) are incorrect because the author never says that he or she likes the things given in these choices.

38. **C** The author's tone is serious, but the author does not reminisce (D), and the author is neither particularly respectful (B) nor sympathetic (A).

39. **A** The quotes around the word "advisors" in the last sentence of the fourth paragraph depicts sarcasm and a bias against the Eisenhower administration. The remaining choices are incorrect because the author does not demonstrate a bias against these groups, even though the author does not always agree with their actions.

40. **C** The author summarizes his thoughts about the price paid by the United States in the last two sentences. The other choices are not correct according to the passage.

41. **B** These charts show that stock prices in the third graph and interest rates in the first graph generally went in opposite directions. (A) is incorrect because

correlation charts do not show a cause-and-effect relationship. (C) is false because the charts do show some relationship. (D) is incorrect because the commodity price chart does not match the stock price chart.

42. **D** The author wants to share what he or she learned about the Hardy Boys books. (A) is incorrect because the author does not describe the practice. (B) and (C) are incorrect because the author does not contrast fact and fiction, nor childhood and adulthood.

43. **A** The word *syndicate* can have many meanings. The context reveals that the word *syndicate* means a publishing business group. (B) and (C) are incorrect because there is no indication of illegal activity. (D) is incorrect because *syndicate* does not mean "large building."

44. **B** The term ghost writer has a specific meaning—it is someone who writes books but does not receive credit. (A) is incorrect here because "ghost" in this context does not refer to a dead person. (C) is incorrect because a ghost writer has a more significant role than influence. (D) is incorrect because a ghost writer has nothing to do with mystical images.

45. **B** The quote supports the nonviolent, nondestructive approach to protest supported by Gandhi. The other choices are incorrect because none of them refer to a wholesale destruction of those who will benefit from an action.

46. **D** The person visited the school and is certainly curious. The person's response to the custodian shows respect. (A) is incorrect because there may be some evidence of timidity as the student tiptoes in the hallway, but there is no evidence of fear. (B) is incorrect because there is no particular evidence of either confidence or optimism. (C) is incorrect because there is no evidence of pessimism, although the tiptoeing may show that the student is unsure.

47. **B** Alpine has a difference of about 40 permits between 1990 and 1995. There are smaller differences in other towns between 1990 and 1995. (A) and (C) are incorrect because these statements include the words "every year" and the chart shows information for only 1990

and 1995. You can't tell from the chart whether or not these statements are true. (D) is incorrect because Bergenfield had the same number of permits in 1990 as Dumont had in 1995.

48. **D** This answer can be found in lines 13 and 14 of the passage. (A) Inoculate means to vaccinate. (B) Experiment means to try out (C) Hydrate means to moisten.

49. **D** The passage contains examples of scientists who opposed Pasteur's theories even though Pasteur had proven his theories scientifically. (A) is incorrect because we see on lines 19–21 that scientists questioned the result for over a decade. (B) is incorrect because there is no connection between anthrax and pasteurization, except for Pasteur himself. (C) is incorrect because the passage documents a pattern of careful scientific work.

50. **C** The passage mentions that Pasteur's early work was at a university dedicated to supporting an important product of the French economy. (A), (B), and (D) are incorrect because they refer to work he did later in his career.

51. **D** The third from last sentence mentions that Pasteur developed vaccines for many diseases. (A), (B), and (C) are incorrect because the passage never mentions that Pasteur had done any of these things. The passage mentions that the rabies vaccine may have first been tried on a boy bitten by a rabid dog.

52. **B** The first sentence in the fourth paragraph explains that the Iroquois had a cohesive society and were adept at fighting. (A) is incorrect because the Iroquois did side with the British, but they lost. (C) is incorrect because the passage never mentions the weakness of other tribes. (D) is incorrect because the number of tribes was not a significant factor compared to choice (B).

53. **D** The second paragraph clearly states that the tribes occupied much of what is now New York State. (A) is incorrect because this choice describes the area conquered by the Iroquois before the Revolutionary War. (B) is incorrect because this choice shows where some Iroquois migrated after the Revolutionary War. (C) is incorrect because this is the name of an Iroquois tribe.

54. **A** The last sentence in the second paragraph explains that the region was called the long house of the Iroquois. (B) is incorrect because the region looked like the long house. (C) and (D) are incorrect because the arrangement of the tribes was not directly related to political ties or to conquest.

55. **C** The first sentence in the third paragraph says the Iroquois economy was based mainly on agriculture. (A) and (B) are incorrect because wampum and corn are mentioned in the paragraph about the economy, but not as the basis for the economy. (D) is incorrect because conquest is not mentioned as a basis for the economy.

56. **A** The first sentence in the passage proposes that there is other life in the universe. (B) is incorrect because the author never suggests the absence of life on earth. (C) is incorrect because the author never suggests that there are humans on other planets. (D) is incorrect because the author compares the entire solar system, not the sun, to the entire cosmos.

57. **C** *Infinitesimal* means very small and *infinite* means without limit or limitless. (A) and (B) are incorrect at least because "large" and "very large" are not synonyms for limitless. (D) is incorrect because "large" is the opposite of *infinitesimal.*

58. **D** The passage is about youth and constantly refers to what youths do and do not know about AIDS. (A), (B), and (C) are either true or can reasonably be implied from the passage, but none of them are the main idea of the passage.

59. **D** This choice paraphrases the third sentence in the paragraph. (A) and (B) are incorrect because they do not describe *how* AIDS can be contracted. (C) is incorrect because it incorrectly describes how AIDS can be contracted.

60. **B** The passage uses many synonyms of the word "unaware" to describe young people's knowledge of AIDS. (A) and (C) are incorrect because someone may characterize another person as "stupid" or "dumb," but a person can't be stupid or dumb about AIDS. (D) is incorrect because "unintelligible" describes a person who can't be understood.

61. **B** (B) paraphrases the next to last sentence in the second paragraph. (A) is a base pairing rule, not a guaranteed outcome of the rules. (C) and (D) are taken directly from the passage, but they are not directly related to this item.

62. **B** This choice paraphrases the last sentence in the passage. All the other choices are taken more or less directly from the passage, but none of these choices have anything to do with coding. (A) This answer is found on lines 12–14, (C) this answer is found on lines 32–33, (D) this answer is found on lines 21–23.

63. **A** This answer paraphrases lines 10–11 in the passage, but in a different order and without numerical information. All of the other lists come directly from the passage as well, but are not associated with nucleotides. (B) lists DNA bases from lines 13–14. (C) lists some terms found on lines 5–7. (D) lists terms from lines 66–69.

64. **D** This famous poster with the words "JOIN or DIE" reflects the sentiment "United We Stand, Divided We Fall," current before the Revolutionary War. The poster suggests the pieces need to be brought together. (A) does not reflect the words "JOIN or DIE." (B) does correspond with bringing pieces together. (C) is incorrect because ratifying a constitution does not have the urgency found in the words "join or die."

65. **D** *Alice in Wonderland*, a fanciful story about a young girl's adventures underground, has underlying figurative meanings and is not to be taken literally. (A) is incorrect because symbolism does not mean in a foreign language. (B) is incorrect because symbolism in this context does not literally mean symbols. (C) is incorrect because nothing in the passage suggests there were no pictures.

66. **C** The context reveals that marginal means explanatory notes written next to the main text. (A) is incorrect because "notes" in this context does not mean musical notes. (B) is incorrect because "marginal" in this context does not mean suspect. (D) is incorrect because the passage indicates that the notes were not written in the book authored by Carroll.

67. **B** The barren landscape and defoliated trees in this print show isolation and cold. (A) is incorrect because the picture does not show action and it is not warm. (C) is incorrect because the picture does not show fluctuation—change. (D) is incorrect because nothing in the picture suggests denseness.

68. **C** There is a three-hour time difference between coasts, and the time is later on the East Coast. It was 11:30 P.M. on Monday in California when you got through. That means it was three hours later, or 2:30 A.M. Tuesday in New Jersey. (A) indicates that the time was three hours earlier on the East Coast, not three hours later. (B) indicates two hours earlier, and (D) four hours later in New Jersey.

69. **B** Consider each Roman numeral in turn.

    I. Incorrect. It does not include a helmet.
    II. Correct. Coveralls can be worn in place of pants and a shirt.
    III. Incorrect. A helmet is missing.

    Only Roman numeral II is correct—(B).

70. **A** This graph is not a perfect reflection of the chart, but it best represents the steady movement up and then down of the temperatures. Graph (B) incorrectly shows that the temperature went straight up, not up gradually. Graph (C) incorrectly shows that the temperature did not go down until late afternoon, and then only partly. Graph (D) incorrectly shows that the temperature went down in the morning and up in the afternoon.

71. **D** The curvature creates an illusion of several different images, including a "three-eared rabbit" and a "running ghost." What images do you see? (A) The light color helps perceive different images, but is not as important as the curvature. Neither mounting at eye level (B) nor the dimensionality (C) creates the illusion of different images.

72. **B** Rewrite the words as symbols: $C = 5 + \frac{1}{2}B$. That formula is the same as $C = \frac{1}{2}B + 5$. None of the other equations or inequalities matches the words in this item.

73. **B** The brawny man standing at the bar appears in lines 26–28. The last mint

julep is ordered in lines 46–47. The correct answer, "The little man stood tiptoe," appears between them on lines 42–43. (A) Haley hastened out in line 25. (C) The gray mist rises in line 3. (D) Tom Loker is recognized in line 24.

74. **B** Haley was startled by a dissonant voice on lines 18–19. (A) It was Tom Loker who looked like a bulldog, lines 33–34. (C) Haley is never described as a little man. (D) It was the little man Marks who was drinking mint juleps, 46–47, 55.

75. **D** On lines 5 and 6 we read that "she (Eliza) disappeared up the bank." (A) The first few lines indicate that this was happening at dusk. (B) Nothing in the passage indicates the slave was brought back to the tavern. (C) Lines 6–9 indicate that the river placed a barrier between the slave and her pursuer.

76. **B** Lines 21–24 suggest this correct answer. (A) Lines 25–28 indicate that it was Tom Loker standing by the door in the corner of the room. (C) Lines 50–53 indicate that Haley met Loker inside the tavern. (D) Lines 54–56 indicate that the little man's name was Marks.

77. **B** It is the dark color. Dark material absorbs more heat than light material.

(A) is incorrect because snow melts more quickly under a black cloth than under a white cloth. (C) is incorrect because white material actually reflects more heat in, as well as away from, the snow. (D) White cloth absorbs less heat because it reflects light better.

78. **B** The author writes that the question still cannot be answered. (A) is true but does not describe our eventual ability to answer the ultimate question. (C) The author does not say that the question will eventually be answered. (D) The author does not say the question cannot be answered.

79. **B** The dust from the horses is the most likely cause of the eerie glow that was seen that morning. (A) A hot day does not produce a glow in the sky. (C) There could not be enough guns to create a strange and eerie glow. (D) An emotional reaction cannot produce an actual glow in the sky.

80. **C** The probability is always ½ regardless of what happens on previous flips. (A) is the probability of flipping four heads in a row. (B) is the probability of flipping two heads in a row. (D) is not related to the probability of flipping coins.

WRITTEN ASSIGNMENT

Show your essay to an English professor or a high school English teacher. Ask them to rate your essay 0–3 using this scale.

3   A well developed, complete written assignment.
Shows a thorough response to all parts of the topic.
Clear explanations that are well supported.
An assignment that is free of significant grammatical, punctuation, or spelling errors.

2   A fairly well developed, complete written assignment.
It may not thoroughly respond to all parts of the topic.
Fairly clear explanations that may not be well supported.
It may contain some significant grammatical, punctuation, or spelling errors.

1   A poorly developed, incomplete written assignment.
It does not thoroughly respond to most parts of the topic.
Contains many poor explanations that are not well supported.
It may contain some significant grammatical, punctuation, or spelling errors.

0   A very poorly developed, incomplete written assignment.
It does not thoroughly respond to the topic.
Contains only poor, unsupported explanations.
Contains numerous significant grammatical, punctuation, or spelling errors.

PART VII

Two Complete ATS-Ws
with Explained Answers

13 PRACTICE ATS-W I (ELEMENTARY)

This practice test contains the types of items you will encounter on the real test, but don't be surprised if the real test seems different. The distribution of items varies from one test administration to another.

Take this test in a realistic timed setting. You should not take this practice test until you have completed your subject matter review.

The setting will be most realistic if another person times the test and ensures that the test rules are followed. But remember that many people do better on a practice test than on the real test.

You have four hours to complete the multiple-choice items and the written assignment. Keep this time limit in mind as you work. Answer the easier questions first. Be sure you answer all the questions. There is no penalty for guessing. You may write in the test booklet and mark up the questions.

Each multiple-choice item has four answer choices. Exactly one of these choices is correct. Use a pencil to mark your choice on the answer sheet provided for this test.

The written assignment immediately follows the multiple-choice items. Once the test is complete, review the answers and explanations as you correct the answer sheet.

When instructed, turn the page and begin.

ANSWER SHEET PRACTICE ATS-W I (ELEMENTARY)

1 Ⓐ Ⓑ Ⓒ Ⓓ	21 Ⓐ Ⓑ Ⓒ Ⓓ	41 Ⓐ Ⓑ Ⓒ Ⓓ	61 Ⓐ Ⓑ Ⓒ Ⓓ
2 Ⓐ Ⓑ Ⓒ Ⓓ	22 Ⓐ Ⓑ Ⓒ Ⓓ	42 Ⓐ Ⓑ Ⓒ Ⓓ	62 Ⓐ Ⓑ Ⓒ Ⓓ
3 Ⓐ Ⓑ Ⓒ Ⓓ	23 Ⓐ Ⓑ Ⓒ Ⓓ	43 Ⓐ Ⓑ Ⓒ Ⓓ	63 Ⓐ Ⓑ Ⓒ Ⓓ
4 Ⓐ Ⓑ Ⓒ Ⓓ	24 Ⓐ Ⓑ Ⓒ Ⓓ	44 Ⓐ Ⓑ Ⓒ Ⓓ	64 Ⓐ Ⓑ Ⓒ Ⓓ
5 Ⓐ Ⓑ Ⓒ Ⓓ	25 Ⓐ Ⓑ Ⓒ Ⓓ	45 Ⓐ Ⓑ Ⓒ Ⓓ	65 Ⓐ Ⓑ Ⓒ Ⓓ
6 Ⓐ Ⓑ Ⓒ Ⓓ	26 Ⓐ Ⓑ Ⓒ Ⓓ	46 Ⓐ Ⓑ Ⓒ Ⓓ	66 Ⓐ Ⓑ Ⓒ Ⓓ
7 Ⓐ Ⓑ Ⓒ Ⓓ	27 Ⓐ Ⓑ Ⓒ Ⓓ	47 Ⓐ Ⓑ Ⓒ Ⓓ	67 Ⓐ Ⓑ Ⓒ Ⓓ
8 Ⓐ Ⓑ Ⓒ Ⓓ	28 Ⓐ Ⓑ Ⓒ Ⓓ	48 Ⓐ Ⓑ Ⓒ Ⓓ	68 Ⓐ Ⓑ Ⓒ Ⓓ
9 Ⓐ Ⓑ Ⓒ Ⓓ	29 Ⓐ Ⓑ Ⓒ Ⓓ	49 Ⓐ Ⓑ Ⓒ Ⓓ	69 Ⓐ Ⓑ Ⓒ Ⓓ
10 Ⓐ Ⓑ Ⓒ Ⓓ	30 Ⓐ Ⓑ Ⓒ Ⓓ	50 Ⓐ Ⓑ Ⓒ Ⓓ	70 Ⓐ Ⓑ Ⓒ Ⓓ
11 Ⓐ Ⓑ Ⓒ Ⓓ	31 Ⓐ Ⓑ Ⓒ Ⓓ	51 Ⓐ Ⓑ Ⓒ Ⓓ	71 Ⓐ Ⓑ Ⓒ Ⓓ
12 Ⓐ Ⓑ Ⓒ Ⓓ	32 Ⓐ Ⓑ Ⓒ Ⓓ	52 Ⓐ Ⓑ Ⓒ Ⓓ	72 Ⓐ Ⓑ Ⓒ Ⓓ
13 Ⓐ Ⓑ Ⓒ Ⓓ	33 Ⓐ Ⓑ Ⓒ Ⓓ	53 Ⓐ Ⓑ Ⓒ Ⓓ	73 Ⓐ Ⓑ Ⓒ Ⓓ
14 Ⓐ Ⓑ Ⓒ Ⓓ	34 Ⓐ Ⓑ Ⓒ Ⓓ	54 Ⓐ Ⓑ Ⓒ Ⓓ	74 Ⓐ Ⓑ Ⓒ Ⓓ
15 Ⓐ Ⓑ Ⓒ Ⓓ	35 Ⓐ Ⓑ Ⓒ Ⓓ	55 Ⓐ Ⓑ Ⓒ Ⓓ	75 Ⓐ Ⓑ Ⓒ Ⓓ
16 Ⓐ Ⓑ Ⓒ Ⓓ	36 Ⓐ Ⓑ Ⓒ Ⓓ	56 Ⓐ Ⓑ Ⓒ Ⓓ	76 Ⓐ Ⓑ Ⓒ Ⓓ
17 Ⓐ Ⓑ Ⓒ Ⓓ	37 Ⓐ Ⓑ Ⓒ Ⓓ	57 Ⓐ Ⓑ Ⓒ Ⓓ	77 Ⓐ Ⓑ Ⓒ Ⓓ
18 Ⓐ Ⓑ Ⓒ Ⓓ	38 Ⓐ Ⓑ Ⓒ Ⓓ	58 Ⓐ Ⓑ Ⓒ Ⓓ	78 Ⓐ Ⓑ Ⓒ Ⓓ
19 Ⓐ Ⓑ Ⓒ Ⓓ	39 Ⓐ Ⓑ Ⓒ Ⓓ	59 Ⓐ Ⓑ Ⓒ Ⓓ	79 Ⓐ Ⓑ Ⓒ Ⓓ
20 Ⓐ Ⓑ Ⓒ Ⓓ	40 Ⓐ Ⓑ Ⓒ Ⓓ	60 Ⓐ Ⓑ Ⓒ Ⓓ	80 Ⓐ Ⓑ Ⓒ Ⓓ

Each item on this test includes four answer choices. Select the best choice for each item and mark that letter on the answer sheet.

Items 1–4.

Ms. Elenora Brown has been teaching seventh grade for just one month. She is having difficulty with discipline and with classroom management. For example, when Ms. Brown checks homework assignments, the students act as though it is free time. They talk, take other's personal property, exchange notes, and just generally make a nuisance of themselves. Sometimes students wander in and out of the class. Many students deliberately do not copy down their homework assignment. Preparing good lessons that are unappreciated by students leaves her frustrated. Ms. Brown has begun to teach in a negative and critical fashion.

1. Ms. Brown's colleague says, "Don't take it personally" about the misbehavior of students in her class. This is good advice because
   (A) the teacher doesn't need to change.
   (B) most seventh graders are unmanageable.
   (C) student misbehavior results from students' needs.
   (D) the teacher must be more authoritative and not so concerned about students.

2. Which of the following is a good suggestion to Ms. Brown about becoming a more effective classroom leader?
   (A) Set up a series of firm precise rules that students should memorize.
   (B) Take steps to establish relationships with peer leaders.
   (C) Discourage cooperative learning experiences.
   (D) Promote competition among class members.

3. The critical approach Ms. Brown has begun to use, compared to a more positive uncritical approach, will generally result in which of the following?
   (A) More learning will take place.
   (B) Less learning will take place.
   (C) More homework assignments will be handed in.
   (D) More parental involvement will take place.

4. To become a more effective classroom manager, Ms. Brown should take steps to ensure that the majority of class time is devoted to
   (A) individual work.
   (B) on-task activities.
   (C) lecturing.
   (D) group work.

5. Students in Ms. Stendel's class are reading a science-fiction story. In the story, Nayr the alien tries to trick the astronauts away from their spaceship so Nayr can look inside. Ms. Stendel wants to ask questions that promote higher-level thinking. Which of the following questions would be most appropriate?
   (A) What are other ways Nayr could have gotten inside the ship?
   (B) How did Nayr trick the astronauts?
   (C) Why did Nayr say he wanted to go inside the ship?
   (D) How many times did Nayr succeed in getting the astronauts away from their ship?

6. Teachers on the Carteret elementary school technology committee are discussing computer use in classrooms. Lee Mombello raises the issue of equity. He says, "In a country where most homes have a computer and the Internet, many of our students have no access to computers outside the school." With this in mind, which of the following is the best policy for the committee to establish about the classroom use of computers?
   (A) "Special after-school computer clubs should be set up for students who do not have a computer at home."
   (B) "Teachers should integrate computers in their teaching whenever possible."
   (C) "Each student should be given his or her own computer to use at school and at home."
   (D) "The school should hire a technology specialist who will help teachers integrate computers in their classrooms."

7. Renita Lopez is teaching language arts in the upper elementary grades and she wants to evaluate students' writing techniques and plan for further writing experiences. Which of the following is the most appropriate choice?
   (A) Administer a standardized grammar test and use the scores as a planning device.
   (B) Use a writing checklist to assess a variety of creative writing samples that include writing summaries and examples.
   (C) Have students prepare a composition on a subject of their choice and holistically evaluate the composition.
   (D) Have students answer a series of higher-level, short-answer questions about a specific writing sample.

8. Sheneoi Goldman is a fifth-grade teacher who conducts science class using the inquiry approach. Which of the following would a person be most likely to observe during Sheneoi Goldman's science class?
   (A) Sheneoi Goldman deliberately does not try out an experiment in advance of the class so everyone in the class is seeing the results together for the first time.
   (B) Sheneoi Goldman tells the students to avoid analyzing thought processes and rather, to rely on what happens in the experiment.
   (C) Sheneoi Goldman presents a problem for the students to solve or a situation for them to explore.
   (D) Sheneoi Goldman asks students to present a problem for the class to solve or a situation for the class to explore.

9. Here is a brief part of a conversation between Alex Whitby, a third-grade teacher, and Marciella Atkins, the school district reading specialist.

   Alex: "Thanks for coming by. I wanted to talk to you about one of my students."
   Marciella: "Which one?"
   Alex: "Savaro—he's still having trouble with reading."
   Marciella: "I remember Savaro from last year in second grade."
   Alex: "I was thinking about more phonics—what do you think?"
   Marciella: "That's OK—just remember that phonics does not help much . . . "

   Which of the following finishes the reading specialist's last sentence?
   (A) to associate sounds with printed letters.
   (B) with reading comprehension.
   (C) to attack new words independently.
   (D) to develop a sight vocabulary.

10. Morina Meridcu is planning to teach a fourth-grade geography lesson. When it comes to ability level, Ms. Meridcu should
    (A) present the lesson below students' ability level.
    (B) present the lesson above students' ability level.
    (C) present the lesson at students' ability level.
    (D) present the lesson in a way that does not take ability level into account.

11. Tara Kirk is concerned about the way she responds to students' questions in science and she wants to develop a more effective approach. The best advice for Ms. Kirk is to respond in which of the following ways?

    I. Encourage exploration of the answer with activities and materials that stimulate curiosity.
    II. Model good responding skills.
    III. Answer all items as quickly and concisely as possible.
    IV. Include children's questions in evaluation techniques.

    (A) I, II
    (B) III, IV
    (C) I, II, III
    (D) I, II, IV

12. Gerard Lancaster is a new teacher who wants to use cooperative learning groups to supplement a teacher-centered approach to social studies instruction. In order to accomplish that task, which of the following should Mr. Lancaster employ when compared to teacher-centered presentations?

    I. More student involvement
    II. More content coverage
    III. More varied outcomes
    IV. More brainstorming

    (A) I, II
    (B) I, III, IV
    (C) III, IV
    (D) II, III, IV

13. Jovina Crockett is planning a lesson to integrate art with haiku, a Japanese poetic form. Which of the following approaches is LEAST likely to meet Ms. Crockett's needs?
    (A) Use the computer as an artistic tool to illustrate the haiku.
    (B) Provide a display of classical Japanese paintings for children to color.
    (C) Provide clay as a means to illustrate their haiku.
    (D) Provide paints and brushes for illustrations to the haiku.

14. Jim Prendergast teaches in a school where most of the students are economically disadvantaged. Mr. Prendergast knows that economically disadvantaged students, as a whole, tend to have lower achievement than other students, leading Mr. Prendergast to which of the following understandings that will enable him to help his students?
    (A) Economically disadvantaged students, as a whole, are usually less capable learners than other students.
    (B) Minority teachers are more effective with minority students.
    (C) Learning expectations should usually be lowered for minority students.
    (D) Economically disadvantaged students usually have fewer enriched learning opportunities at home.

15. Gina Selberding is a beginning teacher in the Herneck School. Gina realizes that she has no criteria whatever for deciding which students to call on to answer a question. Which of the following is the best criteria for Ms. Selberding to use?
    (A) Be sure students know who will answer a question before it is asked.
    (B) Ask questions of the entire class, then call on a student.
    (C) Ask questions of students who are not paying attention.
    (D) Ask questions of students who usually have the correct answers.

16. John Cohen is a new sixth-grade teacher who seems to be having every problem that a new teacher can have. But his main problem this day is trying to maintain attention during a lesson. Which of the following actions on John's part is most likely to be effective?
    (A) He stands where he can see the entire class.
    (B) He limits the number of students who participate in question-and-answer sessions.
    (C) He ensures that the material being taught is very difficult.
    (D) He does not proceed with the lesson if even a single student is not paying attention.

17. Sam Meletto, a second-grade teacher, and the principal are discussing Sam's reasons for instituting a whole language program in his classroom. Which among the following is the best reason Sam Meletto could give?
    (A) Whole language instruction is widely accepted.
    (B) It is not necessary to teach word recognition.
    (C) Children comprehend more after using a whole language approach.
    (D) Children have a better attitude toward reading.

18. Jaedo Purmen, a second grade teacher, says he has found modeling to be an effective form of instruction, meaning that he is most likely to
    (A) show students how to construct replicas of historic buildings.
    (B) respond courteously to students' questions.
    (C) tell students when they have mispronounced a word.
    (D) demonstrate students' inappropriate behavior.

19. Lucien Cardot joined the child study team for a meeting because of a second-grade student in his class. Most of the team members favor a special education classification because of the child's very low test scores. Mr. Cardot says, "From what I've seen, the problem is with the testing and not with the child," most likely meaning

(A) tests used by the school are inappropriate and should be discontinued.

(B) some students' difficulty with tests masks their true capability.

(C) the person administering the tests was not a qualified examiner.

(D) the members of the child study team are too removed from the classroom and do not have an appropriate concern about the welfare of students.

20. Damaris Jones and one of his students are discussing the student's most recent report card. Mr. Jones chooses his words carefully to have the most impact, and finally decides on these. "Your grades would have been better if all homework assignments were handed in." Which of the following approaches has the teacher decided to use?

(A) positive reinforcement

(B) reverse psychology

(C) threats

(D) negative reinforcement

21. The school year has just begun and Mr. Lamum Ngu realizes that his class is culturally and linguistically diverse. Which of the following actions by Mr. Ngu would be the most appropriate modification of the objectives or plans to meet the needs of this class?

(A) Modify the objectives to focus more on basic skills.

(B) Modify the objectives to reduce their difficulty level.

(C) Modify the plans to teach the class in the foreign language.

(D) Modify the plans to focus on the cultural heritage of those in the class.

22. Lisa is a student in DeShala Washington's third-grade class. At a parent-teacher conference, Lisa's mother says she has heard about the school using a basal reading program and asks what basal reading programs are NOT good for. Which of the following would be Ms. Washington's best response?

(A) Skills are taught and developed in a systematic sequential manner.

(B) One should meet individual differences and needs of the child.

(C) A basic vocabulary is established and reinforced.

(D) Manuals provide a detailed outline for teaching.

Items 23–24.

Ms. Lorene Archibald, a third-grade teacher, prepared a chart for students in her class to complete. Ms. Archibald has small stickers of a child walking, a school bus, a car, a bike, and a rail car for students to put on the chart. Students come up to the chart and put a sticker over the word or phrase that describes how he or she gets to school.

HOW I GET TO SCHOOL

Walk	Bus	Car	Bike	Rail/Train

23. Ms. Archibald is most likely having students complete this activity in order to
    (A) gather information about how students get to school.
    (B) help students learn about different modes of transportation.
    (C) give students experience with graphing.
    (D) give students an important opportunity for tactile experiences.

24. A student who recently arrived in the United States does not speak English, and does not know the words "car," "bus," and so on. The most appropriate action that Ms. Archibald can take with this student is to
    (A) say the word in the child's native tongue so that the child can participate in the activity.
    (B) help the student pronounce the words in English.
    (C) not involve the child in the lesson so he or she will not be embarrassed.
    (D) refer the student for English-language help.

25. Elizabeth Del Corso is an experienced fifth-grade teacher. Ms. Del Corso notices that one student in her class has particular difficulty when he is reading the problems in the mathematics textbook. In an effort to help this student, it would be most appropriate for Ms. Del Corso to recognize that this difficulty is most likely to be the result of
(A) faulty word identification and recognition.
(B) inability to locate and retain specific facts.
(C) deficiencies in basic comprehension abilities.
(D) inability to adapt to reading needs in this content field.

26. Luraine Watson is arranging the desks for her fourth-grade class at the beginning of the school year. Which of the following arrangements is LEAST appropriate?

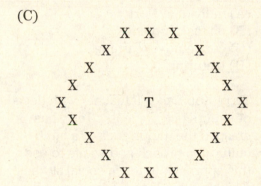

27. The Carson Hills school district is preparing a pamphlet about effective schools to distribute to teachers. Which of the following choices should be listed as characteristic of effective schools in the pamphlet?

    I. A climate of high expectations
    II. Accountability for student performance
    III. Eliminating standardized tests

    (A) I only
    (B) I and II
    (C) III only
    (D) II and III

28. Cindy Weiss is concerned about how she uses her class time in her departmentalized fifth-grade English class. She realizes after a year of teaching that she must learn to be an effective classroom manager, which means that she will take steps to ensure that the majority of class time is devoted to
    (A) individual work.
    (B) on-task activities.
    (C) cooperative learning.
    (D) lecturing.

29. Terry Koolfian is a teacher with decades of experience. Recently, Terry has grasped the importance of a multicultural approach and wants to use this approach to teach social studies, which means Terry's approach will most appropriately include
    (A) a comparison of how different cultures respond to similar issues.
    (B) how people from different cultures contribute to world events.
    (C) how people around the world have common characteristics.
    (D) how events in one part of the globe influence the rest of the world.

30. There is frequently a lot of movement and activity when students in Francois le Bente's class are getting ready to go outside for recess, and it can be difficult to maintain discipline. At these times Mr. le Bente needs to recall that, above all, students usually expect the teacher to be
    (A) very assertive.
    (B) extremely understanding.
    (C) a tough taskmaster.
    (D) an authority figure.

31. Tom Karel has a number of students in his class who are significantly below grade level in reading. Mr. Karel realizes that he needs to adapt social studies instruction for these students. Mr. Karel's choice among the following options would be appropriate EXCEPT to
    (A) use instructional materials that have a lower reading level.
    (B) use instructional materials with less difficult concepts.
    (C) read information about social studies to the students.
    (D) use recorded tapes that contain social studies information.

32. Frank Rios is a primary teacher who is incorporating authentic assessment in his evaluation techniques. That means that Mr. Rios will
    (A) collect and evaluate students' work.
    (B) use only tests provided by the publisher of the books he uses.
    (C) evaluate only students in real situations outside of school.
    (D) collect evaluative information from other teachers.

Items 33–34.

Mr. Adolphus Batsawani is a fifth-grade teacher with high standards. This has created a few run-ins with parents. Mrs. Sivar is one of those parents. "My Tim doesn't finish his tests in Mr. Batsawani's class because the tests are too long," Mrs. Sivar tells the principal. "It is certainly not because he's fooling around," she adds. Mrs. Price, another parent, thinks it is unfair for her daughter Estelle to get a "B" in Mr. Batsawani's class when all her test grades are "A." "So what if she misses a few assignments?" snaps Mrs. Price. Mr. Allen says it is unfair for his son Sam to have to take a test when Sam was absent the previous day. He says, "I don't care if Sam knew about the test at the beginning of the week. And I certainly don't care that Mr. Batsawani sent home a test guide. Sam wasn't in class the day before and he shouldn't have to take the test."

33. It would NOT be appropriate for Mr. Batsawani to respond to which of the following requests from a parent?
(A) Please show me a folder of my child's work and point out areas of needed remediation.
(B) Please show me a folder of my child's work and point out areas of possible acceleration.
(C) Please show me a report of individual students' test scores so that I can tell how my child is doing.
(D) Please show me how my child is doing compared to the average class performance.

34. Which of the following is LEAST likely to enable Mr. Batsawani to promote good communication with parents?
(A) Make phone calls to parents.
(B) Write personal notes on report cards.
(C) Initiate a series of home/school letters.
(D) Meet with groups of parents to discuss individual student achievement.

Items 35–36.

There is a school board meeting tonight. Items on the agenda include a budget discussion and a discussion of a tracking system for a fifth-grade mathematics program based on standardized test results. The meeting is open to the public. Harvey Rios, a teacher in the district but not a town resident, is in the audience to support pro-school board members who want the school budget passed. Registered voters in the community vote on the budget at the same time that they vote for school board candidates. A large group of parents will be at the Board of Education meeting.

35. Which of the following describes the most appropriate action for Mr. Rios?
(A) Tell parents that the school needs their support and ask them to get out and vote.
(B) Tell parents to vote yes on the school budget.
(C) Tell the parents that the voting records are clear and to vote for the pro-school candidates.
(D) Tell parents that a vote for antibudget candidates is a vote against school programs.

36. An opponent of the tracking system could most effectively argue against this approach before the board by saying
(A) "The standardized tests used to place students in the program are deliberately designed to trick minority students."
(B) "Tracking programs have been shown to consistently discriminate against minority students."
(C) "The best teachers are always assigned to the highest and lowest classes."
(D) "The school administration cannot be counted on to accurately report test scores."

37. Betty Ann Hotop is helping her first-grade students learn about counting. She uses shapes as counters and makes sure students point to a shape each time they say the next counting word. What is the most likely reason why she is using this approach?

(A) Ms. Hotop wants to be sure the students are paying attention to what they are doing.

(B) Ms. Hotop wants to be sure students are developing eye-hand coordination.

(C) Ms. Hotop is going to ask the students questions about the shapes once they have finished counting.

(D) Ms. Hotop wants to be sure the students are not just saying counting words.

38. A fourth-grade student in Geovanna Savorsi's class hands in an assignment, containing the writing sample shown below.

Based on this sample, Ms. Savorsi should concentrate on which of the following with that student?

  I. Subject-verb agreement
 II. Pronouns
III. Sentence fragments

(A) I only
(B) I and II
(C) II and III
(D) I and III

39. Lucy Small is a fifth-grade teacher who has heard that a student in her class has AIDS, but she is not sure which student it is. When Ms. Small inadvertently sees his health record she correctly concludes that Louis is the one. Once she has reasonably reached this conclusion, she

(A) has the right to refuse to have Louis in her class because of concerns about her own personal safety.

(B) should keep this information to herself, even though it may be considered important by others in the school who have families.

(C) has a responsibility to inform parents of other students in the class so that these parents may safeguard their children's safety.

(D) has a legal responsibility under New York law to confidentially inform other teachers so that they may protect students in their classes.

40. A voucher program is one in which students use public funds to attend nonpublic schools. In New York, as a general rule, vouchers are legal when

(A) the student's family incomes are below the poverty level.

(B) the student is not attending a religious school or a school owned or controlled by a religious group.

(C) parents make the choice between religious and nonreligious schools.

(D) the school district test scores fall below an established level for three continuous years.

Items 41–42.

Frank Damico, a special education teacher, is working with Kathy McCoy in Kathy's fifth-grade class that includes mainstreamed students. Mr. Damico and Ms. McCoy have regular meetings with the parents of mainstreamed students in the class.

41. Which of the following best describes Frank Damico's role in the classroom?
(A) Observe the mainstreamed students to identify the out-of-class support they need.
(B) Teach the entire class cooperatively with the teacher.
(C) Help the mainstreamed students during the teacher's lesson.
(D) Observe the nonmainstreamed students to get tips on their successful learning styles to pass on to the special education student.

42. During one meeting, a parent expresses extreme concern about how her child James is doing in school. The parent is concerned that continued academic problems will make it impossible for her son to attend college or to be a success in life. Which of the following choices is the best response for these teachers to give?
(A) "Don't be concerned; we are confident that James will do fine and be successful."
(B) "We enjoy working with James and we have the highest hopes for him."
(C) "That James is still in a special education setting at this age indicates that there are likely some real problems that may or may not be resolved over time."
(D) "We are sorry you feel that way but we just cannot discuss these things with parents."

43. Lucie Montelone's class is reading a science fiction story about space travel. Which of the following approaches by Ms. Montelone is most likely to help students differentiate between science fact and science fiction?
(A) She should guide students to understand that science fiction stories are creative writing and not based on science fact.
(B) She should guide students as they identify examples of science fact and science fiction based on the story they just completed.
(C) She should ask students to work independently to make their own list of science fact and science fiction.
(D) She should ask students to work independently as they identify examples of science fact and science fiction in the story they just completed.

44. Dr. Samson, the school principal, was explaining to a group of beginning teachers that children can learn vicariously, meaning children can
(A) learn by doing.
(B) learn through a wide variety of activities.
(C) learn if there is a clear structure.
(D) learn from others' experiences.

45. At a "Back-to-School-Night" Frances Zimolo, a second-grade teacher, displays student work and explains to parents in her brief presentation that it is not a conference time. But one parent corners Ms. Zimolo and asks about her child's progress. Which of the following is the most professional response Ms. Zimolo can make?
(A) "I'm sorry. I am not prepared to discuss your child's progress with others here."
(B) "When would you like to meet to discuss your concerns?"
(C) "Would you please call the office to arrange a conference time?"
(D) Answer the parent's questions as quickly and quietly as possible.

46. Punishment can be an effective way to change a student's behavior when
    (A) the whole class is involved.
    (B) it involves pertinent extra work.
    (C) it is used for limited and specific reasons.
    (D) it makes the teacher feel better.

47. Les Levy is preparing for "back-to-school" night. He plans to explain cooperative learning groups and he is typing a list of the practices consistent with this instructional approach. Which of the following is LEAST likely to appear on Mr. Levy's list?
    (A) Group members themselves devise a working plan.
    (B) Group members are actively involved in learning.
    (C) Groups include ten to twelve members.
    (D) The teacher presents the project or topic to be worked on.

48. Each Friday a group of teachers from the Roosevelt Elementary School get together after school at Jim Stanley's restaurant. It seems that they talk about every administrator and about every problem they have had during the week. In fact, this after-school get-together
    (A) may be common practice in many schools but its actually illegal under New York law.
    (B) gives any administrator mentioned at the meeting the right to suspend the teacher.
    (C) gives school administrators the right to take disciplinary action against teachers in the group.
    (D) is fine as long as they do not discuss confidential information.

49. Entu Geranhi reads a story to her primary class about a sailor on an old-time sailing boat. She asks each student to write one sentence about the story. One student's writing contains this sentence.

> He had enuf rope.

Which of the actions listed below best addresses the problem in the sentence?
    (A) instruction on phonics-based word attack skills
    (B) instruction on context-based word attack skills
    (C) instruction on the use of homonyms
    (D) instruction on variable spelling phonemes

50. Sylvia Negbutu is a new teacher who seeks to use a constructivist approach to teaching. Which of the following is most consistent with that approach?
    (A) Ms. Negbutu encourages students to respond quickly and alertly to questions.
    (B) Ms. Negbutu encourages students to construct complex models of their thought processes.
    (C) Ms. Negbutu encourages students to elaborate on their initial responses.
    (D) Ms. Negbutu discourages students from creating metaphors.

51. A teacher using Gardner's Multiple Intelligences as the basis for instruction is most likely to do which of the following?
    (A) Implement interdisciplinary units.
    (B) Help students learn about each of the intelligences.
    (C) Eliminate assessments.
    (D) Allow students to determine criteria for quality.

52. Elma Topper is discussing one of her second-grade students with the school principal. The student has difficulty pronouncing some printed words. The problem may reflect all of the following EXCEPT
(A) phonetic analysis.
(B) sight vocabulary.
(C) language comprehension.
(D) context analysis.

53. Iraidia Lonia is a member of a committee to formulate a policy for calculator use in the school district. There are a wide variety of opinions, but which of the choices below would be most appropriate for Ms. Lonia to recommend?
(A) Calculators should be banned from classrooms until high school.
(B) Calculators should not be used when the reason for the lesson is to teach computation.
(C) Calculators should not be used to add, subtract, multiply, or divide. These operations should be completed only with "paper and pencil."
(D) Calculators should be used only to check "paper and pencil" computations.

54. Priscilla Mitchell constructs her own content-valid multiple-choice test to assess performance on a social studies unit. One student correctly answers 91 percent of the questions, while another student gets 89 percent correct. How confident should Ms. Mitchell be about assigning grades according to the school grading rules shown below?

SCHOOL GRADING RULES	
A	91–100
B	81–90
C	71–80

(A) Very confident—the teacher should just follow the grading rules.
(B) Very confident—the difference between the grades is clear.
(C) Somewhat confident—the test is content-valid and probably measures important concepts.
(D) Not confident—the errors of measurement in the test could eliminate the meaning of the difference between the scores.

55. Gina Telione just finished teaching a three-day unit on nouns. She wants to determine whether or not the students learned the material in the unit before going on. Which of the following assessment techniques would be best for Ms. Telione to use?
(A) Obtain and have the students complete standardized assessment.
(B) Prepare and have the students complete a teacher-made assessment.
(C) Observe students' writing over the next week.
(D) Review writing that students have previously completed.

56. Stan Powell makes extensive use of portfolio assessment in his anthropology class, so he knows the most significant difficulty with portfolio assessment reliability is that

(A) students put samples of widely different types of work in their portfolio.

(B) scoring machines don't work reliably with materials in the portfolio.

(C) different teachers place different emphasis on the portfolios when giving grades.

(D) different teachers assign widely different grades to the same portfolio.

57. A soccer game over the weekend led to a reaction among some students from the Del Rios Elementary School. The students did not like many of the referee's decisions. On Monday, all students wore replica team jerseys to school and decided on their own to leave the school grounds during lunch to show how they felt. In all likelihood, these students

(A) were just expressing their free speech rights and should not be interfered with.

(B) were a model of democracy and truly represent American values.

(C) were not doing anything wrong because they were not on the school grounds.

(D) were violating school rules and might be disciplined.

58. Repeated testing of a fourth-grade student in Ray Maw's class reveals an IQ in the 110 to 115 range, but standardized test scores that are two or more years below grade level. Which of the following is the most appropriate interpretation of these test scores?

(A) The student is a poor test taker.

(B) The student's achievement and potential match.

(C) The student is gifted.

(D) The student has a learning disability.

Items 59–60.

Lucille Davenport is meeting with parents of a student in her fifth-grade class to interpret their child's test scores. These scores include the results of a standardized achievement test that show the student at the 34th percentile in mathematics. The reading test shows a grade equivalent of 6.3. The average reading score reported for the school district is 6.8. The English test shows a grade equivalent of 6.6. A criterion-referenced test shows that a student has mastered 75 percent of the science objectives for that grade level. Ms. Davenport also has a folder with representative samples of the student's writing. In Ms. Davenport's opinion, these writing samples are well above average for the school.

59. How would Ms. Davenport explain the mathematics test score?

(A) "This means that your child did better than all but 34 students on this test."

(B) "This means that your child did better than all but about 34 percent of the students who took this test."

(C) "This means that your child did better than about 34 percent of the students who took this test."

(D) "This means that your child has better mathematics ability than about 34 percent of the students who took this test."

60. The parents ask for your overall assessment of their child based on these results. Which of the following is the most appropriate response?
(A) "We can't really draw any meaningful conclusions from these results."
(B) "The results indicate that your child may do better when evaluated in real-world settings."
(C) "The results indicate that your child does markedly better in English than in mathematics."
(D) "The results indicate that your child performs better in science than in reading."

61. Ezequiel Sanchez administers an end of chapter test from the teacher's edition of a language arts text to students in his fourth-grade class. In all likelihood, this is a
(A) portfolio evaluation.
(B) standardized test.
(C) norm-referenced test.
(D) summative evaluation.

Items 62–63.

Suzanna Lilanni teaches English and writing to the upper elementary grades. Ms. Lilanni is currently teaching a unit that includes creative writing, writing journals, and following directions.

62. Which of the following would be most appropriate for Ms. Lilanni to use to evaluate students' writing techniques and plan for further writing experiences?
(A) Administer a standardized grammar test and use the scores as a planning device.
(B) Use a writing checklist to assess a variety of students' writing samples.
(C) Have the students hand in a composition of their choice.
(D) Have the students answer a series of short-answer questions from a specific reading selection.

63. Ramona is a student in this class who writes well, understands verbal directions, but often has trouble understanding written directions. Her difficulty might be related to all of the following EXCEPT
(A) auditory discrimination.
(B) visual discrimination.
(C) sight vocabulary.
(D) context clues.

64. The personal journals that students write in class should NOT be used
(A) as a record of feelings.
(B) to share their thoughts with others.
(C) as a means of expressing thoughts.
(D) as a means for writing ideas.

65. Lucinda Crawford uses holistic scoring to evaluate her fifth-grade students' writing. She will make a brief presentation to the Board of Education about this method. This is best described as a scoring technique in which
(A) essays are scored using advanced imaging technology.
(B) essays are scored by several readers who do not discuss the essay.
(C) readers rank essays relative to the "whole" of essays written for that testing cycle.
(D) readers rank essays based on the overall impression, not on a detailed analysis.

66. Pam is a fifth-grade student who is extremely anxious about tests. Which of the following is NOT an effective way for her teacher, Ms. Rosa, to respond?
(A) Give extra time, when practical for students to finish the test.
(B) Don't draw attention to the student by providing emotional support.
(C) Reduce tension before a test with humor.
(D) Use alternative assessment.

Items 67–68.

A fifth-grade student has been classified as a special education student. The child study team, which includes Jeremy Jones, the student's fifth-grade teacher, classified the student as learning disabled. The child study team is deciding the appropriate placement for this student, discussing the basis for the placement and discussing the different strategies to help this student learn.

67. Which of the following describes an appropriate placement strategy for this student?
 (A) Place the student in a self-contained class with other learning disabled students and send the student out for music and art specials.
 (B) Place the student in a fifth-grade class with support from a special education teacher.
 (C) Place the student in a self-contained class with other learning disabled students and send the student to a fifth-grade class for some subjects.
 (D) Place the student in a fifth-grade class and meet with the parents to arrange extra tutoring.

68. Which of the following best describes an effective approach for Mr. Jones to use with this learning disabled student?
 (A) Use large-print books.
 (B) Apply highly relevant skills with a minimum of practice.
 (C) Provide brief assignments and auditory learning.
 (D) Permit the student to test out of requirements.

69. Kisa Amman is called to an emergency meeting along with other teachers in the school. School administrators are concerned that just released tests results have again fallen below the school's goal level. The administrators are primarily concerned because
 (A) they think teacher effort needs to be improved.
 (B) they think the test scores may have been falsified.
 (C) parents may have the legal right to remove students.
 (D) the Commissioner of Education in New York does not have the power to invalidate the scores.

70. An aid has been assigned to Ms. Stanair's first-grade class because there are more students than the district usually allows. Which of the following represents the LEAST appropriate instructional duties for Ms. Stanair to assign to the aid?
 (A) Help preschool children dress themselves.
 (B) Duplicate instructional worksheets.
 (C) Read to small groups of students.
 (D) Help manage difficult children.

71. The assignment of a special education child to an appropriate learning environment is most likely based on which of these education laws?
 (A) PL 99-457
 (B) PL 98-199
 (C) The Emancipation Proclamation
 (D) PL 94-142

Items 72–74.

It is Holly Ritzkovik's first month in school. She is concerned about maintaining discipline, keeping the students interested and on task, having an effective management style, and just surviving. The principal comes by to observe the class and notices that the teacher calls on only about 40 percent of the students and that too much teacher-centered instruction is taking place. The principal also notices that classroom management needs to be improved and that students are often confused about transitions during the lesson. The principal has a conference with the teacher following the observation.

72. Which of the following is the most constructive professional advice Ms. Ritzkovik could expect the principal to give during the conference?
    (A) "Try to call on about 65 percent of the students during any lesson."
    (B) "Make a check on a list of names, a seating chart, or something like that, and try to get to everyone."
    (C) "Research shows that student participation is important, so try to call on all the students."
    (D) "I can see why you don't call on some of these students—they're very difficult—but do your best."

73. The principal notices that several of Ms. Ritzkovik's students are discipline problems just to gain her attention. Which of the following is the best advice the principal could give for dealing with the attention-seeking students?
    (A) "Point out misbehavior each time it occurs."
    (B) "Deliberately ignore appropriate behavior when it occurs."
    (C) "Send students to the office after several misbehaviors."
    (D) "Ignore the misbehavior whenever possible."

74. Which of the following is the most appropriate way for Ms. Ritzkovik to alert students to a transition from group work to a whole-class activity?
    (A) Say, "Time's up—put away your work."
    (B) Use a recognized signal, such as putting the lights on and off.
    (C) Stand silently in front of the room and wait for students to realize that you want their attention.
    (D) Begin making the presentation and then wait for students' attention.

75. Ellen Archibald is about to engage her third-grade class in a lesson on the value of coins. Which of the following should Ms. Archibald say at the beginning of the lesson to have the best chance to motivate students?
    (A) "Hi, class—I have some make-believe coins that look like real coins. I'll hold them up and tell you what each coin is worth."
    (B) "Here are some make-believe coins. Pretend I am a bank. We'll say the value of the coin as you put the coins in."
    (C) "Does anyone know when coins were first used? It is interesting because coins were used a long time ago."
    (D) "Before we begin, let me review with you the value of each one of these coins. Knowing the value of the coins is the secret to our lesson today."

368 Practice ATS-W I (Elementary)

76. Marcie Sola-Vega is a first-year teacher and she carefully planned a lesson and wrote an excellent lesson plan. Once the lesson was underway, Ms. Sola-Vega's observation of students indicates the plan is very clearly not working. In light of this, Ms. Sola-Vega should
    (A) stay with the plan and analyze later why the plan was not successful.
    (B) stay with the plan and discipline any students disrupting the lesson.
    (C) stay with the plan and give other work to those students who can't keep up.
    (D) abandon the plan and try another approach.

77. Samantha Smithson is a third-grade teacher who has just finished reviewing the mathematics assignments her students completed in the last few weeks. Based on her assessment, Ms. Smithson decides to reschedule subjects so that mathematics is first thing in the morning and reading is after a recess but before lunch. Which of the following is the most appropriate response to her plan?
    (A) This is poor planning because the students will be late from recess.
    (B) This is good planning, because if her math lesson runs over, she can always cut out recess.
    (C) It doesn't make any difference when she schedules these subjects, as long as she gets them in somewhere.
    (D) This is good planning because the students have a break before reading.

78. When it comes to the general characteristics of elementary school students,
    (A) all ethnic groups adapt equally well to school.
    (B) boys have more adjustment problems than girls do.
    (C) girls are more physically active than boys of the same age.
    (D) primary students rebel against the teacher's authority.

79. Students come from varying types of families, but overall, which of the following does NOT accurately characterize the American family?
    (A) A majority of families have mothers who work.
    (B) An increasing number of children are "latchkey" children.
    (C) Less than 10 percent of American families have a mother (as a homemaker), a father (as the breadwinner), and children.
    (D) Families are groups of people living together who are related to one another.

80. The gifted and talented (G&T) program in the Almay School has always been self-contained. That is, May Riverbark, the G&T teacher, had always taught students in her own classroom. Then the Almay School implemented a collaborative teaching program that includes the G&T teacher. This most likely means that Ms. Riverbark will
    (A) meet with students' parents to discuss the G&T curriculum.
    (B) work on an interdisciplinary team to plan the G&T curriculum.
    (C) teach both G&T and learning disabled students.
    (D) teach with classroom teachers in their classrooms.

WRITTEN ASSIGNMENT

Write a lesson plan on the topic below. Use the lined pages that follow. Write your lesson plan on this topic only. A lesson plan on another topic will be rated Unscorable (U).

Teachers are asked to suggest goals and objectives for different grades and subject matter areas. A goal is a more general statement about what should be accomplished at the end of a school year or at the completion of a teaching unit. An objective is a more specific statement of expected learning outcomes. Here is one example of a goal.

GOAL: Students should read on grade level by the end of third grade.

Devise your own goal for an elementary school grade level or elementary school subject matter area.

Write the goal and include the grade level or subject area the goal is intended for. Then write an essay appropriate for a group of teachers in New York State that:

- explains why this is an important goal for the grade level or subject area;

- gives examples of learning experiences that could help a child reach that goal;

- describes how to assess whether or not a student has achieved the goal.

PRACTICE ATS-W I (ELEMENTARY)

Explained Answers

1. **C** This is good advice because teachers are authority figures and a student's misbehavior toward an authority figure usually reflects who the student is. (A) is incorrect. The teacher may need to change, but it's still not personal. (B) is incorrect because most seventh graders are not unmanageable. (D) is incorrect because "don't take it personally" has nothing to do with not being concerned about students' misbehavior.

2. **B** Peer leaders and peer pressures have the most impact on students this age. (A) is incorrect because students will not necessarily follow rules just because they are firm or just because the teacher asks that the rules be memorized. (C) is incorrect simply because Ms. Brown will not become more effective because she uses cooperative learning experiences. (D) is incorrect because promoting competition among students may turn the students against one another, but that will not make Ms. Brown a more effective leader.

3. **B** Students learn less when teachers are negative and critical; being negative and critical is very different from having high expectations. (A) is incorrect because less learning actually takes place. (C) and (D) are incorrect because a negative and critical approach will not increase homework participation and parent involvement. However, as the scenario shows, there will likely be an increase in parent complaints.

4. **B** Good classroom managers create on-task learning opportunities, and research clearly shows that students learn more when they spend more time on task. Each of the remaining choices could be an effective management technique, but none carries the proven assurance of more time on task.

5. **A** The question in this choice fits the Analysis category, which is at the upper end of Bloom's scale. The remaining choices contain questions that ask from information and knowledge about the story. These questions fit Knowledge and Comprehension categories at the lower end of Bloom's Taxonomy.

6. **B** This policy statement gives the best guidance to ensure that students have the most opportunities to use computers. (A) and (C) are incorrect because the committee's work is focused on the computer use in classrooms and these policies do not address that area. (D) is incorrect because this policy is not within the committee's control, and it holds little promise of helping since it would require additional approval to implement.

7. **B** This choice describes the best way to consistently determine a student's writing ability, and to prepare for the future. The teacher gathers specific information that can be used for future plans. (A) is incorrect because standardized grammar tests do not reveal detailed information about a student's writing. (C) is incorrect because holistic evaluations reflect the evaluator's view of the overall quality of the writing. A holistic evaluation does not yield a specific analysis that can lead to instructional plans. (D) is incorrect because it evaluates reading, not writing.

8. **C** This choice describes the essence of the inquiry approach, to solve problems as a way to understand scientific principles. (A) is incorrect because a teacher must have prior experience with an experiment so he or she can guide students. (B) is incorrect because students analyze their thought processes when using the inquiry approach. (D) is incorrect because the inquiry approach is student centered not student directed.

9. **B** The reading specialist was most likely going to say phonics does not address word meaning or reading comprehension. Phonics primarily addresses word recognition and word pronunciation. Each of the remaining choices describes a benefit that can be derived directly from the phonics approach.

10. **C** Students learn best when the lesson is at their level of ability. Students become too frustrated when asked to do some-

thing they cannot do. Naturally, there is a difference between ability level and achievement level. Students frequently learn successfully when reasonably challenged beyond their achievement level, but not beyond their ability level. Lessons at advanced achievement levels can be adapted to a student's ability level. (A) is incorrect because teaching below an ability level may not cause a problem, but it is not what Ms. Meridcu should do. (B) is incorrect because a lesson above a student's ability level may prove too frustrating for the student. (D) is incorrect because Ms. Meridcu should take ability level into account.

11. **D** Consider each Roman numeral in turn, and then choose your answer.

 I. Correct. It is a good technique to handle a question with encouragement for more explanation.
 II. Correct. It is effective to demonstrate how to respond to questions.
 III. Incorrect. It is generally not a good idea to answer quickly. Ms. Kirk may be able to help the student find the answer for himself or herself.
 IV. Correct. Students' questions often reveal what is most difficult for them to understand and it is a good technique to include their questions in evaluations.

 I, II, and IV are correct—(D).

12. **B** Consider each Roman numeral in turn, and then choose your answer.

 I. Correct. Group learning means more student involvement.
 II. Incorrect. Cooperative learning groups do not lead to more content coverage. In fact, teacher centered lessons would most likely lead to more content coverage.
 III. Correct. The more people involved, the more varied the outcomes.
 IV. Correct. A cooperative learning group means more brainstorming.

 I, III, and IV are correct—(B).

13. **B** This is the least effective method because this choice, alone, does NOT integrate haiku with fine arts because only art is displayed. Each of the remaining choices describes an effective way of integrating haiku and art.

14. **D** Economically disadvantaged students are not less capable, but as a group economically disadvantaged students do have fewer home learning opportunities. This leads to lower achievement scores. (A) and (C) are factually incorrect stereotypes about minority students. (B) is incorrect because there is no evidence that minority teachers are more effective with minority students. Effective teaching is related to factors other than ethnicity.

15. **B** It is generally most appropriate to address questions to the entire class. This maximizes the number of students who are thinking about the answer. (A) is incorrect because calling on a student before you ask the question may mean others in the class will not try to formulate an answer. (C) is incorrect because this approach may bring a student back into the lesson, but it is not the best criteria for Ms. Selberding to use. (D) is incorrect because this approach severely limits the number of students who will actively participate in a class.

16. **A** The best advice, and the only good advice, among the four choices is to stand where you can see all the students. (B) is incorrect because Mr. Cohen should not limit the number of students who participate, even though he will probably not be able to involve everyone. (C) is incorrect because Mr. Cohen will likely frustrate these sixth graders if the material is consistently very difficult. (D) is incorrect because this rigid approach may actually create discipline problems.

17. **D** Students develop a better attitude toward reading when they use the real literature found in a whole language approach. (A) is incorrect because it may be reassuring that an approach is widely accepted, but that is never the best reason to use it. (B) is incorrect because word recognition must always be taught. Students can't read if they can't recognize words. (C) is incorrect because research does not uniformly support the conclusion that students comprehend better after using a whole language approach. Rather, it seems a combination of approaches, including

aspects of the whole language approach, best develops reading comprehension.

18. **B** Modeling means the teacher demonstrates the behavior students should replicate. (A) is incorrect because classroom modeling does not refer to this hobby. (C) is incorrect because just telling a student to do something is not modeling. (D) is incorrect because a teacher would not model incorrect behavior for students to copy.

19. **B** Mr. Cardot means that some students are not able to show their true achievement on a test. It seems he has observed something to make him believe that's the case for this child. (A) Mr. Cardot never says the tests are inappropriate. (C) and (D) Mr. Cardot never implies that the test administrator was not competent, or that the child study team did not want to act in the best interests of this child.

20. **D** One example of negative reinforcement means explaining how to improve positive outcomes. (A) Positive reinforcement is praise or rewards for good work. (B) Reverse psychology is suggesting the opposite of what you want a student to do. (C) Threats, or bullying, are not appropriate classroom techniques.

21. **D** It is most appropriate to alter the objectives or plans to focus on the cultural heritage of those in the class. It is not appropriate to adopt the other practices in a culturally and linguistically diverse class. A teacher should not assume that students need (A) basic skills instruction, (B) reduced difficulty, or (C) to have the class taught in a foreign language.

22. **B** This choice is correct because a basal reading program is not designed to meet the individual needs of students. Note the word NOT in the item. A basal program is typically designed to be used with all the students in a class. A basal program must be supplemented to meet the individual needs of students. The remaining choices describe some of the characteristics of a basal reading program.

23. **C** Putting stickers on this chart creates a pictograph, which is one way to graph information. (A) is incorrect because

Ms. Archibald has more direct ways to gather this information. (B) is incorrect because students may learn something about different modes of transportation but this is not the most likely reason Ms. Archibald is conducting this activity. (D) is incorrect because placing stickers on a chart does not give these young students useful tactile experiences.

24. **B** Using the ESL (English as a Second Language) approach is the most appropriate step because the child will be best served if he or she can communicate with others in their class. (A) is incorrect because using the child's native language does not further the child's mastery of English. (C) is incorrect because it is best if the child participates in the lesson with the teacher's help and support. (D) is incorrect because this may help, but it does not respond to the immediate situation in the classroom and is not the teacher's most appropriate action.

25. **D** Ms. Del Corso notices the reading difficulty when the student is reading mathematics problems. This indicates that the difficulty is reading in the context of mathematics and there is no mention that the reading problem occurs elsewhere. The remaining choices are all potential causes of reading difficulties, but not this reading difficulty, even though they may contribute to the problem in some way.

26. **C** This arrangement makes it too difficult for the teacher to see all the students, and Ms. Watson must always have her back to at least some of them. Having students out of sight, particularly on the first day of class, is not a good idea. The other chair arrangements are acceptable, particularly when compared to (C).

27. **B** Consider each Roman numeral in turn. Then choose your answer.

   I. Correct. High expectations are a hallmark of effective schools.
   II. Correct. Students do better when teachers and administrators are held accountable for their performance.
   III. Incorrect. Standardized tests are used in effective schools.

   I and II are correct—(B).

28. **B** More time on task is among a relatively few classroom practices shown to enhance learning. It has a proven and more powerful impact than all the other choices listed. There is room in the classroom for all of the other choices. However, if Ms. Weiss had to choose, as you do, she would choose (B).

29. **A** It is the comparison of cultures that creates a multicultural approach to teaching social studies. This approach emphasizes the varying responses across cultures. The intent of multicultural social studies education is to help students recognize differences and yet develop a unified bond among the students. The emphasis is on cultures in this country. The remaining choices may be interesting in a classroom, but they do not best characterize a multicultural approach.

30. **D** Students expect the teacher to be an authority figure. Students may complain, but an authority figure is what students expect and what it is usually best to give them. (A), (B), and (C) are incorrect because some authority figures may be very assertive, or extremely understanding, or tough taskmasters. None of these specific strategies serve Mr. le Bente as well as having students associate him with an authority figure.

31. **B** Just because a student is reading below grade level does *not* mean they cannot understand social studies topics that are on or above grade level. Do not adapt instruction to include less difficult topics on the basis of a low reading level. Each of the remaining choices represents an acceptable way to adapt social studies instruction for students reading significantly below grade level.

32. **A** Authentic assessment means Mr. Rios will observe students as they work or review students' actual work as described in this choice. (B) is incorrect because Mr. Rios would not uses tests as a part of authentic assessment, although he may use them for other purposes in his class. (C) is incorrect because authentic assessment does not have to be conducted in real-life settings. (D) is incorrect because Mr. Rios would not rely on evaluative information from other teachers as a part of authentic assessment.

33. **C** A teacher should never show a parent individual test scores from a child other than their own. (A) and (B) are incorrect because a parent could reasonably be interested in this information and Mr. Batsawani should share it with the parents. (D) is incorrect because reports about average performance are usually available in schools and if it is available for his class, Mr. Batsawani should share it with the parent.

34. **D** Note that the question asks for the choice LEAST likely to help Mr. Batsawani promote communication. The communication generated by this choice is likely to lead to parents talking among themselves or with school administrators. The teacher should never discuss individual test scores with groups of parents. The remaining choices are examples of effective techniques for promoting good communication with parents.

35. **A** This action furthers the teacher's aims and does not run the risk of alienating parents. (B) is too self-serving; it does not give parents a reason to vote yes, and may not further the teacher's goal. (C) and (D) are incorrect because they inject Mr. Rios into town politics, in which he has an interest but no standing, and would likely not further his goal.

36. **B** Minority students' standardized test scores tend to fall below their actual ability and that is one of the reasons minority students are disproportionately represented in the lower tracks of a tracking system. (A) is incorrect because the flaws in standardized tests are not deliberately designed for that purpose, but that is often the outcome. (C) is incorrect because this statement is not necessarily true, and is more properly a suggestion for how teachers are assigned to classes. (D) is incorrect because as a general rule, administrators do accurately report scores.

37. **D** Just because a student can say counting words in order does not mean the student can count. You may have seen a child correctly count to five as the child counts seven objects. It is the correspondence

between the counting words and the objects being counted that indicates a child is actually counting. (A) and (B) are incorrect because the activity is not designed to focus attention or to develop eye-hand coordination, but it may help. (C) Ms. Hotop may ask students about the shapes, but that is not the primary reason for the activity.

38. **A** Analyze the writing sample. The second sentence contains the grammatical error. The singular subject "I" does not agree with the plural verb "are." Consider each Roman numeral in turn.

    I. Correct. Ms. Savorsi should concentrate on subject-verb agreement because of the agreement error in the second sentence.

    II. Incorrect. The sample contains no pronoun errors.

    III. Incorrect. The sample contains no sentence fragments.

    Only I is correct—(A).

39. **B** Health information about students, and particularly about students with AIDS, is confidential and should not be shared. (A) is incorrect because a teacher has no right to have a child with AIDS removed from his or her class. (C) is incorrect because teachers are not permitted to inform anyone that a student has AIDS. (D) is incorrect because Ms. Small should not inform other teachers that Louis has AIDS.

40. **C** The Supreme Court ruled in 2002 that vouchers were constitutional if there was a choice between religious and non-religious schools, and if parents, not the government, decided which school their child would attend. Voucher programs in New York State are legal for that reason, but the state is not required to offer a voucher program. (A) is incorrect because voucher programs do not have to take income into account. (B) is incorrect because students are permitted to use vouchers to attend religious schools. (D) is incorrect because a voucher program does not have to require that schools fall below established criteria for three years.

41. **C** This choice accurately describes why the special education teacher is in the class-

room, to help special education students while the teacher conducts the lesson. (A) is incorrect because Frank Damico's job is to be the support, not to arrange for support. (B) and (D) are incorrect because Mr. Damico's responsibility is not with nonmainstreamed students, although he may spend some time working with nonmainstreamed students.

42. **B** This is the best response to give a parent. It is positive and truthful, but it neither holds out too much hope nor is too negative. (A) is incorrect because this choice is too positive and unrealistically raises a parent's expectations. (C) is incorrect because this response is likely the most candid of the four responses, but it is too stark and it is not the kind of response that should be given at a parent-teacher conference. (D) is incorrect because this response unnecessarily puts the parent off.

43. **B** Guiding students as they work is a very effective strategy for teaching reading. Picking out science fact and science fiction in a space exploration story is certainly the best kind of guidance among the choices given. (A) is incorrect because most science fiction stories contain some science fact. (C) and (D) are incorrect because working independently is one of the least effective ways to learn to pick out science fact and science fiction because it lacks interaction with Ms. Montelone and with other students.

44. **D** It's a definition; vicarious learning means to learn from the others' experiences rather than from direct experience. None of the other choices reflects the definition of vicarious learning.

45. **B** This nonconfrontational response is professional and it furthers the teacher's goals. (A) and (C) are not technically incorrect, but they are not the most professional response and they do not further the teacher's goals. (D) A teacher should never discuss an individual child's work with the child's parent(s) when others are around.

46. **C** Punishment means denial of privileges such as being kept after school. It does not mean corporal punishment. Punishment is an ineffective way to change a

student's behavior except when used for very limited and specific reasons. (A) is incorrect because punishing the entire class is not required to change one student's behavior. (B) is incorrect because extra work is not required for punishment to be effective. (D) is incorrect because there is no known correlation between a teacher feeling better and effective punishment.

47. **C** Groups with ten or twelve members are too large for effective interaction. Cooperative learning groups are typically limited to six group members. The remaining choices describe essential elements of cooperative learning groups.

48. **D** This kind of after-school, off-campus meeting is fine, as long as teachers don't discuss students' confidential information. There is no indication that they do. (A) This meeting is not illegal. (B) and (C) are incorrect because teachers have the right to criticize school administrators.

49. **D** This student is a phonetic speller. "Enuf" is misspelled, but the student followed phonetic rules. This student needs instruction in the alternative spelling used for phonemes (sounds associated with letters and groups of letters). For example, English spelling uses the letters "gh" to represent the "f" sound as in enough. Using many spellings for the same sound can make English a difficult language to learn. (A) and (B) are incorrect because word attack skills lead to the correct pronunciation of "enuf." (C) is incorrect because "enough" and "enuf" sound the same, so they are homonyms. However, confusing homonyms is not the problem here.

50. **C** A constructivist approach encourages students to build their own understanding of concepts. One important way to do this is for students to build on their initial responses. (A) is incorrect because a more reflective approach to questions is in keeping with the constructivist approach. (B) is incorrect because this is not the kind of construction that constructivists have in mind. (D) is incorrect because the constructivist approach encourages students to create metaphors.

51. **A** Gardner's theory supports the use of interdisciplinary units. It holds that students have many intelligences, not just a cognitive intelligence. Interdisciplinary units promote utilization of these multiple intelligences. (B) is incorrect because students don't need to know about the intelligences. (C) and (D) are incorrect because there is nothing in Gardner's theory that supports the elimination of assessments nor having students establish the criteria for quality.

52. **C** You do not have to understand the meaning of a word to properly pronounce it. Note the word EXCEPT in the item. Both word recognition and comprehension are important parts of reading instruction. (A) and (B) are incorrect because a child might not be able to sound out the word phonetically, or the word might not be a part of the child's sight vocabulary. (D) is incorrect because the context of the word reveals the correct pronunciation, so a problem with context analysis could lead to difficulty pronouncing a word.

53. **B** This is the most common way to limit the use of calculators. If students are learning a computation method, calculators should not be used. (A) is incorrect because calculators are now required on many tests and in many real life situations as well. It would not be in the student's best interest to ban them. (C) is incorrect because calculators can be very useful for completing complex computations involving these operations. (D) is incorrect because this sort of checking might happen, but calculators should not be limited "only" to this use.

54. **D** The teacher should not be confident. Errors of measurement that occur on all teacher-made tests quite likely eliminate any meaning in the small difference between these scores. (A) is incorrect because the teacher should not be confident, whether or not she follows the grading rules. (B) is incorrect because a difference of 2 or 4 percent between scores on a teacher-made test may be clear, but it means very little. (C) is incorrect because content validity means the test actually measures the

content in the social studies unit. Content validity does not mean the difference noted in the scores is meaningful.

55. **B** In a brief unit such as this one, a teacher-made assessment is almost always best. There may also be an appropriate assessment available from a text publisher or other source, but this is clearly the best among the choices given. (A) is incorrect because standardized tests are used to establish an achievement level, or to compare results between students or groups of students. Standardized tests are not particularly useful for finding out whether or not a student has learned something. (C) is incorrect because the item states that the teacher wants to know whether the students have learned about nouns before going on. While observing students' written work is an excellent assessment technique, there is not enough time to employ that technique and gather the information needed here. (D) is incorrect because reviewing students' previous work, alone, will not help the teacher determine what they learned since that time.

56. **D** Reliability means the same work consistently receives the same evaluation. Many schools that implemented portfolio assessment had to alter their policies because different teachers assigned widely different grades to the same portfolio. Clear rubrics or standards have to be established for portfolio assessment to be effective. (A) is incorrect because it is not the diverse group of work students put in portfolios that causes the problem. Rather, it is the way teachers assess these samples. (B) is incorrect because machines do not typically score the materials in a portfolio. (C) is incorrect because this may be an issue in some circumstances; however, it is not an issue of reliability.

57. **D** These students couldn't just decide themselves to leave school grounds during school hours; school hours include lunch. (A) and (B) are incorrect because it's one thing to express your free speech rights, or to represent democracy, and another thing to leave school grounds without permission. (C) is incorrect because the fact that the students left the school grounds without permission is the problem.

58. **D** This is the classic test-based definition of a learning disability—at or above average ability but achievement two or more years below grade level. (A) is incorrect because there is nothing in this record to indicate that the student is a poor test taker, and the IQ score of 110 to 115 may indicate the child is not a poor test taker. (B) is incorrect because the student's achievement is well below the student's potential. (C) is incorrect because these IQ test results are not high enough for a gifted classification.

59. **C** This choice is the correct interpretation of percentile. The percentile is the percentage of students who took the test and received a lower score. That means that Ms. Davenport's child scored better than 34 percent of those who took the test. (A) is incorrect because the percentile does not refer to students in the class. (B) is incorrect because this is a description of a student who scored better than about 66 percent of the students who took the test. (D) is incorrect because a standardized achievement test does not measure ability.

60. **B** The writing sample that Ms. Davenport believes is above average for the class *may* indicate that this student does better on authentic assessments. (A) is incorrect because there is a meaningful conclusion shown in choice (B). (C) is incorrect because there is no basis for this conclusion. Both the writing sample and the mathematics test score show good performance. (D) is incorrect because there is no basis to compare these results. The reading results are from a standardized test. The science results are from a criterion-referenced test, which shows the objectives a student has mastered.

61. **D** A summative evaluation assesses what a student learned about a specific objective or objectives. (A) is incorrect because a portfolio evaluation relies on samples of students' actual work. (C) and (D) are incorrect because standardized test and norm-referenced test are essentially the same type of test.

These tests have been standardized on a large population of students. End of chapter tests are not standardized.

62. **B** Evaluation of students' writing is distinct from mastery of specific English skills. Ms. Lilanni's evaluation of a student's writing must be based on actual writing samples. Using a checklist helps ensure that the writing will be evaluated consistently. (A) is incorrect because this choice does not use actual writing samples. (C) is incorrect because this choice does not include an assessment and would rely on only one sample. (D) is incorrect because this choice evaluates reading, not writing.

63. **A** Auditory discrimination refers to hearing and a hearing problem would not be a cause of difficulty understanding written instructions. Difficulty with written instructions has to do with reading or some other visual problem such as those reflected in choices (B), (C), and (D).

64. **B** Personal journals are just that—personal—and they are not meant to be shared with others. There are other types of journals that can be used to achieve the ends noted in the other answer choices.

65. **D** Holistic grading is based on the evaluator's informed impression of the writing sample, not a detailed analysis. (A) This choice may remind you of a hologram, but it has nothing to do with holistic scoring. (B) is incorrect because tests scored holistically are often evaluated by several readers, but this does not happen in Ms. Crawford's class. (C) is incorrect because holistic scoring is not about this kind of whole.

66. **B** This is what Ms. Rosa should *not* do; she should give Pam extra support. Ms. Rosa does not want a fifth-grade student to do poorly on a test because of test anxiety. Choices (A), (C), and (D) represent appropriate ways to respond to a test-anxious child.

67. **B** This choice represents the least restrictive environment that meets the student's needs for additional support. (A) and (C) are incorrect because they represent learning environments that are more restrictive for the student. (D) This choice will not provide the additional support the child needs.

68. **C** Learning disabled students benefit most from brief, structured assignments and auditory opportunities for learning. (A) is incorrect because large-print books are most appropriate for visually impaired students. (B) is incorrect because it is good to provide highly relevant skills, but learning disabled students need practice. (D) is incorrect because learning disabled students can do well on a test one day and not know the skills and concepts on that test the next day.

69. **C** Under the federal No Child Left Behind Act, parents have the right to remove their children from "failing schools." (A) is incorrect because administrators might see teacher effort as a reason for the low scores, but this is not their primary concern. (B) is incorrect because there is no evidence that this is a concern. (D) is incorrect because the Commissioner of Education in New York State *can* invalidate test scores if he or she believes there is just cause.

70. **B** Duplicating instructional worksheets is the least useful endeavor for an aid working in an instructional capacity. Choices (A), (C), and (D) all describe activities that are more useful than the activity described in (B).

71. **D** Public Law 94-142 was originally called the "Education of All Handicapped Children Act" and is now codified under the name "Individuals with Disabilities Education Act" (IDEA). This special education act was the first significant intervention in public schooling, and it is the only federal act listed that could be the basis for the decision.

72. **A** This choice is best because it gives the teacher a specific recommendation to follow. Choice (B) is incorrect because the advice to "try to get to everyone" is too vague." Ms. Ritzkovik could believe she was trying to reach everyone and only get to 30 percent of the students. (C) is incorrect because this advice is similar to Choice (B) but now the teacher is told to "try to call on all the students." It is often impossible to call on all the students and there is no minimum standard to meet. (D) is incorrect because the advice to "do your best" is

almost permission not to call on a higher percent of students in the class.

73. **D** It is best to ignore the behavior whenever possible because when a student is misbehaving to get attention, reprimanding the student just increases the behavior. Choices (A) and (C) are incorrect because they give students the attention they want. (B) is incorrect because Ms. Ritzkovik should make an extra effort to reward positive behavior exhibited by attention-seeking students. This approach may reduce the number of times students misbehave just to get attention.

74. **B** This approach is cueing, which is designed to let students know that a transition will occur soon, but not immediately. Using a recognized signal alerts students and gives them time to put away their work. (A) and (D) are incorrect because they represent too rapid a transition and do not give students an opportunity to adjust. (B) is incorrect because this approach will likely take too long and you may never achieve your goal, unless "standing there" is a recognized signal.

75. **B** This choice draws attention to the coins and actively involves students in the lesson. (A) is incorrect because this choice might sound interesting, but it does not involve students in the lesson. (C) is incorrect because the question of where coins came from may be interesting to some, but usually not to a class of primary students. (D) is incorrect because it is not a motivation, it is an anticipatory set designed to focus students on the lesson.

76. **D** Plans often fail, and for many reasons. It is a reality of teaching, particularly for beginning teachers. If a plan is clearly failing, Ms. Sola-Vega should try to find alternative ways to teach the lesson. The remaining choices recommend that Ms. Sola-Vega "stick with" her plan and give varying reasons why this is the correct approach. But she should not stick with a failed plan. That's not to say she should abandon a plan at the first sign of trouble. However, Ms. Sola-Vega should let the plan go if it is "very clearly not working."

77. **D** It is a good plan because it provides students with a break before reading. Reading does not have to be the first subject taught. (A) is incorrect because the students might not be late from recess. This is not a basis for criticizing the plan. There are always things that can happen during a day to create a problem for any plan. (B) is incorrect because the recess is a regular part of the school day and cannot be "cut out" by the teacher. (C) is incorrect because it does make a difference. For example, Ms. Smithson should not schedule reading as the last thing in the day.

78. **B** It is a research fact that about twice as many boys as girls have problems adjusting to school. (A) is incorrect because minority students adapt more poorly to school than majority students. (C) is incorrect because girls are not more physically active than boys the same age. (D) is incorrect because primary students typically do not rebel against the teacher's authority.

79. **D** This choice does *not* reflect the modern American family. The other choices do accurately describe aspects of the American family, including (A) a majority of families have mothers who work. (B) When the responsible adult or adults at home both work, students let themselves into an empty house after school. That's what "latchkey child" means. (C) It may be because there is only one parent, or it may be because both parents work, but a very small number of American families have one parent who stays home.

80. **D** Collaborative teaching generally means that special education teachers work in regular classrooms along with the classroom teacher. This situation will most likely apply to Ms. Riverbark. Choices (A) and (B) may still be a significant part of Ms. Riverbark's job, but the main impact of collaborative teaching will most likely move her into classrooms. (C) is incorrect because she may come into contact with learning disabled students in classrooms, but this is not the main impact of the shift to collaborative teaching.

WRITTEN ASSIGNMENT

Show your lesson plan to an Education professor. Ask him or her to rate your lesson plan 0–3 using this scale.

3   A well developed, complete lesson plan.
Shows a thorough response to all parts of the plan.
Clear objective and lesson plan parts.
A lesson that is free of significant planning errors.

2   A fairly well developed, complete lesson plan.
It may not thoroughly include all parts of an effective plan.
Fairly clear objective and lesson plan parts.
It may contain some significant planning errors.

1   A poorly developed, incomplete lesson plan.
It does not contain most parts of an effective plan.
Contains an unclear objective, poor planning.
It contains some significant planning errors.

0   A very poorly developed, incomplete plan.
It does not contain any elements of an effective plan.
Contains only poor planning.
Contains numerous significant planning errors.

14 PRACTICE ATS-W II (SECONDARY)

This practice test contains the types of items you will encounter on the real test but don't be surprised if the real test seems different. The distribution of items varies from one test administration to another.

Take this test in a realistic timed setting. You should not take this practice test until you have completed your subject matter review.

The setting will be most realistic if another person times the test and ensures that the test rules are followed. But remember that many people do better on a practice test than on the real test.

You have four hours to complete the multiple-choice items and the written assignment. Keep this time limit in mind as you work. Answer the easier questions first. Be sure you answer all the questions. There is no penalty for guessing. You may write in the test booklet and mark up the questions.

Each multiple-choice item has four answer choices. Exactly one of these choices is correct. Use a pencil to mark your choice on the answer sheet provided for this test.

The written assignment immediately follows the multiple-choice items. Once the test is complete, review the answers and explanations as you correct the answer sheet.

When instructed, turn the page and begin.

ANSWER SHEET PRACTICE ATS-W II (SECONDARY)

1 Ⓐ Ⓑ Ⓒ Ⓓ		21 Ⓐ Ⓑ Ⓒ Ⓓ		41 Ⓐ Ⓑ Ⓒ Ⓓ		61 Ⓐ Ⓑ Ⓒ Ⓓ	
2 Ⓐ Ⓑ Ⓒ Ⓓ		22 Ⓐ Ⓑ Ⓒ Ⓓ		42 Ⓐ Ⓑ Ⓒ Ⓓ		62 Ⓐ Ⓑ Ⓒ Ⓓ	
3 Ⓐ Ⓑ Ⓒ Ⓓ		23 Ⓐ Ⓑ Ⓒ Ⓓ		43 Ⓐ Ⓑ Ⓒ Ⓓ		63 Ⓐ Ⓑ Ⓒ Ⓓ	
4 Ⓐ Ⓑ Ⓒ Ⓓ		24 Ⓐ Ⓑ Ⓒ Ⓓ		44 Ⓐ Ⓑ Ⓒ Ⓓ		64 Ⓐ Ⓑ Ⓒ Ⓓ	
5 Ⓐ Ⓑ Ⓒ Ⓓ		25 Ⓐ Ⓑ Ⓒ Ⓓ		45 Ⓐ Ⓑ Ⓒ Ⓓ		65 Ⓐ Ⓑ Ⓒ Ⓓ	
6 Ⓐ Ⓑ Ⓒ Ⓓ		26 Ⓐ Ⓑ Ⓒ Ⓓ		46 Ⓐ Ⓑ Ⓒ Ⓓ		66 Ⓐ Ⓑ Ⓒ Ⓓ	
7 Ⓐ Ⓑ Ⓒ Ⓓ		27 Ⓐ Ⓑ Ⓒ Ⓓ		47 Ⓐ Ⓑ Ⓒ Ⓓ		67 Ⓐ Ⓑ Ⓒ Ⓓ	
8 Ⓐ Ⓑ Ⓒ Ⓓ		28 Ⓐ Ⓑ Ⓒ Ⓓ		48 Ⓐ Ⓑ Ⓒ Ⓓ		68 Ⓐ Ⓑ Ⓒ Ⓓ	
9 Ⓐ Ⓑ Ⓒ Ⓓ		29 Ⓐ Ⓑ Ⓒ Ⓓ		49 Ⓐ Ⓑ Ⓒ Ⓓ		69 Ⓐ Ⓑ Ⓒ Ⓓ	
10 Ⓐ Ⓑ Ⓒ Ⓓ		30 Ⓐ Ⓑ Ⓒ Ⓓ		50 Ⓐ Ⓑ Ⓒ Ⓓ		70 Ⓐ Ⓑ Ⓒ Ⓓ	
11 Ⓐ Ⓑ Ⓒ Ⓓ		31 Ⓐ Ⓑ Ⓒ Ⓓ		51 Ⓐ Ⓑ Ⓒ Ⓓ		71 Ⓐ Ⓑ Ⓒ Ⓓ	
12 Ⓐ Ⓑ Ⓒ Ⓓ		32 Ⓐ Ⓑ Ⓒ Ⓓ		52 Ⓐ Ⓑ Ⓒ Ⓓ		72 Ⓐ Ⓑ Ⓒ Ⓓ	
13 Ⓐ Ⓑ Ⓒ Ⓓ		33 Ⓐ Ⓑ Ⓒ Ⓓ		53 Ⓐ Ⓑ Ⓒ Ⓓ		73 Ⓐ Ⓑ Ⓒ Ⓓ	
14 Ⓐ Ⓑ Ⓒ Ⓓ		34 Ⓐ Ⓑ Ⓒ Ⓓ		54 Ⓐ Ⓑ Ⓒ Ⓓ		74 Ⓐ Ⓑ Ⓒ Ⓓ	
15 Ⓐ Ⓑ Ⓒ Ⓓ		35 Ⓐ Ⓑ Ⓒ Ⓓ		55 Ⓐ Ⓑ Ⓒ Ⓓ		75 Ⓐ Ⓑ Ⓒ Ⓓ	
16 Ⓐ Ⓑ Ⓒ Ⓓ		36 Ⓐ Ⓑ Ⓒ Ⓓ		56 Ⓐ Ⓑ Ⓒ Ⓓ		76 Ⓐ Ⓑ Ⓒ Ⓓ	
17 Ⓐ Ⓑ Ⓒ Ⓓ		37 Ⓐ Ⓑ Ⓒ Ⓓ		57 Ⓐ Ⓑ Ⓒ Ⓓ		77 Ⓐ Ⓑ Ⓒ Ⓓ	
18 Ⓐ Ⓑ Ⓒ Ⓓ		38 Ⓐ Ⓑ Ⓒ Ⓓ		58 Ⓐ Ⓑ Ⓒ Ⓓ		78 Ⓐ Ⓑ Ⓒ Ⓓ	
19 Ⓐ Ⓑ Ⓒ Ⓓ		39 Ⓐ Ⓑ Ⓒ Ⓓ		59 Ⓐ Ⓑ Ⓒ Ⓓ		79 Ⓐ Ⓑ Ⓒ Ⓓ	
20 Ⓐ Ⓑ Ⓒ Ⓓ		40 Ⓐ Ⓑ Ⓒ Ⓓ		60 Ⓐ Ⓑ Ⓒ Ⓓ		80 Ⓐ Ⓑ Ⓒ Ⓓ	

Each item on this test includes four answer choices. Select the best choice for each item and mark that letter on the answer sheet.

Items 1–4.

Wayne Yarborough is in his fourth year as a social studies teacher in Roosevelt High School. He is giving some thought to the way he teaches. While teaching a social studies lesson, Mr. Yarborough can get the student's interest but he is not so good at maintaining that interest. Wayne uses a wide variety of questions as he teaches and is very interested in changing and reinforcing appropriate student behavior.

1. Mr. Yarborough has the best chance of maintaining student interest in the lesson if:
   (A) he is animated.
   (B) his objectives are clear and unambiguous.
   (C) the students understand that what they are learning will help them learn other material later.
   (D) there are no choices available to students.

2. When questioning students, which of the following techniques should Mr. Yarborough generally follow?
   (A) Make sure students know who will answer a question before it is asked
   (B) Ask questions of the whole class
   (C) Ask questions of students who are not paying attention.
   (D) Ask questions of students who usually have the correct answers.

3. Mr. Yarborough knows that modeling is one appropriate way to modify behavior. Which of the following is an example of a good modeling technique?
   (A) Respond courteously to students' questions.
   (B) Show students how to construct replicas of historic buildings.
   (C) Demonstrate students' inappropriate behavior.
   (D) Stress the importance of appearance and show students how to dress.

4. Which of the following would be an appropriate way for Mr. Yarborough to reinforce student behavior?

   I. Grading on the basis of performance
   II. Praising appropriate behavior
   III. Ignoring inappropriate behavior

   (A) I, II
   (B) I, III
   (C) II, III
   (D) II

5. During a chemistry lesson, Samantha Lione notices that Emetria, a student in her class, is very anxious about remembering the symbols for elements. Which of the following is NOT an effective way for Ms. Lione to respond to Emetria's needs?
   (A) Don't draw attention to Emetria by providing emotional support.
   (B) Give extra time when practical for Emetria to learn the notation.
   (C) Reduce the tension with a little humor.
   (D) Don't criticize Emetria for lack of progress.

Items 6–9.

Ungu Zmbui is a new ninth-grade teacher in her first month of teaching. She is having difficulty with discipline and with classroom management. Particular problems seem to arise when she is distributing books and other materials. While usually quite effective, Ms. Zmbui can teach in a negative fashion. She is unsure of how to deal with parents and has had some difficulties with a few of them.

6. Which of the following would educators generally agree is the best strategy for Ms. Zmbui to follow when placing or distributing books and supplies in a classroom?
   (A) Use group monitors to pass them out.
   (B) Have students line up alphabetically at the teacher's desk.
   (C) Have books and supplies available at several locations around the room.
   (D) Place needed books and materials in each student's desk before school.

7. In order to be an effective classroom leader, Ms. Zmbui should
   (A) establish and post a series of firm, precise rules that students should memorize and follow.
   (B) establish lines of communication with peer leaders.
   (C) prevent students from engaging in cooperative learning experiences.
   (D) establish competitive situations among class members.

8. Which of the following is LEAST likely to promote good communication with parents?
   (A) Make phone calls to parents.
   (B) Write personal notes on report cards.
   (C) Initiate a series of home/school letters.
   (D) Meet with groups of parents to discuss individual student achievement.

9. As an effective classroom manager, Ms. Zmbui should be most careful to take steps that ensure the majority of class time is devoted to
   (A) individual work.
   (B) on-task activities.
   (C) lecturing.
   (D) group work.

10. Chuck Galesky has been teaching a few years but like most newer teachers he still has some problems with discipline. He overhears the assistant principal say "Chuck should try a more 'with-it' teaching approach to handle his discipline problems," most probably meaning Mr. Galesky is
    (A) always aware of new disciplinary techniques.
    (B) always aware of current popular trends among students.
    (C) always aware of what is happening in the classroom.
    (D) well respected by other teachers.

Just before the beginning of the school year Maritza Gonzalez finds out that she has a problem student, Lucretia, in her class. Many teachers complain about Lucretia, and about her unwillingness to do work or to be cooperative. Ms. Gonzalez leaves school saying, "Just what I need—I better rest up so I'm ready for this problem child." Using the same scenario, another teacher calls Lucretia's parents to open up a line of communication.

11. Which of the following best summarizes the description above about the two different reactions to words that a problem child is in the class?
(A) This is an example of proactive vs. reactive teachers. Ms. Gonzalez is proactive; the other teacher is reactive.
(B) This is an example of reactive vs. proactive teachers. Ms. Gonzalez is reactive, the other teacher is proactive.
(C) This is an example of one teacher knowing the parents and Ms. Gonzalez not knowing the parents.
(D) This is an example of two proactive teachers with different styles.

12. Frank Carmody usually uses a lecture approach to present his history lessons. Which of the following approaches is most likely to help Mr. Carmody enhance instruction?
(A) Begin the lesson with a motivation.
(B) Focus his instruction on the entire class and avoid making eye contact with individual students.
(C) Walk around the room while he delivers his lecture.
(D) Choose a topic above the student's ability level.

13. Lisa Germanio has significant discipline problems with her ninth-grade students. However, if Ms. Germanio were teaching high school seniors, she would find that discipline is less difficult because
(A) it is left to the administration.
(B) it is the parent's concern.
(C) students are less resistant.
(D) teachers are less authoritative.

14. When it comes to getting along in the school, Aaron Ruben's colleagues say that a school is a society in itself, meaning
(A) all races, creeds, and ethnic backgrounds will be represented in a school.
(B) the school reflects the larger community.
(C) students in the school reflect the society in particular and the country as a whole.
(D) a school has its own structure of formal and informal relationships, character, and practices.

Items 15–19.

A group of teachers meet with a school psychologist and a social worker to discuss some of their students' problems. One common problem is drug and alcohol abuse, and Harold Ramirez reports that a number of students discuss this problem with him. Cindy Gareki reports that a senior discussed her sexual abuse as a child. The student did not identify who the abuser was.

A number of teachers, including Beth Alugu and Fred Maarzan, reported that a large number of their students have dropped out of school or are thinking about dropping out of school. During the meeting, the group also discussed whether a particular student in Lee Bouce's class would benefit from an alternative learning environment.

15. Health professionals know that the abuser discussed by the student with Cindy Gareki is most likely a
(A) teacher or coach.
(B) relative or family member.
(C) convicted sexual abuser.
(D) stranger.

16. Which of the following would NOT be an appropriate intervention for Mr. Ramirez to suggest when the alcohol abuse, drug use, or child abuse discussed at the meeting is suspected?
(A) Go through a student's locker because the student smelled of alcohol.
(B) Pay particular attention to principles of classroom management.
(C) Provide awareness programs that focus on drug and alcohol use.
(D) Report suspected child abuse to proper authorities.

17. The counselor who is familiar with research on drug use would most likely say that which of the following choices represents the percent of students who have used illegal drugs, other than alcohol, before they graduate from this high school?
(A) 90 percent
(B) 70 percent
(C) 45 percent
(D) 25 percent

18. Which of the following problems of the student in Lee Bouce's class would probably NOT be helped by the alternative learning environment discussed at the meeting?
(A) drug abuse
(B) alcohol abuse
(C) child abuse
(D) dropping out

19. The most effective plan this group can devise to prevent students from dropping out of school is to
(A) have students who have dropped out describe what happens when a student drops out of school, and arrange other presentations and discussions.
(B) provide students with a list of national statistics on dropouts.
(C) provide positive support and alternative learning environments.
(D) provide for parent conferences to discuss keeping students in school.

Items 20–24.

Frank Zaranga is the principal of Archer High School. He holds regular faculty meetings, and the agenda for one recent meeting is shown below.

AGENDA
1. Teachers' rights and responsibilities
2. Quality schools—effective schools
3. Board of Education role and responsibility

During the meeting, Mr. Zaranga distributes handouts, raises issues, and discusses situations about these agenda items.

20. Which of the following on the list below describes free speech that teachers are entitled to exercise without risk?
(A) Criticize the decisions of the school board and superintendent in a letter published by a local newspaper.
(B) Disclose a student's confidential school records to help the student get educational services.
(C) Organize rallies during school hours that disrupt the school but improve student learning.
(D) Make statements *away* from school that interfere with the teaching performance.

21. All of the teachers attending this meeting enjoy a number of employment related rights, including which of the ones shown on this list?

I. Immunity from civil suits for job-related activities
II. Academic freedom to teach what they wish
III. The freedom to associate out of school with any group
IV. Immunity from dismissal once tenured

(A) II
(B) III
(C) I, III
(D) IV

22. Responsibilities primarily attributed to local school boards include:

I. Employ and supervise a superintendent.
II. Assign teachers and staff to schools and designate their responsibilities.
III. Assign individual pupils to schools.
IV. Evaluate district goals.

(A) I, II, IV
(B) II, III
(C) I, IV
(D) I, III, and IV

23. In general, the characteristics of effective schools include all the following EXCEPT
(A) a climate of high expectations
(B) a high proportion of instructional time spent on task
(C) strong and effective leadership
(D) eliminating standardized tests

24. Mary Inoua is a school librarian who is discussing legitimate actions concerning books in school libraries, and she mentions that
(A) school officials may remove books from school libraries.
(B) parents can prevent school boards from removing books from school libraries.
(C) individual teachers may prevent their students from reading books in school libraries.
(D) books may not be removed from school libraries solely because a school official disagrees with its content.

Items 25–29.

Ingrid Johanssen is a science teacher who plans to begin the lesson by saying, "OK class, today we're going to learn about photosynthesis." The teacher wants to model photosynthesis for the students. She plans to write prerequisite competencies for the lesson on the board. Ms. Johanssen plans to use an inquiry approach and wants to motivate the students as much as possible.

25. Which of the following is the most powerful overall motivation Ms. Johanssen could use in the class?
(A) praise
(B) grades
(C) privileges
(D) learning

26. Which of the following best describes a prerequisite competency Ms. Johanssen plans to write on the board?
(A) the knowledge and skills a teacher must possess to teach an objective
(B) a sub-objective to the main objective of the lesson
(C) the basis for admitting students when they transfer from another school district
(D) the knowledge and skills students must possess to learn an objective

27. Which is the best strategy for Ms. Johanssen to follow after she has asked a question?
(A) Call on a student immediately and expect a quick answer.
(B) Wait for a student to call out the answer.
(C) Pause before calling on a student and expect a quick answer.
(D) Pause before calling on a student and give four or five seconds to answer.

28. Approximately what percent of questions should Ms. Johanssen expect to be answered correctly?
(A) 100 percent
(B) 75 percent
(C) 50 percent
(D) 25 percent

29. Ms. Johanssen arranges her students in cooperative learning groups to work on photosynthesis, usually meaning
(A) Ms. Johanssen will cooperate fully with the students.
(B) Ms. Johanssen will give each group specific instructions on how to proceed.
(C) a person from each group will report the group's findings.
(D) each group of students will gather information about photosynthesis from the local Agriculture Department Cooperative Extension.

Items 30–31.

Ellen Echevira plans to teach a unit to her advanced history class that will lead them to discover concepts. To that end, Ms. Echevira will ask a number of questions during the lesson. At the end of the unit she will administer a test from the teacher's edition of the text.

30. Which of the following words best describes the discovery approach to teaching?
(A) deductive
(B) skill
(C) concrete
(D) inductive

31. In all likelihood, the test Ms. Echevira will give is a:
(A) formative evaluation.
(B) standardized test.
(C) norm referenced test.
(D) summative evaluation.

Items 32–37.

Mike Rosspaph is the high school mathematics teacher and the department chairperson. He is reviewing the testing and assessment results for classes in the department. Mike uses a standardized mathematics test with high reliability to measure achievement in department classes. Students' average normed scores are significantly lower in his department than the average normed scores from districts with the same socioeconomic status. Mr. Rosspaph also knows that scores on the PSAT (Preliminary Scholastic Achievement Test) are used to decide which high school students receive Merit Scholarships. He is concerned about the impact that low PSAT scores will have on students in the school.

32. What do we know about the standardized test from the description given above?
   (A) The test is shipped on time.
   (B) The test is consistent.
   (C) The test predicts success in college.
   (D) The test can be used repeatedly without fear of cheating.

33. What action, if any, is indicated by the average normed scores reported above?
   (A) No action; the average normed scores are about where they should be.
   (B) The mathematics curriculum and teaching methods should be evaluated.
   (C) The national standards for mathematics should be reviewed.
   (D) The test company should be contacted and told not to use average scores.

34. Overall, Mr. Rosspaph knows that
   (A) college success correlates more significantly with PSAT scores than with high school grades.
   (B) the PSAT score is just like an IQ score.
   (C) the PSAT is a projective test.
   (D) girls score lower on the PSAT and boys get more Merit Scholarships.

35. Which factor below will correlate most significantly with overall student achievement of all high schools including this high school?
   (A) socioeconomic status
   (B) intelligence
   (C) cooperativeness
   (D) motivation

36. Mr. Rosspaph receives results of a norm-referenced test that indicate that a student has an IQ of 97, leading to the conclusion that the
   (A) student has below average intelligence.
   (B) student's intelligence is in the normal range.
   (C) student is mildly retarded.
   (D) standard deviation of the test is 3.

37. Which of the following could Mr. Rosspaph recommend to teachers as a way to implement authentic assessment in their classrooms?
   (A) Collect and evaluate student work.
   (B) Use a standardized test.
   (C) Use only tests that have been authenticated.
   (D) Ask students to evaluate each other.

Items 38–42.

Faith Bisone is teaching a United States history class that is culturally and linguistically diverse. Many of the students in her class have a first language other than English, and many come from homes where English is not spoken. Ms. Bisone knows that the minority students in her class, as a whole, tend to have lower achievement scores than other students. She wants to familiarize herself with the difficulties these students have and with the teaching approaches that will be effective in her classroom.

38. The data about the achievement of minority students leads Ms. Bisone to the valid conclusion that:
    (A) minority students are less capable learners than other students.
    (B) the parents of minority students care less about their children's education.
    (C) learning expectations should be lowered for minority students.
    (D) minority students have fewer enriched learning experiences at home.

39. Which of the following describes an acceptable approach to modifying the objectives or plans for this class?
    (A) Modify the plans to teach history topics about the parents' home countries.
    (B) Modify the objective to adjust its difficulty level.
    (C) Modify the plans to include direct instruction in English.
    (D) Modify the plans to account for the cultural heritage of those in the class.

40. Which of the following is consistent with Ms. Bisone using an ESL approach with a group of LEP students from the class?
    (A) Use context clues to help students identify English words.
    (B) Teach mathematics in the student's first language.
    (C) Help students learn their native language.
    (D) Encourage regional and local dialects.

41. Ms. Bisone could help the students in her class who are having difficulty in school by providing all of the following EXCEPT
    (A) a quiet place to work.
    (B) exceptions to classroom rules.
    (C) a flexible schedule.
    (D) a warm, supportive atmosphere.

42. Which of the following is an appropriate curriculum alteration for Ms. Bisone to make to accommodate the needs of students who are recent immigrants in her class?
    (A) Lower the expectations for the group.
    (B) Limit the amount of homework.
    (C) Teach in the native language.
    (D) Require English proficiency to make progress in school.

43. Throughout American history, schools have received waves of immigrant children. Which of the following best depicts the way in which schools have reacted to the most recent wave of immigration?
    (A) The academic atmosphere of our schools is not affected by the ethnic and cultural backgrounds of the students.
    (B) Recent immigrant groups are accustomed to the academic atmosphere of American schools.
    (C) There is no longer a need for schools to deal with the cultural differences of students.
    (D) The schools have noted a shift toward cultural pluralism.

44. If you were preparing to conduct a workshop on the changing American family, which of the following would be most helpful to keep in mind?
    (A) Families are no longer the predominant influence in the early lives of children.
    (B) The nature of the American family has changed for the better.
    (C) Schools have no influence on children's values.
    (D) School programs developed for those students of the changing American family cannot replace effective parenting.

Items 45–47.

Carolee Horlieb is an English teacher who wants to assess a student's understanding of a lesson while students are writing. Ms. Horlieb is trying to decide whether to teach a moderate amount or a lot of information and whether to teach below, at, or above grade level. The students in her English classes are able students with a lower socioeconomic status. That is, these students are poor children, largely from single-parent families where no one in the family has graduated from high school.

45. Which of the following is an effective instructional strategy for Ms. Horlieb to use in this class?
    (A) Do not be too encouraging.
    (B) Lower learning expectations.
    (C) De-emphasize mastery of the material.
    (D) Provide a structured learning environment.

46. Which of the following most accurately characterizes how Ms. Horlieb could conduct the desired assessment?
    (A) She should use a standardized test.
    (B) She should observe students during the lesson.
    (C) She should devise and write a quiz for students to complete.
    (D) She should use a test from a textbook publisher.

47. Which of the following activities indicates that Ms. Horlieb is using extrinsic motivation?
    (A) She discusses the book *20,000 Leagues under the Sea.*
    (B) She identifies similarities in students' clothing.
    (C) She discusses the Federal Reserve Bank.
    (D) She identifies the points students can earn for class participation.

48. When completing an assignment, most successful learning takes place when students work
    (A) independently in school.
    (B) supervised by a parent at home.
    (C) supervised by the teacher.
    (D) on a computer.

49. Stan Joacmen is concerned about the level at which he should teach his foreign language classes. The best advice a colleague could give Mr. Joacmen from the following choices is to teach students
    (A) at their achievement level but above their ability level.
    (B) below their achievement level and below their ability level.
    (C) below their achievement level and above their ability level.
    (D) above their achievement level but at their ability level.

50. Stan Heligo is writing objectives based on the Taxonomy of Educational Objectives: Cognitive Domain, which means that he would teach which of these topics to be at the highest level of this taxonomy?
    (A) Evaluate a book.
    (B) Understand a reading passage.
    (C) Analyze a written paragraph.
    (D) Apply a mathematics formula to a real situation.

51. Inu Hgadu is a language teacher who is considering four different approaches to mastery and instructional time. Which of the following approaches that Ms. Hgadu is considering is most likely to result in successful learning?
    (A) Expect mastery and use all class time for learning activities.
    (B) Expect mastery and use some class time for discussing other issues.
    (C) Don't expect mastery and use all class time for learning activities.
    (D) Don't expect mastery and use some class time for discussion of other issues.

52. Ecchumati Mirandi is a new teacher who is reviewing the way she asks questions in her history class. Which of the several guidelines below should Ms. Mirandi most consistently follow when asking questions?
    (A) Ask complete questions.
    (B) Address questions to individual students.
    (C) Ask difficult questions to challenge students.
    (D) Address questions to the entire class.

53. Akando Shkaaboy is an English teacher who begins each lesson with a general overview of an English topic before teaching the topic to the class. Mr. Shkaaboy is using an approach called
    (A) anticipatory set.
    (B) metacognition.
    (C) inquiry learning.
    (D) advanced organizer.

Items 54–56.

Elaine Davies is a science teacher who has several special education students in her classes. Ms. Davies must be aware of the privacy requirements, particularly the privacy requirements of students' confidential records. At the same time she must plan lessons based on the student's IEP. Chad Keredo is a special education teacher who joins Ms. Davies in her room for three classes.

54. Which of the following could Ms. Davies do and still be in compliance with federal privacy requirements for confidential records of minor children?
   (A) Allow the natural father, who does not have child custody, to see his child's confidential school records.
   (B) Refuse to let an unrelated legal guardian see the child's confidential records.
   (C) Refuse a parent's request to show the child his or her own confidential records.
   (D) Inform parents they have no right to see their child's records without the minor child's permission.

55. Students are completing a brief writing assignment at their seats. Alma, the only special education student mainstreamed in one class tells Ms. Davies that she wants her help with the assignment. Which of the following is Ms. Davies most appropriate response?
   (A) Without explaining why, Ms. Davies asks Mr. Keredo to come over and help Alma with her work.
   (B) Ms. Davies says, "Oh, I'm not supposed to do this, but let me see if I can help."
   (C) Ms. Davies comes over, says, "OK," and helps Alma.
   (D) Ms. Davies explains gently and carefully so that Alma will understand that Mr. Keredo is there just to help her, and that she, Ms. Davies, will get Mr. Keredo so that he can provide very special help for her.

56. Ms. Davies and Mr. Keredo work together to adapt instruction to meet student's IEP guidelines. Which of the following choices best describes their responsibility for preparing lessons according to the IEP guidelines?
   (A) They should follow the IEP guidelines as closely as possible but they should also use their common sense and experience if some provisions are impractical.
   (B) They should set aside their own experience with the special education students and implement the guidelines exactly as described in the IEP.
   (C) They should implement the spirit of the IEP guidelines, but not when the implementation interferes with overall instruction in the class.
   (D) They should modify plans to come as close to the IEP guidelines as possible so that the classroom teacher does not have to work with the special education students.

57. Students are upset about a school board decision to cancel the senior prom. Students can show their displeasure with this decision without the possibility of legal interference from school officials by
   (A) publishing editorials in the school newspaper.
   (B) wearing large buttons that say "PROM POWER" while in school.
   (C) refusing to attend classes.
   (D) placing advertisements in the school newspaper.

Items 58–59.

The district's secondary curriculum committee is meeting for the first time this year to formulate a set of instructional goals. A teacher from each department is at this first meeting. The committee will try to agree on a basic definition of an instructional objective and to agree on what resources these objectives should come from.

58. As the committee does their work, which of the following is the LEAST appropriate source of instructional objectives?
   (A) national professional organizations
   (B) commercial textbooks
   (C) parents
   (D) current school district's objectives

59. Which of the following best characterizes an instructional objective?
   (A) It describes how the teacher will teach the class.
   (B) It describes the average achievement for all students at a grade level.
   (C) It describes the books and materials to be used to teach a lesson.
   (D) It describes what a student should know or be able to do.

60. In a seminar to help teachers understand their legal rights, an attorney could mention that which of the following would generally be the most valid grounds for a teacher's suit against a school district?
   (A) not granting tenure to a teacher who is pregnant
   (B) firing a nontenured black female without providing a specific reason concerning her performance
   (C) firing a tenured white male with more experience than a black male teacher who was not fired
   (D) actively recruiting black and Hispanic faculty to the exclusion of white faculty members

Items 61–62.

Lisa Pismenny is a student in Ms. Anderson's English class who writes well, understands verbal directions, but often has trouble understanding written directions. Lisa is trying very hard to become the best writer she can be.

61. Lisa's difficulty might be related to all of the following EXCEPT
   (A) auditory discrimination.
   (B) visual discrimination.
   (C) sight vocabulary.
   (D) context clues.

62. Ms. Anderson gave Lisa this advice: "The best thing students can do just before they start to write is
   (A) decide on the best order for presenting ideas."
   (B) have a clear beginning."
   (C) decide on the audience and purpose."
   (D) support the main idea."

63. Ezequiel Sanchez uses a computer-based multimedia encyclopedia in his social studies class. The multimedia encyclopedia includes hypertext links in most of its articles. To help understand how to use the hypertext links, Mr. Sanchez would best explain that
(A) the links tie together very (hyper) important ideas in the passage.
(B) clicking on a link gives additional information.
(C) the links move or vibrate to draw attention to important ideas.
(D) clicking on a link with a mouse cursor changes the link's color.

64. Felipe Victorino uses a token economy system to motivate students during a unit in his business class. Which of the following actions is most consistent with Mr. Victorino's approach?
(A) Mr. Victorino provides token (symbolic) reinforcement for work completed by students as opposed to real or meaningful reinforcement.
(B) Mr. Victorino distributes subway and bus tokens for reinforcement since this approach was pioneered in urban areas where many students took buses and subways to school.
(C) Mr. Victorino posts a description of how students can earn points and how students may exchange a certain number of points for a more tangible reward.
(D) Mr. Victorino posts a "token of my appreciation list" on the bulletin board and lists the names of students who perform outstanding work.

65. Rolanda Alvarez wants to conduct an ongoing assessment of her ninth-grade English class. Which one of the following actions on the part of the teacher would NOT indicate that the assessment was underway?
(A) Ms. Alvarez walks around the room regularly observing students' writing.
(B) Ms. Alvarez reviews students' written work at the end of the day.
(C) Ms. Alvarez assigns students an in-class composition about the environment.
(D) Ms. Alvarez collects and reviews daily performance samples of students' work.

Items 66–67.

Fran Ragovan keeps a portfolio of written work for students in her ninth-grade English class. In Ms. Ragovan's opinion, Rodney's writing sample is well above average for ninth grade at her school. A standardized language arts test administered last month shows Rodney has a writing grade equivalent of 7.9, which is above average for his class.

66. Which of the following is the best description of Rodney's language arts achievement?
(A) Rodney's writing test scores are above grade level.
(B) Rodney is writing below average for his class.
(C) Rodney needs intensive help in writing.
(D) Rodney seems to do better when evaluated with an authentic assessment.

67. Which of the following is the most reasonable explanation of why Rodney's standardized test score is below grade level, but above average for that class?
    (A) The student answered fewer questions correctly for the ninth-grade level.
    (B) The class did worse on average than the entire group who took the test.
    (C) Half of those who take the test are below average.
    (D) The averages are different because the number of students in each group is different.

68. Jim Brehm is a mathematics teacher who is going to introduce students to the number pi (3.14159…). Mr. Brehm plans to use the Internet to research the number. Which of the following could Mr. Brehm tell students would be LEAST helpful?
    (A) "Use a search engine to look up pi."
    (B) "Send e-mails to others to find out about pi."
    (C) "Type in a Web address that seems related to pi."
    (D) "Go to a chat room to discuss pi with others."

69. At the start of each technology class John Siegrist writes a "problem" on the board for his technology students to analyze and solve. Which of the following describes the most effective technique Mr. Siegrist can use to assess students' work?
    (A) observation
    (B) standardized test
    (C) cooperative learning
    (D) written work

70. Zulma Tolonio is a science teacher and some of her students have difficulty understanding the resistance (R)—fulcrum (F)—effort (E) characteristics of levers. Which of the following activities could Ms. Tolonio do to best help her students understand these concepts?
    (A) Arrange a variety of levers RFE, FRE, and FER order so the students can demonstrate where to place a lever on a fulcrum to reduce or increase effort.
    (B) Have students classify a group of pictorial representations of levers into RFE, FRE, and FER groups.
    (C) Read a textbook description of each type of lever and listing examples under each type.
    (D) Chart the resistance and effort levels of different types of levers.

71. Juan Herndido works hard to provide positive reinforcement for student behavior, which means that he would likely NOT
    (A) grade on the basis of performance.
    (B) praise appropriate behavior.
    (C) explain to students that they will gain privileges for good behavior.
    (D) stop giving correcting comments when inappropriate behavior stops.

72. In New York State, which of the groups listed below has overall legal responsibility for education?
    (A) the federal government
    (B) the State of New York
    (C) local school boards
    (D) local town and county governments

73. Joacim Jumundu has gathered a number of long newspaper articles about whales. He uses these articles to help students read science effectively. Which of the following approaches on his part will most likely help students identify the main idea(s) of each article?
(A) Mr. Jumundu has students work independently and summarize for themselves the main point(s) of each article.
(B) Mr. Jumundu has students work in cooperative learning groups to summarize and present the main point(s) of each article.
(C) Mr. Jumundu presents a brief summary of the main point(s) of each article.
(D) Mr. Jumundu prepares a brief summary of the main point(s) of each article and distributes them to his students.

74. Mr. Louis Derma is a first-year teacher. In his first evaluation, the supervisor recommends that Mr. Derma employ formative evaluation of students' writing in his class. Louis mentions the recommendation to some friends and colleagues. He receives advice summarized in the choices below. Which of the following advice should Mr. Derma take?
(A) You should engage in discussions with all of your students.
(B) You should keep a portfolio of students' writing samples.
(C) You should use the Iowa Test of Basic Skills.
(D) You should have an end of unit test.

Yi Ti is a music teacher who receives a composition from a student that includes this selection. Every teacher is a writing teacher, and Ms. Ti reviews the writing and considers how to best help this student.

> I sat in the audience while my sister play the clarinet. I saw her play while I sit there. I guess I will never be a profesional musician.

75. Ms. Ti is most likely to help improve this student's writing by providing instruction in which of the following areas?
(A) nouns
(B) pronouns
(C) spelling
(D) verbs

76. A school-wide goal is to integrate mathematics across the curriculum and to use estimation first to be sure an answer is reasonable. Dan Kelleher wants to incorporate this goal in his geography class. The *best* example of what he would ask his students is to estimate
(A) the sum of the height of three mountains 6,294 feet, 3,094 feet, and 7,892 feet, before the students find the answer with a calculator.
(B) the distance between two towns.
(C) the number of rocks in a rockslide.
(D) the volume of a lake.

77. Wayne Esposito teaches a unique computer repair class where he uses a cooperative learning approach. All of the following might occur in Mr. Esposito's class EXCEPT
    (A) students get help from other students.
    (B) groups of two to six students work together.
    (C) group members consult with the teacher.
    (D) the teacher summarizes students' work.

78. Norman Chestnut is a tenth-grade teacher who decides to use Gardner's multiple intelligences as the basis for instruction in his class. That means that Mr. Chestnut will most likely
    (A) implement interdisciplinary units.
    (B) help students learn about each of the intelligences.
    (C) eliminate assessments.
    (D) allow students to determine criteria for quality.

79. In her ten years as a superintendent of schools Dr. Kim Morgan has learned that, generally speaking, class discipline problems are most difficult during:
    (A) grades 2–3.
    (B) grades 5–6.
    (C) grades 8–9.
    (D) grades 11–12.

80. Weekly planning differs from individual lesson plans in that
    (A) weekly plans fit lessons and other activities into available time periods during the week, while lesson plans detail the lessons.
    (B) weekly plans detail the lessons, while lesson plans fit into available time periods during the week.
    (C) weekly plans should be prepared each week, while lesson plans should be prepared at the beginning of the year.
    (D) weekly plans are usually kept by the teacher, while lesson plans are usually submitted written in a plan book.

WRITTEN ASSIGNMENT

Write an essay on the topic below. Use the lined pages that follow. Write your essay on this topic only. An essay on another topic will be rated Unscorable (U).

Computers are an indispensable part of everyday life. There was a time when computers in schools were limited to technology classes and business classes. Today, computers, computer software, and the Internet are integrated throughout the curriculum, and there are appropriate ways to use a computer as part of instruction in almost every subject or discipline

---

Choose a secondary subject area such as English, foreign language, history, or mathematics, but not technology.

Choose a topic in that area which can be taught using the Internet or computer software.

Write the topic and the subject area or discipline. Then write an essay appropriate for a group of teachers in New York State that:

- explains why this is an appropriate topic to be taught with the Internet or computer software;

- describes which features of the software or of the Internet you would use during instruction;

- gives examples of how you engage students with the software or with the Internet to help them learn the topic.

PRACTICE ATS-W II (SECONDARY)

Explained Answers

1. **B** Clear and unambiguous objectives are fundamental and crucial to maintaining interest. There is a difference between students being responsive and students being interested in a lesson. (A) is incorrect because an animated presentation may maintain students' interest in the teacher, but not in the lesson at hand unless the teacher has clear objectives in mind. (C) is incorrect because students are typically not interested in a lesson because it holds the promise of subsequent understanding. (D) is incorrect because leaving students with no choice does not maintain their interest.

2. **B** Mr. Yarborough should address questions to the entire class. This increases the likelihood that students will be paying attention and actively thinking about an answer. (A) is incorrect because this technique focuses on just one student and only that student will be thinking about an answer to the question. (C) is incorrect because this is a poor questioning technique, although some teachers use it to bring students back into the discussion. (D) is incorrect because this is a poor questioning technique that keeps the majority of students from full participation.

3. **A** Modeling means Mr. Yarborough does things in the way he wants his students to copy or emulate. This choice shows that he is engaging in exactly that kind of behavior. (B) is incorrect because this is a different kind of model than the one Mr. Yarborough has in mind. (C) is incorrect because Mr. Yarborough would not model inappropriate behavior to be copied. (D) is incorrect because talking about the ways things should be or showing people how things should be is not modeling how things should be.

4. **A** Consider each Roman numeral in turn. Then choose your answer.

   I. Correct. This is an example of reinforcing behavior.
   II. Correct This is also a way to reinforce student behavior.

   III. Incorrect This is not a way to reinforce behavior, but rather a negative reinforcement.

   I and II are correct—(A)

5. **A** Note the word NOT in the question. This choice describes the inappropriate course of action for Ms. Lione to follow. It is fine for Ms. Lione to provide emotional support even if other students notice. Choices (B), (C), and (D) are all appropriate ways to respond to a student who is anxious about memorizing facts.

6. **C** This technique makes books and supplies readily available and reduces administrative and behavioral problems. (A) is incorrect because this process just increases interaction problems between the student monitors and the students they are distributing the books to. (B) is incorrect because every teacher has seen the pushing and shoving that goes on in this situation, and it wastes time. (D) is incorrect because this approach is an inefficient use of teacher time. Besides, it will not be appropriate when the materials are needed later in the day.

7. **B** Peer leaders are much more important to these students than Ms. Zmbui is. Students at this age will follow peer leaders and Ms. Zmbui can harness this developmental trait to help her with discipline. (A) is incorrect because students do not follow rules just because the rules are firm, or because the rules have been posted. Students certainly don't follow rules because they have been asked to memorize them. (C) is incorrect because cooperative learning activities are effective, but using them or not using them will not, themselves, help Ms. Zmbui become a better classroom leader. (D) is incorrect because there is nothing about competition among students that will make Ms. Zmbui a more effective leader, and the practice actually creates problems in the class.

8. **D** This choice identifies the approach that Ms. Zmbui should not use. It is improper

to discuss individual student achievement with groups of parents. Even if the parents seem to agree to share the results, the practice can only lead to problems. The remaining choices give examples of ways to promote effective communication with parents.

9. **B** There is very little in education about which we are absolutely sure—but time on task is one of them. It is well established that students learn more when they spend more time on task. Ms. Zmbui's main goal as a classroom manager is to promote learning, and this is clearly the best choice. The other choices can be effective forms of classroom management, but none of them can even match the proven positive impact of time on task.

10. **C** The answer to this is common sense, but it also fits Kounin's definition of what "with-it" teaching means. (A) is incorrect because just being aware of techniques does not mean you use them. (B) is incorrect because this choice means "with-it" in one sense, but it does not describe an approach to teaching. (D) is incorrect because the respect from peers described in this choice is not an approach to teaching.

11. **B** Ms. Gonzalez is reactive while the other teacher is proactive. Generally speaking, proactive teachers are the best classroom managers. (A) is incorrect because Ms. Gonzalez is not proactive. (B) is incorrect because many teachers don't know parents at the beginning of the school year, and this should not stop a teacher from making contact. (D) is incorrect because the other teacher is proactive, not Ms. Gonzalez.

12. **A** Research shows that starting a lecture with a motivation, compared to the other choices, is the most effective way to enhance instruction. (B) is incorrect because it is good to make eye contact with students during a lecture. (C) is incorrect because walking around the room, alone, does not enhance instruction. (D) is incorrect because a topic above students' *ability* level will detract from the effectiveness of a lecture.

13. **C** During the first two years of high school students tend to follow peer leaders. By the last two years of high school students are more responsive to adult authority. (A) and (B) are incorrect because they apply as equally to ninth graders as to seniors. (D) is incorrect because teachers who are constructively authoritative are usually best at discipline.

14. **D** The school has its own society that must be appreciated and "mastered" by beginning teachers. This is frequently a teacher's first step to success in a school. (A), (B), and (C) are incorrect because the word "society" in this question does not refer to the larger society or the larger community. A school's society is unique to that school.

15. **B** Most abused children suffer abuse at the hands of a relative or family member. It is possible that anyone in the other three categories listed might abuse a child, and they cannot simply be ruled out. And child abuse by a teacher or some other public figure tends to be more widely known. However, the likelihood that one of these people will be the abuser is greatly diminished when compared to those listed in choice (B).

16. **A** This choice identifies the most inappropriate action for Mr. Ramirez. A teacher does not have the right to search students' lockers without administrative direction and approval. School administrators may direct and oversee a locker search in some circumstances. The other choices represent effective ways to respond to the problems raised by those at the meeting and described in the scenario.

17. **B** Studies indicate that, overall, about 70 percent of high school students use illegal drugs other than alcohol. This percentage soars when alcohol, illegal for most high school students, is included. The percentage may vary somewhat from school to school, but overall it typically does not fall as low as (C) 45 percent or (D) 25 percent, nor rise as high as (A) 90 percent.

18. **C** The emotional problems caused by child abuse are too severe to respond to an alternative learning environment. It is possible, but not guaranteed, that students who are (A) drug abusers,

(B) alcohol abusers, and (D) potential dropouts can be helped by an alternative learning environment.

19. **C** Students are least likely to drop out when the school provides extra support and when school officials and teachers find some way to keep the student interested in school. (A) This choice may be effective with some students, but overall, potential dropouts do not respond well to being told what things will be like. (B) is incorrect because just providing statistics about how many students drop out is unlikely to discourage any student from dropping out. (D) is incorrect because parent conferences are a good idea, but will not, themselves, prevent students from dropping out of school.

20. **A** Teachers are permitted to criticize school board members and school officials. Of course, this may not always be the wise thing to do, particularly for new teachers. (B) is incorrect because a teacher may never disclose a student's confidential records for any reason. That does not stop a parent from disclosing that information. (C) is incorrect because it goes without saying that a teacher can't do anything to disrupt the functioning of a school. (D) is incorrect because teachers can't do anything that will interfere with their teaching performance without putting themselves in jeopardy, even if they do it away from school.

21. **B** Consider each Roman numeral in turn. Then choose your answer.

    I. Incorrect. Teachers can be sued civilly for job-related activities.

    II. Incorrect. Teachers do not have academic freedom and they must teach the curriculum specified by the school district.

    III. Correct. Teachers have freedom of association, but not necessarily freedom in activities that arise from that association.

    IV. Incorrect. Tenured teachers can be dismissed for cause or as part of a staffing reduction.

    Only III is correct—(B).

22. **C** In a sense, a school board is responsible for everything in a district and very little can happen without some sort of approval from the board. In practice, the board has a more limited number of primary responsibilities. Consider each Roman numeral in turn. Then choose your answer.

    I. Correct. This is one of the board's most important responsibilities.

    II. Incorrect. This is primarily an administrative responsibility.

    III. Incorrect. The board may make policy about school assignment, but very rarely actually assigns a student to a school.

    IV. Correct. This is another of the board's most important responsibilities. The board has a responsibility to ensure that the long-term and short-term goals are being met.

    I and IV are correct—(C).

23. **D** Note the EXCEPT in the question. Standardized tests are not an *essential* feature of effective schools. But most effective schools use standardized tests in some manner. (A) High expectations, (B) time on task, and (C) strong, effective leadership are incorrect because these are essential features of effective schools.

24. **D** School boards cannot remove a book from a school library just because a school official or school board member objects to its content. However, school boards may remove books from school libraries for other reasons. Public libraries are bound by different rules than school libraries. (A) is incorrect because school officials may not, themselves, remove books from a school library. (B) is incorrect because if a school board appropriately removes a book from a school library there is nothing a parent can do to prevent it. But a parent could petition the board to reconsider their decision. (C) is incorrect because teachers may not prevent students from reading books found in a school library.

25. **B** Grades remain the primary motivation for students to do work in school. (A) praise (C) privileges, and less so (D), the opportunity to learn, all contribute to a

student's motivation. These other choices are but a secondary consideration compared to (B).

26. **D** A prerequisite competency refers to some skill or knowledge a *student* must possess to learn a competency. In the sense used here, competency does *not* refer to teachers. (A) is incorrect because a competency refers to what the *student* must learn or do. (B) is incorrect because a prerequisite competency comes before the main objective; it is not a part of the main objective. (C) is incorrect because the term prerequisite competency does not apply to admission or transfer requirements.

27. **D** Ms. Johanssen should use this method because it gives students a chance to think about the answer and keeps the answer to a reasonable length, which maintains students' interest. (A) is incorrect because calling on students quickly does not give them adequate time to formulate a response. (B) is incorrect because calling out answers makes for a chaotic process. (C) is incorrect because nothing is gained by forcing students to answer quickly when a few more seconds would permit a full and complete answer.

28. **B** Among the choices given, it would be best for Ms. Johanssen to ask questions that will be answered correctly about 70 percent of the time. This provides for a mix of difficult and easier questions. This guideline will foster a range of questions that will not be too frustrating for students and will offer opportunities for discussion. (A) is incorrect because the questions would be too easy if Ms. Johanssen expected all the questions to be answered correctly. (C) and (D) are incorrect because an intended correct answer rate of 50 percent or 25 percent would indicate the questions were too difficult and too frustrating for students.

29. **C** Students in cooperative learning groups devise their own plan and work actively together to gather information. Usually, one member of the group reports the group's findings. (A) is incorrect because this kind of cooperation does not describe cooperative learning groups. (B) is incorrect because the

teacher gives cooperative learning groups the topic, but group members themselves devise a working plan. (D) is incorrect because a cooperative learning group may do this, but working with Cooperative Extensions does not describe cooperative learning groups.

30. **D** The discovery approach proceeds inductively from examples and details to generalizations and conclusions. (A) is incorrect because deductive teaching is like direct teaching where students first learn the generalization and then the details and examples. (B) is incorrect because the discovery approach is most effective for teaching concepts, not skills. (C) is incorrect because some say that discovery teaching goes from the concrete to the abstract, but just the term "concrete" does not identify the discovery approach.

31. **D** A summative evaluation sums up what the student has learned in a chapter or lesson, and that is the intent of the test Ms. Echevira is giving. (A) A formative evaluation is used to determine what will be taught in the future. Ms. Echevira's test may help some with that, but it is not the main purpose of the test. (B) and (C) are incorrect because a standardized test and a norm referenced test serve the same purpose: to compare a student with the performance of many other students. Ms. Echevira's test does not serve that purpose.

32. **B** The description says the test is reliable, which means that it is consistent from one administration to the next. (A) is incorrect because the reliability mentioned in the description has nothing to do with shipping. (C) is incorrect because the description says nothing about the tests predicting success in college. (D) is incorrect because there is nothing in the description to indicate the test can be used many times without the likelihood that someone will cheat. Repeated usage of the same test may well compromise its content.

33. **B** Test scores that are significantly lower than those from comparable districts are a source of concern. An evaluation of the curriculum and methods used in the school is indicated by these results.

(A) is incorrect because some action is indicated, and that action may be revealed by an evaluation of the curriculum and methods. (C) is incorrect because this might be a good idea as a part of the overall evaluation of the school's curriculum and methods. But just reviewing national standards does not address the issue of low test scores. (D) is incorrect because average scores on normed tests are an effective and appropriate way to compare comparable school districts.

34. **D** Girls score generally lower on the mathematics section of the PSAT than boys. Even though the gap is narrowing, girls tend to be discriminated against for Merit Scholarships. As recently as a few years ago, girls received about 45 percent of the Merit Scholarships. (A) is incorrect because college success correlates more significantly with high school grades than with PSAT scores. (B) is incorrect because an IQ test, and the resulting score, measure ability, while the PSAT includes sections designed to measure achievement. (C) is incorrect because a projective test is a psychological test to help determine personality traits, and this does not describe the PSAT.

35. **A** Overall student achievement in a high school correlates most highly with the overall socioeconomic status (SES) of students in the school. That is, the more wealthy the families in the school, the better students perform overall on tests. (B) is incorrect because individual student achievement may correlate highly with intelligence scores, but overall, the scores of all tests in the school correlate most highly with SES. (C) cooperativeness and (D) motivation, however measured, do not correlate as highly with overall test scores as does SES.

36. **B** IQ tests have a mean of 100 and a standard deviation of 10, and IQ scores from 90 to 100 are in the normal range. That means that 97 is in the normal range, and the other choices are incorrect. There is no evidence from this score that this student is mentally retarded.

37. **A** Authentic assessment means a teacher collects and reviews students' actual work or observes students while they are working. (B) and (C) are incorrect because tests are not used in authentic assessment, and there is no process called test authentication. (D) is incorrect because authentic assessment is based on the teacher's own observation and not on the observations or evaluations of students in the class.

38. **D** Minority students as a whole are *not* less capable, but as a whole they do have fewer opportunities for learning at home, which tends to lower achievement scores. (A) is incorrect because minority students are not less capable. (B) is incorrect because parents of minority students are as concerned about their student's education as other parents are. (C) is incorrect because Ms. Bisone should not lower learning expectations for her students. High expectations lead to more learning.

39. **D** The acceptable approach is for Ms. Bisone to modify the plans to account for the cultural heritage of the students in her class. (A) is incorrect because the topics should be those regularly taught in the school's United States history courses. (B) is incorrect because the objective should be at the same difficulty level, although Ms. Bisone may adapt her teaching approach. (C) is incorrect because it is fine for Ms. Bisone to help her students understand English in the context of learning history. But she should not adapt her objectives to become English objectives.

40. **A** Every teacher is a reading teacher. ESL means English as a Second Language, while LEP means Limited English Proficiency. Teaching English as a Second Language includes using context clues to identify words. (B) is incorrect because teaching mathematics in the first language is an example of bilingual education. (C) is incorrect because teaching English as a Second Language does not include instruction in the foreign language. (D) is incorrect because standard spoken English is the goal, and ESL instruction does not encourage regional or local dialects.

41. **B** A student will not be helped by permitting him or her to ignore certain classroom rules. Children who have problems in school because of the cultural and linguistic adaptations can benefit from (A) a quiet, private place to work, (C) a flexible schedule, whenever possible, and (D) a warm and supportive atmosphere.

42. **B** Children from immigrant families will often not benefit from extensive homework because there may not be help available from parents. (A) is incorrect because lowering expectations does not help these students. (C) is incorrect because teaching in the native language will not help these students, who will need to master English to enjoy viable careers. This is different from helping children make the transition from their native language to English, which could be helpful. (D) is incorrect because this requirement is not helpful since English proficiency is beyond the capability of most of these students. However, it may be useful to ask students to *make progress* toward English proficiency.

43. **D** This choice means that the cultural identities of children have become more pronounced, and this is what has happened in American schools. (A) is incorrect because the academic atmosphere is always affected by students' backgrounds and this is even more noticeable today. (B) is incorrect because recent immigrant groups tend not to be from Europe and so these students are not accustomed to the European atmosphere of American schools. (C) is incorrect because there is even more need to deal with students' cultural differences because students' cultural identities are more pronounced than in the past.

44. **D** Parents and families have *the* overwhelming impact on children. School programs, no matter how effective, can never replace the role of parenting. (A) is incorrect because families are and always have been the main influence on children during their early years and nothing has happened to change this. It is just that the American family is different now than it was a few generations ago. (B) is incorrect because the nature of the American family has changed for the worse, particularly where children are concerned. (C) is incorrect because schools have a significant influence on the lives of children, but not the profound influence that families have.

45. **D** A clear, structured learning environment is always an effective approach to teaching. This does not mean that structure is rigid, but rather a comfortable and predictable environment for students. (A) is incorrect because it is difficult to imagine being too encouraging, and encouragement does not mean doing work for the students. (B) lowering learning expectations and (C) de-emphasizing mastery are ineffective instructional strategies.

46. **B** Ms. Horlieb should observe and evaluate students while they are working. Ms. Horlieb can't give any kind of a test while the lesson is underway. She would not be able to administer the test or the quiz described in the other choices.

47. **D** An extrinsic motivation is some sort of overt reward, such as points to be earned. Just discussing those points can be motivating. The other choices do not represent extrinsic motivation, although they might be a good introductory motivation for a lesson, depending on the lesson and on students' interests.

48. **C** Students typically learn most when they are supervised by a teacher. (A) is incorrect because some students may learn most when they work independently, but that is not typical. (B) is incorrect because some parents are capable of appropriate supervision, but that is not usually the case. (D) is incorrect because some students may learn most while they complete an appropriate assignment on the computer, but that is not where most successful learning occurs.

49. **D** Achievement level refers to what students know, while ability level refers to what they are capable of learning. It is best to teach more than a student already knows, but within their ability to learn. Instruction can be adapted to teach very advanced concepts within a student's ability. (A) and (C) are incorrect because Mr. Joacmen should not

teach above students' ability. It will prove too frustrating. (B) is incorrect because Mr. Joacmen should not teach less than what students already know.

50. **A** Evaluation is at the sixth and highest level of Bloom's Cognitive Taxonomy. (C) analysis is the fourth level, and (D) application is the third level. (B) comprehension is at the second level on this hierarchy of learning objectives.

51. **A** Students learn best when mastery, a thorough understanding of a topic, is expected and all of the class time is used for instruction. (B) Using some class time for noninstructional activities interferes with learning. This is a matter of concern since noninstructional activities can take up a significant portion of class time. (C) and (D) are incorrect because students learn best when the teacher expects mastery, even if mastery is not achieved.

52. **D** Ms. Mirandi should consistently ask questions of the entire class to keep every student engaged in the learning process. (A) It is not a bad idea to ask complete questions, but this is not the choice that she should most consistently follow. (B) It is fine to ask some questions of individual students and (C) she should ask difficult questions to challenge students, but none of these choices should be followed as consistently as (D).

53. **D** A general overview of a lesson best describes an advanced organizer. (A) is incorrect because an anticipatory set is a brief activity or event at the start of the lesson that engages students and focuses their thoughts on the lesson objective. An anticipatory set does not provide a general overview of the lesson. (B) is incorrect because using metacognition a teacher would show students how to think about their learning, that is, how to actively monitor and regulate mental processes. (C) is incorrect because in inquiry learning, teachers ask students to "discover" generalizations by working from specific examples to general ideas.

54. **A** Ms. Davies should always show a child's record to a natural parent, unless there is a court order preventing it. The scenario mentions no such order. (B) A

legal guardian, whether related to the student or not, has the same rights as parents. (C) The parents have the right to request that a minor child see his or her own records. (D) Minor children do not decide whether or not parents see their records.

55. **C** It is appropriate for Ms. Davies to help every student in the class. Mr. Keredo would have given the same response if a nonmainstreamed student asked for help. Mr. Keredo has specific responsibilities but that should not interfere with helping all the students in the class. The remaining answer choices represent inappropriate ways for Ms. Davies to respond to the situation.

56. **B** The IEP is a legal document and it must be implemented as written. Parents may take action if provisions of an IEP are just ignored. The other choices are incorrect because teachers are not in a position to alter or ignore any of the IEP's provisions. But a teacher should bring problems with an IEP to the attention of the responsible person to see if a revision is possible.

57. **B** Public school officials cannot interfere when students use inoffensive speech, which includes spoken words and symbols or words displayed on their person. However, students may not engage in offensive speech or interfere with the operation of the school. (A) and (D) school newspapers are the school's property and school officials can control the content of these papers. (C) students cannot refuse to attend classes.

58. **C** Parents have a vital role themselves, and through the Board of Education, in setting the overall goals for the district. However, this group is least knowledgeable about instructional objectives and they are the least appropriate source among those given for instructional objectives. The other choices all represent appropriate sources of instructional objectives.

59. **D** An instructional objective is a clear description of a student's knowledge or performance. (A) is incorrect because this choice describes the procedures used to help students reach the objective. (B) is incorrect because this

choice describes a normed test result. A criterion-based test would be used to find out whether or not students had learned lesson objectives. (C) is incorrect because this choice describes the learning materials used during a lesson.

60. **C** School districts may not employ "reverse discrimination" when removing teachers, although it is permissible to use the practice when hiring teachers. (A) A teacher can't be denied tenure because she is pregnant. However, there is nothing about being pregnant that ensures a teacher will receive tenure. (B) Nontenured teachers have virtually no employment rights, and administrators or the Board of Education need only say they are not pleased with a teacher, or say they think they can do better. (D) Districts are permitted to recruit in this manner.

61. **A** This choice is correct because it has to do with listening and *not* reading. Note the word EXCEPT in the item. Difficulty with auditory discrimination does not itself interfere with reading. Early hearing problems can inhibit reading and writing development. However, Lisa writes well and understands verbal directions. The remaining choices could be the cause of Lisa's trouble understanding written directions.

62. **C** A student must have an audience and a purpose in mind before writing. (A) is incorrect because the order of presentation is important, but this must come after writers know who they are writing for and why they are writing. Each of these factors may change the order of presentation. (B) and (D) are incorrect because they are things that are done after the writing begins, not before.

63. **B** Clicking on a hypertext word reveals a definition or underlying meaning. Hypertext links to word definitions hold tremendous promise for reading instruction. (A) is incorrect because the links do not tie together "hyper" ideas. (C) is incorrect because links do not usually move or vibrate to draw attention. (D) is incorrect because a link may change color when clicked, but that is to let you know you have visited that link before.

64. **C** A definite reward schedule, some means of giving rewards (points, paper coupons, plastic tokens), and a means of redeeming tokens or points are the essential ingredients of a token economy. (A) The word "token" in this choice means figurative, and does not mean a real token to be handed out to children.

65. **C** Note the word NOT in the item. Assigning an in-class composition, by itself, does not indicate that an ongoing assessment is underway. There must be some evidence that the composition is being assessed. The remaining choices do indicate that an ongoing assessment is underway. (A) is incorrect because observing students as they work is a very effective ongoing assessment approach. (B) is incorrect because the teacher regularly reviews students' daily work. (D) is incorrect because daily performance samples are collected and reviewed.

66. **D** The only conclusive information in Rodney's profile is that he appears to do better on authentic assessment. Authentic assessment gives students an opportunity to demonstrate achievement that may not show up on standardized tests. (A) is incorrect because his score of 7.9 is below average for ninth grade. (B) is incorrect because the last sentence says his writing score is above grade level for his class. (C) is incorrect because a score one year below grade level and an above average writing sample do not support the need for intensive help in writing.

67. **B** The grade level is based on the entire national group of students who took the test. It is quite common for test scores of a class, of a school, or of a school district to be higher or lower on average than the national average. (A) and (D) are just meaningless statements about test scores. (C) This statement is generally true. More or less half of the students nationally who take a standardized test are below grade level. But this statement does not explain the student's test score situation.

68. **C** The least helpful way to find information is to just type in a Web address. Frequently, information about a subject

is not found at a Web address with that name. There are many different suffixes (.com, .edu, .gov, .net, and so on). A student would have to choose the correct suffix as well as the correct Web name. (A) is incorrect because using a search engine is the best way to locate information on the Internet. (B) and (D) are incorrect because these can be effective ways to get information on the Internet. They are more effective than just typing in the Web address, but less effective than using a search engine.

69. **D** Students may be working on the problem at different times of the day. The best approach is for students to submit written samples of their solutions for the teacher to review. (A) is incorrect because students will not be working on the solution for the entire class, and there will not be enough time to observe all the students. (B) is incorrect because Mr. Siegrist's problems are not part of a standardized test. The teacher presents the problems. (C) is incorrect because cooperative learning is not itself an assessment tool.

70. **A** You don't have to know these science concepts to answer the question. It is always best to help students learn science through actual experience. Choices (B), (C), and (D) are incorrect. Each of these choices has value, but none is as good as actual experience.

71. **D** This is not an example of positive reinforcement, or of any kind of reinforcement. The remaining choices are all examples of positive reinforcement

72. **B** The Constitution of the United States of America does not specify which governmental entity has the responsibility for education. But the constitution states the responsibilities not specifically assigned shall be the province of the states. In every state, including New York, the state has the responsibility for education. The State of New York may assign some of its responsibilities to (C) and (D) school boards and local town governments.

73. **B** This is exactly the situation in which cooperative learning groups excel. Students learn from interaction in the group, from the presentation made by

other groups, and from your reaction and other's reactions to the presentations. (A) is incorrect because working independently is one of the least effective approaches to reading comprehension because it lacks interaction with teachers and other students. (C) and (D) are incorrect because the approach involves direct instruction in which the teacher just provides the information.

74. **B** Formative evaluation helps a teacher plan future lessons for a student. Samples of a student's writing best furthers that goal. (A) is incorrect because a discussion with a student may help a teacher, particularly if the discussion follows a review of the student's writing. But a discussion is not the best opportunity. (C) is incorrect because the Iowa Test of Basic Skills is more useful when standardized scores are indicated. (D) is incorrect because an end of unit test is also more useful as a summative evaluation of writing skills, but not as an evaluation of a student's writing.

75. **D** The student's writing contains several verb tense shifts. In the first sentence "sat" is past tense, while "play" is present tense. In the second sentence, "saw" is past tense, while "sit" is present tense. (A) and (B) are incorrect because the nouns and pronouns are used correctly. (C) is incorrect because the only spelling error is in the last sentence.

76. **A** A reasonable answer to a problem usually means to a computation problem. This is the best example because students frequently make key entry errors when they use a calculator. A student can tell if the answer is reasonable if he or she estimates first. (B), (C), and (D) are incorrect because estimation in these measurement examples does not ensure that an answer is reasonable.

77. **D** In authentic assessment the students summarize the results of their cooperative work. Choices (A), (B), and (C) are incorrect. All of these choices are characteristics of cooperative learning groups.

78. **A** Gardner's theory of multiple intelligences supports the use of interdisciplinary units. Gardner says that students have many intelligences and interdisciplinary

units promote simultaneous use of these intelligences. (B) is incorrect because Gardner does not say that students should know about the intelligences. (C) and (D) are incorrect because Gardner's theory does not support the elimination of assessments or of students establishing the criteria for quality.

79. **C** It is during these grades that students turn most to peer groups and are most resistant to authority. The activity that one sees in the early grades and the maturity later in high school typically present fewer discipline problems than (C).

80. **A** A weekly plan allocates available time to lessons. (B) is incorrect because the plan descriptions are reversed in this choice. (C) is incorrect because the first part is correct but the second part is not practical because not enough is known at the beginning of the year to prepare these plans. (D) is incorrect because it is usually just the opposite. Teachers usually hand in plan books containing weekly plans.

WRITTEN ASSIGNMENT

Show your essay to an Education professor or a teacher. Ask him or her to rate your essay 0–3 using this scale.

3   A well developed, complete written assignment.
Shows a thorough response to all parts of the topic.
Clear explanations that are well supported.
An assignment that is free of significant grammatical, punctuation, or spelling errors.

2   A fairly well developed, complete written assignment.
It may not thoroughly respond to all parts of the topic.
Fairly clear explanations that may not be well supported.
It may contain some significant grammatical, punctuation, or spelling errors.

1   A poorly developed, incomplete written assignment.
It does not thoroughly respond to most parts of the topic.
Contains many poor explanations that are not well supported.
It may contain some significant grammatical, punctuation, or spelling errors.

0   A very poorly developed, incomplete written assignment.
It does not thoroughly respond to the topic.
Contains only poor, unsupported explanations.
Contains numerous significant grammatical, punctuation, or spelling errors.

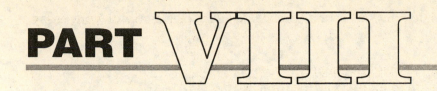

PART VIII

Beginning a Career in Teaching

15 GETTING CERTIFIED IN NEW YORK

Office of Teaching Initiatives
5N Education Building
Albany, New York 12234
(518) 474-3901
(TTY for the deaf: In New York 1-800-622-1220—Out of New York 1-800-855-2880)

Web Page Address: *www.highered.nysed.gov/tcert/*

This chapter explains how to get certified in New York. The Teacher Certification Web page contains complete information about New York State teacher certification along with a wide range of other information of interest to teachers.

To obtain a teacher certification application or to get more information about teacher certification you may call the Office of Teaching at the number given above. Access to Office of Teaching representatives is very limited. You may also contact the Office of Teaching through the contact link on the web site.

CERTIFICATION SUMMARY

New York State offers teacher certificates in many different areas. This summary describes the most common certification requirements. More detailed certification requirements are given in the chapter.

New York offers two primary certificate types—initial and professional.

Initial certificates generally require an undergraduate degree, required education courses, student teaching, and passing scores on the LAST, the ATS-W, and the appropriate CST.

Initial certificates may be obtained by completing an approved teacher certification program at a New York college or by applying directly to the New York State Education Department. You may also qualify through the Interstate Certification Compact or the Northeast Regional Credential, although these certificates are normally valid for a limited time.

Professional certificates generally require a provisional certificate, a related graduate degree, and three years of teaching experience. A professional certificate is maintained through the completion of 175 hours of professional development activities every five years.

Previously issued provisional and permanent certificates are still in force and have their own regulations.

REQUIREMENTS AND PROCEDURES

FORMS OF CERTIFICATION EFFECTIVE FEBRUARY 2004

There are three forms of certification:

This is a brief overview of the certification regulations that take effect in February 2004. You should check with your college or the New York State Education Department for details about the certificates you plan to pursue.

Initial Certificate. The Initial Certificate requires a bachelor's degree and is valid for three years, but issuance may be delayed up to two years after program completion.

Testing Requirements.
Liberal Arts and Sciences Test (LAST)
Assessment of Teaching Skills Written (ATS-W)
Appropriate Content Specialty Test (CST) (except for Speech and Language Disabilities).

This certificate might be extended for one year upon completion of 24 semester hours of approved graduate study. While this certificate may not be renewed, it might be reissued, with completion of additional professional development.

Professional Certificate. The Professional Certificate is issued to those who hold the Initial Teaching and who receive an appropriate master's degree and complete three years of teaching experience, including one year of mentored teaching experience.

Testing Requirements.
No additional tests are required, except that the CST is required for Speech and Language Disabilities.

The Professional Certificate is maintained through the completion of 175 hours of professional development activities every five years. The activities follow the school district's professional development plans, and the requirement is adjusted for those not teaching in a public school.

Transitional Certificate. This certificate is issued to candidates in intensive, school-based teacher preparation programs and entry-level teachers in specific career and technical subjects.

Transitional A Certificate—the first certificate to teach a specific career and technical subject within the field of agriculture, health, or a trade

Transitional B Certificate—the first certificate obtained by a candidate enrolled in an alternative teacher certification program

Transitional C Certificate—the first teaching certificate obtained by a candidate holding an appropriate graduate academic or graduate professional degree and enrolled in an intensive program leading to a professional certificate

CERTIFICATES ISSUED BEFORE FEBRUARY 2004

Provisional and permanent certificates issued before February 4, 2004 are still in force and have their own regulations. Generally, holders of a provisional certificate must earn a master's degree, pass the appropriate CST and the Assessment of Teaching Skills—Performance to receive a permanent certificate. Permanent certificates are generally valid for the life of the holder.

WAYS TO OBTAIN CERTIFICATION

There are five ways to obtain teacher certification.

We strongly recommend that you try to obtain your teaching certificate through an approved program at a college or university. The approved program route is the most direct and the most trouble free certification route.

Approved Program

A person may complete a teacher education program in a New York college or university and be recommended for a certificate provided that program has been registered by the State Department of Education as leading to the designated certificate. There are more than 2,000 individual programs of preparation in New York. Programs in colleges and universities must give consideration to the certification requirements.

Direct Application

An individual may submit an application, official transcripts of all collegiate study and test scores to the Department. These materials are evaluated in accordance with the pertinent Regulations. If the applicant's preparation, test scores, and moral character satisfy the requirements, the appropriate certificate is issued. If there are deficiencies, the applicant is so informed. This evaluation process for most certification areas is also available through the regional certification offices maintained in the majority of Boards of Cooperative Educational Services; but certificates are issued only by the State Education Department.

Interstate Certification

New York has interstate contracts with 40 other states and jurisdictions. A person certified in one of the contract states who meets the conditions of the contract is eligible for conditional certification in New York, until the person meets the New York testing requirements.

Northeast Regional Credential

The Northeast Regional Credential does not include all the certificates issued by New York State. Current state participants in the credential include CT, DC, ME, MA, NH, NY, RI, and VT. This credential is issued to those who hold a valid teaching certificate in a participating state. The credential is valid in all participating states.

National Board for Professional Teaching Standards (NBPTS)

Anyone who holds a NBPTS certificate qualifies for a regular New York State certificate without completing any NYSTCE examinations. National Board Certification includes a significant program of testing.

HOW TO APPLY FOR CERTIFICATION

If you are completing an approved program, your college or university will help you apply for certification. If you are not completing an approved program you need an individual evaluation. Submit the materials described below.

You must submit these documents to begin the certification process.

- a completed certification application with the current application fee
- official transcripts from all your colleges

You must submit these documents before you can obtain teacher certification.

- verification that you completed approved training for identifying and reporting child abuse
- verification of completed testing requirements
- copies of any valid teaching certificates
- affidavit of good moral character

CERTIFICATION TITLES

The titles of the teaching certificates issued by New York are given below.

Early Childhood Education (Birth–2)
Childhood Education (1–6)
Generalist in Middle Childhood Education (5–9)

Students with Disabilities

Students with Disabilities (Birth–grade 2)
Students with Disabilities (Grades 1–6)
Students with Disabilities (Grades 5–9)
Students with Disabilities (Grades 7–12)
Deaf and Hard of Hearing (All Grades)
Blind and Visually Impaired (All Grades)
Speech and Language Disabilities (All Grades) TSSLD

English

English Language Arts (5–9)
English Language Arts (7–12)

Languages

Language other than English (specified) (5–9)
Language other than English (specified) (7–12)

Mathematics

Mathematics (5–9)
Mathematics (7–12)

Biology

Biology (5–9)
Biology (7–12)

Chemistry

Chemistry (5–9)
Chemistry (7–12)

Earth Science

Earth Science (5–9)
Earth Science (7–12)

General Science

General Science (5–9)
General Science (7–12)

Physics

Physics (5–9)
Physics (7–12)

Social Studies

Social Studies (5–9)
Social Studies (7–12)

Special Subjects

Dance (All Grades)
Health Education (All Grades)
Music (All Grades)
Physical Education (All Grades)
Theater (All Grades)
Visual Arts (All Grades)

Literacy and Second Language

Literacy (Birth–Grade 6)
Literacy (Grades 5–12)
English to Speakers of Other Languages (All Grades)

Media and Technology

Library Media Specialist (All Grades)
Educational Technology Specialist (All Grades)
Technology Education (All Grades)

Other Certificates

Agriculture (All Grades)
Family and Consumer Sciences (All Grades)
Business and Marketing (All Grades)
Specific Agricultural Subject Titles (Specified) (Grades 7–12)
Specific Family and Consumer Science Titles (Specified) (Grades 7–12)
Specific Technical Subject Titles (Specified) (Grades 7–12)
Specific Trade Subject Titles (Specified) (Grades 7–12)
Specific Health Occupations Subject Titles (Specified) (Grades 7–12)
Specific Business and Marketing Subject Titles (Specified) (Grades 7–12)

Certificates Available as Extensions or Annotations of Existing Teaching Certificates

Certificate extensions and annotations may require graduate courses or a graduate degree and field work or other experience, along with the Content Specialty Test for that field in which the extension is sought. Check with your college or the New York State Education Department for details.

Extensions and Annotations

Bilingual Education extension of most teaching certificates.

Middle Childhood Education (grades 1 through 6) extension of a certificate for teaching common branch subjects in the lower (PreK–3) and upper (4–6) elementary grades (PreK–6)

Middle Childhood Education (grades 7–9) extension of a certificate in English language arts (7–12), language other than English (7–12), mathematics (7–12), biology (7–12), chemistry (7–12), earth science (7–12), physics (7–12), or social studies (7–12)

Gifted Education extension to any classroom teaching certificate

Coordinator of Work-Based Learning Programs for Career Awareness or Career Development Extension to Any Classroom Teaching Certificate

Language other than English (specified) (grades 1–6) (birth–grade 2) extension to certificate in a language other than English (grades 7–12) or a certificate in a language other than English (grades 5–9) or a language other than English (grades 7–12)

American Sign Language extension to any classroom teaching certificate

General Science (grades 5–9) extension to any certificate in science (grades (5–9)
General Science (grades 7–12) extension to any certificate in science (grades 7–12)

Severe or Multiple Disabilities annotation to a certificate listed above under Students with Disabilities

COLLEGES AND UNIVERSITIES WITH APPROVED TEACHER CERTIFICATION PROGRAMS

The following is a partial list of New York colleges offering state approved teacher certification programs. Read the college catalog and check with the college's education department to be sure that a program is state approved before you begin.

COLLEGE	ADDRESS	PHONE
Adelphi University	Box 701 Garden City, NY 11530	516-877-3462
Alfred University	P.O. Box 786 Alfred, NY 14820	607-871-2214
Bank Street College of Ed.	610 W. 112th St. New York, NY 10025	212-875-4469
Canisius College	2001 Main St. Buffalo, NY 14208	716-888-2397
CUNY - Brooklyn College	School of Education Avenue H & Bedford Ave. Brooklyn, NY 11210	718-951-5214
CUNY - Herbert H. Lehman	250 Bedford Park Blvd. West Bronx, NY 10468-1589	718-960-4993
CUNY - Hunter College	695 Park Ave., Box 393 New York, NY 10021	212-650-3959
CUNY - Queens College	65-30 Kissena Blvd. Flushing, NY 11367	718-997-5220
CUNY - College of Staten Island	2800 Victory Blvd. Staten Island, NY 10314	718-982-3723
Colgate University	Hamilton, NY 13346	315-824-7253
College of Mount St. Vincent	Riverdale, NY 10471	718-405-3285
College of New Rochelle	Castle Place New Rochelle, NY 10801	914-654-5578
College of St. Rose	432 Western Avenue Albany, NY 12203	518-454-5257
Columbia - Teachers College	525 West 120th Street New York, NY 10027	212-678-4050
Cornell University	Dept. of Ed., Stone Hall Ithaca, NY 14853	607-255-2207

COLLEGE	ADDRESS	PHONE
Daemen College	4380 Main Street Amherst, NY 14226	716-839-3600
Dowling College	Idle Hour Boulevard Oakdale, NY 11769	516-244-3171
D'Youville College	Division of Ed., 320 Porter Ave., Buffalo, NY 14201	716-881-7629 716-274-1540
Elmira College	Elmira, NY 14901	607-735-1922
Five Towns College	305 North Service Road Dix Hills, NY 11746-6055	516-424-7000
Fordham University	East Fordham Road Bronx, NY 10458	212-636-6400
Hartwick College	Oneonta, NY 13820	607-431-4841
Hobart and William Smith Colleges	Geneva, NY 14456	315-781-3640
Hofstra University	126 Hofstra University Hempstead, NY 11550	516-463-5745
Houghton College	Houghton, NY 14744	716-567-9672
Iona College	715 North Avenue New Rochelle, NY 10801	914-633-2210
Ithaca College	Muller Faculty Ithaca, NY 14850	607-274-1488
Keuka College	Keuka Park, NY 14478	315-536-5277
LeMoyne College	Syracuse, NY 13214	315-445-4658 718-488-1055
LIU - C.W. Post Center	C.W. Post Campus of LIU, N. Blvd. Greenvale, NY 11548	516-299-3006
Manhattan College	4513 Manhattan College Parkway Bronx, NY 10471	212-749-2802
Marist College	Poughkeepsie, NY 12601	914-575-3000
Marymount Manhattan College	221 East 71st Street New York, NY 10021	212-517-0501
Medaille College	18 Agassiz Circle Buffalo, NY 14214	716-884-3281
Mercy College	555 Broadway Dobbs Ferry, NY 10522	914-674-7350
Molloy College	1000 Hempstead Avenue Rockville Centre, NY 11570	516-678-5000

COLLEGE	ADDRESS	PHONE
Mount St. Mary's College	330 Powell Avenue Newburgh, NY 12550	914-569-3268
Nazareth College	Smyth Hall, Rm. 335, 4245 East Ave. Rochester, NY 14610	716-586-2525
New School for Social Research	66 West 12th Street New York, NY 10011	212-229-5600
New York Institute of Technology	268 Wheatley Rd., P.O. Box 170 Old Westbury, NY 11568	516-686-7516
New York University	NYU/SEHNAP, 70 Washington Sq. So., New York, NY 10012	212-998-5033
Niagara University	Niagara University, NY 14109	716-286-8557
Nyack College	Nyack, NY 10960	914-358-1710
Pace University - New York City	1 Pace Plaza New York, NY 10038	212-346-1603
Pratt Institute	200 Willoughby Avenue Brooklyn, NY 11205	718-636-3637
Rensselaer Polytechnic Institute	Troy, NY 12180	518-276-6906
Roberts Wesleyan College	2301 Westside Drive Rochester, NY 14624	716-594-6610
Russell Sage College	45 Ferry Street Troy, NY 12180	518-270-2403
St. Bonaventure University	St. Bonaventure, NY 14778	716-375-2201
St. Francis College	180 Remsen Street Brooklyn, NY 11201	718-522-2300
St. John Fisher College	3690 East Avenue Rochester, NY 14618	716-385-8366
St. John's University - Jamaica	Grand Center & Utopia Parkways, Jamaica, NY 11439	718-990-1308
St. John's University - Staten Island	300 Howard Avenue Staten Island, NY 10301	718-390-4545
St. Joseph's College	245 Clinton Avenue, Brooklyn, NY 11205	718-636-6800
St. Lawrence University	Canton, NY 13617	315-379-5861
St. Thomas Aquinas College	Rte. 340, Sparkill, NY 10976	914-398-4154
Sarah Lawrence College	Bronxville, NY 10708	914-395-2374
School of Visual Arts	209 East 23rd Street New York, NY 10010	212-592-2600
Siena College	Loudonville, NY 12211	518-783-2968

COLLEGE	ADDRESS	PHONE
Skidmore College	Saratoga Springs, NY 12866	518-584-5000
SUC - Brockport	Room 207, F.O.B. Brockport, NY 14420	716-395-2510
SUC - Buffalo	GC 510, 1300 Elmwood Avenue Buffalo, NY 14222	716-878-4214
SUC - Cortland	P.O. Box 2000, D-206, Cornish Hall Cortland, NY 13045	607-753-2701
SUC - Fredonia	Fredonia, NY 14063	716-673-3449
SUC - Geneseo	Erwin 107 Geneseo, NY 14454	716-245-5560
SUC - New Paltz	OMB 102 New Paltz, NY 12561	914-257-2800
SUC - Old Westbury	P.O. Box 210, Old Westbury, NY 11568	516-876-3099
SUC - Oneonta	Administration Bldg., 337 Oneonta, NY 13820	607-436-3456
SUC - Oswego	611 Culkin Hall Oswego, NY 13126	315-341-2102
SUC - Plattsburgh	Hawkins Hall 107 Plattsburgh, NY 12901	518-564-3066
SUC - Potsdam	Potsdam, NY 13617	315-267-2535
SUNY - Albany	Education 113 1400 Washington Avenue Albany, NY 12222	518-442-5001
SUNY - Binghamton	Vestal Parkway East Binghamton, NY 13901	607-777-2833
SUNY - Buffalo	553 Baldy Hall, 3435 Main Street Buffalo, NY 14206	716-645-2461
SUNY - Col. of Environmental Science	Syracuse, NY 13210	315-470-6366
SUNY - Stony Brook	Soc. & Behavioral Sci. Bldg. 109 Steele Hall Stony Brook, NY 11794	516-632-7055
Syracuse University	School of Education Syracuse, NY 13244-1120	315-443-4751
Union College	Union Avenue Schenectady, NY 12308	518-388-6361
University of Rochester	421 Lattimore Rochester, NY 14627	716-275-1009

Utica College of Syracuse University	Burrstone Road Utica, NY 13502	315-792-3090
Vassar College	Box 31 Poughkeepsie, NY 12601	914-437-7361
Wagner College	Staten Island, NY 10301	718-390-3464
Wells College	Aurora, NY 13026	315-364-3252
Yeshiva University	245 Lexington Avenue New York, NY 10016	212-340-7788

16 GETTING A TEACHING JOB

There are specific steps you can follow to increase your chances of getting the teaching job you want. There are no guarantees, but you can definitely improve the odds. Let's begin with a discussion of job opportunities.

WHERE ARE THE TEACHING JOBS?

There are teaching jobs everywhere! This writer served on the board of education in a small suburban town with about 80 teachers in a K-8 school district. It was the kind of place most people would like to teach. There were between two and five teaching openings each year, for six years. But you could hardly find an advertisement or announcement anywhere.

About the only people who knew about the jobs were administrators and teachers in the district and surrounding districts, the few people who read a three-line ad that ran once in a weekly paper, and those who called to inquire about teaching jobs. Keep this information in mind. It is your first clue about how to find a teaching job.

The *Occupational Outlook Handbook*, released by the federal government, predicts that teaching opportunities for elementary and secondary school teachers will increase faster than all occupations as a whole during the next 10 years. The book predicts a much faster increase in jobs for special education teachers.

Other sources predict an increased need for mathematics, science, and bilingual teachers during this same period. Experience indicates that the opportunities for teachers certified in more than one area will grow much faster than average as well.

Some publications predict that the population of elementary age school children will increase about 10 percent by 2008. There are about 215,000 public school teachers in New York State. A 10 percent increase would mean about 237,000 public school teaching positions in 2008.

The growth in the school age population and the increased retirement rate will probably produce a large numer of teaching jobs during the next decade. You need only one.

HOW CAN I FIND A JOB?

Before discussing this question, let's talk about rejection. Remember, you need only one teaching job. If you are interested in 100 jobs, you should be extremely happy with a success rate of 1 percent. A success rate of 2 percent is more than you need, and a very high success rate of 5 percent will just make it too hard to decide which job to take.

Rejection and failure are part of the job search process. Be ready; everyone goes through it.

OKAY, I'M READY TO BEGIN. HOW DO I FIND A JOB?

Begin by deciding on the kind of teaching jobs you want and the geographic areas you are willing to teach in. There is no sense pursuing jobs you don't want in places you don't want to go.

Write your choices here.

These are the kind of teaching positions I'm interested in.

_____   _____

_____   _____

These are the counties, towns, places, areas, or locales I'm willing to teach in.

_____   _____

_____   _____

You can change your mind as often as you like. But limit your job search to these choices.

Follow the guidelines presented below. You must actually do the things outlined here. Reading, talking, and thinking about them will not help.

Make and use personal contacts (network)

Find out about every appropriate teaching position

Apply for every appropriate teaching position—go to every interview

Develop a good resume

Develop a portfolio

Use the placement office

MAKE AND USE PERSONAL CONTACTS (NETWORK)

You will not be surprised to learn that many, if not most, jobs are found through personal contacts. You must make personal contacts to maximize your chances of finding the job you want. Take things easy, one step at a time, and try to meet at least one new person each week.

Find a way to get introduced to teachers, school administrators, board of education members, and others who will know about teaching jobs and may influence hiring decisions. The more people you meet and talk to, the better chance you will have of getting the job you want.

Get a mentor. Get to know a superintendent or principal near where you want to teach, and ask that person to be your mentor. Tell them immediately that you are not asking for a job in their district. (That will not stop them from offering you one if they want to.) Explain that you are just beginning your teaching career and that you need help learning about teaching jobs in surrounding communities and about teaching in general. Ask your mentors to keep their eyes and ears open for any openings for which you are qualified. You can have several mentors if you want to. Listen to their advice.

You already have a lot of contacts through your friends and relatives. Talk to them all. Tell them you are looking for a teaching job and ask them to be alert for any possibilities. Ask them to mention your name and your interest in a teaching position to everyone they know.

FIND OUT ABOUT EVERY APPROPRIATE TEACHING POSITION

The contacts you have and are making each week will help you keep abreast of some teaching opportunities. Follow these additional steps. Look in every paper every day distributed in the places you want to teach. Don't forget about weekly papers.

Call all the school districts where you want to teach. Ask the administrative assistant or secretary in the superintendent's or principal's office if there are current or anticipated job openings in the district. If you are in college or a recent graduate, visit or contact the placement office every week and ask your professors if they know about any teaching opportunities. Contact the regional BOCES (pages 440–442) for information about jobs and recruitment fairs.

APPLY FOR EVERY APPROPRIATE TEACHING POSITION— GO TO EVERY INTERVIEW

Apply for every teaching position that is of the type and in the location(s) you listed. No exceptions! Direct application for a listed position is probably the second most effective way to get a job. The more appropriate jobs you apply for, the more likely you are to get one. It is not unusual for someone to apply for more than 100 teaching positions.

Go to every interview you are invited to. Going to interviews increases your chances of getting a job. If you don't get the job, it was worth going just for the practice.

Your application should include a brief cover letter and a one-page resume. The cover letter should follow this format: The first brief paragraph should identify the job you are applying for. The second brief paragraph should be used to mention a skill or ability you have that matches a district need. The third brief paragraph should indicate an interest in a personal interview. Every cover letter should be addressed to the person responsible for hiring in the school district.

DEVELOP A GOOD RESUME

A good resume is a one-page advertisement. A good resume highlights the things you have done that prospective employers will be interested in. A good resume is not an exhaustive listing of everything you have done. A good resume is not cluttered.

For example, say you worked as a teacher assistant and spent most of your time on lunch duty and about 10 percent of your time conducting whole language lessons. What goes on the resume? The whole language experience.

Your resume should include significant school-related experience. It should also include other employment that lasted longer than a year. Omit noneducation-related short-term employment. Your resume should list special skills, abilities, and interests that make you unique.

An example of a resume using a format that has proven successful appears in this chapter. This resume combines the experience of more than one person and is for demonstration purposes only.

An outline of a resume you can copy, to begin to develop your own resume, is also included in this chapter. If you are interested in two different types of teaching positions, you may have two resumes. Go over your final resume and cover letters with a placement officer or advisor and show them to teachers and school administrators.

Derek Namost
33 Ann Street
Kearning, NY 12345
(555) 555-5555
derekn@zyxwv.net

Objective: Elementary School Teacher
Special Education Teacher
Secondary History Teacher

Education: BS History—Collegiate College (minor in education)   2001
MS in Education at Long Key College in progress

Certification: Teacher of Special Education
Teacher of Elementary Education

Experience: **Lincoln School District,**   2001–present
Elementary School Teacher Fifth Grade

- Teach in a student-centered elementary school
- Prepare and teach individualized lessons geared to student needs
- Use computer software and CD-ROM's to teach mathematics
  and motivate students
- Collaborate on an interdisciplinary team
- Integrate instruction in science, language arts, and social studies

Southern Pines School District,   2001–2004
Secondary School Special Education Teacher

- Planned and taught modified classes for classified students
- Modified the curriculum to meet the individual needs of students
- Taught modified science and social studies courses to classified students
- Assisted students with class assignments, self-management, and
  study skills
- Collaborated with class and subject matter teachers

Watson School,   Spring 2001
Student Teacher, Preschool Class

- Collaborated in teaching a class of preschool students

Honors: Kappa Delta Pi, Phi Delta Kappa

Coaching/ Coach, varsity soccer team   2001–2004
Advising: Advisor, mathematics team   2001–2004
Interested in coaching and advising after-school activities

Special Extensive experience using computers, including the Internet,
Skills: desktop publishing, PowerPoint, multimedia, and CD-ROM's

References: References are available on request

RESUME WORKSHEET

_____

_____

_____

(_____) _____ - _____

_____ @ _____ . ____

Objective:

Education:

Certification:

Experience:

Honors:

**Coaching/
Advising:**

**Special
Skills:**

References:

DEVELOP A PORTFOLIO

Develop a portfolio to show to potential employers. Choose four or five lesson plans you like. Rewrite them extensively to incorporate all the elements of a good lesson plan. Carefully type them in final form and include them in your portfolio. Include examples of your student's work that you believe will be well received by a principal or superintendent. You may want to take pictures of a classroom you've worked in showing class arrangement and bulletin boards. Include other materials to show your familiarity with current teaching methods. Be sure to show your portfolio to your education advisor and a principal before you show it to prospective employers. Make changes in the portfolio as they recommend.

USE THE PLACEMENT OFFICE

If you are a college student or graduate, use the school's placement office. Set up a placement file that includes recommendation letters from professors, teachers, and supervisors. It's handy to have these references on file. If a potential employer wants this information, you can have it sent out from the placement office instead of running around.

College placement offices often give seminars on job hunting and interviews. Take advantage of these.

WHAT TIME LINE SHOULD I FOLLOW?

Let's say you are looking for a job in September and you will be certified three months earlier in June. You should begin working on your personal contacts by September of the previous year. You should start looking for advertisements and tracking down job possibilities during January. Have your placement file set up and a preliminary resume done by February. You can amend them later if you need to. Start applying for jobs in February.

ANY LAST ADVICE?

Stick with it. Follow the steps outlined here. Start early and take things one step at a time. Remember the importance of personal contacts. Remember that you need only one teaching position. Let people help you.

JOB SEARCH CONTACTS

THE URBAN TEACHING ACADEMY

The Urban Teaching Academy (UTA) is a college program that offers a wide variety of state approved teacher certification programs. Most UTA students are placed in paid teaching positions in the New York City schools while taking teacher certification courses. The UTA has had an over 90 percent success rate placing its students in paid teaching positions upon graduation.

If you want to teach in New York City call the UTA at one of the numbers below.

Urban Teaching Academy

1-718-518-7710, Ext. 4438

BOCES and school districts are listed on the following pages by county. The Board of Cooperative Educational Services offices (BOCES) are listed first. The school district listings show the approximate number of students in each district and school.

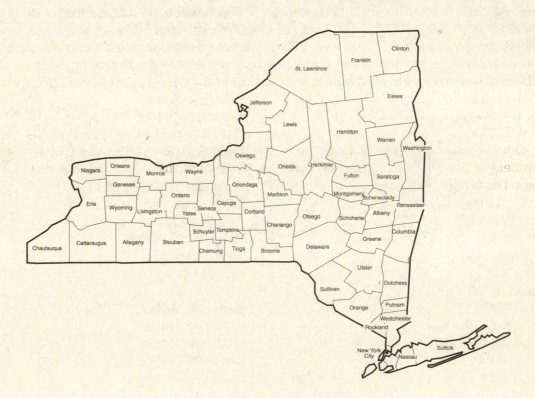

NEW YORK COUNTY MAP

BOCES

Boards of Cooperative Education Services (BOCES) offices are located throughout New York State. BOCES coordinate the efforts of local school districts and these offices are a good starting point for a job search. BOCES Web sites frequently list the teaching jobs available in that region. Job fairs are often listed through BOCES, and you may find other job bank information at these sites. In at least one case, the Putnam-Northern Westchester BOCES has an on-line application system that processes job applications for most of the schools in that region.

A complete list of BOCES offices with contact information is given below. For a map of BOCES locations and for clickable Web links visit the link below.

www.emsc.nysed.gov/mgtserv/BOCES/

Broome-Delaware-Tioga
435 Glenwood Road
Binghamton, NY 13905-1699
(607) 763-3309
www.btboces.org

Capital Region
1031 Watervliet-Shaker Road
Albany, NY 12205
(518) 456-9215
www.capregboces.org

Cattaraugus-Allegany-Erie-Wyoming
1825 Windfall Road
Olean, NY 14760
(716) 376-8200
www.caew-boces.wnyric.org

Cayuga-Onondaga
5980 South Street Road
Auburn, NY 13021
(315) 253-0361
www.cayboces.org

Champlain Valley
P.O. Box 455
1585 Military Turnpike
Plattsburgh, NY 12901
(518) 561-0100
www.cves.org

Delaware-Chenango-Madison-Otsego
6678 County Road 32
Norwich, NY 13815-3554
(607) 335-1233
www.dcmoboces.com

Dutchess
5 BOCES Road
Poughkeepsie, NY 12601
(845) 486-4800
www.dcboces.org

Erie 1
355 Harlem Road
West Seneca, NY 14224-1892
(716) 821-7001
www.erie1boces.org

Erie 2—Chautauqua-Cattaraugus
8685 Erie Road
Angola, NY 14006
(716) 549-4454 / 1-800-228-1184
e2ccb.org

Franklin-Essex-Hamilton
P.O. Box 28
3372 State Route 11
Malone, NY 12953
(518) 483-6420
www.fehb.org

Genesee Valley
80 Munson Street
LeRoy, NY 14482
(585) 658-7905 or (585) 344-7905
www.gvboces.org

Hamilton-Fulton-Montgomery
25 West Main Street–Suite One
Johnstown, NY 12095-0665
(518) 762-4634
www.hfmboces.org

Herkimer-Fulton-Hamilton-Otsego
352 Gros Boulevard
Herkimer, NY 13350
(315) 867-2022
www.herkimer-boces.org

Jefferson-Lewis-Hamilton-Herkimer-Oneida
20104 State Route 3
Watertown, NY 13601
(315) 779-7010 or (315) 377-7009
www.boces.com

Madison-Oneida
4937 Spring Road
Verona, NY 13478-0168
(315) 361-5510
www.moboces.org

Monroe #1
41 O'Connor Road
Fairport, NY 14450
(585) 383-2200
www.monroe.edu

Monroe 2—Orleans
3599 Big Ridge Road
Spencerport, NY 14559
(585) 352-2410
www.monroe2boces.org

Nassau
718 The Plain Road
P.O. Box 1034
Westbury, NY 11590-0114
(516) 396-2200
www.nassauboces.org

Oneida-Herkimer-Madison
P.O. Box 70
4747 Middle Settlement Road
New Hartford, NY 13413-0070
(315) 793-8560
www.oneida-boces.org

Onondaga-Cortland-Madison
6820 Thompson Road
Syracuse, NY 13221
(315) 433-2602
www.ocmboces.org

Orange-Ulster
53 Gibson Road
Goshen, NY 10924-9777
(845) 291-0110
www.ouboces.org

Orleans-Niagara
4232 Shelby Basin Road
Medina, NY 14103
1-800-836-7510 Ext. 201
www.onboces.org

Oswego
179 County Rt. 64
Mexico, NY 13114
(315) 963-4222
www.oswegoboces.org

Otsego-Delaware-Schoharie-Greene
Frank W. Cyr Center
Stamford, NY 12167
(607) 652-1209
www.oncboces.org

Putnam-Northern Westchester
200 BOCES Drive
Yorktown Heights, NY 10598-4399
(914) 248-2300
www.pnwboces.org

Questar III
10 Empire State Boulevard, 2nd Floor
Castleton, NY 12033
(518) 477-8771
www.questar.org

Rockland
65 Parrott Road
West Nyack, NY 10994
(845) 627-4701
www.rockland.org

St. Lawrence-Lewis
P.O. Box 231
Canton, NY 13617
(315) 386-4504
www.sllboces.org

Schuyler-Chemung-Tioga
459 Philo Road
Elmira, NY 14903
(607) 739-3581
www.sctboces.org

Steuben-Allegany
6985 Technology Way
Hornell, NY 14843-0586
(607) 324-7880
www.saboces.org

Suffolk 1 (East)
201 Sunrise Highway
Patchogue, NY 11772
(631) 289-2200
www.sricboces.org

Suffolk 2 (West)
507 Deer Park Road
Dix Hills, NY 11746
(631) 549-4900
www.wsboces.org

Sullivan
6 Wierk Avenue
Liberty, NY 12754-2151
(845) 292-0082
www.scboces.org

Tompkins-Seneca-Tioga
555 Warren Road
Ithaca, NY 14850
(607) 257-1551
www.tstboces.org

Ulster
175 Route 32 North
New Paltz, NY 12561
(845) 255-3040
www.ulsterboces.org

Washington-Saratoga-Warren-Hamilton-Essex
10 Lacrosse Street
Hudson Falls, NY 12839-1415
(518) 746-3310
wswheboces.org

Wayne-Finger Lakes
131 Drumlin Court
Eisenhower Building
Newark, NY 14513-1863
(315) 332-7284
www.wflboces.org

Westchester (Southern)
17 Berkley Drive
Rye Brook, NY 10573
(914) 937-3820
www.swboces.org

SCHOOLS

There are about 215,000 public school teachers and about 2,811,000 public school students in New York State. About 1,030,000 of these students (about 37 percent) are in New York City public schools. About 65 percent of all public school students are in school districts in the New York City metropolitan area.

Given below is a complete list of public school districts, by county, with enrollment figures current at press time.

Following the list you'll learn how to find contact information, and more detailed reports, for each school district in the list.

SCHOOL DISTRICT LIST BY COUNTY

School District	Number of Students	School District	Number of Students
ALBANY *13 Districts*	**40,427**	Deposit	724
Albany	9,368	Harpursville	1,087
Berne-Knox-Westerlo	1,111	Johnson City	2,550
Bethlehem	5,034	Maine-Endwell	2,694
Cohoes	2,117	Susquehanna Valley	2,159
Green Island	3,311	Union-Endicott	4,563
Guilderland	5,667	Vestal	4,372
Maplewood	3,190	Whitney Point	1,903
Menands	3,233	Windsor	2,060
North Colonie	5,619		
Ravena-Coeymans-Selkirk	2,327	**CATTARAUGUS** *13 Districts*	**16,038**
South Colonie	5,734	Allegany-Limestone	1,430
Voorheesville	1,292	Cattaraugus-Little Valley	1,195
Watervliet	1,424	Ellicottville	678
		Franklinville	964
ALLEGANY *12 Districts*	**7,987**	Gowanda	1,474
Alfred-Almond	727	Hinsdale	494
Andover	413	Olean	2,553
Belfast	458	Pioneer	1,077
Bolivar-Richburg	937	Portville	170
Canaseraga	322	Randolph Academy	990
Cuba-Rushford	142	Randolph	1,511
Fillmore	721	Salamanca	484
Friendship	325	West Valley	3,018
Genesee Valley	727		
Scio	474	**CAYUGA** *7 Districts*	**11,748**
Wellsville	1,441	Auburn	4,930
Whitesville	300	Cato-Meridian	1,271
		Moravia	1,161
BROOME *13 Districts*	**32,108**	Port Byron	1,153
Binghamton	6,244	Southern Cayuga	1,069
Chenango Forks	1,826	Union Springs	1,123
Chenango Valley	1,926	Weedsport	1,041

School District	Number of Students	School District	Number of Students
CHAUTAUQUA *18 Districts*	**23,246**	Germantown	725
Bemus Point	888	Hudson	2,256
Brocton	764	Kinderhook	2,341
Cassadaga Valley	1,349	New Lebanon	634
Chautauqua Lake	971	Taconic Hills	1,874
Clymer	483		
Dunkirk	2,158	**CORTLAND** *5 Districts*	**7,661**
Falconer	1,441	Cincinnatus	720
Forestville	608	Cortland	2,805
Fredonia	1,896	Homer	2,448
Frewsburg	1,026	Marathon	1,050
Jamestown	5,163	McGraw	638
Panama	771		
Pine Valley	798	**DELAWARE** *12 Districts*	**7,160**
Ripley	413	Andes	153
Sherman	551	Charlotte Valley	466
Silver Creek	1,277	Delhi	1,053
Southwestern	1,738	Downsville	353
Westfield	951	Franklin	336
		Hancock	508
CHEMUNG *3 Districts*	**12,889**	Margaretville	548
Elmira	7,310	Roxbury	351
Elmira Heights	1,117	Sidney	1,405
Horseheads	4,462	South Kortright	360
		Stamford	487
CHENANGO *8 Districts*	**9,573**	Walton	1,140
Afton	700		
Bainbridge Guilford	1,024	**DUTCHESS** *14 Districts*	**46,980**
Georgetown-So. Otselic	470	Arlington	9,993
Greene	1,374	Beacon	3,488
Norwich	2,222	Dover Plains	1,821
Oxford	971	Hyde Park	4,729
Sherburne-Earlville	1,787	Millbrook	1,185
Unadilla Valley	1,025	Northeast	876
		Pawling	1,377
CLINTON *8 Districts*	**13,183**	Pine Plains	1,472
Ausable Valley	1,415	Poughkeepsie	4,542
Beekmantown	2,085	Red Hook	2,332
Chazy	597	Rhinebeck	1,269
Northeastern Clinton	1,689	Spackenkill	1,785
Northern Adirondack	1,129	Wappingers	12,111
Peru	2,304		
Plattsburgh	2,072	**ERIE** *29 Districts*	**138,031**
Saranac	1,892	Akron	1,684
		Alden	2,069
COLUMBIA *7 Districts*	**9,620**	Amherst	3,169
Berkshire	279	Buffalo	41,589
Chatham	1,511	Cheektowaga	2,431

School District	Number of Students	School District	Number of Students
Cheektowaga-Maryvale	2,545	**FULTON** *7 Districts*	**9,349**
Cheektowaga-Sloan	1,477	Broadalbin-Perth	1,896
Clarence	4,763	Gloversville	3,118
Cleveland Hill	1,578	Johnstown	2,070
Depew	2,414	Mayfield	1,148
East Aurora	2,094	Northville	526
Eden	1,841	Oppenheim-Ephratah	431
Evans-Brant	3,339	Wheelerville	160
Frontier	5,645		
Grand Island	3,205	**GENESEE** *8 Districts*	**10,495**
Hamburg	3,970	Alexander	1,046
Holland	1,314	Batavia	2,703
Hopevale	122	Byron-Bergen	1,271
Iroquois	2,909	Elba	609
Kenmore	8,871	Le Roy	1,433
Lackawanna	2,005	Oakfield-Alabama	1,113
Lancaster	6,109	Pavilion	903
North Collins	734	Pembroke	1,417
Orchard Park	5,127		
Springville-Griffith Institute	2,388	**GREEN** *6 Districts*	**7,714**
Sweet Home	3,899	Cairo-Durham	1,819
Tonawanda	2,379	Catskill	1,790
West Seneca	7,636	Coxsackie-Athens	1,641
Williamsville	10,725	Greenville	1,419
		Hunter-Tannersville	537
ESSEX *11 Districts*	**4,909**	Windham-Ashland	508
Crown Point	339		
Elizabethtown	404	**HAMILTON** *7 Districts*	**658**
Keene	192	Indian Lake	201
Lake Placid	931	Inlet	26
Minerva	144	Lake Pleasant	102
Moriah	817	Long Lake	101
Newcomb	69	Piseco	18
Schroon Lake	290	Raquette Lake	13
Ticonderoga	1,096	Wells	197
Westport	262		
Willsboro	365	**HERKIMER** *11 Districts*	**11,038**
		Bridgewater-West Winfield	1,459
FRANKLIN *7 Districts*	**8,632**	Dolgeville	977
Brushton-Moira	895	Frankfort	1,145
Chateaugay	608	Herkimer	1,281
Malone	2,509	Ilion	1,794
Salmon River	1,452	Little Falls	1,157
Saranac Lake	1,669	Mohawk	970
St. Regis Falls	347	Poland	721
Tupper Lake	1,152	Town of Webb	377
		Van Hornsville-Owen Young	3,233
		West Canada Valley	2,924

School District	Number of Students	School District	Number of Students
JEFFERSON *11 Districts*	**17,931**	Fairport	7,126
Alexandria Central	682	Gates-Chili	5,123
Belleville-Henderson	582	Greece	13,559
Carthage	2,949	Hilton	4,438
General Brown	1,547	Honeoye Falls-Lima	2,606
Indian River	3,480	Penfield	4,958
La Fargeville	540	Pittsford	5,935
Lyme	359	Rochester	34,526
Sackets Harbor	465	Rush-Henrietta	5,873
South Jefferson	1,991	Spencerport	4,312
Thousand Islands	1,181	Webster	8,478
Watertown	4,155	West Irondequoit	3,973
		Wheatland-Chili	933
LEWIS *5 Districts*	**4,765**		
Beaver River	1,054	**MONTGOMERY** *5 Districts*	**7,852**
Copenhagen	602	Amsterdam	3,734
Harrisville	418	Canajoharie	1,100
Lowville	1,436	Fonda-Fultonville	1,602
South Lewis	1,255	Fort Plain	931
		St. Johnsville	485
LIVINGSTON *8 Districts*	**9,839**		
Avon	1,158	**NASSAU** *56 Districts*	**207,909**
Caledonia Mumford	1,180	Baldwin	5,437
Dalton-Nunda	966	Bellmore	1,308
Dansville	1,741	Bellmore-Merrick CHS	5,678
Geneseo	2,966	Bethpage	2,955
Livonia	2,180	Carle Place	1,517
Mount Morris	645	East Meadow	8,081
York 2	1,003	East Rockaway	1,264
		East Williston	1,752
MADISON *10 Districts*	**11,992**	Elmont	4,101
Brookfield	258	Farmingdale	6,502
Canastota	1,570	Floral Park	1,553
Cazenovia	1,822	Franklin Square	1,940
Chittenango	2,571	Freeport	6,935
De Ruyter	496	Garden City	4,058
Hamilton	741	Glen Cove	3,160
Madison	467	Great Neck	5,920
Morrisville-Eaton	911	Hempstead	6,940
Oneida	2,589	Herricks	3,874
Stockbridge Valley	567	Hewlett-Woodmere	3,223
		Hicksville	5,066
MONROE *18 Districts*	**119,225**	Island Park	799
Brighton	3,593	Island Trees	2,783
Brockport	4,573	Jericho	3,125
Churchville-Chili	4,511	Lawrence	3,714
East Irondequoit	3,499	Levittown	8,005
East Rochester	1,209	Locust Valley	2,231

School District	Number of Students	School District	Number of Students
Long Beach	4,322	New Hartford	2,709
Lynbrook	3,105	New York Mills	564
Malverne	1,836	Oriskany	775
Manhasset	2,624	Remsen	644
Massapequa	8,179	Rome	6,076
Merrick	1,944	Sauquoit Valley	1,298
Mineola	2,706	Sherrill	2,376
New Hyde Park	1,656	Utica	8,885
North Bellmore	2,542	Waterville	1,061
North Merrick	1,287	Westmoreland	1,178
North Shore	2,623	Whitesboro	3,894
Oceanside	6,312		
Oyster Bay	1,487	**ONONDAGA** *18 Districts*	**76,717**
Plainedge	3,474	Baldwinsville	5,801
Plainview	4,874	East Syracuse	3,675
Port Washington	4,706	Fabius	946
Rockville Centre	3,643	Fayetteville-Manlius	4,605
Roosevelt	2,793	Jamesville-Dewitt	2,722
Roslyn	3,163	Jordan-Elbridge	1,727
Seaford	2,720	La Fayette	1,130
Sewanhaka CHS	8,266	Liverpool	8,490
Syosset	6,485	Lyncourt	341
Uniondale	6,334	Marcellus	2,169
Valley Stream #13	2,186	North Syracuse	9,940
Valley Stream #24	1,072	Onondaga	1,047
Valley Stream #30	1,524	Skaneateles	1,874
Valley Stream CHS	4,439	Solvay	1,809
Wantagh	3,488	Syracuse	21,963
West Hempstead	2,405	Tully	1,269
Westbury	3,793	West Genesee	5,162
		Westhill	2,047
NIAGARA *10 Districts*	**34,695**		
Barker	1,098	**ONTARIO** *9 Districts*	**18,023**
Lewiston-Porter	2,400	Canandaigua	4,173
Lockport	5,714	East Bloomfield	1,131
Newfane	2,097	Geneva	2,635
Niagara Falls	8,636	Gorham-Middlesex	1,651
Niagara-Wheatfield	3,982	Honeoye	1,093
North Tonawanda	4,765	Manchester-Shortsville	953
Royalton-Hartland	1,717	Naples	977
Star Point	2,804	Phelps-Clifton Sp.	2,120
Wilson	1,482	Victor	3,290
ONEIDA *15 Districts*	**37,388**	**ORANGE** *18 Districts*	**65,289**
Adirondack	1,614	Chester	993
Camden	2,756	Cornwall	2,983
Clinton	1,661	Florida	883
Holland Patent	1,897	Goshen	2,869

School District	Number of Students	School District	Number of Students
Greenwood Lake	720	**PUTNAM** *6 Districts*	**16,839**
Highland Falls	1,229	Brewster	3,698
Kiryas Joel	217	Carmel	4,957
Middletown	6,347	Garrison	299
Minisink Valley	4,385	Haldane	866
Monroe-Woodbury	7,164	Mahopac	5,255
Newburgh	12,512	Putnam Valley	1,764
Pine Bush	6,028		
Port Jervis	3,432	**RENSSELAER** *12 Districts*	**23,116**
Tuxedo	594	Averill Park	3,466
Valley CSD (Montgomery)	5,215	Berlin	1,046
Warwick Valley	4,596	Brittonkill	1,381
Washingtonville	5,122	Brunswick (Brittonkill)	4,602
		Hoosic Valley	1,235
ORLEANS *5 Districts*	**7,930**	Hoosick Falls	1,280
Albion	2,683	Lansingburgh	2,458
Holley	1,397	North Greenbush	20
Kendall	1,056	Rensselaer	1,067
Lyndonville	797	Schodack	1,219
Medina	1,997	Troy	4,966
		Wynantskill	376
OSWEGO *9 Districts*	**24,687**		
Altmar Parish	1,699	**ROCKLAND** *9 Districts*	**41,852**
Central Square	4,907	Clarkstown	9,196
Fulton	3,857	East Ramapo (Spring Valley)	9,152
Hannibal	1,761	Edwin Gould Academy	173
Mexico	2,688	Haverstraw-Stoney Point	8,072
Oswego	4,974	Nanuet	2,164
Phoenix	2,474	Nyack	2,908
Pulaski	1,229	Pearl River	2,409
Sandy Creek	1,098	Ramapo	4,506
		South Orangetown	3,272
OTSEGO *12 Districts*	**9,230**		
Cherry Vall.-Springfield	664	**ST. LAWRENCE** *17 Districts*	**16,901**
Cooperstown	1,159	Brasher Falls	1,023
Edmeston	581	Canton	1,492
Gilbertsville-Mt. Upton	562	Clifton-Fine	366
Laurens	450	Colton-Pierrepont	397
Milford	472	Edwards-Knox	694
Morris	464	Gouverneur	1,773
Oneonta	2,131	Hammond	342
Otego-Unidilla	1,255	Hermon-Dekalb	388
Richfield Springs	681	Heuvelton	639
Schenevus	382	Lisbon	587
Worcester	429	Madrid-Waddington	780
		Massena	2,838
		Morristown	447
		Norwood-Norfolk	1,155

School District	Number of Students	School District	Number of Students
Ogdensburg	2,012	Bath	1,973
Parishville-Hopkinton	487	Bradford	313
Potsdam	1,481	Campbell-Savona	1,195
		Canisteo	921
SARATOGA *12 Districts*	**35,087**	Corning	5,649
Ballston Spa	4,477	Greenwood	196
Burnt Hills	3,413	Hammondsport	689
Corinth	1,256	Hornell	1,980
Edinburg	82	Jasper-Troupsburg	583
Galway	1,218	Prattsburgh	545
Mechanicville	1,379	Wayland	1,786
Saratoga Springs	6,905		
Schuylerville	1,660	**SUFFOLK** *71 Districts*	**258,227**
Shenendehowa	9,233	Amagansett	112
South Glens Falls	3,269	Amityville	3,122
Stillwater	1,322	Babylon	2,001
Waterford	873	Bay Shore	5,705
		Bayport-Blue Point	2,447
SCHENECTADY *6 Districts*	**22,154**	Brentwood	16,138
Duanesburg	947	Bridgehampton	128
Mohonasen	4,223	Center Moriches	3,896
Niskayuna	3,281	Central Islip	6,488
Schalmont	2,245	Cold Spring Harbor	2,046
Schenectady	8,448	Commack	7,321
Scotia-Glenville	3,010	Comsewogue	7,065
		Connetquot	4,635
SCHOHARIE *6 Districts*	**5,432**	Copiague	1,390
Cobleskill-Richmondville	2,177	Deer Park	4,211
Gilboa-Conesville	393	East Hampton	1,988
Jefferson	295	East Islip	5,212
Middleburgh	1,018	East Moriches	714
Schoharie	1,176	East Quogue	434
Sharon Springs	373	Eastport	1,042
		Eastport-South Manor CHS	1,159
SCHUYLER *2 Districts*	**2,260**	Elwood	2,462
Odessa-Montour	892	Fire Island	52
Watkins Glen	1,368	Fishers Island	51
		Greenport	651
SENECA *4 Districts*	**5,185**	Half Hollow Hills	9,192
Romulus	622	Hampton Bays	1,752
Seneca Falls	1,533	Harborfields	3,414
South Seneca	1,042	Hauppauge	4,012
Waterloo	1,988	Huntington	4,081
		Islip	3,608
STEUBEN *14 Districts*	**18,395**	Kings Park	3,973
Addison	1,226	Lindenhurst	7,601
Arkport	645	Little Flower	96
Avoca	694	Longwood	9,867

School District	Number of Students	School District	Number of Students
Mattituck	1,562	**TIOGA** *6 Districts*	**8,976**
Middle Country	11,015	Candor	973
Miller Place	2,974	Newark Valley	1,444
Montauk	406	Owego-Apalachin	2,379
Mount Sinai	2,390	Spencer-Van Etten	1,168
North Babylon	155	Tioga	1,194
Northport	6,211	Waverly	1,818
Oysterponds	115		
Patchogue	9,142	**TOMPKINS** *7 Districts*	**12,528**
Port Jefferson	1,158	Dryden	1,928
Quogue	110	George Jr. Republic	149
Remsenburg	174	Groton	1,140
Riverhead	4,896	Ithaca	5,525
Rocky Point	3,657	Lansing	1,357
Sachem	15,311	Newfield	966
Sag Harbor	932	Trumansburg	1,463
Sagaponack	17		
Sayville	3,629	**ULSTER** *10 Districts*	**28,566**
Shelter Island	261	Ellenville	1,878
Shoreham-Wading River	2,685	Highland	1,895
Smithtown	9,801	Kingston	8,155
South Country	4,708	Marlboro	2,067
South Huntington	6,248	New Paltz	2,386
South Manor	936	Onteora	2,229
Southampton	1,686	Rondout Valley	2,798
Southold	1,013	Saugerties	3,412
Springs	550	Wallkill	3,658
Three Village	7,993	West Park	88
Tuckahoe Common	315		
Wainscott	11	**WARREN** *9 Districts*	**11,205**
West Babylon	4,902	Bolton	287
West Islip	5,894	Glens Falls	2,607
Westhampton Beach	1,815	Glens Falls Common	184
William Floyd	10,267	Hadley-Luzerne	1,119
Wyandanch	2,216	Johnsburg	424
		Lake George	1,100
SULLIVAN *8 Districts*	**11,353**	North Warren	633
Eldred	725	Queensbury	3,862
Fallsburg	1,395	Warrensburg	989
Liberty	1,857		
Livingston Manor	645	**WASHINGTON** *11 Districts*	**10,533**
Monticello	3,592	Argyle	788
Roscoe	282	Cambridge	1,129
Sullivan West	1,617	Fort Ann	624
Tri-Valley	1,240	Fort Edward	561
		Granville	1,477
		Greenwich	1,241

School District	Number of Students	School District	Number of Students
Hartford	609	Hawthorne Cedar Knolls	301
Hudson Falls	2,361	Hendrick Hudson	2,833
Putnam	45	Irvington	1,930
Salem	829	Katonah-Lewisboro	4,112
Whitehall	869	Lakeland	6,322
		Mamaroneck	4,649
WAYNE *11 Districts*	**17,862**	Mount Vernon	10,412
Clyde-Savannah	1,045	Mt. Pleasant-Blythedale	132
Gananda	1,204	Mt. Pleasant-Cottage	253
Lyons	1,100	Mt. Pleasant CSD	10,072
Marion	1,155	New Rochelle	10,011
Newark	2,663	North Salem	1,412
North Rose-Wolcott	1,674	Ossining	4,033
Palmyra-Macedon	2,261	Peekskill	2,896
Red Creek	1,100	Pelham	2,473
Sodus	1,478	Pleasantville	1,710
Wayne	2,809	Pocantico Hills	330
Williamson	1,373	Port Chester	3,527
		Rye	2,633
WESTCHESTER *47 Districts*	**144,160**	Rye Neck	1,369
Abbott	87	Scarsdale	4,508
Ardsley	2,284	Somers	2,983
Bedford	4,035	Tuckahoe Central	980
Blind Brook-Rye	1,281	UFSD-Tarrytowns	2,348
Briarcliff Manor	1,690	Valhalla	1,368
Bronxville	1,460	White Plains	6,594
Byram Hills	2,657	Yonkers	24,830
Chappaqua	4,055	Yorktown Central	4,183
Croton-Harmon	1,520		
Dobbs Ferry	1,326	**WYOMING** *5 Districts*	**5,568**
Eastchester	2,609	Attica	1,833
Edgemont	1,798	Letchworth	1,296
Elmsford	914	Perry	1,114
Greenburgh	1,885	Warsaw	1,094
Greenburgh Eleven	403	Wyoming	231
Greenburgh-Graham	286		
Greenburgh-North Castle	202	**YATES** *2 Districts*	**2,963**
Harrison	3,360	Dundee	923
Hastings-on-Hudson	1,674	Penn Yan	2,040

School District	Number of Students	School District	Number of Students
NEW YORK CITY		**MANHATTAN**	
Over 40 districts		High School District 71	49,270
Approximately 1,030,000 students		District 1	8,095
		District 2	21,825
		District 3	14,245
BRONX		District 4	19,543
High School District 72	49,725	District 5	14,660
District 7	15,942	District 6	30,120
District 8	22,226		
District 9	32,190		
District 10	41,602	**QUEENS**	
District 11	27,403	High School District 77	72,305
District 12	19,304	District 24	33,890
		District 25	24,008
		District 26	15,583
BROOKLYN		District 27	34,920
High School District 73	54,600	District 28	25,682
District 13	16,109	District 29	26,040
District 14	19,400	District 30	29,600
District 15	21,893		
District 16	11,230	**STATEN ISLAND**	
District 17	28,140	District 31	38,220
District 18	19,020		
District 19	24,608		
District 20	27,340		
District 21	24,600		
District 22	29,300		
District 23	14,200		
District 32	16,290		

There are significant other enrollments in the BASIS high schools, in Chancellor's districts and schools, in alternate schools, and in the citywide special education district.

JOB CONTACT INFORMATION OUTSIDE NEW YORK CITY

The link below takes you to alphabetical links for all of the school districts in the state. Click on a school district and you will find additional links for all of the schools, public and private, in that district. Click on a school link for basic contact information.

http://www.nysed.gov/admin/admindex.html

The link below takes you to school report cards and more information about public schools in New York State. The year at the end changes each spring. For example, the report cards for 2003–2004 will be posted in the spring of 2005. To access these report cards, replace the 2003 in the link below with 2005.

http://www.emsc.nysed.gov/repcrd2003/

JOB CONTACT INFORMATION IN NEW YORK CITY

For information about teaching in New York City visit the link below.

www.teachny.com/

CONTACT INFORMATION FOR CERTIFICATION IN OTHER STATES

New York is bordered by five states, Connecticut, New Jersey, Massachusetts, Pennsylvania, and Vermont, and by Canada. You should consider pursuing certification in one or more of these states.

The links below will give you certification information for states outside New York, and for Canada. These links are current at press time, but they may change. If a link is broken, search on-line for "Name of State" "Teacher Certification."

(Type *www.* before the Web address given below.)

Alabama	*alsde.edu/html/sections/section_detail.asp?section=66*
Alaska	*educ.state.ak.us/TeacherCertification/home.html*
Arizona	*ade.state.az.us/certification/*
Arkansas	*arkedu.state.ar.us/teachers/index.html*
California	*ctc.ca.gov/*
Colorado	*cde.state.co.us/index_license.htm*
Connecticut	*state.ct.us/sde/dtl/cert/index.htm*
Delaware	*deeds.doe.state.de.us/*
District of Columbia	*k12.dc.us/dcps/teachdc/index.html*
Florida	*firn.edu/doe/bin00022/home0022.htm*
Georgia	*gapsc.com/*
Hawaii	*doe.k12.hi.us/personnel/teachinginhawaii.htm*
Idaho	*sde.state.id.us/certification/*
Illinois	*isbe.net/teachers/*

Indiana	*state.in.us/psb/*
Iowa	*state.ia.us/boee/*
Kansas	*ksbe.state.ks.us/cert/cert.html*
Kentucky	*kyepsb.net/*
Louisiana	*doe.state.la.us/DOE/asps/home.asp?l=CERTIFICATION*
Maine	*state.me.us/education/*
Maryland	*state.md.us/education/*
Massachusetts	*doe.mass.edu/educators/e_license.html*
Michigan	*michigan.gov/emi/*
Minnesota	*cfl.state.mn.us/licen/*
Mississippi	*mde.k12.ms.us/license/*
Missouri	*dese.state.mo.us/divteachqual/teachcert/*
Montana	*opi.state.mt.us/index.html*
Nebraska	*nde.state.ne.us/tcert/tcmain.html*
Nevada	*ccsd.net/HRD/NVDOE/*
New Hampshire	*ed.state.nh.us/Certification/teacher.htm*
New Jersey	*state.nj.us/njded/educators/license/1111.htm*
New Mexico	*sde.state.nm.us/div/ais/lic/index.html*
North Carolina	*ncpublicschools.org/employment.html*
North Dakota	*state.nd.us/espb/*
Ohio	*ode.state.oh.us/Teaching-Profession/*
Oklahoma	*sde.state.ok.us/home/defaultie.html*
Oregon	*tspc.state.or.us/*
Pennsylvania	*teaching.state.pa.us/teaching/site/*
Rhode Island	*ridoe.net/teacher_cert/*
South Carolina	*scteachers.org/*
South Dakota	*state.sd.us/deca/OPA/*
Tennessee	*state.tn.us/education/lic_home.htm*
Texas	*sbec.state.tx.us/SBECOnline/*
Utah	*usoe.k12.ut.us/cert/*
Vermont	*state.vt.us/educ/license/*
Virginia	*pen.k12.va.us/VDOE/newvdoe/teached.html*
Washington	*k12.wa.us/cert/*
West Virginia	*wvde.state.wv.us/certification/*
Wisconsin	*dpi.state.wi.us/dpi/dlsis/tel/licguide.html*
Wyoming	*k12.wy.us/ptsb/*
Department of Defense Schools	*odedodea.edu/pers/employment/*
Canada	*http://www.ctf-fce.ca/e/teaching.htm*